THE SHADOW GOSPEL

THE SHADOW GOSPEL: HOW ANTI-LIBERAL DEMONOLOGY POSSESSED U.S. RELIGION, MEDIA, AND POLITICS

WHITNEY PHILLIPS AND MARK BROCKWAY

The MIT Press
Cambridge, Massachusetts
London, England

The MIT Press
Massachusetts Institute of Technology
77 Massachusetts Avenue, Cambridge, MA 02139
mitpress.mit.edu

The MIT Press would like to thank the anonymous peer reviewers who provided comments on drafts of this book. The generous work of academic experts is essential for establishing the authority and quality of our publications. We acknowledge with gratitude the contributions of these otherwise uncredited readers.

This book was set in Bembo Book MT Pro by New Best-set Typesetters Ltd. Printed and bound in the United States of America.

Library of Congress Cataloging-in-Publication Data

Names: Phillips, Whitney, 1983- author. | Brockway, Mark, author.
Title: The shadow gospel : how anti-liberal demonology possessed U.S. religion, media, and politics / Whitney Phillips and Mark Brockway.
Description: Cambridge, Massachusetts : The MIT Press, 2025. | Includes bibliographical references and index.
Identifiers: LCCN 2024020095 (print) | LCCN 2024020096 (ebook) | ISBN 9780262552271 (paperback) | ISBN 9780262383011 (epub) | ISBN 9780262383028 (pdf)
Subjects: LCSH: Conservatism—United States. | Right-wing extremists—United States. | Christianity and politics—United States. | Culture conflict—United States. | Political culture—United States. | Mass media—Social aspects—United States. | Church and state—United States.
Classification: LCC JC573.2.U6 P493 2025 (print) | LCC JC573.2.U6 (ebook) | DDC 320.520973—dc23/eng/20241118
LC record available at https://lccn.loc.gov/2024020095
LC ebook record available at https://lccn.loc.gov/2024020096

10 9 8 7 6 5 4 3 2 1

EU product safety and compliance information contact is: mitp-eu-gpsr@mit.edu

To Anne, Matthew, and the City of Eugene

CONTENTS

PREFACE

In the days leading up to the 2024 presidential election, Donald Trump accused the Democratic Party of being "demonic," said that former House Speaker Nancy Pelosi was an "evil, sick, crazy" word-that-starts-with-a-B ("*Buh-*," he teased), and openly fantasized about his enemies being shot.[1] These statements aligned with the Trump campaign's final messaging push about enemies within and enemies at the gates. Trump's Madison Square Garden rally, held a week before the election, embodied this spirit; speakers called Democratic nominee Kamala Harris "the devil" and "the antichrist" and described the "whole fucking" Democratic Party as "a bunch of degenerates," among other invectives.[2]

The fact that Trump won swiftly and decisively, and beyond that, gained votes across almost every demographic group despite all the vitriol and controversy that swirled in the lead-up to November 5, seems to point to a powerful and growing cult of personality. We make a very different argument in this book. Trump hasn't built a cult of *personality*. Trump has inherited a cult of *demonology*, the origins of which extend back to the Cold War and center on a shape-shifting liberal devil mapped sometimes onto nefarious "elites," sometimes onto economic leftism (which also rails against elites, but that's just details), sometimes onto the institutional Democratic

---

[1] "WATCH: Trump Calls Democrats 'Demonic,' Alludes to Shooting at Reporters at Pennsylvania Rally," *PBS NewsHour*, November 4, 2024, https://www.youtube .com/watch?v=i4lAAxJbPng; Meryl Kornfield, "Trump at Final Rally Hints at Profane Insult of Pelosi That 'Starts with a B,'" *Washington Post*, November 5, 2024, https://www.washingtonpost.com/politics/2024/11/05/trump-insult-pelosi/; "WATCH: Trump: Let's Put Liz Cheney with '9 Barrels Shooting at Her,'" *PBS NewsHour*, November 1, 2024, https://www.youtube.com/watch?v=bnAjz6F6p5E.
[2] KOMO News, "'She Is the Antichrist,' Kamala Harris Called 'Devil' and 'Antichrist' during Trump Rally in NY," October 28, 2024, https://www.youtube.com /watch?v=FpIFu_8qJfc.

Party, and sometimes, simply, onto things demonologists don't like. This is a devil that spans partisan lines and defies logical coherence.

Throughout the 2024 campaign, Trump and his surrogates, boosted by a sprawling rightwing media apparatus, seized every opportunity to highlight how the family, God, conservatives, and America were endangered by the liberal devil. All discursive roads inevitably lead back to that threat: what the liberal-leftist-elite-Democrat-Marxist *them* was doing to pull the country into hell, a framing that simultaneously allowed Trump to position himself as the nation's savior.

To tell this story, especially after the July 2024 near-miss attempt on Trump's life in Butler, Pennsylvania, Trump would at times use explicitly religious symbolism and visuals. He posted one such image to X, formerly Twitter, of the Archangel Michael, a stand-in for Trump, raising a sword to slay Satan, a stand-in for Trump's enemies.[3] More often, Trump and his allies cast off religious rhetoric entirely to make wholly secular claims about liberals' corrosive influence in schools, Big Tech, media, and the government. Whether forwarded by Trump or his MAGA faithful, whether outright religious or secular, these claims typically had very little to do with policy. In fact, the less specific detail or evidence the claims contained, the better, including what, exactly, made someone one of the liberal *them*.

As incessant as it was in its messaging about liberal/leftist evil, indeed as disciplined as it was in that messaging, the Trump campaign was not pursuing a conventional electoral strategy centered on broad public outreach. Trump stuck to MAGA-friendly audiences. He did not actively court swing voters. He simply wasn't focused on persuading lots of different kinds of people to vote for him. Instead, he focused on making the liberal devil bigger by attaching its threat to more people (anyone who challenged Trump) and more places on the map (anywhere that didn't support Trump) and more ideas (anything that didn't align with Trumpism). The center became the left. The right became the left (the "wrong" kind of right, anyway; just ask Liz Cheney). And it all needed to be vanquished. If anti-liberal demonology were a normal electoral strategy, then Trump and his deputies could put down their swords, having handily slain their devil.

---

[3] Donald Trump (@realDonaldTrump), "Saint Michael the Archangel, Defend Us in Battle," X, September 29, 2024, https://x.com/realDonaldTrump/status/1840550305085141221.

But for demonologists, the enemy is never vanquished. Once one issue or group of people is crushed, the threat will simply hop to another issue or group. There will always be more liberals to fight.

Finalizing this book as the election unfolded has been a surreal experience. So many of the things that were assumed to be new lows, or at least new weirdnesses, during the last few months can be traced back ten, twenty, fifty, eighty years, including claims that centrist politicians are Communists, the equation of diversity, equity, and inclusion efforts with the apocalypse, and endless talk about Satan among us, particularly when that talk is secular. This book explores the histories of these and other seemingly novel political developments, explains how they are tethered to changing media systems and structures, and shows how anti-liberal media and their messages emerge from shadow versions of Christianity and conservatism that are not grounded in theology or ideology, and indeed, are the *enemies* of theological Christianity and ideological conservatism.

The prognosis the book offers isn't a good one. What it provides is a way to make sense of what just happened, starting with the insight that Trump's victory wasn't actually a victory for Trump. It was a victory for demonology. As a mode of thinking and political ethos, demonology can be resisted. But it has to be identified as a possessing spirit first.

November 8, 2024

Eugene, Oregon
Syracuse, New York

ACKNOWLEDGMENTS

As we worked on this book, we drew from so much clarifying and sometimes terrifying scholarship spanning media and cultural studies, religious studies, and political science. We are especially indebted to the work of Carol A. Stabile, Nicole Hemmer, Michelle Nickerson, Heather Hendershot, Sara Diamond, Jason Bivins, Anthony Nadler, Doron Taussig, and Daniel Wojcik. Wojcik's framings of avertive apocalypticism and dark enchantment were especially influential to our thinking, and his comments on our final draft were enormously helpful. Others have also provided thoughtful feedback and sound boarding: thank you to Jordan and Anne for constant insights and support and to Michelle D. Brock for the generous exchange of ideas at such a pivotal moment in the editing process. Many thanks to A. W. Ohlheiser for the comments and conversations as we began to find our way through the project. Thank you, Andy, for the careful line edits and salvation from misspellings and other mistakes that in any other context would be funny (and long before that, for listening to the smash and clatter as the project started to take shape). We are also deeply thankful for the book's reviewers, whose feedback significantly shaped the book's final revisions and encouraged us to think more broadly about how our argument fit within existing literature and discourses.

At the MIT Press, we are grateful for the entire production team; a big thank you to Gita Manaktala for her encouragement, enthusiasm, curiosity, and vision (the list goes on) throughout the process. Suraiya Jetha's editorial support is also much appreciated, as is the copyediting work of Stephanie Sakson and Kathleen Caruso and the cover design work of Emily Gutheinz.

From Mark specifically: I owe much thanks and appreciation to Dave Campbell, Geoff Layman, Allen Hertzke, and Allyson Shortle for their mentorship and enthusiasm for the study of religion and politics. Thank you to the Political Science and Religion Departments at Syracuse University for their support through the long writing process. Thank you to Anne, whose love, support, and patience kept me going through the peaks and valleys of writing the book. Thanks to Matthew for distractions and fun when sorely needed. And, last, deep gratitude for Whitney, whose tireless and herculean efforts, not to mention incredible knowledge, are the only reason the project came to fruition through times of my own personal struggles.

From Whitney specifically: Thank you, *thank you*, to my amazing, accomplished, truly wonderful colleagues in the School of Journalism and Communication at the University of Oregon. I am aware that I cannot stop saying how nice everyone here is—although nice doesn't fully capture it. It's the feeling of sitting in an all-school meeting and thinking, this is the best. Call it whatever you want, it is just so exciting to get to say thank you so much. And my SOJC students! You have been such a joy to work with, I'm a lucky Oregon duck. Similarly, and with equal delight, I offer daily appreciation to the City of Eugene Parks and Open Space Department—what a place this is, and what a great job you all do to keep it imminently runnable. Thank you, enormously, to Mark: in a thousand years I couldn't have written this book or anything that resembled this book without your insight and support and patience with my rewrites and expertise on so many things that I got to learn from you. And Anne: thank you for your good cheer and encouragement to us both; I love our Friday ritual and am truly sorry for just how many voice memos about anticommunism you had to hear from the other room. Also to Moo, Vati (thanks for the front yard daffies!), El, Culdro, the Storyteller, the Great Singer, Dum and Max (hurray for your new house!), Dad, Carol, Mrak, Phil, Paola, Wandor, Colin, MA, SA, Regina, Seth, Gretchen, Alex (Hi Gil! Hi Tilly!), Nick, Leah, Mike, Nicole, Theresa, Wesley, Adriene, Anthony, Rachel, Erik, Norah, Jesse, Joan, Claire, Brandy, Bonsey, Alien Twin, Lorax, Everett, Stevie, Finny, Kato forever, John's ghost forever.

INTRODUCING THE SHADOW GOSPEL

THE WAR ON CHRISTMAS IS A WAR ON YOU

Fox News host John Gibson may have written the book *The War on Christmas*, but as far as he's concerned, credit for popularizing the war belongs to his former colleague Bill O'Reilly. "It wasn't really me," Gibson explained in a 2016 interview. "When Bill made it an issue, it went mega."[1]

Gibson, who mentions several times in his book that he is not a devout Christian, is both correct and not quite right. The War on Christmas, which is said to reflect liberals' efforts to remove all vestiges of Christmas from public life and replace them with the rhetorical equivalent of a bowl of cold oatmeal, is now synonymous with Fox News. And Bill O'Reilly did indeed popularize the phrase with a now-infamous 2004 Fox News segment lamenting the various Christmastime traditions—like being greeted with "Merry Christmas!" at a grocery store—that the liberals and their foot soldiers in the ACLU (American Civil Liberties Union) were allegedly whittling away.[2] They did it because they could, O'Reilly said, and because they were too weak to accomplish any of the other sweeping cultural changes they were gunning for. Christmas, though, was a place for them to start—and who knows what they would go after next.

With each passing year, the War on Christmas grew increasingly coordinated. At least, so said O'Reilly and the other prime-time hosts at Fox News, providing as much comedic fuel for *The Daily Show* as it did reactionary fuel for *The Rush Limbaugh Show*.[3] So, when the Christmas tree outside Fox News' headquarters was set on fire by an unhoused man struggling with addiction on December 8, 2021, the network had nearly twenty years of branding to leverage.[4] The fire was evidence of a War on Christmas Trees, which pointed to the broader War on Christmas, which pointed to an even broader War on Christians, which ultimately was a war on *you*, the Fox News viewer. Fox News contributor Reverend Jacques DeGraff likened the fire to the attack on Pearl Harbor, adding that "these colors don't run," referencing the post–September 11 rallying cry of American hawkishness.[5]

Whatever John Gibson, Bill O'Reilly, or any other Fox News personality might think, however, the network can't take credit for inventing the notion of a War on Christmas. In 1959, the conspiratorial John Birch Society published a pamphlet titled "There Goes Christmas?!," which blamed the United Nations and Communists for the holiday's de-Christing, an argument that echoed virulent anti-Semite Henry Ford in his 1921 pamphlet "The International Jew."[6] References to a War on Christmas were also present in the work of *National Review* writers Peter Brimelow and John O'Sullivan in the 1990s, which Brimelow officially codified into a litany in 2000;[7] this rhetoric was right at home within the incendiary rhetoric of Evangelical radio at the time[8] and the "huge movement" of Christian grievance the programs stoked.[9] This is not to say that *all* Evangelicals were concerned about the alleged War on Christmas. For many Christians, a pervasive worry was that there wasn't *enough* Christ in Christmas,[10] and that materialism and commercialization had obscured the true "reason for the season."[11]

The War on Christmas, however, was a good wedge issue. It was also a good ratings grab, which is how the war went mainstream. Before Fox News stormed the battlefield, the people airing concerns about attacks against Christmas—seen as a proxy for Christians generally—were those embedded in conservative media, church, and legal networks. What Fox News and Bill O'Reilly did was to bring the war to everyone else. The result is that, since 2004, the War on Christmas has become a holiday tradition.

PARENTAL WARNING: EXPLICIT CONGRESSIONAL TESTIMONY

In 1984, a small group of wives of prominent U.S. politicians and business figures found themselves deeply disturbed. Their children were being exposed to sexually explicit song lyrics performed by the likes of Prince and Madonna, and they were worried about the effect the lyrics might have on their families and society as a whole.[12] Four of these wives, most prominently Tipper Gore, whose husband was Democratic senator Al Gore, and Susan Baker, whose husband was Republican U.S. Treasury secretary James Baker, formed the Parents Music Resource Center (PMRC). The goal of the PMRC was to lobby the Recording Industry Association of America (RIAA) to include a warning label on explicit records, and the goal of doing that was to protect children and families from the corrosive influence of rock music on kids' value systems. It wasn't just the glamorization of drug use, sex, and rebelliousness that concerned the PMRC, captured in the PMRC's "Filthy Fifteen" litany of worst offenders. It was the alleged link between rock music and suicide. Somebody needed to think of the children.

Many people already were. The Parent Teacher Association had been trying to make headway with the RIAA on precisely this issue, to no avail.[13] The PMRC, in contrast, was much harder to ignore, particularly after the Senate Commerce, Science, and Transportation committee—which included four senators whose wives were PMRC members—announced that they would hold a public hearing on the need for a parental advisory label on records. On the day of the hearing, senators on both sides of the aisle decried the "outrageous filth"[14] and "danger to society"[15] the music industry was producing. A parade of expert witnesses bolstered the senators' concerns by emphasizing how music negatively affects behavior, with one musicologist focusing on the dangers of subliminal messaging. The correlation between rock music and teenage suicide was a recurring worry. But there were dissenters. Musicians Dee Snyder of Twisted Sister, John Denver, and Frank Zappa were called to testify on behalf of the music industry, resulting in a number of sensationalist, overtly comical moments involving the recitation of naughty words into the congressional record. The circus-like atmosphere of the testimony, not to mention all the gratuitous F-bombs, ensured that the hearings would be, as Tipper Gore mused in her 1987 book, "the hottest ticket in town all year."[16]

The PMRC was a secular organization—in name, anyway. In practice, the PMRC and its mission had strong ties to the Christian Right, particularly James Dobson's organization Focus on the Family. PMRC's first meeting had been held in a church and featured youth minister Jeff Ling, who ultimately testified at the 1985 Senate hearing.[17] Its public service video "Rising to the Challenge" was produced by media company Teen Vision, then headed by Bob DeMoss, who was later hired as Focus on the Family's "youth culture expert."[18] Susan Baker, one of the founding members of PMRC, sat on Focus on the Family's board of directors.[19] Further, much of the "evidence" cited in the 1985 Senate hearings, including the dubious link between teen suicide and rock music, was taken from Evangelical sources.[20] The hearings also drew from equally dubious claims about "backmasking," which Evangelical preachers and other media figures claimed contained satanic messages. Some of these Evangelicals insisted that listening to rock music was literally demonic.[21] Others, like the St. Paul, Minnesota, ministry duo the Peters Brothers, were more measured in their arguments, particularly when they appeared on cable television.[22] According to the Peters Brothers, rock music and its "backmasked" messages led teens astray from good morals—and toward more figurative demons like premarital sex and drug use. They were cited in the 1985 PMRC hearings.[23] Post-hearing, the PMRC continued secularizing Evangelical messages, including in the "Satanism Research Packets" they mailed to concerned parents.[24]

The PMRC did not, however, advertise their ties to Evangelicalism and groups like Focus on the Family.[25] And when mainstream media, particularly cable news, covered the 1985 hearings, controversy over "backmasking" and general fears about the dangerous influence of rock music further obscured the Evangelical origins of the panic. This was about our children and families; this was about porn rock and suicide. How could you not support the former and how could you not want to do something about the latter? By the time the Explicit Lyrics sticker finally made its debut in 1990, it had already become part of the pop-cultural backdrop. Of *course* we needed to think about the children.

COVID FREEDOM FIGHTING

Early in the COVID-19 pandemic Donald Trump seemed prepared, even eager, to take credit for the development of a COVID vaccine and hawk it as Trump-branded merchandise.[26] Once the vaccine was available, however, vaccinations were roped into the same Fox News–orbit discourse as masks, social distancing, and lockdowns. Even the Trump-allied Republican leaders who weakly affirmed the value of vaccines reinforced the consensus Party message: "but you shouldn't be forced to take it." Republican governors Ron DeSantis of Florida, Kristi Noem of South Dakota, and Greg Abbott of Texas were on the front lines of the antivax fight, outright banning vaccine requirements for businesses and vaccine mandates for state employees.[27] As with so many other COVID issues, religious freedom became a rallying cry. Republican representative Madison Cawthorn of North Carolina encapsulated the COVID freedom slush pile when he railed against the Biden administration's plan for door-to-door vaccine outreach. "Think about what those mechanisms could be used for. They could then go door-to-door to take your guns. They could go door-to-door to take your Bibles."[28]

Conservative media took this stance even further, entertaining all kinds of conspiracy theories about the vaccine.[29] Fox News was relentless in its "just asking questions" vaccine coverage, as hosts and guests regularly challenged the safety of the Covid vaccine, pushed disproven COVID treatments—including an ineffective malaria drug and horse dewormer whose primary effect on humans was to tear up one's stomach lining—and railed against the fascism of vaccine mandates.[30] (This, of course, despite the fact that Fox News maintained a strict vaccine requirement for employees, including prime-time talent.[31]) Between late June and early August of 2021, conservative media watchdog group Media Matters for America found that 63 percent of all Fox News segments about the vaccine included false and misleading information.[32] Fox's COVID coverage correlated to vaccine rates among Fox News viewers during that same timeframe that were much lower than the national average.[33] Fox News wasn't the only antivax game in town; rightwing networks like Newsmax and One America News, which many Trump supporters turned to when they felt Fox News wasn't pro-Trump enough, also pushed antivax messages, so much so that their audiences were twice as likely as Fox News audiences to resist vaccination.[34]

Just as it was for pro-Trump political leaders, concern over religious freedom remained a common theme of conservative anti-vaccine media.[35] People should be able to make healthcare choices in accordance with their religious faith, the argument went, and the threat to the tenet "my body my choice" was further proof of creeping leftist authoritarianism (never mind that many of the people shouting that slogan were also anti-abortion).[36] Fox News host Tucker Carlson underscored the leftist threat when he argued that Christianity was being phased out in favor of the "cult of Coronavirus," evidenced, in part, by the "vaxed" vaccination status necklace worn by New York State Governor Kathy Hochul (an "unelected governor of a dying state with bad weather," Carlson sneered).[37] By this same logic, Carlson argued in another segment that vaccine mandates in the military were an effort to purge "sincere Christians."[38]

The "sincere Christians" leading the National Association of Evangelicals who supported the vaccine weren't making similar arguments.[39] In fact, reflecting the position of religious leaders around the globe, Christian leaders, including Pope Francis, resoundingly encouraged COVID vaccinations.[40] And yet there were plenty of Evangelicals, including some pastors, who decried vaccine mandates and also claimed that Christians were being purged from public life because of them.[41] Some used social media to offer "religious exemption" letters to help sidestep workplace vaccine requirements. "We're not anti-vaxxers," one Oklahoma pastor and Republican U.S. Senate candidate explained. "We're just pro-freedom."[42]

IF NOT CHRISTIANITY, THEN WHAT?

Each of these three cases, like all the cases we'll be exploring in this book, promote the interests of conservative—and implicitly white—Christians in the United States. At the same time, there's something disorienting about the Christianity on display.

First, the War on Christmas case points to two Christianities. Calls to put Christ back in Christmas emerge from biblical teachings and focus on individual Christians' relationships with God. In contrast, the War on Christmas is broadcast through secular channels and focuses on the perceived threat that Christians in the United States are no longer free to be Christian in public and, by extension, are no longer free to be Christian anywhere. The PMRC case illustrates how influential Christian messages can become once they shed any direct connections to the church and emerge, seemingly secularized, from the mouths of those who have significant public platforms but not necessarily meaningful connections to Christianity—and who just might be Democrats. The COVID vaccine case further underscores the disconnect between beliefs informed by the Bible and beliefs informed by rightwing media. It also shows how the invocation of Christianity by such media—however biblically untethered it might be—serves rhetorically as shield and sword.

In these cases, the religion on display isn't exactly religious. As claims about threats to Christians, Christmas, or children are filtered through cable television and other mass media, they might lose some of their religious content; they might not mention God at all, and focus instead on freedoms allegedly under attack. And yet for those who believe them, the messages carry all the weight and moral authority of a sermon from the pulpit or passage from the Bible.

So what exactly is happening? In this book, we call the not-quite-religion on display the shadow gospel. The *gospel* part of the shadow gospel refers to eighty years of densely overlapping messages about a historically ungrounded, hyperbolized liberal devil. Three frames shape the gospel's messages. The first is outright conspiracism, which posits cadres of scheming liberals in the government or within institutions such as journalism, with granular detail given to the alleged plots and ringleaders themselves. Outright conspiratorial messages are most likely to be designated as "extreme" and tend to be most salient within far-right networks, though they also filter into mainstream conservative spaces. The second is the *anti-* frame, which forwards staunch if abstract opposition to all things liberal, whether those things are described as such by self-identifying liberals or are coded as liberal by conservatives. Anti- messages are predicated on grievance, feed into narratives about beleaguered conservatives, and are a recurring focus of rightwing media. The third is the *pro-* frame, which is expressed as positive support for ideals such as the family, freedom, and America. These messages are least obviously partisan and most likely to spread beyond rightwing circles.

The *shadow* part of the shadow gospel refers to the versions of conservatism and Christianity that have been conjured through anti-liberal messages. Just as a shadow is tethered to but cannot be equated with the solid object casting it, the shadow gospel is tethered to but cannot be equated with conservative ideology or Christian theology. What emerged in the mid-century media environment and expanded over the decades is a shadow realm of false histories and half-truths that uses the language of faith and family—and caricatures of what a liberal is—to exalt the category of "real" Americans, to hell with everyone else.

This analysis begins with mid-century Evangelical and rightwing activist —and later, institutional Republican—networks because that is where shadow gospel messages first emerged and thrived. Although the messages were swiftly adopted toward partisan political ends (namely, to help elect more Republicans), they were not the *product* of partisan politics. Their origins were, instead, strikingly nonpartisan. It is therefore unsurprising that, in the end, the messages that eventually were politicized did not stay confined to the political right; and neither did their implications. As later chapters will show, shadow gospel messages have also circulated widely within the political left—at least, what gets called "the left." More on that caveat soon.

The relationship between left and right is central to the story we're telling. That said, *this is not a book about polarization*. In fact, our underlying argument is that the polarization frame misses something important when it attributes the chaos of the U.S. political landscape to intensifying clashes between leftwing liberals and rightwing conservatives. People are obviously clashing, and intensely. Our claim is that the left/right polarization framework does not fully explain why. The framework we present instead is one of possession by the shadow gospel, which transcends conventional partisan categories. The result is that we are not merely asking readers to consider how the shadow gospel has taken hold of the MAGA (Make America Great Again), Trumpist, Evangelical *them*. We are also asking readers to consider how the shadow gospel has become an animating spirit in the United States more broadly.[43] To modify the old saying, the devil you know is much easier to exorcise than the devil you don't.

THE SHADOW GOSPEL, NOT THE CHURCH GOSPEL

As hinted above, our analysis challenges how politics in the United States has for decades been understood: through the prism of *left* and *right*. Central to this left/right focus is the conventional account of how Christian conservatism, particularly Evangelicalism, came to dominate the rightwing, and by extension, the U.S. political landscape. We will be telling a different story entirely about religious influence in the United States, with major implications for the basic coherence of the notions of "left" and "right."

However, the conventional account of Evangelical influence remains a significant part of our study. That account goes like this. In the 1970s, very conservative Republican and Evangelical leaders came together to push the Republican Party platform toward more conservative positions on issues like abortion and same sex marriage.[44] This was an advantageous arrangement for both groups; Republicans benefited because Evangelicals were an untapped but increasingly powerful voting bloc that would give the Party an electoral advantage,[45] and Evangelicals benefited because it put them and their interpretation of biblical teachings in the driver's seat of policy-making.[46] The synergy between Evangelicals and Republicans is what allowed Evangelicalism's "Three Bs" of belonging, belief, and behavior[47] to remake U.S. politics.

Appropriately, our shadow gospel book project started with a discussion of Evangelical influence. It took the form of a January 6, 2021, email exchange between Brockway, a religion and politics scholar whose work focuses on secularism, Evangelical activism, and Evangelical party influence, and Phillips, a media studies scholar whose early work on internet trolling evolved into a political communication and journalism focus, with much energy devoted to rightwing conspiracy theories. Like many people in the United States and around the world, we were both trying to make sense of the violence and chaos at the U.S. Capitol as it unfolded. Brockway, at the time Phillips's colleague at Syracuse University, messaged to ask whether the trolls Phillips had studied on 4chan were Evangelical, since the visual rhetoric of the Capitol rioters included a heady mix of trolling memes, Christian symbolism, and antagonistic Trump support.[48] Phillips was surprised by this question. Trolls in the early days of 4chan had delighted in mocking and harassing Christians; they definitely weren't Evangelical.[49] But the more we talked about the role of religion, or at least the role of Christian symbology, within rightwing political networks, the more we realized that there was something strange about the relationship between religious and secular media, and something even stranger about the relationship between religious and secular belief.

The conversations that followed—many more emails, COVID quarantine Zooms, and countless voice memos—uncovered another oddity: the anomalies generated by the conventional account of Evangelical influence. Most conspicuous is the fact that since the early 1980s—the time of Evangelical Christianity's supposed rise in cultural influence—Evangelicalism has remained stagnant in terms of numbers of believers.[50] Measured as a percentage of the population, there are no more Evangelicals today than there were in the 1980s; Evangelicals now, as then, make up about a quarter of the population.[51] Evangelicals have not even grown as a percentage of the Republican Party since the Reagan era.[52] What has changed is the secular population, which has risen sharply since the 1980s.[53] The numbers suggest that the last forty years have been a conversion and outreach failure for Evangelicals, rather than a period of increasing influence and power. Indeed, the only significant rise in Evangelical identification during the last four decades came under the Trump presidency, but, critically, that was not accompanied by a similar rise in church attendance.[54]

Further, while activists might have been able to link Republican Party machinery with Evangelical leadership during the 1970s, the full fusing of Republican and Evangelical identity within the churchgoing public didn't happen until the 1990s.[55] This is to say nothing of how improbable the forging of Republicanism with Evangelicalism was in the 1970s; it might seem like a natural fit from our contemporary perspective, but pre-Reagan Republicans and Evangelicals were far from monolithic.[56] The idea that a few rightwing activists single-handedly changed the course of U.S. politics in the 1970s is compelling, but is complicated by the fact that these same activists were unable to make overwhelming electoral headway for another twenty years. Social science research conducted by Clyde Wilcox in the 1980s adds to this complication. In his study of the Religious Right, Wilcox identified significant demographic and attitudinal similarities between Christian rightwingers of the 1950s and the Religious Right of 1980s that couldn't have been engendered by Republican organizing because it pre-dated that organizing by decades.[57] Wilcox's work suggests that the Republican Party *inherited* a powerful (if ideologically slippery) coalition, but can't be credited with building it.

What became clear to us was that the existing stories—about Evangelicalism and about rightwing activism—were incomplete. Something besides Evangelical believers, churches, and theological tenets themselves had powered Evangelical influence within the Republican Party and U.S. culture. The argument we developed over the subsequent two years was that *a* gospel had fueled the relationship between the religious and the secular; *a* gospel had fundamentally shaped, and was continuing to shape, the American landscape. But it wasn't the church gospel.[58]

DEMONOLOGY AND DISCONNECTION

By arguing that Evangelicalism is not in the driver's seat of U.S. culture and politics—at least not in the way the conventional account would suggest—we are not swapping out one religious influence for another. Specifically, we are not positing a white Christian nationalist explanation.

Christian nationalism can seem like a close fit, particularly when considering the shadow gospel's MAGA manifestations. It is certainly the framework with the most cultural traction, largely because so many Christian leaders and groups have taken up the cause of fighting it within their own ranks.

In these contexts, many cite the January 6, 2021, attack on the U.S. Capitol as the moment they realized the dangers of such a belief system, particularly given the prevalence of Christian rhetoric used by pro-Trump insurrectionists. Of course, January 6 wasn't a stand-alone event, and worry over white Christian nationalism isn't restricted to that one day. As an example, in a *Time* magazine article focused on the "Christians against Christian Nationalism" movement, discussion of the insurrection pivots to reflections on the 2022 Buffalo massacre, in which a white supremacist opened fire on a supermarket in a predominantly Black neighborhood.[59]

Like so many of the articles that highlight the dangers of white Christian nationalism, the *Time* article posits the racist "Great Replacement" theory as the link between *white Christianity* and *nationalism*. This theory maintains that nonwhite non-Christians are trying to overrun the country, thereby replacing the "real" Americans. The Buffalo shooter took the Great Replacement narrative to its grotesque extreme. However, rightwing media and Republican politicians have promoted versions of the theory—some watered-down, some full-throated—even if they don't describe it as "replacement" as such. For instance, former House Speaker Newt Gingrich stated on Fox News just a few months prior to the Buffalo shooting that leftists were trying to "drown traditional, classic Americans with as many people as they can who know nothing of American history, nothing of American tradition, nothing of the rule of law."[60] Fox News' Tucker Carlson—host of the most popular show on cable until he was fired from the network as it navigated a costly 2020 election defamation case—also played a central role in promoting the theory, as he'd all but signed his name to the idea of "replacement."[61]

The prominence—and danger—of Great Replacement discourses animates a great deal of academic research focused on white Christian nationalism and the threat it poses to democracy.[62] Empirical research conducted by sociologists Samuel Perry and Philip Gorski has been especially influential in articulating white Christian nationalist belief. As Perry and Gorski describe it, white Christian nationalism is a reactionary and increasingly anti-democratic fundamentalist worldview that seeks to establish the United States as a Christian nation and ensure that Christians are central to that nation.[63] Perry and Gorski emphasize that white Christian nationalism can take secular and semi-secular forms, but ultimately it emerges from all the *stuff* of Christianity, just warped and directed toward exclusionary ends. Perry and Gorski identify specific indicators of white Christian nationalism,[64] which they measure by asking respondents to assess their agreement with statements such as, "The success of the United States is part of God's plan" and "The federal government should advocate Christian values."[65] These indicators, like the belief system they index, are grounded in theology. These indicators are also grounded in ideology. They point to something specific, consistent, and ultimately coherent.

In contrast, the case studies we were beginning to explore for this book project—including our three opening cases—were not consistently or coherently grounded in theology or ideology. They were not even grounded in *identity*, at least not in the cut-and-dried identity categories said to carve up the U.S. electorate. The messages swirling in our ever-expanding pile of cases were not restricted to conservatives or Republicans or Christians. They often *targeted* conservative Republicans. They also often targeted Christians, including Evangelicals, most frequently those who pushed back against false claims that the 2020 election had been stolen from Donald Trump, or who followed basic COVID mitigation protocols—or who merely acknowledged that COVID was real.

The overarching strangeness suffusing these cases has historical precedent. Historian Richard Hofstadter, famous—and for some, infamous—for grounding the "paranoid style" of U.S. politics in a good-versus-evil apocalypticism, identified all kinds of strangeness in the Christianity and, as he described it, "pseudo-conservatism" he was analyzing in the 1960s.[66] He argues, presciently, that the anticommunism animating conservatism during the Cold War was influenced by Christian fundamentalism.[67] He also argues presciently that the fundamentalism on display was better described as a religious style than a grounded theology, since it wasn't clear "how many evangelical right-wingers adhere to a literal view of Scripture and other fundamentalist tenets."[68]

Pulling from 1960s survey data about the Christian Anti-Communism Crusade analyzed by political scientist Raymond Wolfinger and others[69]—which decades later was reexamined by Clyde Wilcox—Hofstadter also notes that the "pseudo-conservatism" he and his colleagues were identifying within the Republican Party wasn't coming from the expected places, like economic concerns. Where Hofstadter continually directed his energy was toward the *style* of this group, with a particular focus on the conspiracism and paranoia that Hofstadter attributed to fringe fundamentalism. What we have come to believe is that Hofstadter was knocking on the door of the shadow gospel. He didn't walk fully in because he restricted his analysis, first, to conspiracism, and second, to the religious fringes. (In our analysis we will highlight the shadow gospel's additional *anti-* and *pro-* registers as well as the fact that it did not emerge from the fringes of fundamentalism, but rather from emergent Evangelical Christianity, which at the time Hofstadter was writing was actively positioning itself as "classic" American Christianity. This is a critical point of divergence between our study and studies focused on white Christian nationalism, which lament the recent takeover of Evangelicalism by white Christian nationalist extremism.[70] Our argument is that what has gripped many Evangelical churches isn't *outside* extremism but rather reflects media and rhetorical dynamics at the core of Evangelicalism's founding.) Still, Hofstadter deserves credit for recognizing that this indeterminate thing, this in-between thing, was something to measure—and to worry about.

Other scholars focused on the Cold War era have pointed to similar unwieldy dynamics and the difficulties of classification, including historian Joel Kovel, who describes America First anticommunism as a semireligious, semi-secular "realm of the shadowy bizarre."[71] But work of this ilk tends to *point* to bizarre political and religious contours rather than fully systematize them, let alone ascribe a stable name to them, and also tends to tether the bizarreness to the Cold War era and anticommunism in particular. What we were seeing over and over, through the decades, confined to rightwing networks and also swirling through the mainstream, was an unwieldy not-quite-this-but-not-quite-that animus that long outlived the 1960s. Our goal was to explain it—and to give it a name.

To do so, we synthesized decades of political science, religious studies, and media history research and analyzed the biographies, communications, speeches, and published works of Evangelical leaders, rightwing media figures, and conservative politicians. The methodological term for this kind of work is conjunctural analysis. What it means is dot-connecting.[72] By identifying historical trends within contemporary events, culminating with the Trump era and all the question marks that loom over the impending 2024 election, the contours of the eighty-year-old thing we were looking at began to emerge. What we were dealing with was the felt sense that the liberal enemy is always at the gates, ready to destroy everything that "real" Americans hold most dear, with "real" referring not just to conservative Christians but to the *right kind* of conservative Christianity—one that is ultimately disconnected from grounded ideological or theological beliefs. Instead, shadow gospel fear and loathing of liberals is a form of *demonology*.

Anthropologist Phillip Stephens Jr., describes demonology as "an elaborate body of belief about an evil force that is inexorably undermining society's most cherished values and institutions."[73] Demonological thinking is different from the more straightforward dynamic of demonization.[74] Demonization is grounded; it points to something that exists in the world and says that it is very bad or even evil.[75] In contrast, demonology is aggressively *un*grounded; it points to a sense of threat mapped onto a fuzzily defined, shapeshifting enemy. Some of these threats may connect to real things in the world: actual external dangers or perceived dangers that take on an almost supernatural quality of malevolence. Very often, though, the threat results from casting shadows and then setting out to defend oneself against them. For contemporary demonological conservatives, the liberal devil is synonymous with "the left" and Democrats. But reflecting the ungroundedness of the demonological framework, the liberal devil can be anyone who seems to align with liberalism—or who simply questions the existence of a liberal devil.

Religion and politics scholar Jason Bivins also employs the term "anti-liberal" to describe some Christians' beliefs, specifically their opposition to government authority and policies. For Bivins, however, "liberalism" refers to the foundational ideology of American democracy, with its valuing of individual over collective rights, and negative freedoms (*freedom from* government restriction) over positive freedoms (*freedoms for* everyone to enjoy equally).[76] In the context of the shadow gospel, the concept "anti-liberal" describes something very different. It points to a nebulous, omnipresent threat said to undermine God, America, the family, and traditional (specifically, conservative) values. Further, it equates the pursuit of diversity, equity, and inclusion as a liberal plot. The result is an aggressive minoritarianism—simply defined as minority interests overruling majority interests—and a basic if unspoken white supremacy. Anti-liberal demonology thus doesn't just oppose liberalism as a vague vessel for evil. It actually *undermines* the foundational sense of liberalism as a structuring framework for democracy.

Ultimately, the vagueness of anti-liberal demonology is what makes it incompatible with ideology and theology. When ideological conservatives oppose left-wing policies, their dissent is based on arguments over specific courses of action, tenets, or proposals. Maybe the arguments are good, maybe the arguments are bad. In either case, ideological conservatives counter what they believe to be worse ideas with what they believe to be better ideas. And when these conservatives find themselves rolling their eyes at the left-leaning friends, colleagues, or family in their lives, they are likely to point to actual conflicts, behaviors, and irritations. Likewise, even the most fundamentalist Christians are rooted in the specificity of biblical teachings. When they talk about external threat, it's a response to the encroachment of the secular world into their religious sphere. The more secular someone is, the less likely they will be moved by such an argument. But it is still an argument about something solid.

In contrast, when an anti-liberal demonologist is confronted by a liberal—at least, by someone who has been accused of being one—the conversation does not center on the specifics of a given tax policy or adopting a biblical principle in practice. Details and coherence are secondary concerns, if they matter at all. What matters most is the fight. This is what many accounts of white Christian nationalism miss, or at least, misidentify. Demonology can look like ideology and theology. But unlike the ideological and the theological, the demonological is not built on arguments or facts. There is no rhetorical solid ground.

As a result, having little or nothing to do with the actual stuff of Christianity is no problem whatsoever. The fact that Fox News was not encouraging people to attend church, that advocates of the PRMC scrubbed mentions of anything overtly religious, that the most prominent "preachers" across each of our opening cases are secular media figures and politicians who made their arguments without guidance from religious doctrines or principles, that the warrior for Christmas John Gibson emphasizes his distance from the church,[77] and that the Buffalo shooter warrior for "Christian values" (whose "Christian values" apparently include racist bloodlust) explicitly states that he is not Christian[78] all fit comfortably within a demonological paradigm where the primary driver isn't how much someone loves God but how much they hate the liberal devil.

Anti-liberal animus also helps reconcile the disconnect between clear irreligiosity and use of Christian rhetoric. When you have zero meaningful ties to the Bible but continue to make vague references to Jesus, the devil, or sin to suit your changing needs, there's nothing you can't aim a God cannon at. Additionally, sidling up to Christianity allows anti-liberals to enjoy the legitimacy afforded by religious affiliation without any of the theological constraints—which as an added bonus allows them to scream religious discrimination any time they are challenged. Thus when critics point to the strikingly unchristian behavior of people like Rush Limbaugh, Alex Jones, and Donald Trump—all of whom at least wink at the idea of "Christian values"—in the hopes of breaking the spell of their popularity, they fail to see that *not* being beholden to religious doctrine is what makes that popularity possible. Freed of those strictures, anti-liberals can say anything, regardless of what they might have said the day before, or the hour before, or the moment before.

Finally, burning opposition to liberalism is how secular proclamations can take on all the religious weight of a divine decree, the fewer concrete details the better. This is how John Gibson could point to all the Christmas trees the liberals *haven't* taken away as proof of their war against Christmas. This is how the Fox and Friends hosts could casually sidestep the Christmas tree arson's motives (or lack thereof); those didn't matter. What mattered is that the fire served as yet more "proof" that the leftist horde was coming for *you*, the Fox News viewer, a point driven home by hosts Brian Kilmeade and Ainsley Earhardt. What the fire revealed, Kilmeade insisted, is that "no city is safe, no person is safe."[79] Earhardt clarified which people Kilmeade meant. "This is personal to you, too, at home now: the Fox Christmas tree vandalized. Arson! And that's personal to you, it's personal to us. This is an American icon. This is our Christmas tree."[80] In these and other cases, the lack of specificity—indeed, the outright incoherence of the claims being made—is what makes the devil stronger.

WHAT IN THE ACTUAL HELL

Up to a point, the imagined liberal devil and its demonological tradition—the feeling, simply put, that (liberal) evil is all around—share some basic characteristics with the Christian devil.

One point of overlap is that, in the Bible, Satan isn't a static figure. As religious historian Elaine Pagels explains, Satan evolves as early Christianity evolves and maps onto different kinds of enemies as they emerge,

reflected in the demonization of Jews, pagans, and heretics, whose opposition to the early Christians was framed as a form of demon possession.[81]
The logic was that Satan worked through one's adversaries. The association
of particular groups with Satan thus functioned as "a way of characterizing one's actual enemies as the embodiment of transcendent forces."[82] This
proved to be an *additive* process of demonization. New enemies appended
to the list of cosmic opponents didn't replace the older enemies. Instead,
the evil accumulated.[83] In their analysis of Satan's influence on the Western
tradition, historians Richard Raiswell, Michelle D. Brock, and David R.
Winter build on this idea, noting that Satan's constructed nature—the fact
that his significance isn't confined to the Bible but rather functions as a com-
posite of people's experiences with adversity—ensures that "every reiteration of the devil serves to expand the devil's perceived field of operation."[84]
It also makes Satan something of a rubbish bin into which you throw all the
bad things.[85]

Similarly, who and what counts as the liberal devil—who and what
gets thrown into *that* rubbish bin—evolves as the early conservative movement evolves. Subsequent chapters highlight how historically grounded
notions of liberals and liberalism—in the 1930s–1940s context of the New
Deal, 1950s–1960s context of Evangelicalism, and 1950s–1960s context of
rightwing media—were sucked into a demonological amalgamation that
flattened liberalism into a singular concept and designated it as the great
destroyer. Raiswell, Brock, and Winter's frame of reiteration helps explain
why it was *this* word, liberal, and not some other word, that became the
go-to label for accumulating evil. "Liberal" is, very simply, *the most satanic
term* in the shadow gospel orbit. It was used in different ways in different contexts by different groups of people over many years. It was able to
amass the most demonic reiterations as conservative networks strengthened
and expanded.

The contemporary understanding of "liberal" that emerged is not a
standalone concept, echoing another of Raiswell, Brock, and Winter's
insights about the Christian devil. As they argue, God and the devil become
"mutually authenticating and mutually contingent."[86] In other words, the
existence of one reinforces the existence of the other. Similarly, contemporary liberalism has come to imply opposition to conservativism. Modern self-identifying liberals would be inclined to frame this opposition *via
negativa*; they believe the opposite of what conservatives believe. Modern

conservatives—certainly those steeped in demonological thinking—would be inclined to frame liberal opposition as an across-the-board, even spiritual, attack.

That general sense of liberal threat has, over the decades, subsumed a dizzying spectrum of bad others that includes "the left" writ large and Democrats, of course, but also the "wrong" kinds of Republicans and Christians, queer people, K-12 teachers, civil rights activists, government bureaucrats, and literally anyone else said to run afoul of the "traditional American values" exalted by the shadow gospel.

Ronald Reagan personifies the shadow gospel dynamic of harnessing placeholder evil. He does so by creating what political scientist Michael Rogin calls a "disembodied self" that Reagan grafted onto whatever policy or economic aim he decided to champion.[87] The subversive—if nebulous— opponents of these aims were used to reinforce the category of the good American in contrast to the monstrous/evil American, both of which were disconnected from major American social and political identities but whose clash was framed by Reagan both apocalyptically and cinematically.[88] We will revisit Reagan and the demonological template he perfected in later chapters. What his presidency emphasizes is that demonology aimed at perceived liberal threats is a natural shapeshifter, just like the devil himself.

A second overlap between the Christian and liberal devil is that they both lend cosmic significance to turmoil and strife. Pagels emphasizes how, among early Christians, conflict took on a very specific world-sustaining importance. Opposition wasn't just opposition. Opposition was a supernatural force,[89] with the fate of the world always hanging in balance.[90] Being threatened in this very particular kind of way—threatened *cosmically*— was central to early Christian identity and community formation.[91] Satan was so important to the story the gospel writers were telling about Jesus that Pagels flatly states that their writings "would make little sense *without* Satan."[92]

The evil liberal, nebulously conceived, is an equally important figure in the development of modern conservatism and its own set of gospels. Subsequent chapters will show that the threat of an apocalypse wrought by liberals lends enormous weight, meaning, and even excitement to fights over everything from tax policy to LGBTQ rights. More foundational than that, liberal evil is the basis of conservative goodness—facilitating an identity that might seem solid and stable but is built on top of shadows.

However, overlaps between the Christian devil and liberal devil can go only so far. The primary difference between the Satan of the Bible and the Satan of the shadow gospel is that, as the archfiend of *shadow* Christianity, shadow gospel Satan was conjured through widespread, mutually reinforcing rightwing media *specifically so that he could be fought*. This devil is, in the end, a mass-mediated target to rail against and rally around.

A second distinction between these two devils is that, while the emergence of Satan within the early Christian tradition may have been narratively necessary, that necessity had a higher and more glorious purpose: bringing about the Second Coming of Christ. Satan is bad, in other words, but the post-apocalyptic outcome is good: a restored, redeemed world.[93] For the Christian faithful, victory over evil is assured. "Those who participate in this cosmic drama," Pagels writes, "cannot lose."[94] In stark contrast, the shadow Christian tradition is not based on the idea that Christ will return after tribulation. There is no promise of a returned messiah or a cleansed word. There is just Revelation Lite: an always and ongoing Armageddon, nothing but horsemen of the liberal apocalypse.[95] Those who participate in *this* cosmic drama cannot stop fighting. Here, the devil is more important than Jesus, if Jesus is even needed at all.

That's not to say that there is *no* Jesus within the shadow Christian framework. In the pages to follow, we chronicle how shadow gospel evangelists, from Evangelical leaders in the 1940s and 1950s to partisans at the vanguard of the 1994 Republican Revolution to pundits at Fox News, promote themselves as the savior of the world they have created for themselves, one that is always teetering at the edge of the end times. A scary prospect, certainly, but as cultural theorist Daniel Wojcik emphasizes, religious apocalypticism is acutely appealing as a form of "dark enchantment."[96] Enchantment as a vernacular religious framework describes how humans create meaning, make sense of things, and enliven their existence in a world seen as drab, mechanistic, and soulless, and which is replete with randomness, adversity, and suffering. "Dark enchantment" is equally enlivening, Wojcik argues, but is derived from the perception of "darker" forces at work in human existence, including demons, evil conspiracies, and various flavors of apocalypticism. As Wojcik explains, it can be exciting to be thrust in the middle of a cosmic end-times drama. One's life takes on newfound significance. And for those who are certain that they are the chosen ones, cosmic significance contributes to heightened self-esteem in the face of perceived evil.[97]

THE POLITICS OF RESENTMENT

The active and aggressive conjuring of the liberal devil by the shadow gospel marks another point of departure between this project and existing political science scholarship. For decades, researchers have described conservatives as reactionary, a framing that dovetails with characteristics of resentment, grievance, and paranoia. The reactionary definition of conservatism often highlights resistance to pluralistic democracy—equal representation within the body politic of various racial, national, and religious groups of different economic classes—that can dovetail into nationalism.[98] Classic texts in this vein include Katherine Cramer's political analysis of Wisconsin conservatives, which argues that economic and cultural resentment in rural communities has intensified distrust of the state and the "liberal elite" said to be running things, as well as Arlie Russel Hochschild's sociological study of Louisiana conservatives, which explores these conservatives' belief that liberal elites have allowed cultural "line cutters" to enjoy unearned and undeserved resources at the conservatives' expense.[99] Jeremy Engels focuses on the violent rhetoric that results from the perceived encroachment of the state (or liberal elites) and argues that it can be understood as *defensive*: they unfairly took something from us.[100]

In these and other accounts, scholars almost always highlight gaps between perceptions of encroachment and the reality of encroachment. And yet conservative pushback against economic, social, or political democratization tends to be described in terms of clear ideological battle lines between advancing liberals and the conservatives either forced to retreat or who defiantly endeavor to stand their ground. The presumption that conservatives have been pushed into a defensive stance by a modernizing, liberalizing culture—one that threatens traditional values and generally upsets The Way Things Were—forms the core of the culture wars thesis. Sociologist James Davison Hunter maps this political binary onto a traditional/modern divide within religious traditions. Drawing from reactionary definitions of conservatism, Hunter states that traditionalists favor protecting time-honored, religiously grounded values in the face of shifting religions, politics, and societies.[101] The conflict of the culture war arises as traditionalists struggle to preserve things and modernists struggle to change them.

By highlighting the demonological conjuring of "liberal" as a unified, historically stable concept—a process that belies the amalgamated and ultimately placeholder quality of the term—the following chapters challenge such a framing. The culture war, we argue, is actually a culture trap. To claim that progressive liberals are the ones policing the boundaries of culture and pushing against traditionalism is to fail to appreciate the decades of shadow gospel evangelizing that sets up a falsely traditionalist morality and then laments that it has been knocked down by its own invented enemy. Put bluntly: the shadow gospel isn't reactionary. The shadow gospel is progressive. It establishes who and what the devil is, throws the first punch, then it insists it was acting in self-defense. And it is convincing.

This book argues against another element of the reactionary politics framework: the common assumption that if we could just find a way to shift people's material conditions, or at least shift their perceptions about their material conditions, they would stop feeling aggrieved and, as a consequence, would stop being reactionary. But what if that's wrong? What if the driver of grievance isn't despair over feeling screwed over, but excitement over getting to live in a cosmic drama and perpetually fighting a custom-made devil? What if the challenge isn't extracting people from pain but extracting them from a shadowy form of comfort derived from a devil they don't just know but prefer?[102]

UNMASKING MYTHS

When we speak of the shadowy realm of liberal devils, conservative messiahs, and perennial apocalypse conjured by the shadow gospel, we are not being literal. Our conceptions of shadow Christianity and shadow conservatism are meant to function as mental shortcuts to help conceptualize, even visualize, the totally divergent ethical, epistemological, and ontological paradigm that emerges from eighty years of intensely resonant Evangelical and rightwing media centered on the dangers of an amalgamated placeholder liberalism.

To be clear, shadow gospel evangelists absolutely use the language of the Book of Revelation to describe the American cultural landscape, and they absolutely refer to liberals as devils and demons and incessantly point to their godlessness.[103] We are not forcing that framework; it's there, front and center, and has been through the decades. Our rhetorical purpose in developing the shadow/shadowy realm theme is to make a very slippery thing feel a bit more solid, so that we can discuss its origins and point to its consequences. This is simply not possible to do when one takes for granted, instead, that Christian-sounding language and self-identification points to biblically based, theologically grounded Christianity or that conservative-sounding language and self-identification points to principled, ideologically grounded conservatism. Sometimes, grounded theology and ideology is what is happening. Sometimes it is not; *often* it is not. The shadow gospel provides a framework for identifying and historicizing when it is not.

Historicization is crucial, as doing so challenges the shadow gospel's most powerful attribute: its ability to make myth. Here we draw from cultural theorist Roland Barthes's conception of myth: claims about the world that have specific causes and histories but which become so commonplace through such intense wraparound and repetition (the term "wraparound" in the context of repeated media messages will emerge as a recurring framework throughout the chapters) that they come to feel natural and necessary, something that could not be otherwise.[104] As myth, they step out into the sunlight convinced of their own reality. They exist beyond argument. They are simply true.

To give a contemporary example, ask anyone who is certain that Christmas is under siege by liberals where they got the idea and they will likely cock their head quizzically. Particularly for those raised on a lifelong diet of demonological media, the evidence is everywhere and has always been everywhere, so much so that the question itself would be jarring. For believers, the existence of a Christmas-assaulting left is perfectly natural and perfectly necessary, yet another example of what *we* have to deal with because of *them*.

The War on Christmas points to another, much more powerful myth that we have already begun to unpack: a historically and linguistically stable *left* and *right*, with the left mapping onto liberals and the right mapping onto conservatives. The political parties are subject to the same directional split; Democrats go left and Republicans go right. From a contemporary American vantage point, liberal and conservative, left and right, Democrat and Republican, is simply how the political landscape is divided, and liberal *versus* conservative, left *versus* right, Democrats *versus* Republicans is simply how electoral politics are fought. This division between left and right is the ultimate example of something that feels like it could not be otherwise. How else would we describe it?

However, as historians Hyrum Lewis and Verlan Lewis argue, the categories of "left" and "right" are much less coherent than our politics would suggest. "Our two political teams have coalesced around the concept of left and right," Lewis and Lewis concede, "but the concepts themselves are fictions."[105] Our account of the emergence of the shadow gospel doubles as an account of the emergence of the myth of left and right—one that hinges on a demonological conjuring of liberal threat equated with leftism and the Democratic Party. We are not saying that liberals, leftists, or Democrats don't exist. Millions of people use the word "liberal" to self-identify and to associate themselves with political positions they feel good about (and also to distinguish themselves from conservatives). Economic leftism is real and so is the activist left. The Democratic Party is the (sometimes uneasy) home of people who describe themselves as liberal and leftist. What we are saying, echoing Lewis and Lewis,[106] is that our stories about "left" and "right" need rewriting.

This poses some complications in how to describe things. The left/right dichotomy is *the* structuring political framework in the United States. It is very difficult to think outside of such an all-encompassing frame. That, however, is precisely our goal; to challenge the assumption that left and right are, like God and Satan, mutually authenticating and mutually contingent. As a result, we use "liberal" and "left" under a blanket disclaimer (and very often, scare quotes). And although we have chosen to employ the term "rightwing" to describe what ultimately is a self-contained media and information ecosystem, "right" does not take for granted an equal and opposite "left." In the chapters that follow, what "right" points to is itself.

Resisting the left/right framing is the first step in pushing back against the culture wars thesis, one set against the backdrop of the politics of resentment. The overarching claim in culture wars resentment narratives is that conservatives feel bad because of what liberals have done to them. Our counterpoint is that it's a particular kind of grievance when you are thrashing against a devil that you invented, and which you also enjoy fighting. Of course, people in this mode can simultaneously be struggling financially or socially or both. But whether spoken by a liberal or conservative, Democrat or Republican, attributing the *cause* of that struggle to the liberal devil is a demonological move, and needs to be interrogated as such.

The culture wars thesis needs pushback for another reason. When forwarded by demonologists, arguments about encroaching liberals ultimately reflect an aggressive push for the "right to enjoy"[107] life without ever having to worry about other people's needs, concerns, or experiences. The assertions that we get to abide by any standards we want, we get to be as exclusionary as we want, and we get to be as cruel as we want are then transformed by demonologists into a reactionary, defensive, and even pitiable stance. Our goal in calling attention to this and other shadow gospel myths—and just as important, in identifying the network processes by which these myths are created and sustained—is to resist false histories about who gets to be comfortable by default, about who represents "real" America, and about who is the savior and who is the devil.

CHAPTER OVERVIEW

Exclusionary beliefs are not specific to the shadow gospel. They are as much woven into the United States' national fabric as are efforts to create a more pluralistic, more diverse, and more just union, and are reflected in a true embarrassment of historical examples, from the Puritans' paranoid, violent, "wellspring of diabolism" aimed at indigenous people in the seventeenth and eighteenth centuries[108] to the Ku Klux Klan's nineteenth-century weaponization of Protestantism to stoke conspiratorial racist and xenophobic fears[109] to the fervor—one that Anthea Butler describes as outright religious[110]—surrounding lynching culture and the Lost Cause narrative embraced by many whites in the post–Civil War U.S. South.

We begin our analysis in the 1940s because this was when the invented liberal devil began to take shape through the emergent gospel of rightwing and Evangelical media. Fundamentally linked to these media, the shadow gospel—the messages themselves and the shadow worlds they created—would evolve through the decades, reflecting changes in media policy, network resources, and conservative audience expectations. "The Realm of the Shadowy Bizarre" (chapter 1) sets the stage for this story with a focus on Cold War anticommunism and its consequences. It highlights the pervasiveness of Christian language and symbology in religious and ostensibly secular anticommunist networks, including within the FBI. It also establishes where, how, and why self-described "100 percent Americans" lobbed demonological attacks against allegedly un-American subversives, forming a shadowy crater into which evil enemies could be accrued.

"Branding Satan" (chapter 2) examines how New Evangelicalism in the 1950s and 1960s and its loosely linked network of parachurch organizations contributed to the shape and scope of the shadow devil by pushing messages about a fundamentally evil liberalism said to be infiltrating education, politics, and pop culture. It also examines how New Evangelicals like Billy Graham reframed Mainline Protestantism as extreme, even outright demonic, in order to claim the throne of mainstream Christianity for themselves. (We use the term "Mainline" to refer to the pluralistic group of Protestant denominations mostly associated with the Federal, later National, Council of Churches. The term "Mainline" emerged in the context of the fundamentalist/modernist divide and would also come to distinguish Mainline from Evangelical Christians like Graham, histories we will revisit in subsequent chapters.) This rhetorical move, in which the New Evangelicals defined what was evil in order to position themselves as America's savior, was foundational to the development of shadow Christianity and shadow conservatism, summed up in the apocalyptic credo, *liberals are evil and we are here to save you.*

Focusing on rightwing media activists of the 1950s and 1960s, including those within the self-described respectable right and those relegated to the "lunatic fringe," "Make Me a Shadow Myth" (chapter 3) foregrounds the shadow gospel's network dynamics. Through dense media wraparound, decontextualization, and opacity, with a powerful amalgamation of pandemonic rhetoric across secular and Evangelical networks, falsely traditional claims about America, conservatism, and Christianity were entrenched as natural and necessary. Claims of liberal bias in media and education, dovetailing with claims of conservative oppression by liberals, followed a similar mythmaking process. The growing ubiquity of these messages lengthened the shadows of Christianity and conservatism. They also helped facilitate a smooth transition into the deeply demonological Reagan era.

"The Culture Wars Are Satanic" (chapter 4) challenges the assumption that the dominant catalyst for the rise of the New Right in the 1970s was faith in God coupled with ideological overlap between conservative Christian and Republican platforms. We argue instead that it was demonology—particularly the expediency of the devil and resonance of apocalypticism—that cohered the New Right. By reframing this well-known story, the chapter highlights the influence not of Christianity as such, but of a shadow Christianity wholly preoccupied with the dangers of an amalgamated liberal evil. It also foregrounds the overlap between demonological *pro-* frames, *anti-* frames, and intense satanic conspiracy theorizing, allowing for a novel critique of the culture wars thesis, encapsulated in the Republican Party's 1994 "Contract with America" and the Christian Coalition's "Contract with the American Family."

This background is foundational for "Religion without Religion" (chapter 5). Evidencing strong Evangelical influence, the shadow gospel messages that circulated in the 1980s and early 1990s emphasized the cosmic good-versus-evil clash between messianic conservatives and a litany of satanic reiterations. However, what these wraparound, decontextualized, highly amalgamated messages ultimately promoted was Revelation Lite: an end times narrative that centered on fighting the liberal devil and that's it. Fox News led this charge, ultimately overtaking Evangelicalism as the hub of shadow gospel messaging. The result was to transform the liberal devil into a good television character.

The above chapters focus on what the shadow gospel did to help mainstream demonological conservatism. "The Left Hates America" (chapter 6) explores what the shadow gospel did *to* liberals, at least to those who found themselves absorbed into the anti-liberal shadow realm. In so doing, the chapter reveals how and when anti-liberal demonologists howling about the dangers of "the left" have been squaring off with an enemy of their own encoding. For decades, white conservative women have played an especially important role in drawing up the blueprints for an allegedly vast complex of liberal influence. The chapter gives these women the credit they're due. It also explores how self-identified liberals have inadvertently fed into liberal shadow boxing. In particular, it highlights Democratic politicians' demonological messaging in the wake of the September 11, 2001, terrorist attacks; subsequent wars in Afghanistan and Iraq; and a political landscape littered with American flag lapel pins.

The book's conclusion, "The Devil You Know," assesses the Trump-Biden years using the two interconnected elements in the shadow gospel: the gospel itself and the shadows it casts. Regarding the specific messages of the gospel, anti-liberal conspiracism is the most conspicuous and of course most visually stunning in the case of January 6. But the gospel's *anti-* framing (anti-woke, anti-trans, anti–critical race theory) and, even more pernicious, its *pro-* framing (pro-family, pro-America, pro-speech) remain enormously powerful in sustaining a shadowy realm over which Donald Trump currently reigns as messiah. All three levels of shadow gospel messaging contribute to an even more vexing outcome: an intensifying demonology that, first, does not hesitate to feed even the most staunchly ideologically conservative Republicans and Evangelicals into the jaws of the shadow realm's demiurge and, second, has been harnessed by people across the political spectrum to cast demonological aspersions on key institutions like journalism, science, and government. Having surveyed this political hellscape, the conclusion then turns to the question: What do we do now?

We do not pretend to have any easy answers. What we do know are the stakes. The shadow gospel is incompatible with a functioning democracy. It needs exorcizing for the benefit of all Americans, regardless of their political affiliation or religious identity.

The only way to start that process is to develop literacy around what the shadow gospel is, beginning most basically by naming it and explaining how to recognize and decode demonological messages. This need is threefold. First, our existing religious and political frameworks, including the tendency to understand our political woes as left/right polarization and to presume that things that look and sound Christian actually are, don't get us where we need to go. What this book offers is a new way of describing the problem so that proposed solutions—including political communications and community outreach efforts—can be more targeted and strategic. Second, literacy around the shadow gospel is needed because of just how easy it is *even for people who identify as liberals and Democrats* to feed into its minoritarian, morally corrosive messages and framings. The third reason is political, though not partisan in the traditional sense. Whatever the outcome in the 2024 presidential election, the shadow gospel is on the ballot. It is time, long past time, to drag it out into the light.

THE REALM OF THE SHADOWY BIZARRE

"Democrats are actually Communist," Georgia representative Marjorie Taylor Greene flatly stated to former White House Advisor Steve Bannon in a podcast interview in 2021.[1] She further claimed that Senator Bernie Sanders, Speaker of the House Nancy Pelosi, and President Joe Biden—among others—had taken an oath to the Communist agenda when they were in college.[2] Several months later, after Greene was removed from Twitter for spreading COVID-19 vaccine misinformation, she attributed the suspension to Communists in Big Tech and the Democratic Party,[3] an accusation she echoed when attacking gay California state representative Scott Wiener for pointing to the rising levels of hate directed at LGBTQ people. Calling Wiener a "Communist groomer," Greene accused him and people like him of trying to "chop off" children's genitals.[4]

Greene isn't alone in her red-baiting (or her homophobic attacks, as we'll discuss in later chapters). *New York Magazine* contributor Ed Kilgore notes that since the 2020 election, Republican politicians have called Democratic politicians Communists with increasing frequency. Donald Trump, South Dakota governor Kristi Noem, and Alabama senator Tommy Tuberville have all flung the invective with America First aplomb, forgoing more anodyne charges of socialism.[5] "Socialism" is already a stretch, Kilgore explains. Its various philosophical articulations advocate for the publicness—of ownership or regulation—of institutions that under capitalism are privately held (healthcare, for instance). Sometimes public ownership or regulation is indeed what leftist politicians are advocating for. Very often, however, "socialism" is little more than a derisive synonym for "liberal." Communism, though, that's an even more puzzling taunt. As a political party, state apparatus, and political ideology, Communism is just so *specific*, prompting Kilgore to ask, do these Republicans even know what Communism is?

The answer is that not knowing what Communism is—or at least not worrying about the specifics—has never been an impediment to Communist fear and loathing. Quite the contrary; ungrounded fears about Communism were pervasive during the Cold War, dramatically expanding the list of who and what qualified as "subversive." The rhetorical pandemonium that resulted from fusing so many disparate identities, groups, and real and imagined threats created a shadowy realm into which any perceived enemy could be plunged. Eventually, one linguistic descriptor would become dominant: that of the liberal synonymous with the left and Democrats. In the 1940s and 1950s, those demonological outlines were just starting to emerge.

ANTI-COMMUNISM AND ANTICOMMUNISM

Following World War II, the Soviet Union and its ruling Communist Party ascended as a global power, positioning it as an economic, military, and ideological competitor to the capitalist West. This was unnerving to many in the United States, especially given the Soviets' interest in acquiring atomic secrets, the risk that they would use those secrets to attack the United States, the atomic weapons they ultimately developed, the global reach of their expansive security agencies, the brutality with which they treated their own citizens and those within their orbit—the list goes on.

Those on the political rightwing were especially concerned; they saw Soviet influence in New Deal policies, through which the federal government, led by Democratic president Franklin Roosevelt, had significantly expanded its social welfare and other public works programs to help pull the country out of the Great Depression. It wasn't just that New Deal policies had pointed the country toward Communism, the rightwing worry went.[6] New Deal leaders, notably Democrat Harry Truman, who served as Roosevelt's vice president and succeeded him as president in 1945, weren't seen as pushing back against Soviet expansion vigorously enough.[7]

The existence of the Communist Party USA—which was founded in 1919 following Russia's Bolshevik Revolution—and other homegrown Popular Front groups advocating leftist causes reinforced concerns about stateside Communism. The causes these groups championed included unapologetically socialist aims, but also zeroed in on civil rights. As feminist media historian Carol A. Stabile explains, many members who otherwise had reservations about formally joining the Party in the 1930s did so because it was the only party in the country actively fighting against racial and economic injustice.[8]

As a state system, Soviet-style Communism was expanding globally. Its sphere of political influence did not include the United States. Groups like the Communist Party USA did not significantly shape U.S. policy even as membership peaked in the 1930s, and by the late 1940s, Party membership had shrunk significantly.[9] Similarly, while Soviet espionage efforts were real, counterintelligence efforts proved to be enormously successful in the post–World War II years.[10] Mid-century America was entering a dangerous game of nuclear brinkmanship with the Soviets, but it was not on the brink of stateside Communist takeover.

The fear that it was and, in fact, that it had already been hopelessly compromised by Communist influence gave way to something much more amorphous than anti-Communism, that is to say, ideologically grounded opposition to Communist bloc states and their loyalists, coupled with concerns, even apocalyptic panic, over nuclear war.[11] That something was *anticommunism*, a term used to denote the special status of this particular "anti-." As historian Joel Kovel explains, anticommunism was "the part of the picture which is primarily about us," that is to say, the United States' ultimately shadowy self-conception.[12] These shadows generated such a strong gravitational pull and ultimately absorbed so many different people, places, and things that, together, they formed a moral black hole in which distinctions between alleged evils melded together.[13]

Reflecting this melding, the line between anti-Communism and anti-communism could be fuzzy. At times, anticommunism pointed to elements of actual Communism, that is to say, what Communist Party members in the United States and around the world were doing or planning to do. At times it could also overlap with the bipartisan political pushback against Soviet-style Communist expansion. Its demonological amalgamation of some real things—real economic and political threats, real geopolitical risks, real nuclear warheads—and a much vaguer preoccupation with a loosely defined but ever-expanding enemy significantly complicated how people discussed the issue. Even when they said the word explicitly, anticommunists were only sometimes talking about Communism as an ideology. Much more frequently, their claims about Communism mapped onto the ideal of "100 percent Americanism," a concept the veteran's group the American Legion popularized at the end of World War II, and which other rightwing groups adopted to signal opposition to anything "alien" to white Christian America, which could be weaponized against just about anything.[14]

Anticommunism in this linguistically disorienting sense took several organizational forms. Some aligned with industry. Communism in the Soviet sense was, after all, a genuine threat to capitalists, meaning that business leaders had an economic incentive—the preservation of their own wealth—to push a 100 percent Americanism agenda regardless of whether they were grounded in anti-Communism or absorbed by black hole anti-communism.[15] Corporate interests, which even then overlapped with Republican political interests, had an additional reason to raise alarms about Communism, already equated with New Deal liberalism: the connection between New Deal liberals and Democrats.

A note, here, on terminology. At the outset of the Cold War in the late 1940s, the demonological shadow realm that aimed its earliest energies at Communism, or what it described as "Communism," ultimately adopted the term "liberal" as the overarching leftist enemy. But that wouldn't fully happen for another three decades. In the 1930s and 1940s, "liberal" had yet to cleanly map onto the contemporary category of "the left" or *necessarily* be linked to the Democratic Party.[16] As Hyrum Lewis and Verlan Lewis explain, "being a liberal" or "opposing liberals" was a unidimensional position. It referred to what someone thought about the size and role of government. Stances on cultural issues were not part of that discussion, and indeed, when those issues were discussed, it was done locally and nonideologically.[17] The only thing that could be gleaned from the label of liberalism was support for the New Deal.[18] People who otherwise seem retrospectively conservative (another word whose meaning hadn't fully developed in the late 1940s and into the 1950s) could embrace such a position, or elements of that position, further highlighting that the connotation of "liberal" then is not the same thing as "liberal" now.

Linguistic caveats aside, one timeless fact remained about post–World War II Democrats and New Deal–supporting liberals: Republicans wanted to beat them in elections. Whatever the ideological reasons (or lack thereof), the corporate push to cast liberalism in the reddest, most subversive light possible thus served what from the Republicans' vantage point was the most important cause of all: their own.[19]

Other anticommunism was populist, bubbling up from various veteran's groups, most prominently the American Legion,[20] local chapters of the conspiratorial John Birch Society,[21] and what historian Michelle M. Nickerson describes as "housewife populism," an expansive organizational effort quite literally built atop the infrastructure of suburban sprawl that trained a generation of rightwing women to identify Communist threats to the family, spread anticommunist propaganda through vast communications networks, and generally troll corporate executives whose Americanism was clocked as less than 100 percent.[22] Astroturf anticommunism (in landscaping, "Astroturf" refers to real-looking artificial grass; in politics, "astroturf" refers to corporate-sponsored grassroots activism) bridged its corporate and popular articulations by creating the impression of mass backlash when in fact the alleged outrage had been engineered by economic or political elites.[23]

Sociologist Sara Diamond describes one such anticommunist activist, Marvin Liebman, whose Committee for One Million—later slyly rebranded as Committee *of* One Million—circulated an enormous amount of anticommunist media coupled with intense lobbying efforts to strengthen American opposition to Communist China. As Liebman bragged in his autobiography, the perception that his group was speaking for one million Americans was far more important than the reality that "What it came down to was one individual—me—with a circle of influential allies who could get all these VIPs to sign the public statements we wrote . . . thus creating the illusion of an enormous people's movement."[24] The more that illusion was, or seemed to be, corroborated by sincere citizen activism, the more it served to affirm the efforts of the thousands of housewife populists and other citizens who really had devoted themselves to anticommunist organizing.

Whether corporate, populist, or astroturfed (and the various ways that astroturf can cultivate genuine grassroots efforts), the specific targets of anticommunist efforts followed two basic tracks. The first focused on the foreign, or the potential encroachment of the foreign, into everyday American life and walked what could be an especially blurry line between anticommunism and anti-Communism; in particular, anticommunists worried about Soviet spies hiding in plain sight in their neighborhoods and schools.[25]

The second track of anticommunism was decidedly domestic. Echoing the imperative of 100 percent Americanism, it demanded obedience to authority, repression of "deviant" tendencies, and, at a very basic level, purity of mind, body, and spirit.[26] Speaking warmly to House Un-American Activities Committee (HUAC) friendly witness Ronald Reagan, HUAC Chairman J. Parnell Thomas promised that the committee would "make America just as pure as we can possibly make it,"[27] an objective FBI director J. Edgar Hoover also endorsed when he proclaimed, "What is American is clean and innocent; what is alien, or Communist, is the introduction of 'slimy wastes' into the body politic."[28]

WHO ARE YOU CALLING A COMMUNIST?

As 100 percent Americanism is defined in contrast to "slimy wastes," those "slimy wastes" demarcate where "real" America begins and ends. Some of these boundaries during the Cold War were unsurprising; echoing HUAC, which maintained a list of subversive individuals and organizations, anticommunist activists singled out members of leftist organizations and people active in the labor movement. They also reached beyond the obvious, beyond the groups that had ties, however tenuous, with actual Communism.

For instance, civil rights activism was explicitly equated with Communism from the very outset of the Cold War[29] and, indeed, had been since the first Red Scare of 1919.[30] On the more extreme edges, groups such as the Klan argued that the civil rights–focused National Association for the Advancement of Colored People (NAACP) was an international Communist front,[31] and avowed anti-Semite George Lincoln Rockwell, leader of the American Nazi Party, insisted that Dr. Martin Luther King Jr. was, variously, a Communist dupe, pawn, and Party member.[32] John Birch Society founder and figurehead of the so-called lunatic fringe Robert Welch cosigned the idea that the civil rights movement was a Communist plot, and in propaganda materials, alleged King's ties to Communist training schools.[33] But the notion that civil rights equaled Communism was far from an extremist position. Throughout the 1960s the FBI aggressively surveilled civil rights leaders, most famously King, on the grounds that such leaders were Communist subversives,[34] and J. Edgar Hoover, echoing a typical anticommunist talking point in an article for the *American Legion Magazine*, stated matter-of-factly that Black Americans were being used as a tool to build a Communist America.[35]

Historian Elaine Tyler May offers an economic explanation for why so many Americans would see civil rights as a Communist front: calls for Black equality would result in wealth redistribution, and anything with the slightest whiff of such horror was seen as hopelessly socialistic.[36] Carol Stabile offers another explanation for why anticommunists were so opposed to civil rights: because Communist Party members, along with other Popular Front groups, supported them, and opposing whatever the Communists supported was what "real" Americans did.[37] Regardless of the specific reason—if there was any logically coherent reason to speak of—the rhetorical equation of civil rights with Communism provided segregationists with convenient cover. "Communism" was what they railed against, coupled with discourses about "states' rights." This allowed the segregationists to express white supremacist ideals without having to use explicitly racist language.[38] Since "Communism" in the shadowy sense connoted that which was not pure, meaning that which was not white—not in the 100 percent American sense, anyway—the label was code that didn't need much decoding.

Beyond civil rights issues, a litany of beliefs, behaviors, and identities believed to fall short of 100 percent Americanism was thrust into anticommunism's demonological maw. Heading into World War II, American Jews in particular were frequent targets. Jews had similarly and just as viciously been targeted only a few decades earlier during the first Red Scare, when many Russian Jews fleeing pogroms immigrated to the United States.[39] The overlap between anti-Semitism and anti-isolationism in the 1930s filtered all the way up to Congress. Some congressional representatives explicitly pointed to Jews as harbingers of Communistic influence (or at the very least immigration), and some pointed to an alleged Jewish conspiracy to enter World War II, which rabid America First anticommunists vehemently opposed.[40]

Throughout the 1930s, Father Charles Edward Coughlin breathed similarly anti-Semitic fire over the radio waves linking Jews with the Communist threat. Through his broadcast sermons—which drew from the work of an equally virulent Catholic anti-Semite, Friar Denis Fahey—Coughlin popularized Jewish subversion myths ripped from the *Protocols of the Elders of Zion*, an anti-Semitic 1903 forgery that posited an alliance between Jewish bankers and Communist Party members said to be plotting to take over the world.[41] Post–World War II, groups like the Klan continued railing against "rich Jews," and the American Nazi Party and associated Christian Identity movement—which not incidentally grew in influence proportionate to the growth of the civil rights movement—proudly promulgated blatant anti-Semitism.[42]

Outside the radical right, however, and particularly following World War II, explicit anti-Semitism became increasingly rare in anticommunist attacks.[43] It would be a mistake, however, to assume that because an anticommunist wasn't saying the word "Jew" that anti-Semitism wasn't subsumed by the same "chains of racist signification" that allowed white supremacists to speak in segregationist code.[44] Just as white supremacists were, to quote Carol Stabile, "hindered in their ability to use openly racist tropes in their more public forums of address" (with an emphasis on *public* communication; private communication was another matter entirely),[45] anti-Semites during the Cold War—always with significant overlap between anti-Semitic thought and white supremacist thought[46]—could restrict their invectives to "Communism" and still disproportionately target Jews in media, education, and science.[47] And not merely as a function of the targets' ethnicity. Many Jews heeding the post–World War II call to reject complicity in the face of injustice aligned themselves with the civil rights movement.[48] Doing so subjected them to the Cold War dynamic of ascribing guilt based on subversive *association*, not specifically subversive *action*.[49] Basically: if it sympathized with a Communist or, by extension, any of the groups under Communist suspicion, then it was a Communist.

Catholicism also landed on anticommunists' subversive activities list. This was a strange irony given the intense anticommunism that many Catholics embraced. Peter Jan Margry explores the "Satanic ambushes" Pope Pius XI ascribed to Communists and their perceived "plot to kill God," claims that Pius used to urge Catholic priests and bishops to take up anticommunist arms in the 1930s.[50] Rightwing Catholic groups across the United States echoed the pope's sentiment, even as other Catholic groups were simultaneously subjected to anticommunist attacks.[51] Additional anticommunist targets included interracial relationships,[52] queerness of any kind,[53] sex education in schools,[54] challenges to patriarchal control,[55] devotion to social responsibility rather than personal gain,[56] sexual activity outside the confines of marriage,[57] overprotective mothering,[58] use of the world "peace,"[59] and, of course, not being Christian, or not being Christian enough, or not being Christian enough in the proper direction, namely, to the political right.

A HOLY WAR THAT DIDN'T NEED RELIGION

That Christianity was so foundational to 100 percent Americanism speaks to an undercurrent of anticommunism that cannot be overstated: just how religious it was. Joel Kovel highlights the institutionalized nature of anticommunist piety, arguing that it "turned into a kind of state religion."[60] In even stronger terms than that, religious historian Dianne Kirby describes the Cold War as one of "history's greatest religious wars."[61] Michelle Nickerson similarly emphasizes the prominence of God in the anticommunist activities of "housewife populists,"[62] and media scholar Heather Hendershot shows in her study of 1950s rightwing media figures that even the anticommunism of the secular right had a religious tinge.[63] Describing rightwing radio in the 1950s, historian Paul Matzko draws the same basic conclusion. "Scratch the surface of any right-wing archive from the 1960s," he observes, "and religion oozes out."[64]

In particular, Evangelicals—specifically "New" Evangelicals like Billy Graham, whose mass-mediated ministry we'll soon be revisiting—actively embraced the relationship between Christianity and anticommunism. This was a natural theological fit; the implicit end-times logic of the Communist threat, which pitted the United States' ultimate good against the Communists' ultimate evil, easily dovetailed into apocalyptic ministries.[65] The relationship between Christianity and anticommunism was also a natural network fit. Mainline Protestants, fundamentalists, and New Evangelicals all recognized the need to build their own Christian "missionary industries," to borrow Sara Diamond's term, with anticommunism as a recurring theme for each.[66]

As we'll see in chapter 2, the New Evangelicals ultimately proved to be the most successful in harnessing mass media (and harnessing anticommunism), helped along by the fact that many of the radio stations carrying ultra-right anticommunist radio shows were owned *by* Evangelicals.[67] These Evangelicals, along with other media-savvy religious figures, coordinated through a tangle of parachurch organizations unbeholden to formal church oversight to compete with and lob red baiting attacks against Mainline Protestant churches deemed soft on Communism.[68] Chapter 2 is also where we'll explore the—on the surface—irony of hunting for Communists in churches, given how religious, and specifically how Christian, anticommunism could be. What that discussion will show is that anticommunist attacks against churches centered on those churches' perceived *liberalism*, allegedly reflected in their charitable, social gospel–focused work.

Parachurch organizations weren't restricted to a singular audience, and neither were New Evangelical media, making it difficult to parse religious and secular anticommunist networks. The religiosity of the ostensibly secular John Birch Society exemplifies the overlap. Throughout the 1960s, the John Birch Society was a highly visible organization—Gallup polls taken in 1965 revealed that 79 percent of voting-age Americans had heard of it[69]—whose rhetorical tactics certainly earned them the label of "lunatic fringe" but whose core concerns about anticommunism and civil rights mirrored those of mainstream conservatism.[70] That the Society suffused its anticommunism with in-your-face Christianity aligned with how in your face Christianity was for anticommunism more broadly.

Most basically, the Society was named after a Christian Missionary killed in Communist China during World War II.[71] It also pleaded for "God's Help" in its motto ("Less government, more responsibility, and—with God's help—a better world") and chapter meetings typically opened with prayer followed by a salute to the American flag.[72] In its early 1960s recruitment videos, the Society even featured Reverend Tim LaHaye, future coauthor of the millenarian *Left Behind* book series and future architect of the New Christian Right (and future recurring character in this book). "I couldn't live with myself today," LaHaye explains, "unless I had joined the only nonreligious organization that has any chance of turning back the greatest enemy our country has ever faced."[73] And in a representative example of its wide messaging reach, the Society's anticommunist film *Communism on the Map* was distributed in 1961 by the anticommunist organization United Evangelical Action, which itself had ties to anticommunist Christian youth ministries.[74]

Reflecting these religious overtones, Carol Conner, daughter of staunch Bircher parents, recalled how her mother described the choice to join the Society. "It was good or evil, life or death, God or Satan," her mother stated.[75] Chapters 2 and 3 will explore the dense overlap of religious and semi-secular anticommunist networks in more detail. The takeaway for now is that, during the Cold War, Evangelicalism and the political right were fundamentally "in relationship," to use an understated phrase from Heather Hendershot.[76]

SEMI-SECULAR ANTICOMMUNISM

However, the holy war of anticommunism wasn't always so obviously religious. It was championed, even facilitated, by people whose Christianity wasn't publicly declared or who otherwise represented decidedly secular institutions. FBI Director J. Edgar Hoover, for example, frequently contributed articles in the explicit capacity of a government official to Christian magazines in which he emphasized in the starkest possible terms the religious stakes of the Communist threat.[77]

In another instance of state lassoing church in order to make an anticommunist point, Congress passed a bill, which President Eisenhower signed into law, to insert the phrase "under God" in the Pledge of Allegiance in 1954. "I pledge allegiance to the Flag and the republic for which it stands, one nation, indivisible, with liberty and justice for all" thus became "I pledge allegiance to the Flag and the republic for which it stands, one nation, *under God*, indivisible, with liberty and justice for all." The push to add "under God" had been pinging back and forth between congressional sponsors of similar bills and the lobbying efforts of the Knights of Columbus, a Catholic fraternal organization, as well as the self-described "patriotic organization" Illinois Society of the Sons of the American Revolution. During debate over the bill, questions about the separation of church and state were not raised on the House or Senate floor, likely because congressional leaders wanted to avoid the accusation that they were soft on Communism, inadequately patriotic, or not Christian enough—which all ultimately meant the same thing.[78] Celebrating this win for Americanism, congressional representative Overton Brooks of Louisiana declared that, by adding "under God" to the Pledge, America was protecting itself from "the rabid Communist" and "pagan doctrine of Communism."[79]

The "spiritual proportions"[80] of anticommunism were reinforced by the overtly religious language used by bipartisan Cold War framers to describe the Soviet threat and the United States' role in meeting that threat[81]—specifically as a Redeemer Nation locked in battle against a Communist beast of the apocalypse.[82] Secretary of State John Foster Dulles, responsible for the United States' Communist containment policy, was particularly instrumental—and particularly theological.[83] In writings to secular and Christian audiences, Dulles drew from his own religious convictions,[84] supplemented by his active involvement in church networks; he took a leadership position within the Federal Council of Churches in the 1940s.[85] (The FCC was an organization that supported the interests of Mainline Protestants, including their interests on the airwaves. Looking ahead to chapters 2 and 3, it pushed back against the more extreme fundamentalist radio programs and, in the process, played a critical if inadvertent role in securing

Evangelical airtime.) Dulles argued that "confidence in our spiritual heritage" was the precondition to an effective Cold War foreign policy[86]—a position with which Billy Graham very much agreed, as we will soon see. Journalist Cedric Belfrage wryly observed that what Dulles understood, and what he so effectively spoke to, was the need for reassurance—at least for those aiming for 100 percent Americanness—that God approved of American policies.[87]

The cleaved moral universe of the Cold War resulted in the enlistment of millions of citizen soldiers into a holy war that often *involved* religious fundamentalism but didn't directly *require* it. Ideological fundamentalism in the form of 100 percent Americanism was sufficient.

A CONSPIRACISM THAT DIDN'T NEED CONSPIRACY THEORIES

Claims about the Subversive Other's schemes to corrode the values and destroy the homeland of the Real American *Us* were conspiracy theories just waiting to be articulated. Birchers and others within the "lunatic fringe" were the most conspicuous in this regard, hewing to the consensus academic definition of conspiracy theory elegantly articulated by Peter Knight as claims about hidden hands and hidden agendas seeking to exert control over a person's life, mind, or body.[88] At their bluntest, these theories pointed to the literal Communist takeover of organizations like the Girl Scouts or the YMCA.[89] They also integrated a number of violently anti-Semitic tropes, subjecting Jews to continued prejudice and suspicion even as more Americans made an effort to control their prejudices in public.

For instance, many of John Birch Society founder Robert Welch's ideas were inherited from Canadian conspiracy theorist and Catholic intellectual leader William Guy Carr.[90] In his 1958 book *Pawns of the Game*, Carr argued that the world's troubles were the result of a Jewish-controlled world conspiracy linked to the subversive Order of the Illuminati. Reflecting something of a break from the fascist tradition of tracing the origins of the Illuminati to a Bavarian revolutionary, Carr parroted details from the *Protocols of the Elders of Zion* to claim that the Illuminati had been founded by Jewish rabbis and high priests. He also claimed that the Jewish Illuminati had literally sold their souls to the devil, creating what Carr described as a "Synagogue of Satan."[91]

"Conscious of his audience," folklorist Bill Ellis deadpans, Welch absorbed Carr's overarching narrative about the Illuminati but omitted any direct references to the Synagogue of Satan—though he did repeat the link between communism and the "cult of Satanism"[92] as well as the idea that the foundations upon which Communism was built emerged from "a uniformly Satanic creed and program."[93]

Housewife populists also embraced feverish conspiracy theories. One example is their 1950s panic over state-sponsored mental health programs, services, and providers, which they argued were smokescreens for Communist indoctrination.[94] Three 1955 community health bills proposed in Sacramento, California, were especially galvanizing; the housewives aggressively and ultimately successfully campaigned against what they saw as the state's effort to undertake mass Communist brainwashing and undermine Christian values.[95] In another 1955 case, they attacked an Alaska community health bill by falsely alleging that it would allow anticommunist "patriots" (synonymous with Christian right-wingers) to be institutionalized.[96]

Other housewife populists spoke more broadly about the potential for children to be "psychologically manipulated by authorities,"[97] with special ire directed at progressive school educators and social psychologists. A whole anticommunist cavalry mobilized against the dangers allegedly posed by such experts, for the understandable reason that many of the experts had come to see racism and nationalism as a public health threat—in turn pathologizing 100 percent Americanism and, by extension, anticommunism itself.[98] To add an even deeper sting, a few of these experts had classified anticommunism as a mental health disorder, or at least a form of derangement.[99]

LEVELS AND LAYERS OF DEMONOLOGY

Not all conservative anticommunists embraced outright conspiratorial thinking. The so-called responsible right, a cluster of publications and individuals that set itself in contrast to the extremity of Bircherism (never mind the fact that until Welch's various 1960s humiliations, he was deeply embedded within "respectable right" circles[100]), avoided such theories.

William F. Buckley Jr., for instance, founder of the "respectable" magazine *National Review* (a publication that, at its founding, took a proud stance against civil rights),[101] initially mocked the "hard-working band of dedicated housewives" convinced of a Communist plot to establish gulags in Alaska.[102] At the same time, Buckley thrashed against the perceived moral and spiritual decay of the United States, which he claimed put the nation on a course to a humanist, relativist, soft-on-Communism welfare state hell.[103] The soul of America was under attack, in other words, maybe not from roving cabals of Communist Party USA camp counselors but from collectivism and other forms of allegedly un-American thinking. This was not conspiracism. But it did butt up against a demonological *anti-* stance that posits pervasive moral corrosiveness attributed to an amorphous enemy. For Buckley that enemy included "relativists" and "humanists," warnings *National Review* writers reinforced in their frequent targeting of the state, "elites," and even the institution of psychiatry.

The magazine's *anti-* orientation was especially apparent in its early preoccupation with "the Establishment": an insidious, elite-driven hivemind implicitly linked to "liberal media bias." Building on the designation of "liberal" in a New Deal context more broadly, "liberal media bias" had a very specific meaning in the 1950s. It attacked the professed objectivity and neutrality of mainstream journalism, a critique rightwing activists also leveled at academia and government. These institutions pursued consensus and an "agreed-upon middle" that opponents said excluded alternative voices and perspectives (we will return to this idea in chapter 3). Liberal media bias was not an accusation that hewed perfectly to party lines; Republicans and Democrats could be accused of having liberal bias.[104] While it lacked a clear partisan charge, it was still a powerful claim, framing mainstream news as deceitful and encouraging readers to question journalists' loyalties.[105]

Even when they railed against the Establishment or the related "Liberal Machine," *National Review* writers steered away from positing an "organized and disciplined body," to quote one *National Review* editor eager to distance his denunciations of the Establishment from conspiracy proper.[106] Those inclined toward conspiracism were not so restrained. By the time the magazine started phasing out the term's usage in 1958, other rightwing groups had embraced the Establishment as a go-to scapegoat, imbuing it with an incandescent conspiracism that ultimately affixed itself to Barry Goldwater's 1964 presidential campaign.[107]

Rightwing criticism of the alleged sources of political and moral rot in the United States, which mixed vigorous anti-Communism with equally vigorous anticommunism, represent a demonology in transition. The black hole of the shadow gospel hadn't yet elevated the term "liberal" to describe a totalizing satanic rubbish bin. But it had begun to absorb a range of enemies, from Communists to relativists to humanists to the Establishment to particular understandings of the word "liberal" tethered to the New Deal and its supporters. Whether something was framed conspiratorially or with an *anti-* stance, whether some of the ideas initially had ideological grounding, once everything fused with everything else, it all came to mean the same thing: the sense of a corrosive, creeping evil, coming to get the *us* of 100 percent America.

DEMON HUNTING IN THE USA

Demonology is a helpful concept because it differentiates the shadowy amalgamation of anticommunism from ideologically grounded claims about Communism subject to the regular laws of gravity (and rhetoric). The demonology frame is useful in another way: it helps highlight demonologists' preoccupation, even obsession, with evil. With its elaborate body of literature focused intently and often grotesquely on the hierarchies, preferred methods of torture, and general goings-on of demons, Christian demonology provides the ultimate model.[108]

Author and literary scholar C. S. Lewis, himself a devout Christian, simultaneously satirized and channeled this demonological tradition in his 1942 novella *The Screwtape Letters: A Devil's Diabolical Advice for the Capturing of the Human Heart*. Epistolary in structure, the book follows the correspondence of Screwtape, a senior demon in Hell's bureaucracy (described in the book as its "lowerarchy"), and Wormwood, a junior demon and Screwtape's nephew. In his letters, Screwtape guides Wormwood in his efforts to snatch his assigned human away from the Christian hearth, imprison his soul, destroy his capacity for love, and turn him into an automaton.

The above sentence is a near word-for-word quote from Joel Kovel, but he was describing a different book entirely: J. Edgar Hoover's 1958 *Masters of Deceit: The Story of Communism in America and How to Fight It*.[109] In this screed, Kovel explains, Hoover describes the stereotypical Communist as a godless, cold, and calculating agent of a totalitarian system, one whose entire purpose was—here comes Kovel's quote, used to highlight the overlap between Lewis's and Hoover's conceptions of the lowerarchy—to snatch Americans "away from the American hearth, imprison their souls, destroy their capacity for love, and turn them into automatons."[110]

The underlying argument of *Masters of Deceit* isn't in itself what makes it an exemplar of anticommunist demonology. It's the obsessive focus Hoover directed to the activities of alleged Communists, something C. S. Lewis himself warns against in an epigraph to the 1982 edition of *The Screwtape Letters*: "There are two equal and opposite errors into which our race can fall about the devils," Lewis writes. "One is to disbelieve in their existence. The other is to believe, and to feel an excessive and unhealthy interest in them." The anticommunist journalist Westbrook Pegler embodies such an interest when he admitted in 1953, "My hates [have] always occupied my mind much more actively than my friendships."[111]

LOSING THE SPECIFICS FOR THE DEMONS

By the time Hoover published *Masters of Deceit*, the number of actual card-carrying Communists in the United States had dipped well below 1939 levels. In 1951, the Party's decline was archly chronicled by the *New York Times*, which reported on anemic Communist Party USA events, the disbanding of Popular Front groups, and dwindling Party membership, estimated between seven and 3,000 members.[112] These estimates were not far off, Cedric Belfrage notes, from the total number of active FBI agents at the time—forcing Hoover to adopt what Belfrage describes as a "fewer Communists, more conspiracy" stance.[113]

But actual Party membership numbers missed the point. For black hole anticommunists, the actual stuff of Communism—its ideological claims, data points, and member rolls—wasn't what mattered. Only its evil did. This point is supported by the fuzziness with which many Americans related to the specifics of Communism even at the height of the McCarthy hearings. One 1953 set of Madison, Wisconsin, person-on-the-street interviews about the nature of Communism revealed answers such as, "I don't know, I'm an American citizen," "Well, they are always sneaking around . . . I don't know too much about them," "I'm not exactly sure," and "I've been trying to find out myself but I've never been able to get a definition."[114]

In a similar vein, a landmark 1954 study conducted by Samuel Stouffer of Harvard University revealed an overwhelming, even vitriolic, opposition to Communism, with 51 percent of the national cross section favoring the imprisonment of an admitted communist and 77 percent in favor of stripping Communists of U.S. citizenship. However, only 3 percent of respondents claimed to have interacted with a Communist, with 10 percent admitting to suspecting someone of being one for such reasons as, "He was always talking about world peace," "He brought a lot of foreign-looking people into his home," "Just his slant on community life and church work. He was not like us," and "I just knew. But I wouldn't know how to say how I knew."[115] Indeed, when pushed on the specifics, many citizens during the Cold War who despised Communism didn't have much to say about the tenets of Communism, had little to no experience with the alleged enemy, or had, in Joel Kovel's words, "only a dim apprehension of what Communism means."[116]

In other words, while anticommunism was the structuring condition of many Americans' lives, Communism itself was, in many ways, just details. This dynamic was ripe for satire, which John Kennedy Toole captured while writing *Confederacy of Dunces* in the early 1960s. In the first chapter of the novel, the main character Ignatius J. Reilly and his mother clash with a New Orleans police officer. An old man bystander named Claude Robichaux attempts to defend Ignatius, declaring wildly that the officer is a "communiss." No reason is given as to why "it's the communiss," in this scene or at any other in which Robichaux makes similar claims. What matters is that he hates them.[117]

A PRO- THAT IS ANTI-

The consequences of black hole anticommunism were vast. Much has been written about the cruelty and injustice of the so-called McCarthy Age, the anticommunist objectives of which were hardly novel to U.S. politics but were championed, Cedric Belfrage muses, with much more daring and noise during the 1950s.[118] What Joseph McCarthy did, what the House Un-American Activities Committee did, what the Hollywood Blacklist did, what the FBI did, what loyalty boards did, what the "informer racket" did, what propagandists in the military and corporate America did, what red-baiting journalists and rightwing Hollywood stars did[119] all worked together through the same demonological logic—sometimes outright conspiratorial, sometimes "respectably" *anti-*—to frighten people into orthodoxy, lower the bar to almost comic proportions of what qualified as "subversion," chilled speech, gutted the scientific community, kneecapped the labor movement, cultivated paranoia among educators, and ruined an untold number of lives in an untold number of ways.[120]

It is easy to look back—as many have—and point to the possessing spirit that took hold of McCarthy and Hoover and all the other inquisitors during the 1950s and early 1960s. It is easy to show how and when things went too far, something that anti-Communists of both parties did loudly and often once McCarthy and the -ism later ascribed to his name proved to be a political liability. But such scapegoating overlooks a critical lesson of the Cold War: that the most enduring successes of black hole anticommunism omitted the word "Communist" entirely and instead embodied the most subtle, most effective, and ultimately most insidious level of pandemonic rhetoric: *pro-* frames, frames celebrating things that everybody likes. At least, frames that look like the things everybody likes, or should like—or else.

During the Cold War, these frames centered on the family and land squarely in the realm of Barthian myth: claims about the world that position themselves as universal, timeless truths, but in fact are historically contingent, something that could have been otherwise. Feminist historian Stephanie Coontz highlights how "family values" emerged as such a myth.[121] Contrary to the Cold War imaginary, the ideal of the white, middle-class, nuclear family didn't exist from time immemorial, only newly threatened by un-American mid-century immorality. It was instead facilitated, even incentivized, by postwar government programs that subsidized suburban life for white middle-class families[122] and reinforced binary gender roles by helping men find work and making motherhood and homemaking the most viable financial option for married women.[123] All the gains in employment and associated independence that women enjoyed during World War II gave way to the "traditional family," which was in fact, as Stephanie Coontz describes, "the most atypical family system in U.S. history."[124]

The ideal of the "traditional family" was further entrenched by government efforts—with J. Edgar Hoover leading the charge[125]—to elevate the white middle-class family as the ultimate bulwark in the fight against Communism. Family security, running parallel with consumerism, thus dovetailed with national security.[126] The containment offered by the "traditional family" moved in two key directions. First, children raised in traditional families would have the emotional and moral fortitude to resist Communist influence,[127] reframing the home explicitly in terms of defensive domesticity.[128] The more 100 percent American babies these families produced (and the more the families consumed to support their needs), the better off the country would be. As May emphasizes, fears about the "wrong" kind of babies overtaking the "right" ones included more than an echo of the eugenics movement; the goal was, very explicitly, to make more white middle-class Protestant babies.[129]

The equation of white, middle-class marital fecundity with patriotism[130] spoke to the second level of containment of the traditional family: female sexuality. According to anticommunist logic, an independent woman was a sexually lax woman who facilitated moral decay and destroyed families. The risks were even higher when she was single.[131] Sexual containment within a heterosexual marriage was therefore paramount: if women's erotic force wasn't harnessed to save the nation, it would be its downfall. Reflecting and reinforcing the sexual containment doctrine, Hollywood films post–World War II rewarded women—both fictional characters and the stars themselves—who embraced a domestic role and punished women who walked a different and implicitly deviant path. In the early 1930s, Hollywood hadn't been so rigid; female characters and offscreen stars could chase their ambitions—break rules, beat odds, and thrive, not just survive—and audiences applauded.[132] After the war, that applause was redirected to those who embraced married life.[133]

Entertainment media of all kinds upheld similarly restrictive norms around the traditional family and its "real" American values, a trend championed by none other than J. Edgar Hoover.[134] Carol Stabile describes the lengths to which Hoover went not just to purge Hollywood and the television industry of "subversives,"[135] but to shape its storytelling. Hoover recognized that entertainment media—and particularly television, with its direct line into Americans' homes—was a way to promote traditional family values and thus protect national security, at least in accordance with anticommunist fever-logic.

So, with the support of studio heads and other powerful media figures, and without any direct links between the Bureau and its vast public relations apparatus,[136] Hoover and his agents quietly consulted on radio and television programs,[137] pushed for law-and-order "copaganda" programming that portrayed the FBI's G-men as chest-thumping American heroes[138] (including efforts to tout the masculine, submachine gun–toting bona fides of Hoover himself),[139] and secretly worked with friendly journalists to generate positive coverage of the FBI and whip up frenzy over alleged subversion.[140] Few Americans would have guessed—or have any idea even today—that Hoover was, in the end, an unrivaled patron of the arts.[141]

The stories that *weren't* told during this time—the result of the chilling effects of anticommunism and resulting purges within the entertainment industry—were, Stabile argues, equally important as the ones that were.[142] This was an era that denied diversity and therefore imagination. "The consensus American television presented in the 1950s existed only by virtue of anti-communists' ability to criminalize dissent, drive dissenters from media industries, and then make it all but impossible to remember that dissent had existed in the first place,"[143] Stabile writes. What was left, what anticommunism universalized, was a *Leave It to Beaver* world of conformist, consumerist, white, implicitly Christian, 100 percent American families. Generations later, millions of Americans remember such shows as documentaries. As Stephanie Coontz flatly reminds us, they were not.[144] Michelle Nickerson similarly considers the other ideas—about culture, about our relationships to each other, about our understanding of difference—that were not allowed to flourish because of anticommunism.[145]

In short, the world could have been different; American values and norms could have been different. As it was, anticommunists did everything they could to train citizens to embrace 100 percent Americanism and to mete out punishment to those who refused. Anticommunists also did everything they could to reinforce a media literacy born of demonology, in which subversion was always present; you just had to know where to look. Stabile describes the resulting reading practices. Patriotic citizens were encouraged to "[peel] away layers of deception to demonstrate the concealed intent of progressive media," to "[read] for subversives' secret intent," and to "undermine their critics by suggesting criticism was red in nature, hysterical, and unfounded."[146] In short, to do what they could to find the demons around which their worlds revolved—and if they couldn't find any at first, to try, try again. Not being able to find the demons right away wasn't proof of their absence. It was proof that they were good at hiding.

BUILDING A BRIDGE TO THE NEW RIGHT

Anticommunists' narrow definition of who counted as a "real" American, and equally important, their crushing of anything that deviated from the false nostalgia of a "simpler time" said to have existed before the subversives threatened to tear us all asunder, is a key source of energy for the shadow gospel.

The following chapter loops back to the beginnings of the Cold War to focus on New Evangelicalism's contributions. Today, Evangelicalism is a mainstream American institution. Yet it began on the post–World War II fringes, achieving its majority status not because it reflected majority interests, but as a consequence of its forward-thinking media savvy, network dominance, and black hole anticommunism, all of which were harnessed by Evangelicalism's most prominent early boosters to emphasize its *traditionalism*: the claim that it was the natural, necessary, and indeed only religious option for 100 percent Americans. A central dynamic of this self-mainstreaming process was its marketing of a specifically liberal evil tethered to the figure of Satan. This wasn't a theologically grounded Satan, however; it was a demonologically ravenous Satan that dragged a series of liberal enemies into the realm of the shadowy bizarre—starting with Christianity itself.

2

BRANDING SATAN

It makes sense that so many people see Billy Graham as the figurehead of Evangelical Christianity.[1] He was an enormously popular evangelist who drew huge crowds and preached the gospel of salvation to parishioners and presidents alike. High-profile political figures regularly sought his counsel, and national publications gave him glowing coverage. In 1954, *Time* magazine placed Graham at the head of Christianity itself, stating that "Billy Graham is the best-known, most talked-about Christian leader in the world today, barring the Pope."[2]

But his ascension as "America's pastor"[3] would have seemed unlikely when he first emerged on the scene. Graham began his ministry as a fundamentalist, a person who takes a strict view of biblical and religious teachings. Despite initially championing the dogma of Christian fundamentalism, Graham also knew how to strategically cast off the strictures of fundamentalism, especially when tailoring his message to the widest possible audience. Youth for Christ, the youth outreach program Graham helped start in the 1940s, exemplified Graham's priorities. Many fundamentalist pastors recoiled at Graham's deft combination of old religious teachings with pointedly modern public relations and branding techniques. As one fundamentalist preacher invited to speak at a Graham-sponsored event complained, "They're trying to run the message out and just put a lot of music and features in."[4] At the same time, Graham's fundamentalism—which included a message of salvation but also sin and the threat of Satan—made Mainline Protestants wary.

Disconnecting from religious traditions and institutions made Evangelicals like Graham enormously and uniquely adaptable—and, stemming from this adaptability, enormously and uniquely powerful.[5] It allowed them, among other rhetorical flourishes, to link their understanding of liberalism—one tethered to notions of modernism, the enemy of fundamentalism according to fundamentalists—with Communism, and Communism with Satan.[6]

This, however, was not the theologically grounded Satan of the Bible inherited from fundamentalism. Instead, it was a rhetorically hollowed-out version of Satan that could be filled with an amalgamation of liberal threats, some of which were based on real obstacles and some of which were imagined or misrepresented.

The first thing the New Evangelicals added to their demonological Satan shell was Mainline Protestantism, allowing them to paint allegedly liberal perspectives within and outside the church as extreme and literally satanic while championing Evangelical Christianity as the only solution to the liberal menace. New Deal liberalism and related charges of liberal media bias had already been flagged as threatening to 100 percent Americanism. What New Evangelicals did was bring the devil—*their* version of the devil—to the anti-liberal fight.

By defining itself as the moral center battling against the liberal forces of darkness,[7] Evangelicalism self-styled as the ultimate bastion of *pro-* frames: not just supportive of American religion, capitalism, and democracy, not just their redeemer, but their logical precondition. These claims sidestepped the theological. Instead, they reflected a religion of communications strategy that rewrote the definitions of who was liberal, who was evil, and who counted as mainstream. America listened.

THE "NEW" EVANGELICALISM

[Billy Graham] is doing more harm to the cause of Jesus Christ than any living man.
—Bob Jones Jr., fundamentalist broadcaster and founder of Bob Jones University, 1966[8]

Billy Graham was part of an emerging movement of "new" Evangelicals born out of the division between the two dominant sides of the American Protestant conflict of the early 1900s: "traditional" fundamentalist Protestantism and "modern" Mainline Protestantism.[9]

Conflict between fundamentalists and modernists had been brewing for decades, reflected in fights over teaching evolution in schools during the Scopes Monkey Trial of 1925,[10] theological debates over biblical inerrancy,[11] and disagreements over the role of the church in engaging with issues such as prohibition, race, and social justice more broadly.[12] In these fights, fundamentalists took a general position of isolationism and strict biblical interpretation, while modernists took a general position of social and theological liberalism characterized by a "living" interpretation of the Bible.[13] As in the previous chapter, the word "liberal" needs some unpacking. In the 1930s and 1940s, and even into the 1950s, "liberalism" within religious contexts described how different groups of Protestants approached the Bible and how they believed they should apply those lessons to society. Mainline Protestants' liberal approach to the Bible pushed them toward social outreach, a path they believed was good and righteous. Fundamentalists had a very different perspective. For them, to be liberal was to turn away from the Bible. It was a form of heresy.

With "liberalism" as the dividing line, the fight between fundamentalists and modernists spilled over into many areas of society, including the radio airwaves.[14] On one side of the divide, fundamentalist radio preachers and revivalists gained huge followings both on and off the air by preaching a message of traditionalism, hellfire, and the importance of individual salvation and conversion.[15] Their message was stark: follow their interpretation of Christianity or go to hell. In contrast, Mainline Protestants focused on making the world a better place with the progressive goal of bringing heaven to earth.

Both fundamentalist and Mainline Protestant preachers had been quick to adopt new communication strategies as part of their respective focus on individual conversion.[16] Both augmented their audiences by holding large, in-person rallies.[17] Thus it was competition as much as theological difference that prompted Mainline Protestants to rally so strongly against fundamentalists and use their connections with powerful businesspeople and government officials to try to quash the fundamentalist radio presence. To this end, the Federal Council of Churches, introduced in the previous chapter as an umbrella organization for many Mainline Protestant denominations, played a key lobbying role. Secretary of State John Foster Dulles— also introduced in the previous chapter—was an especially prominent FCC booster. He was in high-profile company. Oil magnate John D. Rockefeller's donations to the Federal Council of Churches accounted for 5 percent of its operating budget, which FCC leaders leveraged to pass regulations severely limiting fundamentalist access to free radio airtime.[18]

HELL IS A PLACE ON EARTH

Ironically, it was the Mainline Protestants' focus on fundamentalism, including their active efforts to restrict fundamentalist radio influence, that allowed New Evangelicalism to emerge as a dominant force within religious media.[19] We will revisit that story shortly. First, we must situate New Evangelicalism in the mid-century religious landscape.

The term "new" was used to delineate an emerging crop of Evangelicals from their revivalist, tent-preaching predecessors who, during the eighteenth and nineteenth centuries, traveled around the American countryside converting souls. Although the term "Evangelical" harkened back to a bucolic image of a revivalist preacher on a mission for Jesus, the objectives of New Evangelicalism were decidedly modern.[20] Loosely connected through the advocacy organization the National Association of Evangelicals (NAE), New Evangelicals aimed to carve out space for themselves in a hostile media environment and to promote their own brand of American Christianity.[21]

A basic element of this brand was its sometimes precarious balancing between fundamentalism and modernism. New Evangelicals embraced the fundamentalists' focus on hellfire and push for individual salvation, but rejected its calls for insularity, which the fundamentalists believed provided protection from temptation.[22] The New Evangelicals also moved away from the fundamentalists' description of a metaphysically removed, physical location of hell containing an eternal tormentor Satan.[23] For one thing, the idea of hell was becoming unpopular.[24] For another, the fundamentalist Satan was *confined*. He required his minions on earth to tempt believers with sin, luring them away from the mortal plane "into the jaws of death, into the mouth of hell."[25] Evangelicals had a different focus: the here-and-now incarnation of Satan and the often vague, nonspecific threat he posed to everyday life by inserting his evil influence into "dangerous" people, behaviors, and media. The fact that he was, in essence, free-range was what made the New Evangelicals' Satan so powerful, a point Billy Graham emphasized in his warnings that Satan's earthly presence was on the rise. This was a literal assertion. By stating that Satan was active everywhere that Graham was preaching, Graham reinforced the idea that no one was safe.[26] No matter how pious or sinless a person was, there was always a satanic influence lying in wait.[27]

The subtle shift from a devil resting in hell to a Satan alive and well in the world was what compelled New Evangelicals to act: they could not, and should not, be insular. Nor could they rest easy just by resisting temptation. To do the Lord's work, they needed to be out in the world and they needed to be ready for battle. This was a fundamentally progressive, change-making stance. The New Evangelicals' approach to Satan thus ran parallel to the progressivism of many Mainline Protestants, with two critical differences. First, New Evangelicals were focused on hell on earth, not heaven on earth. Second, their solution wasn't to make the world a better place through the Mainline social gospel. It was to make the world a better place by exorcising its demons.

WHITENESS AND THE NEW EVANGELICALS

The New Evangelicals' rejection of the social gospel is reflected in their tepid support for civil rights and overall embrace of white centrality. Graham and other New Evangelicals may not have adopted the strictly segregationist attitudes of denominations like the Southern Baptists or white fundamentalists, but pointedly, and speaking to a more implicit kind of segregationist sentiment, Black Protestant churches were not invited to join the NAE.[28]

Further, many New Evangelicals, including Graham, shared messages on race that at best were mixed and at worst were overtly racist. In one example, Graham was interviewed by a *New York Times* reporter during the 1963 civil rights demonstrations in Birmingham, Alabama, led by Dr. Martin Luther King Jr. Describing King as his "good personal friend," Graham told the reporter that he thought King should "put the brakes on a little bit" on the grounds that good progress was already being made and because Graham "seriously doubt[ed]" that Black people in Birmingham even supported the protests. He then expressed his desire for "a period of quietness in which moderation prevails."[29]

King, who at that moment was sitting in a Birmingham jail cell after being arrested for demonstrating, subsequently penned his "Letter from Birmingham Jail" in which he chided "moderate white clergy" for talking out of both sides of their mouths: expressing support for civil rights, but only insofar as it wasn't too disruptive to white people.[30] The hedging between outright racism and full support of the civil rights movement characterizes the subtle but effective effort by New Evangelicals to cordon themselves off from Black Protestants.[31] (In contrast to the New Evangelicals' ambivalence on race, one that defaulted to the segregationist status quo, the largest southern Protestant denomination, the Southern Baptist Convention [SBC], was actively segregationist and would be a vocal opponent of the civil rights movement. Notably, the SBC did not join the NAE, although they would eventually align with Evangelicals in the 1970s after dropping their segregationist fights.[32])

For their part (and perhaps because they weren't invited into it), Black Protestant denominations sidestepped the fundamentalist/modernist debate that New Evangelicals had thrown themselves into. Instead, these churches retained conservative, even fundamentalist, religious theology in tandem with strong calls for racial and social justice.[33] In other words, Black Protestants were both fundamentalist and modernist, compared with the New Evangelicals, who were neither fully fundamentalist nor modernist. Black Protestant denominations thus provide a key counterpoint to New Evangelicals; theirs was the road not taken by figures such as Graham.

A RELIGION OF COMMUNICATION STRATEGY

The New Evangelicals didn't just enter the fundamentalist/modernist debate. They harnessed it strategically, forming numerous parachurch organizations that existed alongside the conventional church and appeared to work toward a similar purpose by spreading the word of Jesus and converting souls.[34] The NAE was most prominent among these organizations. It worked coast to coast to ensure that New Evangelicals were well represented and, to the extent possible, shielded from fundamentalist and Mainline attacks. Their energies were well spent. While Mainline Protestants chased down fundamentalist bogeymen, New Evangelicals and their parachurch appendages steadily built a religion centered on strategic communications.[35]

EVASIVE MANEUVERINGS

New Evangelical success had not been guaranteed. Initially, regulatory restrictions, coupled with pushback from both fundamentalists and Mainline Protestants, created an enormous uphill battle for Evangelicals.[36] Fundamentalists, as mentioned, already had a strong radio presence—too strong for the Mainline's tastes—and, from the outset, weren't pleased by the Evangelicals' emergence.[37] Fundamentalists didn't object to the basic fact that Evangelicals were on the radio. Rather, they took issue with their use of "popular" tactics like music, celebrity speakers, and high production values, all of which rankled the fundamentalist impulse toward insularity and strict theological adherence.[38] Mainline Protestants lobbed criticisms from the other side of the fence: the New Evangelicals were too fundamentalist, too focused on damnation and sin. Needless to say, New Evangelicals did not like being in both the fundamentalists' and Mainline Protestants' crosshairs.

Of the two threats, the biggest came from Mainline Protestants, whose radio programmers wanted to protect Mainline airtime and restrict the fundamentalists'.[39] Unlike their upstart Evangelical counterparts, Mainline Protestant organizations and programmers were already well connected to the largest radio networks, such as the National Broadcasting Company and Columbia Broadcasting System. In the 1930s and 1940s, many stations within these networks allotted a certain amount of free airtime to public service announcements, which included religious radio.[40] The majority of this airtime was given to programs under the umbrella of the Federal Council of Churches and their Mainline radio programs such as *National Vespers*, hosted by Harry Emerson Fosdick.[41] Fosdick and others used their media pulpit to wade into the fight against fundamentalism and, later, to rally against New Evangelicals.

This would have been reason enough for the New Evangelicals to dislike Fosdick and the Mainline institutions he represented. But they had an even deeper reason for their animus. Although he saw himself as a centrist,[42] Fosdick's calls for theistic evolution, racial and economic justice, and peace placed him firmly in the liberal camp. The fact that he represented a threat to their airtime *and* to their beliefs intensified the New Evangelicals' growing fears of a specifically liberal source of censorship.[43]

New Evangelicals then needed to contend with the economic challenges caused by radio stations' strict control over free airtime. Unlike Mainline Protestant broadcasters, New Evangelicals were forced to purchase commercial airtime at great expense. This meant, first, that donations from listeners were necessary to sustain programming.[44] To stay afloat, they had to make sure that their messages would appeal to wide audiences and that they were fostering listener involvement and engagement. Thus many programs read viewer letters live on air, embraced a bombastic tone when it was right for the audience (more on hosts' rhetorical strategies soon), and devoted significant airtime to courting donations.[45] Mainline Protestants, in contrast, didn't need to worry as much about developing a mass following—they would get their airtime either way. But Evangelicals did need to worry. And they needed to hustle. The result—ultimately born of restriction—was that Evangelical programming was much more engaging, and therefore more popular. It had to be.

And yet the New Evangelicals' future remained uncertain. The Federal Radio Commission, frightened by the growing number of independent religious radio stations, deemed most religious broadcasting propaganda.[46] The result of this policy was that many radio stations were forced to close during the late 1930s and into the 1940s, sending their programs packing and creating the impetus among Evangelicals to start organizing to protect their access to the airwaves. Those early organizational efforts would eventually form the NAE in 1942. The Federal Radio Commission also prohibited programming it saw as too one-sided, a particularly onerous requirement for messengers who were disinclined to host those who might challenge their hellfire worldviews.[47] Due to the non-controversial nature of their messages and their existing connections to regulators and radio station owners, Mainline Protestant radio programs were largely spared these regulatory restrictions. Further restrictions in the late 1930s that specifically targeted fundamentalist radio had entrenched the idea among the more incendiary religious broadcasters that religious radio was under attack.

In response to these threats, the NAE established the National Religious Broadcasters in 1944.[48] Its mandate was to transcend previous denominational, theological, and organizational boundaries to protect Evangelical media interests against the power of the Federal Council of Churches and government regulators. However, their goal was not to create a new religious denomination based on theological or practical differences with fundamentalist Christians. Instead, the goal of the NAE, via the NRB, was to communicate their version of Christian ideas and, more important, to protect their mechanisms of communication.[49]

Again, protection was needed. Under the new regulations governing radio, the Federal Council began issuing complaints throughout the 1930s and 1940s on behalf of Mainline broadcasters and lobbying Congress for increased regulation of Christian radio programs.[50] What was particularly worrying for Mainline Federal Council members was that, in the NRB's own words, Evangelical broadcasters were not accountable to denominational constraints. They could do, and were doing, exactly what they wanted.[51]

The creation of the NAE, NRB, and other parachurch organizations had profound impacts on the landscape of religious broadcasting. At first, the

NAE had few friends in the broadcasting and corporate world, and their efforts to lobby for greater consideration in regulatory changes of the early 1940s were unsuccessful.[52] But Walter Maier, a recent addition to the NAE and the NRB, was persistent in his efforts to lobby Congress for regulatory considerations. Eugene Bertermann, the NRB president from 1957 to 1975, also lobbied the Federal Communications Commission directly, and by the 1970s, U.S. presidents were speaking at NRB conventions.[53] Thanks to these advocacy efforts, Evangelical radio was able to grow into a productive industry through the 1940s and 1950s despite restrictions and regulatory threats.[54] In turn, up-and-coming Evangelicals like Billy Graham were able to leverage the NAE's successes to build their own organizations and followings.[55] Evangelicals like Graham were also able to leverage the successes of the Federal Council of Churches, which worked to push the most incendiary fundamentalists off the air[56]—but that is a story for chapter 3.

SELLING THE LIBERAL THREAT

An important consequence of the ascendancy of Evangelicals and their associated communication networks was that the primary source of religious conflict shifted from a fundamentalist/modernist divide to an Evangelical/liberal divide. This tension, like the original clash between traditionalism and modernism, had been simmering for some time. In a 1945 op-ed entitled "The Cancer of Liberalism" published in *The Calvin Forum*, Clarence Bouma, a central figure in the formation of the NAE, underscores the dangers of liberalism within Protestantism. "In every large denomination of our land," he explains, "the cancer of theological Liberalism has been eating away in recent decades. The supernaturalism of Scripture is either attacked or silently undermined. . . . The policy of peace at any price must make way for the solemn calling to champion the truth at any cost.[57] Bouma identifies the "virus" of liberal Christianity as the enemy of real Christianity. He also calls for action against this liberalism, reinforcing the stark contrast with the insular tendencies of fundamentalist Christians. This fight isn't just practical, the outcrop of strategic pushback against a demonized opponent. It's also *spiritual*, reflecting the cosmic pushback against a demonological threat.

And yet the Evangelicals' anti-liberal fights, central to the very founding of the NAE, were indeed very practical and very strategic, stemming from the fact that Mainlines were actually trying to neutralize Evangelicals. But because their opposition to liberals was demonological, the fighting didn't stop when the battle was won. As Evangelicals' communication platforms grew and began outpacing Mainline Protestants in terms of market share, the focus of the Evangelicals' anti-liberal enmity shifted from liberal Protestantism specifically to liberalism—at least, what was described as liberal—in culture more broadly. The resulting messages had little connection to theological debates. Instead, they focused on Evangelicalism's role in combating the liberal threat, one that might, like Satan himself, emerge from anywhere at any time.

POPULAR DEMONOLOGY

The network of loosely connected yet complementary parachurch organizations developed by the NAE was a response, at least in part, to fears of federal broadcasting regulation. But parachurch organizations ended up providing much more than an outreach insurance policy. The overlapping, self-reinforcing, demonological messages these organizations circulated— which could run the gamut from outright conspiratorial to *pro-* to *anti-* depending on the audience—helped secure Evangelical dominance for decades to come by placing them at the center of the fight against liberalism. Communism was an early bogeyman, but Evangelicalism's anti-liberal black hole would absorb a range of cultural and political threats—and religious competitors.

NOT YOUR PARENTS' CHRISTIANITY

American youth were a key parachurch audience. Billy Graham's Youth for Christ, Bill Bright's Campus Crusade for Christ, and Henrietta Mier's Sunday school movement[58] all sought to spread the good word of Christianity—the Evangelical version of Christianity—to young people around the country.[59]

Because these organizations were formally and informally connected to the NAE by shared goals and advocacies, they needed to maintain a certain level of message discipline. At the same time, the lack of connection to a formal church denomination gave significant leeway and even incentive for parachurch leaders to remain flexible and adaptive to local audiences. The effort to remain plugged in nationally and locally resulted in a great deal of messaging overlap across organizations. Messages targeted to local chapters'

interests echoed similar messages to the ones heard on NAE-backed programs, which themselves echoed similar messages to the ones encountered
at local meetings and outreach events.[60]

Worry over rock music was one issue linking local and national outreach
campaigns. Evangelical radio programs reflected on the demonic origins
of rock[61] and so did youth-focused parachurch materials, which circulated
the same repackaged messages through multiple publications. The racist
pamphlet "Jungle Madness in Modern Music" by William Ward Ayer, for
instance, which attributes the "satanic assault" of rock music to its African origins, appeared as a stand-alone publication but was also reprinted
as Youth for Christ material and was featured as recommended reading in
Baptist Standard magazine.[62] Similarly, when David A. Noebel of Christian
Crusade called Columbia Records the "home of Marxists minstrels" at a
youth rally in 1968, his message was repeated in the pages of the Boy Scouts'
Boy's Life magazine.[63] In another pamphlet by Noebel titled "Communism,
Hypnotism and the Beatles," he alerts readers to a "devilish" Communist
scheme to use rock music to invade the minds of the youth.[64] Ironically,
rather than encouraging youth to listen to old-fashioned gospel hymns,
Evangelical youth outreach would rely on similar lively music to the music
they criticized. Of course, when they did it, it was perfectly godly.

The wide range of anti-rock and other pamphlets produced for youth
parachurch organizations hewed to a basic theme: focus on how you deliver
the message and how you are perceived. Very little was offered in the way of
theological content or instruction. Fundamentalists unsurprisingly rankled
at the foregrounding of messaging over the message. But it was a sound
marketing strategy. Focusing on *form* successfully pushed young Christians
who were drawn to the lively music and active engagement of the New
Evangelicalism away from their parents' comparatively dour fundamentalism and competitively dull Mainline Protestantism.

It wasn't all bright wholesome *pro-* frame fun with Jesus, though; the
Evangelical messages these youth encountered were often dark and violent,
and told of indeterminate, unpredictable, evil threats.[65] So, while Youth
for Christ participants waved flags and sang American hymns, they were
also subject to a litany of *anti-* frames that dovetailed with apocalyptic
conspiratorial messages.[66] In one Youth for Christ pamphlet titled "Why I
Believe in Youth for Christ," Pastor Oswald J. Smith identifies a whole host
of threats that young Evangelicals needed to battle. He states, "Youth for

Christ faces the challenge of invading five worlds—the Roman Catholic, the Communist, the pagan, the Protestant and the world of false religions. All these worlds need to be evangelized. The three opponents which Youth for Christ must face are false religions, nationalism and communism. These three are the great enemies of Christianity."[67]

Evangelical youth were trained to recognize these enemies in music, movies, and even their parents' church through loose demonological chains of association. If someone or something was connected to anything Evangelicals already feared, that fear would be transferred to the newest threat. Through these rhetorical efforts, Evangelical youth were primed to go to war with mainstream culture—in turn helping Graham and others intervene directly in the secular and political spheres.[68] This, however, was not a future-tense war. Evangelical youth were told that the war had already come—and that it was their sacred duty to fight, despite not entirely knowing who the enemy was or would be.

EVANGELICAL SELF-BRANDING

Whether outreach was targeted to youth or adult believers, New Evangelicals' competitive advantage over Mainlines and fundamentalists was a result of savvy marketing choices prompted by the need to differentiate their religious brand.[69] This need was especially pressing when the content of their messages—for instance, regarding Communism, Catholicism, or postwar demographic changes—overlapped in substance with both fundamentalists and Mainline Protestants. Like the New Evangelicals, these groups spoke to topical and political issues. Like the New Evangelicals, they used frames of good versus evil.

What was different about the New Evangelicals—indeed, what was revolutionary—was *how* they communicated.[70] Drawing from the language and rhetorical flourishes of the previous generation of fundamentalist preachers active in radio in the 1920s and 1930s, they cloaked their often-apocalyptic messages in religious traditionalism. Evangelical radio preachers used "virtual" altar calls invoking the image of the revival tents of the previous century, which asked listeners to recommit themselves to Jesus while sitting in their armchairs at home.[71] Many programs also used gospel and traditional music[72] extensively in their programming, again to invoke an old-fashioned sensibility. Charles Fuller's *Old Fashioned Revival Hour*, which shared predominantly biblical messages, is a prime example. In one sermon, Fuller set up ominous claims that the Soviets would invade Jerusalem and bring about the end times with several old-time gospel hymns.[73]

At least, this was the production strategy when the programs targeted older people. By making the programs seem more traditional, and therefore more trustworthy, they were better positioned to capture (and scare) the target audience.[74] In contrast, efforts targeting young people completely eschewed traditionalism for contemporary music, popular media, and celebrities, and was often sold with a chipper, "Yeah Jesus!" high five, despite reinforcing the same kinds of apocalyptic messages and imagery as were presented to adult audiences, and despite denouncing so many of the things young people liked, including music and sex.[75]

The ability to be modern when they needed to be and traditionalist when they needed to be allowed New Evangelicals to seamlessly adapt their message to fit many situations, graft on ideas that were completely outside the boundaries of *actual* religious traditions, and position themselves as the paragons of "classic" American Christianity for many different groups. Whether the message was packaged as old-timey and traditional for older audiences or bright and boppy for younger audiences, the underlying character of the message was the same: Christianity is in danger, America is in danger, and *you* are in danger, but we will prevail if we all fight together.

ENTER SATAN

Messages of sin and Satan were as central to this media strategy as was the Evangelicals' rhetorical flexibility and savvy marketing skills. Satan, of course, had long been a prominent figure in American religion and made periodic appearances in popular culture as well. For example, during prohibition, Satan was said to use liquor to tempt men to sin and capture their souls for hell.[76] For New Evangelicals, Satan was much more visceral and his dominion more present.[77]

He was also a Satan without qualities, allowing a wide range of threats to be absorbed into his shadowy realm. Sometimes Evangelicalism would posit the satanic contours of an invented threat, for instance, by declaring particular behaviors immoral. Other times, Evangelicalism would take an existing threat and drag it into the shadows, for instance, by latching onto the military aggressions of the Soviets and rendering the overall idea of Communism evil. Doing so allowed figures like Billy Graham to add a key dynamic to the figure of Satan: that of conversion. Not the conversion of souls but the conversion of *society*, guided by the principle that where liberalism went, Satan followed.

Because it had been denounced as a bastion of liberalism, the Mainline Protestant church was easily linked to the figure of Satan. Harold Ockenga, one of the NAE's first leaders, spoke of the devil in Mainline Protestantism during his speech at the convention that formed the NAE. As he explained, "There has been a lapse into modernism. Satan has captured another organization which had been designed originally to oppose him."[78]

Ockenga's fervor in painting Mainline Protestantism as demonic was, like so much of the Evangelicals' messaging, highly strategic. To gain a following, Evangelicals couldn't just convert nonbelievers. There simply weren't that many around in 1940s America. Instead, their task was to reach out to what Ockenga called the "unvoiced Christian multitudes" in both the fundamentalist and Mainline denominations. Critically, this outreach centered on renouncing existing fundamentalist and Mainline Christian denominations as bastions of Satan in order to unite Christians against liberalism. Ockenga makes this point directly, stating, "Satan's greatest stronghold is the division of Christians into denominations as they are today. . . . The division is between those who believe in Christ and the Bible, and those who reject Christ. . . . Now is the time to forget all these differences and join together as one with the Crucified One."[79]

Ockenga's claim is that if you belonged to another denomination and did not leave it to join the new, ostensibly non-denominational parachurch movement—that is to say, to enlist in the Evangelical anti-liberal vanguard—you were aiding and abetting Satan. The core of new Evangelicalism's effort to capture followers was to paint all other religions as dangerous and of the devil.

DESPERATELY SEEKING SATAN

Evangelicals did not restrict their ire to liberal religion. Since everything politically, societally, and culturally was a potential hotbed of liberal-thus-satanic influence, the Evangelical fight against Satan had to tackle each potential outcropping.[80] Young people were seen as particularly vulnerable to satanic influence through Communism, popular music, and modern (a term always implying "liberal") ideas.[81] Parachurch leaders thus worked overtime to spread anti-satanism messaging and actively reflected on how best to package the messages for Evangelical youth. As Robert A. Cook, the second president of Youth for Christ, says in a Youth for Christ pamphlet, "Remember that the devil's crowd in show business never presents anything until it is polished and is sure of going over. Can we, who name the blessed name of Jesus, and profess to have his Holy Spirit dwelling within, dare to present anything to our rally audiences without being deeply serious about it, and having had it well prepared? Think it over. . . . It must be happy, informal, and appealing to young people."[82] Put more simply, make sure the messages are as fun as Satan's media. In fact, make it look just like Satan's media—kids love it—with the implied reassurance, echoing the thumbs-up for rock music so long as it was used to promote Evangelicalism, that it's only satanic when liberals are producing it.

However slick the production values might have been and whatever audience it may have been created for, an underlying focus of New Evangelical demonological messaging was *sin*, which was shorthand for the influence of the amorphous satanic threat in one's own life. A 1958 Billy Graham sermon focused on the question, "What's wrong with America?" emphasizes the pervasiveness of sin and further emphasizes that Christianity (specifically, his version of Christianity) is the only solution. You might assume, Graham says in the sermon, that the existential threats to the nation—including racial tensions, crime, war, and nuclear weapons—are the result of social problems. "But Jesus said you're wrong," Graham states, "the problems of the world are not social. The social problems are only symptoms of a deeper problem. The problems of the world are not illiteracy . . . poverty . . . it's not social injustice. . . . He said our problems originate from within and he called it S.I.N."[83]

The language of sin might seem innocuous, but for Graham and those listening, the use of sin would have conjured demonic imagery. Graham then removes any ambiguity about what was lurking just around the corner. "We are told that sin is of the devil," he says. "Jesus said he that committeth sin is of the devil."[84] Because societal problems are a result of sin, and because sin is a product of the devil, the fight against perceived societal problems is therefore reframed as a fight against evil. Solving societal problems, in turn, requires active efforts to root out sinful people as incarnations of Satan. That is the only way to transform and convert society.

The placeholder nature of these evil incarnations made them an especially powerful tool of disconnection. By focusing on satanic threats inside and out of church, and doing so through parachurch organizations that were not beholden to the limitations of religious dogma or practices, New Evangelicals could direct their anti-liberal demonology to anyone or anything they deemed threatening. This is precisely the rhetorical strategy they used to temper the mainstream appeal of Mainline Protestantism. Prior to the New Evangelicals' emergence, the term "mainstream" was a theological distinction that separated denominational boundaries and referred primarily to Mainline Protestants.[85] New Evangelicals wanted to be part of this "mainstream" without having to adopt the liberal religious and social beliefs of the Mainline Protestants.[86] Characterizing existing denominational boundaries and the denominations themselves as instruments of Satan helped them do that.

HARROWING THE MAINSTREAM

The consequences and indeed the rhetorical genius of this move cannot be overstated. By pointing to things that were already mainstream—notably the Mainline Protestant church but also pop culture mainstays like rock music—and calling them tools of the devil, New Evangelicals worked to position themselves as the *true* mainstream. In so doing, they didn't just champion an American identity tethered to Evangelicalism; they touted the cultural centrality of Evangelicalism in the struggle for individuals' souls and every other aspect of American life. Ockenga of the NAE argued this point directly when discussing the secularism that he claimed had "flooded America." "Unless we can have a true revival of evangelical Christianity, able to change the character of men and build up a new moral fibre, we believe Christianity, capitalism and democracy, likewise, to be imperiled."[87]

Ockenga's assertion is that the core tenets of American identity—Christianity, capitalism, and democracy—are under threat from secularism, used as a vague catchall word for liberalism and Communism. The key to saving all three is Evangelicalism. What appears at first glance to be a call to individual morality is therefore, instead, a declaration of Evangelical supremacy *over* Christianity, capitalism, and democracy. Because without Evangelicalism, none of the other three things could exist.

This would have been an impossible—and extremely controversial—argument for Mainline Protestantism or fundamentalism to make. But because Evangelicals had actively disconnected themselves from the theological strictures of both, they could shape their religious ethos to reflect their conception of an America that, simply put, needed Evangelicalism to survive.

OPPORTUNIST ANTICOMMUNISM

New Evangelicals' strategic use of anticommunism helped reinforce their assertion that Evangelicalism was America's only hope. In so doing, they added a cosmic dimension to the sense of widespread threat many already attributed to Communist encroachment. By positioning themselves as the central bulwark against the threat, New Evangelicals also positioned themselves as the supreme protectors of the family, American society, and Christianity itself.[88] Fighting Communism from the New Evangelical perspective wasn't merely to fight *for* these ideals, however. It was to fight *against* Satan and his efforts to destroy the family, America, and Christianity. In his 1954 article in *The American Mercury* titled "Satan's Religion," Billy Graham emphasized the apocalyptic stakes:

> No amount of words at the United Nations or peace conferences in the Far East is going to change the mind of Communism. It is here to stay. It is a battle to the death—either Communism must die, or Christianity must die, because it is actually a battle between Christ and anti-Christ. Has it ever occurred to you that the Devil is a religious leader, and millions are worshiping at his shrine today? While it is true that his religion is anti-Christ and anti-God, it must be classified as a religion nevertheless. And it must be an alluring one, for millions of the world's population at this hour can be counted as his devoted followers. The name of this present-day religion is: Communism.[89]

Graham also points to popular media, education, and politics as seedbeds of Communism. He explains, "The mysterious pull of this satanic religion is so strong that it has caused some citizens of America to become traitorous, betraying a benevolent land which had showered them with blessings innumerable. It has attracted some of our famous entertainers, some of our keenest politicians, and some of our outstanding educators."[90] Like other New Evangelicals, Graham's proposed solution to the Communist—and therefore satanic—menace was to be found in "conservative and Evangelical Christianity" and required religious anticommunist efforts in media, politics, and education. To weather the satanic storm, the nation needed a spiritual revival; and Graham made explicitly clear that only the Evangelicals could lead it.

Graham's message was reflected in a 1961 NAE study guide titled "The Christian Answer to Communism" that detailed the many paths of Communist infiltration in American society: labor, minorities, youth, education, and religion, all of which needed Evangelical harrowing. Reflecting their intense focus on youth, Evangelicals took these anticommunist messages directly into schools, lobbying school boards and throwing themselves into local politics to address alleged Communist infiltration.[91] The fruits of one campaign in Tulsa, Oklahoma, resulted in graduating seniors being gifted a copy of J. Edgar Hoover's *Masters of Deceit*. Another Evangelical-led battle in1960s Anaheim, California, centered on alleged Communist infiltration through sex education, which activists linked to the "dynamic duo of Satan and the Communists" threatening the innocence of students and families.[92]

THE RED MAINLINE

But Evangelicals' most potent mobilization of anticommunist messaging, just like its most potent weaponization of anti-liberal demonology, was against religion itself. This point might seem counterintuitive from a contemporary standpoint, but for many during the Red Scare of the 1940s and 1950s, religion, more than schools, politics, or even Hollywood, was fertile ground for fears of Communist creep. Indeed, in the "100 Things You Should Know about Communism" series produced by the House Un-American Activities Committee, religion was the first topic covered after the introductory pamphlet on the United States as a whole:

60. *Are Communists trying to corrupt religion in the U.S.A.?*

Yes.

61. *What is their method?*

The Communist Party of the United States assigns members to join churches and church organizations, in order to take control where possible, and in any case to influence thought and action toward Communist ends.

It forms "front organizations," designed to attract "fellow travelers" with religious interests.

It tries to get prominent religious leaders to support Communist policies, disguised as welfare work for minorities or oppressed groups. In the words of Earl Browder, former head of the Communist Party of the U.S.A.:

"... By going among the religious masses, we are for the first time able to bring our anti-religious ideas to them."[93]

As HUAC's concern attests, the image of Communists infiltrating churches—particularly *liberal* churches—was already extremely powerful. New Evangelicals harnessed those existing fears to tie Mainline Protestant denominations to Communism (again, always presented with a satanic tinge) by focusing on the Mainline liberal social gospel. The result was that many believers turned on their own denominations. In the pamphlet "Is There a Pink Fringe in the Methodist Church? If So, What Shall We Do about It?," the Committee for the Preservation of Methodism named dozens of Methodist leaders it suspected as having ties to Communism and was especially critical of the Methodist Federation for Social Action.[94] Echoing the HUAC pamphlet, any charitable or social work by a church was seen as a gateway to Communism.

IT'S NOT SUBVERSION WHEN WE'RE DOING IT

Thanks to its aggressive anticommunist self-branding efforts, New Evangelical Christianity became *the* safe haven for 100 percent Americanism, making it the perfect partner in the FBI's fight against Communism and related fight against the "slimy wastes,"[95] as Hoover called them, that purportedly made America less pure, less Christian, and less white.[96] As Lerone A. Martin outlines in his damning account of the FBI's role in propping up Evangelical Christianity, what made Evangelicalism especially attractive to Hoover was its "just right" Goldilocks position between radical fundamentalism and liberal Mainline Protestantism, coupled with its persistent championing of white Christian values. What resulted from the partnership, Martin argues, is nothing less than the transformation of white Christian nationalism into a faith.

But in focusing on the FBI and Hoover, Martin's account undersells the extent to which Evangelicalism had *designed itself* to fill the role of reliable anticommunist partner. Hoover was without a doubt an opportunist, but so were the New Evangelicals, who leveraged their disconnection from established religious traditions to frame Mainline Protestants—previously the country's mainstream religious ballast—as Communist radicals, dangerous subversives, and literally demonic, making them fundamentally unfit to occupy the country's moral center. Hoover parroted Evangelical messages about sin and society and (Evangelical) Christianity as the solution. He also bought into the myth of traditionalism and "classic" Americanism that New Evangelicals had so deftly espoused, and which they positioned themselves inside by making their own advocacy look like America's true religion, aligned with nationalism and capitalism, all in the name of protecting the country from "Satan's religion." Put very bluntly, Hoover could only do what he did because the Evangelicals did what they did.

What the Evangelicals were after, however, was not necessarily white Christian nationalist domination, as Martin suggests. New Evangelicals were certainly white, with that whiteness manifesting perhaps not as violent racism but as lukewarm support for civil rights—and only so long as things didn't get too "disruptive."[97] Additionally, by racially segregating their movement by not including Black Protestants, Evangelicals further reinforced the idea that mainstream America was white America.[98] Whatever lip service they might have paid to "spreading the word," New Evangelicals did not seek to expand ad infinitum. Instead, they sought to center the mainstream around an insular white conservative identity.

But there is something strange lurking in the rest of the descriptor "white Christian nationalism." Without question, New Evangelicals used a great deal of patriotic-sounding God and Country language. But they were not nationalists. They were not committed first and foremost to the interests of the United States. They were committed first and foremost to the maintenance of their own demonology, which pointed to American religious, political, economic, and cultural institutions as potential avenues for liberal subversion. By insisting that it was the country's only reliable protection against the liberal threat, Evangelicalism positioned itself as America's savior. By positioning itself as America's savior, *it positioned itself as more important than America*. But rather than being denounced as a subversive organization, Evangelicalism continued to be lauded by institutions like the FBI—and to laud itself—as subversion's holy warrior.

MOVING INTO THE CENTER

Evangelicalism's self-centering as the mainstream by demonizing the alternatives, self-branding as "classic" American Christianity, and self-positioning as the barrier to an amalgamated liberal evil, helped facilitate its full, swift integration into American culture and politics.

Graham, of course, seamlessly transitioned from fringe religious figure to "pastor to the presidents,"[99] a title that came with deep political connections to powerful public officials—despite being viewed as apolitical.[100]

That Graham, the anticommunist, anti-liberal firebrand, would appear in
the same sentence as the word "apolitical" only underscores the incredible
success of his and other New Evangelicals' mainstreaming efforts, which
functioned almost like an invisible shield around their radical, apocalyptic,
satanic paranoia.

Graham wasn't the only New Evangelical figure embraced by the establishment. Billy James Hargis, host of the Christian Crusade organization
and radio program, routinely espoused strong anticommunist messages as
well as messages against segregation, the United Nations, and a host of other
anti- topics.[101] And yet Hargis gained the confidence of many high-profile
political figures, was invited to speak before Congress, and at least for a
time had the ear of J. Edgar Hoover. Eventually, the tides turned for Hargis when the Mainline Protestants and the Federal Council of Churches,
boosted by the Kennedy administration's public stance against rightwing
extremism, regained their regulatory foothold in the mid-1960s. (More on
that story in chapter 3.) Still, through the 1950s, New Evangelicals—and
especially Billy Graham—were able to weave their messages into the fabric
of American culture and politics and then claim, convincingly, that the tap-
estry had always looked that way.

Ironically, the New Evangelicals' position within the mainstream
was further reinforced by the presence of even more extreme and much
louder rightwing figures whom the establishment rejected. Carl McIntire, for example, a fundamentalist pastor and radio preacher we will also
be revisiting in chapter 3, railed against government radio regulation and
used his radio program to actively spread rabidly anticommunist and anti-
liberal messages.[102] He often criticized Graham for being too involved with
Mainline Protestants, which he, just like Graham, described as seedbeds of
Communism. But Carl McIntire did not enjoy the stealth mode that came
with being seen as mainstream and therefore "apolitical." McIntire, like
Hargis, ultimately paid a high price for falling short of that status—one
that paid dividends to figures like Graham, whose lack of pushback only
reinforced the idea that Evangelicalism was the center and that everyone
else just revolved around it. Increasingly, the orbiters included Mainline
Protestants, who by the late 1960s had begun to retreat from the world of
media, large public gatherings, and youth outreach and organizations.

All the better for the New Evangelicals—or by then, just Evangelicals,
no qualifier needed. From the center they had created for themselves, they

were able to raise an increasingly shrill alarm about morality and the corrosive sinfulness of cultural liberalism. They had won, and in winning, got to define who and what counted as evil.

Thus when cultural critics mark the distinction between "fringe" Evangelicals like Pat Robertson and Bob Jones and "mainstream" Evangelicals like Billy Graham, they are missing the point. New Evangelicalism, which was founded by Graham and others like him, preached radical, apocalyptic, conspiratorial beliefs from the fringes and spread those beliefs in a savvy, media-centered effort to shape American culture. What changed was the definition of the mainstream and the definition of the fringe—definitions that Evangelicals themselves helped rewrite. The following chapter will show how rightwing media undertook a similar effort to reframe their fringe positions as mainstream by calling upon a vast anti-liberal demonology—minus the actual figure of Satan. Although they too would get to Satan eventually.

MAKE ME A SHADOW MYTH

There Ronald Reagan was, all Hollywood smiles, standing at the podium behind a large "Change Your World" banner at the 1983 National Association of Evangelicals meeting.[1] The title of the speech, "Evil Empire," seems to preview anticommunism as usual. But this was not a speech focused merely on empire. Reagan was equally focused on *evil*, contrasted with the venerable American traditions of religion and morality.

At different points in the speech, these traditions are described as enduring, strong, and reflective of the majority, and also corroded but reemerging thanks to the tireless work and prayers of the people in the room. The audience, by extension, is framed as hardscrabble upstarts and keepers of the American fire, embodiments of both renewal and continuity. In contrast are the secularists, who use the cover of government to threaten the values that ensure America's goodness and greatness. Reagan offers two examples. First, they provide birth control pills to teenage girls (and then, he snipes, have the audacity to describe the girls as "sexually active" rather than "promiscuous"). Second, they resist prayer in public schools. Both undermine parental choice, and therefore family values, and therefore American values, and therefore American democracy.

The Soviet adversary doesn't appear in the speech until Reagan has laid out his case against the stateside secularists. The Soviets are introduced as a collection of nameless, faceless, white-collared bureaucrats, which Reagan equates with the paper-pushing denizens of Hell's lowerarchy from C. S. Lewis's *The Screwtape Letters*. As Reagan describes them, they could be any cog in any broad mechanism of state control, made all the more dangerous by their quiet tones and talk of peace and brotherhood. Do not listen to this snake-tongued logic, Reagan implores, claiming that if history teaches us anything, it's that "simpleminded appeasement or wishful thinking about our adversaries is folly. It means the betrayal of our past, the squandering of our freedom"[2]—an echo of the same warning he'd given about the threats of U.S. secularists.

Reagan's weaving of domestic concerns about American goodness and greatness into talk of Soviet threat reflected how much had changed in the Cold War landscape since the HUAC days.[3] By 1983, Communism as a global force was on the decline, something Reagan himself admits in the speech. There had been and would continue to be punctuated flare-ups in response to leftist revolutions around the world; and some pockets of red baiters remained. But anticommunism as a state religion was simply no longer necessary. The Red Scare was largely over.[4]

That did not mean, however, that the underlying fear was eradicated. Instead, it *shapeshifted*, with the facelessness and implied interchangeability of the godless white-collar bureaucrats Reagan describes serving as an example. Reagan's demonological message about the dangers of the secular state was not new. It was the legacy of the rightwing media landscape of the 1950s and 1960s. Through a smoldering amalgamation of conspiratorial, *anti-*, and *pro-* messages, this landscape—and the audiences that collided within it—transformed claims of liberal media bias, liberal gatekeeping, and conservative oppression into pandemonic Barthian myth. Like all myths of this type, rightwing myths could have been otherwise. They were the products of network affordances, regulatory shifts, capitalist incentive structures, and a host of other variables related to the choices people made or didn't make. The shadow gospel's disconnection from these histories is its ultimate source of power, just as the power of Satan within 1940s and 1950s Evangelicalism hinged on its *everywhereness*. That which is not grounded in anything can be everything.

GROUNDING CONSERVATISM

Ideals around "classic" America born of anticommunism and "classic" Christianity born of Evangelicalism were products of the early Cold War media environment successfully sold as enduring truths. "Classic" conservatism has the same basic provenance and dependence on media, though it didn't fully cohere until the end of the Cold War.

The story begins with a spotlight on what the American rightwing was actually thrashing against immediately following World War II, before shadow gospel networks and energies began to generate their own gravity. That enemy, introduced in chapter 1, was the consensus-based institutional mainstream—described as the agreed-upon middle or "vital center"—that was upheld by journalism, government, and educational institutions. People on the far left and the far right rankled at the center's aggressive claims of neutrality, as it was never actually neutral.[5] However, as historian Nicole Hemmer explains, it was the activists on the right who were most successful at mobilizing against the center, over time convincing a plurality of the population that it was a bastion of the left.[6] Significantly, rightwing activists' anti-liberal crusade didn't begin as a shadow campaign. It had for a time been connected to ideology and history. So that is what we must start with: what was true.

TRUTH: RIGHTWING POLITICS WERE MARGINALIZED IN THE 1930s AND 1940s

In the 1930s, a creeping sense that capitalism had failed, that the New Deal was the way forward, that unions were necessary, and that fascism was an existential threat pushed artists, writers, and intellectuals—and indeed, much of the country—sharply to the left. Those on the political right, who railed against the New Deal and its collectivist, big-government policy framework, found themselves significantly out of step with the mainstream.[7]

Being opposed to the New Deal was one thing. Being opposed to World War II was another, a position embraced by many on the political right. The clearest articulation of isolationist sentiment came from the America First Committee, a publicity organization founded by rightwing businessmen and law students. Although the AFC leveraged its connections well, growing to 450 chapters and a quarter million members, isolationists in the late 1930s found themselves very profoundly on the wrong side of public opinion.[8] They were often branded as "disloyal, or naive, or even outright admirers of Adolph Hitler,"[9] with leftists especially quick to accuse rightwing isolationists of being pro-fascist.[10] Anti-Semites like aviator Charles Lindbergh did the leftists' jobs for them when he claimed that the "Jewish-controlled media" in consort with the Roosevelt administration and the British were conspiring to push the country into World War II.[11] Not all America First Committee members embraced such explicit anti-Semitism, but the committee refused to denounce Lindbergh's comment,[12] and even those who didn't posit outright Jewish conspiracies often pointed to Communist ones.[13]

After the attack on Pearl Harbor in 1941, isolationist sentiment persisted in smaller numbers and was increasingly marginalized; even the AFC disbanded after the attack. As a result, Nicole Hemmer explains, isolationism quickly "scooted to the far fringes of American politics."[14] Those who maintained public isolationist sentiment were blacked out by both political parties and the mainstream press. Unsurprisingly, the isolationists did not appreciate this. Future rightwing publishing powerhouse Henry Regnery, for instance, railed against the elites who he claimed were muzzling public opinion (specifically, his) and sought to develop new media channels for rightwing voices, which would function as messaging workarounds for rightwingers.[15] One such effort was his isolationist, anti-UN *Human Events* newsletter, framed as a direct response to the silencing of isolationists' nonconformist ideas.[16]

Outside the specific context of isolationism, the mainstream press and other institutions regularly ridiculed those on the rightwing for what was seen as excessive worry over Communism. This was during a time when even direct affiliation with the Communist Party and other leftist causes didn't carry political risk. So when one of the witnesses testifying before the 1938 Dies Committee, an early articulation of the House Un-American Activities Committee, suggested that Hollywood stars like Shirley Temple were being used for Communist propaganda, the mainstream press collectively snorted with laughter. Even the U.S. Secretary of Interior publicly mocked the idea.[17]

During this period, it would not be accurate to describe those on the right as "conservative"; that word wasn't yet a widely adopted synonym for the rightwing. Yet it is still possible to ascribe continuity between the "ideological components, institutions, and political actors" that had begun to align during the World War II era and the conservative movement that would emerge, fully formed, in the 1960s[18]—due largely to the work of media activists like Henry Regnery, who were beginning to build out the nascent movement's communications networks. Despite not always agreeing on what they should call themselves, those on the right were in agreement about two basic things. First was a deep and abiding disdain for liberalism and the left,[19] so much so that defining themselves against *them* helped coalesce a growing sense of *us*[20]—even if their definitions of liberalism and the left could vary.[21] The second thing these future conservatives of America believed was that they were on the outside of the mainstream looking in. And about that, they were correct.

TRUTH: THE CONSENSUS-BASED MAINSTREAM HAD NO PLACE FOR
THE RIGHTWING IN THE 1950s

Heading into the 1950s, rightwing positions remained, according to Nicole Hemmer, definitionally controversial: "out of the mainstream, not in step with political consensus."[22] Nor were these positions in step with mainstream broadcasting. The regulatory climate at the time was simply not hospitable to rightwing perspectives.[23]

A major driver of this outsider status was the rightwingers' strong opposition to unions, which initially aligned with some combination of anti-Communism and anticommunism but dovetailed, at least ostensibly, into concerns over worker's choice and general opposition to bigness in various forms: in labor, in government, and in business.[24] Rightwing activists knew their concerns were being "yawned away" by those who saw big labor, big government, and big business as ultimately positive countervailing forces.[25]

These activists were not alone in the fight: there was a natural overlap between their interests and industrialists who opposed unions for economic reasons, prompting industry to throw their support and their money behind the networks that rightwing activists were building.[26] So it wasn't true that there was *no* support for the rightwing; it just wasn't coming from the consensus-based mainstream. For these rightwing activists, however, the term "consensus" didn't fully capture the dynamic. For them, it reflected a stifling conformity that didn't just create a center, but created an inside and an outside—and a roadblock to insider-ness that was specifically stymying them.[27]

Being pushed outside and disliking the view was, as noted above, what prompted figures like Regnery to begin developing alternative rightwing media. He was joined by a cadre of fellow travelers, including William Rusher, whom William Buckley chose as publisher of the *National Review*; Buckley himself, golden child of the rightwing media scene following his anti-secularism screed *God and Man at Yale*; and Clarence Manion, an anti-UN ideologue whose radio show would make him one of the country's most prominent rightwing voices. Each of these men had elite backgrounds and were well-connected to some of the wealthiest and most powerful people in the country.[28] And yet they found themselves in exile—or at least, decided to exile themselves[29]—because they clashed with the mainstream consensus.

Although Regnery, Buckley, and the like built their brands on their out-sider status, they framed their policy and cultural positions as traditional, timeless, and aligned with a natural order ruled by God[30]—one they said was directly threatened by modernism, relativism, secularism, and collec-tivism. In this way, Michelle Nickerson argues, they positioned themselves as defenders of faith and moral absolutes and positioned their movement with all the characteristics of a crusade, one necessary to wrest the country from the brink of destruction.[31]

The dark force against which they were crusading was the so-called liberal machine that allowed only system-supporting views and blocked out everything else.[32] As discussed in chapter 1, the charge of "liberalism" wasn't the same then as it is now; complaints about the liberal machine, the Establishment, or Liberal Line (the acceptable range of public discourse) could be applied to Democrats or Republicans, and mapped broadly onto the idea of the "Eastern elites" who supported federal growth, collectivism, and the specific policies and general spirit of the New Deal.[33] In short, even as they railed against liberalism, rightwing activists didn't position them-selves within a strict, clearly demarcated, partisan split—not yet.

Critically, Hemmer emphasizes, the rightwing media activists who launched salvos against the Establishment and its orthodoxies weren't opposed to orthodoxy as such; they were opposed to orthodoxies that did not foreground Christianity, free-market economics, or their version of traditionalism.[34] Nor was the goal of these activists to encourage main-stream media to include more rightwing perspectives.[35] The goal was to remake public opinion to be more in step with their own orthodoxies. This meant taking the fight to two key liberal, that is to say, consensus-based, strongholds: media and higher education, not incidentally the two spaces where rightwing media activists had the strongest existing connections. Their college and university efforts took the form of massive campus out-reach, to which we will return shortly.[36] Regarding media, the explicit goal was to erode faith in the mainstream press and to provide audiences with rightwing alternatives.[37]

It is possible to speak directly to these activists' motives because *they* spoke so directly to their motives. For example, in a memorandum sent to Regnery and other rightwing figures about fundraising for his *National Review* project, Buckley explained that the purpose of such a magazine would be to change the national political climate. The goal, in short, wasn't to reflect public opinion; it was to remake it.[38] This was a fight that needed *winning*, not something to find middle ground on.[39]

Thus it might have been true that the agreed-upon middle of the liberal machine didn't give those on the right a seat at the table. What was also true is that rightwingers like Buckley didn't *want* a seat at the mainstream table. They wanted their own table in their own room—and they wanted that room to set the standard for the rest of the neighborhood.

TRUTH: RIGHTWING MEDIA WERE UNDER ATTACK IN THE 1960s

By the 1960s, the term "conservative" had reached critical mass, and so had a very specific conservative identity. A major component of this identity was the consumption of conservative media,[40] creating a dividing line between media that were conservative and media that were mainstream. The latter was something one watched or listened to; the former reflected who someone was. Grievance rhetoric suffused conservative media at this time and, by extension, suffused conservative identity, encapsulated by Clarence Manion's lamentation in 1964 that "All tools of persuasion— radio, TV, literature, precinct work—must be used [to spread the conservative message], because the Liberal-Socialist-Communists are IN THERE, and we Conservatives are OUT HERE."[41]

The marginalization of conservatives was dubious up to a point, given the very strong connection between rightwing media and industry.[42] These claims were also belied by just how successful rightwing media had been throughout the 1950s, as their broadcasts reached huge swaths of the population. For a beleaguered minority on the brink of extension, they were remarkably prominent and profitable. At the same time, there was some basic truth to the claim that conservatives were under attack, stemming, ironically, from how popular they had become.

To start, those lumped into the category of far right found themselves the object of significant mockery within the mainstream press during the 1960s.[43] Journalists had particular fun going after the John Birch Society, especially after the 1960 leak of Robert Welch's *The Politician*, which accused President Eisenhower of being a Communist.[44] The resulting flurry of media coverage denounced what it described as rightwing extremism and applied the label to all conservatives who flirted with Bircherism. This included figures like Barry Goldwater, who identified with the self-described respectable right, cringed at Welch's tackiness, yet actively

avoided alienating Birch Society members, whose votes or financial contributions (or both) were needed.[45]

Writing in very broad strokes, journalists and other cultural critics
played up the caricature of the "paranoid right" across hundreds of articles,
editorials, and other media, including pop songs.[46] They framed rightwingers as kooks and crazy old ladies who zoomed around Southern California
blanketing every strip mall in sight with anticommunist pamphlets (the
impetus behind the song "Little Old Lady from Pasadena").[47] They lingered
on Welch's candy-making background for maximum comedic effect ("And
while the peppermint popped and the popsicles purred . . .").[48] In short,
they had a field day. Robert Kennedy echoed this perspective during his
first press conference as attorney general. When asked his thoughts about
the far right, he asserted that Birchers and their ilk were "ridiculous" and
"in the area of being humorous."[49]

The pushback against the so-called radical right—and all the other conservatives subsumed by that label—wasn't restricted to popular media, nor
was it restricted to Democrats and others on the left; a number of Republicans also worried about growing influence of rightwing extremism.[50]

President Kennedy was especially concerned. Through their constant
agitations and controversies, the rightwing was normalizing radical politics. Those politics, bad on their own, also threatened Kennedy's chances at
reelection if they siphoned votes away from pro-segregationist Dixiecrats.[51]
It's difficult to know which of those concerns was the primary animating
force, but in either case, Kennedy's administration began hitting the rightwing where it hurt the most: in the pocketbook, the result of an IRS audit-
ing program targeting political action organizations. Of the twenty-four
organizations identified as "radical," the fifteen whose tax exemption was
revoked were rightwing. The result wasn't just an increased tax burden for
the organizations themselves. Donations to those organizations—primarily
made by ultra-wealthy conservatives—were no longer tax-deductible.[52]

But it was Kennedy's Federal Communications Commission that caused
the most damage to the rightwing. Enter the Fairness Doctrine, which first
emerged in a 1949 FCC report that removed the existing and highly onerous injunction against editorializing in broadcasting. The new directive
was that broadcasters *should* report on controversial issues, and when they
did, they needed to include multiple viewpoints. The doctrine was only

sporadically enforced until the early 1960s, when it became the weapon of choice against rightwing media.[53]

There were two basic reasons that rightwing radio was particularly vulnerable to Fairness Doctrine complaints. First, the Doctrine, as explained by the FCC, aimed to address controversial content related to segregation, integration, and racism, regardless of whether the broadcasters hid their racist attacks behind euphemisms like Americanism, anticommunism, or states' rights. Black civil rights activists deserved to have their views publicized as well, the FCC maintained, particularly given white Southern broadcasters' efforts to spread falsehood or block information about civil rights issues.[54] Rightwing positions on segregation and race—like so many other rightwing positions—were inherently controversial,[55] and actively used all the racist dog whistles identified by the FCC's "we see what you're doing" guidance. Conservatives pointed to that language as proof that they were being specifically targeted.[56] They weren't totally wrong. Rightwing broadcasters were disproportionately impacted because rightwing broadcasters were in disproportionate violation.

Another reason that rightwing media ran afoul of the Fairness Doctrine was that conservative media actively rejected the idea of "balanced" news coverage. They believed that their programs were the answer to liberal bias in news—an idea we take for granted now, but which didn't fully sharpen as a conservative media critique until the 1960s, spurred on by Fairness Doctrine fights.[57] Rightwing broadcasters were thus philosophically disinclined from showing the other side, because, from their perspective, they *were* the other side[58]—an attitude that, as Nicole Hemmer states, cultivated the rightwing norm that their bias was "an appropriate journalistic value."[59] These broadcasters also believed that their views were "classic" American views. To give the "other side" any airtime was to give America's enemies free publicity.[60] Of course, the FCC saw things differently, highlighting the fundamental impasse between the conservative and mainstream consensus worldview, particularly around notions of the "public interest." For the FCC, what the rightwing broadcasters were saying hurt the public interest because it was divisive, one-sided, and racist. Conservatives, in contrast, believed that what hurt the public interest was not having their perspectives broadcast.[61]

That the Fairness Doctrine was an enormous liability for rightwing broadcasters is not in question. What is in question is how actively the

Kennedy administration worked to weaponize the Doctrine—and the FCC more broadly—against the rightwing.[62] Regardless of motives. Kennedy's FCC delivered a series of blows to what Paul Matzko calls the "radio right." Two groups in particular worked overtime to ensure this outcome: the Democratic National Convention, which helped direct Fairness Doctrine complaints against specific broadcasters,[63] and the Mainline Protestant National Council of Churches—previously known as the Federal Council of Churches, the religious advocacy organization introduced in the previous chapter—which worked with every regional Council of Churches to coordinate rightwing radio monitoring programs, keep track of stations that aired "attack programs," and generate FCC complaints against those stations.[64] The DNC's dog in the fight was political. The NCC's dog was spiritual; liberal clergy were deeply worried about rabidly anticommunist radio preachers such as Carl McIntire and Billy James Hargis, who they believed were "poisoning the minds of our people who believe anything if told often enough."[65]

The NCC's efforts boosted and were boosted by a simultaneous U.S. Senate Commerce Committee investigation into the so-called radical right, to which the NCC contributed a list of offending broadcasters. Ultimately, the NCC got what it wanted out of this investigation, which was a 1967 clarification of the Fairness Doctrine that shifted the burden of responsibility to the broadcaster, who was now required to reach out to targeted parties or else risk losing their license with the FCC.[66] Before, the burden had been on the individual who had been targeted, and who needed to *hear* the attack in order to request equal response time (hence the NCC's efforts to monitor the airwaves, so that they could, in turn, notify the target and help them lodge a complaint). This new rule made it much easier, as Matzko explains, to "clobber" stations by sending along threats that the FCC would rain down regulatory fire if the stations didn't drop controversial programs from their lineup.[67] Independent stations had to make a difficult financial call: keep the programming on-air and risk losing their FCC license or comply with the free airtime requests and hemorrhage profits. Or drop the program entirely; problem solved.[68]

For many stations, the choice was easy. Complying with the NCC's demands to drop a program was cheaper and safer than the alternatives.[69] The number of stations carrying rightwing broadcasters, particularly rabid anticommunists like McIntire and Hargis, thus dropped precipitously[70]—an outcome that could not have come at a more opportune time for Evangelical media figures, who suddenly found their path cleared of pesky fundamentalists like McIntire and other competitors like Hargis, who technically was an Evangelical as well but didn't know how to activate the political stealth mode enjoyed by the likes of Billy Graham.

Given the long-standing mistrust of the government coupled with their growing complaints of liberal media bias, it is unsurprising that conservative audiences were so quick to believe that the cancellations were part of a coordinated government censorship campaign.[71] What was missing from this account was the role played by the market. Conservative radio programming was unquestionably targeted. It was also a business liability.

That the market spoke as loudly as the FCC in Fairness Doctrine fights of the 1960s is a detail lost to history. So is the rightwing activists' disinterest in having a seat at the mainstream table in the 1950s and the deep unpopularity of rightwing positions in the 1930s and 1940s. The narrative that emerged instead—and persists to this day—is of a mainstream, traditionalist, unwavering conservatism rooted in Christianity that has been blocked by liberal gatekeepers simply because conservatives hold different views. This is a compelling story, and it is clearly a galvanizing story—all the more reason to explore how we *got* that story, how specificity gave way to myth.

SPREADING THE GOOD WORD

It's not possible to talk about the Christian gospel without considering the dynamics of network spread. Jesus was, essentially, a broadcaster, a role captured in the parable of the sower: one who "freely disseminates his seeds in democratic fashion," allowing audiences to make their own meaning from what they encounter.[72] The early seeds of the shadow gospel also spread widely but were less open to interpretation by rightwing audiences given the demonological amalgamation into which they were cast. The dense swirl of conspiratorial messages about the liberal enemy, messages that emphasized opposition to that enemy but not specifically their secret plots, and messages that forwarded abstract positives grafted onto the good conservative "us" ensured that everything, ultimately, came to mean the same thing: *liberals are at the gates*. Intense media wraparound, the decontextualization of messages, and the opacity of who was casting the seeds had a similarly profound effect on the gospel that emerged: mythic and deeply misleading versions of American values, Christianity, and conservatism that claimed truth and righteousness but were lacking in both.

AMALGAMATION AND MEDIA WRAPAROUND

In describing the contemporary online rightwing ecosystem, computer scientist Kate Starbird and her team use the term *echo-system* to describe densely self-referential and self-reinforcing messages that appear to come from multiple sources—and can therefore be described as wraparound—but are in fact slightly repackaged and reframed versions of the same information. People look here and there, see what appears to be confirmation everywhere, and consequently have every reason to assume that the claims they encounter are true. If they weren't, why would everyone come to the same conclusions? Because this is the *illusion* of source diversity, not actual source diversity, it allows for all kinds of false and harmful information to be experienced as fact.[73] Digital networks are perfectly calibrated for echo-systems. But the same basic dynamics fueled the gravitational pull of anti-liberalism in the 1950s and 1960s. Here we use the term "anti-liberalism" with a nod to previous caveats: "liberal" was adopted in different ways by different groups during this two-decade period. It would be years before "liberal" would fully take on its contemporary function as place-holder evil specifically aligned with "the left" and Democrats. Still, opposition to liberals was what helped coalesce the rightwing, so "anti-liberal" remains descriptive even as the category was in flux during the 1950s and 1960s.

The first element facilitating anti-liberal messaging wraparound—and consequently the *amalgamation* of those messages—was the cozy relationships between anti-liberal figures. These affinity networks operated at several levels. One was the "mutual reinforcing relationships," as Nicole Hemmer calls them, between rightwing media activists and other prominent conservatives who boosted each other's work, pooled resources, and promoted shared crusades.[74] An additional level of overlap was between rightwing media producers and corporate funders. The radio show *Manion Forum*, for instance, received help from a range of industry sources thanks to Clarence Manion's approach of harnessing "the interpersonal connections between businessmen to win contributions."[75] Grassroots donations to rightwing programs were also important,[76] but the impact of rich funders—including rightwing media patrons such as oil tycoons J. Howard Pew and H. L. Hunt—in reinforcing a closed gravitational system can't be overstated.[77]

Many of these same industrialists fed money and resources into Evangelical networks; J. Howard Pew, for example, who had been committed to "bring[ing] capitalism to Christianity and businessmen into the church"[78] since the end of World War II, helped fund the John Birch Society, Billy Graham's ministry, Graham's parachurch magazine *Christianity Today*, and Bill Bright's Campus Crusade for Christ.[79] Sunbelt businessmen cut from the same cloth as Pew—a man whose efforts to evangelize often had little to do with saving souls and instead focused on saving capitalism, equated with what Pew described as "our American way of life"[80]—poured enormous amounts of money into a range of Evangelical causes.[81] Its links to the business world were so strong, historian Darren Grem states, that Evangelicalism must be understood as "one of the longest and most thorough-going business-backed movements in modern American history."[82]

Anti-liberal *audiences* were also densely overlapping. These overlaps go back to the early 1940s. One example is Nazi-sympathizing minister Gerald L. K. Smith and his publication *The Cross and the Flag*, which brought together a variety of mothers' groups under the banner of Christian moral crusading. Smith's outreach, in turn, helped boost the visibility and recruiting power of prominent anticommunist women, whose organizing work proved integral to the expansion of the conservative movement.[83]

The interconnections between anti-liberal audiences—some aligned with rightwing or outright fascist ideology, some housewife populist, some Evangelical—persisted through the 1950s and into the 1960s, helping to blur the lines between explicitly religious shows like Carl McIntire's and shows like the *Manion Forum* that might have taken "classic" Christianity as its backdrop but weren't religious per se. Perhaps surprisingly, these audience overlaps were not due to the same kinds of chummy interpersonal overlaps that existed between secular(ish) rightwing media such as the *Manion Forum* and the *National Review*; Nicole Hemmer emphasizes that Cold War religious programming, that is to say, programs hosted by Evangelicals or fundamentalists, stood apart.[84]

It was the audiences that grouped these programs together. They were the ones who saw pandemonic parallels between religious and secular media; they were the ones who pinged between shows, in the process creating a cross-referencing collective.[85] Central to this audience were groups of segregationist women who functioned as hubs between outright white supremacist mothers and other conservative women who implicitly or explicitly linked the concept of family values with the maintenance of existing social and racial hierarchies.[86] Matzko sums this idea up, noting that "to be a conservative in the 1960s almost invariably meant support for Jim Crow segregation."[87]

Fused anti-liberal networks resulted in fused anti-liberal messaging, both in terms of shared ideas and in terms of shared materials. Housewife populists played an especially key role by staging boycotts (often with the signal-boosting help of rightwing media figures),[88] organizing study groups,[89] circulating newsletters and other media about common causes,[90] opening rightwing bookshops,[91] and furnishing rightwing materials to local schools.[92] Anti-liberal ideas and materials were also spread via the early use of computer databases. Radio fundamentalists like Billy James Hargis identified these databases as key to spreading "weekly doses of apocalyptic warnings," as historian Dan Carter describes them, via "computer-generated 'personalized' mailings,"[93] an approach other rightwing organizations cannily adopted, mailing out hundreds of thousands of pamphlets and other materials pushing messages about the latest liberal (or secular, or collectivist, or relativist, depending on which terms were used) threats to America.[94]

Alabama Governor George Wallace, of "segregation now, segregation forever" infamy, was a close ally of Billy James Hargis and enjoyed significant support from networks of white Southern Baptists, the key religious opponents of integration (and who would later be identified as Evangelicals, though they were not officially part of the NAE). Leveraging both sets of connections, Wallace drew from the databases and technical know-how of the Christian Anti-Communism Crusade to reach out to supporters directly with campaign communications.[95]

Wallace's outreach efforts are instructive for two reasons. First, they reveal the networking savvy of anti-liberals and the early role that computer systems played in their success. Second, his ability to parlay targeted messages into mainstream visibility demonstrates that anti-liberals weren't the only groups amplifying and therefore helping amalgamate anti-liberal messages. Mainstream news media were also signal-boosters, particularly via television. Reporters might have justified their coverage of Wallace as southern gothic gawkery, but still gave him enormous amounts of free airtime. Never one to miss the opportunity afforded by a spotlight, Wallace made bold conspiratorial claims linking the civil rights movement with "subversion," a whole range of *anti-* claims about the federal government, and just as many *pro-* claims that provided cover for segregationists to argue that their opposition to civil rights was about states' rights and freedom, not race.[96]

Wallace's pandemonic communications, aided by the mainstream news media, help explain how anti-liberals of various stripes could encounter the same claims, or at least variations on the same *themes*, through countless overlapping affinity and media networks. The information system that emerged, Hemmer explains, had a "different network of authorities, a different conception of fact and accuracy, and a different way of evaluating truth claims."[97] This included a robust firewall against conflicting or contradictory evidence. Everything fed into accusations of liberal bias or exclusionary treatment, even when the evidence pointed in the other direction, for instance, when news outlets took a critical stance toward people or policies designated as liberal. That merely provided an opportunity to point to all the other instances of alleged bias.[98]

DEMONOLOGICAL DECONTEXTUALIZATION

The intense iterative messaging and audience ping-ponging of such a system facilitated equally intense decontextualization, resulting in the extreme difficulty, Heather Hendershot notes, of tracing the circulation of Cold War anti-liberal messaging.[99] And that's for researchers who would very much like to. For Evangelicals and rightwingers and conservatives and segregationists and anybody else steeped in anti-liberal messages, it would have been enormously difficult to discern basic information such as where a particular claim originated, with whom, or when. History, the ultimate contextualizing force, falls away when you can no longer access it or don't realize that there are histories to trace.

Hatred of the UN is an example. The conviction that the UN was bad—or as many on the rightwing argued, that it was outright evil—transformed over time into a generalized conservative position. But at one point, resistance to the UN, like resistance to liberalism generally, was embraced for many reasons by many groups. Birchers railed against the UN as part of a plot to "destroy all religious beliefs and customs," including alleged efforts to replace Christmas decor with UN symbols in department stores.[100] Rightwing media figures railed against the UN for a range of reasons, including concerns that the organization would infringe on citizen freedoms, that it would give rise to a one-world government, and that it would empower "primitive people" in developing nations.[101] Conservative women's groups railed against the UN as the antithesis of the family;[102] segregationist women as a sign of U.S. supplication to the "developing, left-leaning, non-white world";[103] and Evangelicals for not having a Christian basis or because of its potential to encroach into the spheres of church and family.[104] Ultimately, these details gave way to a rhetorical position akin to frozen orange juice concentrate: a homogeneous slush untraceable to the specific fruit that had been squeezed.

THE QUALITY OF OPACITY

The wraparound, amalgamation, and decontextualization that characterized anti-liberal media worked to obscure where messages came from. They also worked to obscure who was connected to whom. For every direct link in the chain—for instance, when William F. Buckley appeared on Clarence Manion's radio program—there were countless indirect links shaping and framing and amplifying anti-liberal messages. Some obscured connections were strategic. For example, like many sunbelt businessmen, J. Howard Pew preferred to remain in the background and avoid publicizing where his money was going.[105] Pew's was a position that Evangelicals like Graham also preferred out of concern that the public would accuse their movement of being a "corporate byproduct."[106]

Other obscured connections were expedient rather than calculated, for instance, the full extent of the relationship between Buckley and Manion,[107] or the quiet but key role the radio right played in boosting the *National Review*.[108] Still other hidden connections were logistic byproducts: the result of so many people sharing so many things through so many networks and, further, of having these people's backgrounds, including Evangelical backgrounds that already were a falsely traditional mythic mashup, fall away through the process of multi-directional sharing. Regardless of these sharers' motives, the outcome of their constant overlap—of resources, messages, and oil tycoons—was simultaneously to confuse where everything was coming from and continually reinforce the boundaries of the closed gravitational system the anti-liberals were helping create.

OPACITY ON CRUSADE

The relationship between the 1960s campus crusades—one for Christ, the other for conservatism—illustrates the process of network opacity and its consequences. On the surface, Campus Crusade for Christ, the parachurch organization founded in 1951 by Bill Bright, and the two main campus conservative groups, Young Americans for Freedom and the Intercollegiate Society of Individualists (later Intercollegiate Studies Institute), don't seem to have much in common. Most basically, the push for individual salvation and biblically grounded religiosity was baked into the mission of Campus Crusade.[109] It was not for YAF or ISI.

For instance, when Stanton Evans—a prominent campus conservative and author of 1961's *Revolt on the Campus*—discussed the results of a demographic survey he and ISI leadership sent out to conservative student leaders and rank and file members, he did not mention any questions directly related to respondents' religion.[110] What the survey focused on instead was the financial background of conservatives (to counter the stereotype that they all had wealthy fathers) and the degree of liberal indoctrination on their campuses (high, according to most respondents).[111] The survey also asked the young conservatives who and what they read most frequently. The Bible wasn't mentioned. Rather, familiar secular sources like Barry Goldwater, William Buckley, the *National Review*, and *Human Events* topped the list.[112] Speaking to the survey results and conservative movement as a whole, Evans unequivocally embraced a traditionalist moral order centering on belief in God.[113] Yet there was no discussion of the need to evangelize or convert.

These apparent differences, however, conceal a tangle of demonological connections. First, the messages that emanated from both crusades had striking rhetorical parallels. Both groups claimed that U.S. universities were breeding grounds for liberal influence and indoctrination.[114] Both embraced language of war, encroachment, and rebellion to position themselves against those influences.[115] And both framed their groups as the antidote to liberalism.[116] Speaking on behalf of the movement, Stanton Evans declared that conservatives had no choice but to change the status quo, as that was the only way to "affirm his tradition."[117] Bright embraced a similar approach through what historian John Turner describes as an "evangelical manifest destiny"[118] perfectly articulated in one of Bright's pamphlets, titled "Come and Help Change the World."[119]

Sources of support and funding for each campus crusade further connected the groups. As mentioned earlier, Campus Crusade was supported by anticommunist networks of Sunbelt businessmen. The oil tycoon Hunt family, comprising father H. L., son W. H., and other son Bunker—the latter of whom also gave to the John Birch Society and to George Wallace[120]—was especially generous with Bill Bright.[121] J. Howard Pew, down-low bankroller of *Christianity Today*, contributed to Campus Crusade's overall mission as well through what Darren Dochuk describes as his "spectacularly large" sphere of influence within New Evangelicalism.[122]

In apparent but not actual contrast, YAF and ISI were supported financially and through signal-boosting by the self-styled responsible conservative side of rightwing media networks, with the *National Review* most closely associated with YAF[123] and ISI most closely associated with *Human Events*.[124] The *Manion Forum* also did its part. In the 1960s it produced joint advertising materials with YAF and provided local chapters with free radio broadcasts to play at their campuses.[125] These were wholly reciprocal relationships, Nicole Hemmer explains; rightwing media helped prop up the college groups, and the college groups helped reinforce a conservative media diet in member students.[126] These relationships also point to the fuzziness between secular and religious networks. Campus Crusade champion H. L. Hunt, for example, was a major funder of the *Manion Forum*,[127] itself a staunch ally of the *National Review*, while J. Howard Pew provided startup funds for *Human Events*, one of the college students' top sources of information.[128]

These were also *college* students; they mingled. Very religious and secular-leaning campus crusaders reinforced messaging overlap through the sharing and recommending of various conservative books, magazines, and films, and social overlap through what Caroline Rolland-Diamond describes as the "festive practices" of conservative and Evangelical students.[129] Focusing on California universities in the 1960s, Rolland-Diamond describes shared outings to the traditional values-touting Knott's Berry Farm[130] and cross-pollinating party scenes, some more and some less wholesome (although the drinking that frequently took place at Greek parties was not accompanied by drug use, sneered at by conservative students as the stuff of dirty hippies)—with many of these parties themed to mock liberals.[131] Campus crusaders also targeted Greek leaders and spring breakers.[132] In short, through a web of shared media and cultural practices best summarized as college students being college students, these groups forged connections even in the absence of formal coordination between groups.[133]

So many of the connections within the burgeoning conservative movement followed exactly this model. People and publications and claims about the world might have seemed to stand alone, paragons of the conservative ideal of proud self-reliance and what Stanton Evans describes as "inner direction" (as opposed to the weakling liberal push for "outer direction").[134] But when you shine a light into those shadows, what supports conservative networks are all the other conservative networks.

FUSION, DISCONNECTION, AND POWER

When describing the kinds of entanglements—ideological, financial, and social—that characterize cases like the campus crusaders, scholars have pointed to fusionism, the mid-century confluence of libertarianism (specifically, laissez-faire economics and emphasis on personal freedoms), moral traditionalism, and anticommunism. The term "fusion" is in reference to the three strains of thought coming together and also to the process by which rightwing activists, recognizing common causes and philosophies, joined forces.[135] In the 1940s and 1950s, Sara Diamond argues, moral traditionalism was critical to fusionist politics, as was libertarian approaches to the market, but ultimately both were overshadowed by anticommunism.[136] It wasn't until the 1960s and 1970s that moral traditionalism emerged as equivalently important to anticommunism, which Diamond attributes to the rise of Evangelicals within the rightwing sphere.[137]

The shadow gospel framework tells a different, much more disorienting story. It also suggests that it was *shadows* that were the glue of the modern conservative movement. Without a doubt, various groups variously identifying with libertarianism, anticommunism, and moral traditionalism fused together in the 1950s and 1960s through the network processes described throughout this chapter. According to the established story, anticommunism is in the driver's seat initially, but then in the mid- to late 1960s is replaced by moral traditionalism. This story is perfectly explanatory, with one enormous snag: "moral traditionalism" as embraced and evangelized by the burgeoning conservative movement wasn't a universal truth. It was itself a product of the mid- to late 1960s: a demonological reaction to an amalgamation of liberalisms. One was from a New Deal context, one was from an Evangelical context, and one was from a rightwing media context. Each added—to gesture back to the book's introduction—an ever-expanding litany of satanic reiterations.

What ends up qualifying as "moral" and naturalized as "traditional" is what was placed in opposition to a disjointed, shapeshifting *them* that ultimately settled on the broad descriptor of "liberal" mapped onto the political left and Democrats. The liberals are immoral, so we are moral. The liberals are subversive, so we are traditional. Repeated enough times, strengthened by a closed media system outfitted with its own experts and forms of sensemaking, the vague sense that *there is something evil here* became a gospel truth that could look ideological or theological, and which could even integrate elements of grounded ideology, theology, and things that were true, but which was, ultimately, shadows fused with other shadows.

USEFUL SUPPRESSION

A case in point is the plight of the beleaguered, censored conservative. With qualification, it is possible to state all the historical facts articulated earlier in the chapter: that rightwing politics were marginalized in the 1930s and 1940s, that the consensus-based mainstream had no place for the rightwing in the 1950s, and that rightwing media were under attack in the 1960s. Contextualizing details complicate this picture, namely, that rightwing policies were deeply unpopular in the 1930s and 1940s, that the rightwing had no interest in being accepted within the consensus-based mainstream in the 1950s, and that what was attacking the rightwing media most directly in the 1960s was capitalism. Still, the facts are the facts: conservative activists through the 1960s faced obstacles.

Things started to shift for Evangelicals first. In 1960, the FCC announced a series of policy changes that created a much more hospitable media environment for religious broadcasting, including the lifting of restrictions on how much time could be spent fundraising on-air. Suddenly emboldened and flushed with cash, Evangelicals began to monopolize the airwaves through programming that aligned with the new financial incentive structures proposed by the FCC[138]—the same FCC whose Fairness Doctrine would soon be used by the NCC and DNC to pummel the more extreme religious broadcasters like Billy James Hargis and Carl McIntire. Billy Graham came out of the dustup just fine, allowing him and likeminded evangelists to monopolize a version of Evangelical Christianity that seemed downright demure in comparison to the likes of Hargis and McIntire.

As the 1960s came to a close, another key change was on the horizon: the slow decline of the Fairness Doctrine, which many people across the political spectrum were happy to put out to pasture. This may have been unavoidable; the doctrine was unclear and unevenly enforced. It had also, with or without the active, quasi-conspiratorial help of the Kennedy administration, successfully kept the lid on the most extreme programs. Once that lid was removed, the airwaves became increasingly heated—to the enormous benefit of conservative media, whose visibility was further compounded by the rise of television and corresponding rise of a second generation of Evangelical leaders such as Pat Robertson and Jerry Falwell.[139]

Despite this advantageous, even victorious, boon for conservative media, claims of liberal censorship and generalized liberal threat didn't just persist, they got *louder*. What had been grounded—if subject to qualification—gave way, over time, to the world of could-not-be-otherwise in which claims were taken as true today, true tomorrow, and true forever, regardless of what actually happened. With that mythic turn, history goes out the window. Nuance goes out the window. The ability to have honest conversations goes out the window.

So does the critically important detail that censorship—both the threat of it and actual instances of mainstream pushback—is the best thing that ever happened to conservatives. There would *be* no conservative movement, at least not as we currently know it, if rightwing media activists hadn't encountered a blackout of their unpopular views and decided to build their own networks. Being pushed out of the mainstream, or at least claiming to have been pushed out after self-exiling, was from the very outset a cornerstone of what would become the "classic" conservative brand. Further, while the Fairness Doctrine burned many rightwing media activists, most obviously those driven off the air, it also cleared space for Evangelicals to grow unchecked, mainstream themselves, and yet allow charges of censorship to remain rhetorically generative as an anti-liberal rallying cry.

Ultimately, then, pushback against rightwing media was a key catalyst for rightwing media, something anti-liberals could unify around and further scaffold their collective identity onto.[140] Clarence Manion captured this tension when he lamented the "censorious atmosphere" on college campuses whenever student-run stations stopped airing his program. But ultimately, Nicole Hemmer explains, "he found the story of suppression useful."[141]

The story of suppression was very useful to the anti-liberal ecosystem overall. It fed into a vague foreboding sense that threat was everywhere

and was coming for *us*, bearers of the immovable and enduring moral traditionalism of American Christian conservatism. The conventional narrative, to be explored in later chapters, that the New Right of the 1970s and
1980s was responsible for bringing "traditional morality" to the cultural
foreground—reflecting all the work of all the Evangelicals listening to
Reagan's "Evil Empire" speech—isn't just missing a step. It's overlooking
what made the New Right possible in the first place.

EVERYTHINGNESS AND THE SHADOW GOSPEL

By the time Reagan delivered his "Evil Empire" speech in 1983, traditionalism in the United States had asserted itself as the moral majority.
Its demonological logic justified every available attack against the vague
and interchangeable *them* plotting to take everything from *us*. Or maybe it
already had? That was just details. Through wraparound, decontextualization, and opacity, with a dizzying amalgamation of pandemonic messages,
the classic American Christian conservatives in Reagan's audience were able
to simultaneously represent tradition and change, continuity and renewal,
fire bearing and fire starting. The past could collapse into the future, and
the present could collapse into both, allowing the exalted moral traditionalist *we* to exist beyond time and beyond logic. To echo an earlier point,
when you aren't connected to anything, you get to be everything.

Reagan's good news for the audience was that they—along with "real"
Americans everywhere—were about to topple the evils of Communism.
And yet conservative Christians needed to forge ahead, past Communism, to the newer and worse threats Reagan highlighted during the first
half of his speech. This is a winnable future, Reagan insisted, because the
people in the room are spiritual warriors, called to heed the banner under
which Reagan stood: Change Your World, with the tail of the letter "g" in
"change" wrapping around a cartoon globe. So rise up, be part of this glorious renewal, and also continue to defend tradition; it's all the same thing.
For Reagan, the victory that was just on the horizon was not an invitation
to rest and rejuvenate. It was a call to harness the spiritual strength of the
conservative movement in order to "terrify and ultimately triumph over
those who would enslave their fellow man."[142] Happily for Reagan, Evangelicals didn't need to be told twice to terrify.

THE CULTURE WARS ARE SATANIC

Triumphant on the heels of Republicans' crushing victory of Democrats during the 1994 midterms, newly sworn-in Speaker of the House Newt Gingrich delivered a speech overviewing the Republicans' plan for the first hundred days of the congressional session. This "Contract with America" forwarded various conservative foreign and domestic policies.[1] The effort to strengthen families was given top priority. Lowering taxes, eradicating welfare, and cleaning up "the streets" (at least, the streets that made white people nervous) was how the Republicans promised to do it. Gingrich made clear what was at stake at this pivotal juncture in U.S. politics. "What is at issue," he proclaimed, "is literally not Republican or Democrat or liberal or conservative but the question of whether or not our civilization will survive."[2] This wasn't the first time Gingrich had waxed apocalyptic. As he stated in 1994, "I see evil around me every day . . . we're on the edge of losing this civilization."[3]

There was, of course, a lie baked into Gingrich's suggestion that his was a neutral, nonpartisan concern about the fate of the republic. He had made abundantly clear in the runup to 1994's so-called Republican Revolution whom he held responsible for America's shuffle toward the apocalypse: liberals, which for him mapped onto "official Washington," namely, lobbyists, most members of the press, and his Democratic colleagues in Congress.[4] Gingrich even had a pet name for them: the "loony left," which he said controlled the "Democratic machine." During a 1988 congressional speech delivered to an empty chamber—but with plenty of cameras, a rhetorical habit of Gingrich's[5]—he explained his reasoning for the epithet. The left's views "are so weird, so far out of touch with reality, so unusual, that no other term was good enough."[6] Gingrich made his case as often as he could. This was a group of people who always lied, who were sick, who were hedonists, and who embraced socialist values.[7] For Gingrich, liberals were the ultimate *them*, whom he accused of personally attacking him, attempting to slow him down, and beating him "around the head and shoulders."[8]

It had been a slow, strange transition from the various definitions of liberal that circulated during the 1950s and 1960s to the hyperpartisan pandemonic definition that crystalized by the 1980s. That definition was the springboard for Gingrich's political career.

Gingrich's language about liberals was in fact the basis of an aggressive and highly coordinated communications strategy involving political strategists, public relations firms, and focus testers designed to help Republican politicians "speak Gingrich" and effectively vilify the left.[9] For instance, in 1990, Gingrich distributed a packet via GOPAC, a Republican political action committee, titled "Language: A Key Mechanism of Control."[10] In it, Gingrich emphasized the importance of going and staying negative. Besides using they/them to describe Democrats as well as "liberal" framed sneeringly (*Atlanta-Journal Constitution* reporter James Salzer found that, on one randomly chosen page of a fundraising letter, Gingrich used "liberal" to describe his opponent seven times[11]), Republicans were encouraged to embrace words such as destroy, sick, traitors, endanger, radical, devour, anti-flag, anti-family, anti-child, bizarre, intolerant, shame, and disgrace when describing Democrats.

The "Contract with America" was more careful than that; its language is civil, reasonable, and adult. It's framed as *pro-* from beginning to end, with pro-family policies as the north star. At least, it sounded that way. Its rhetorical implications were all *anti-*, which is another way of saying all Gingrich. For instance, the statement that the transfer of power from Democrats to Republicans reflected "the beginning of a Congress that respects the values and shares the faith of the American family"[12] implicitly asserted that Democrats didn't respect those values or share that faith—thus pitting them *against* the American family. In describing their commitment to acting "with firmness in the right, as God gives us to see the right,"[13] a confusing Abraham Lincoln quote, the Republican conference further emphasized their divine decree to act, implicitly contrasted with the Democrats, who were not similarly exalted by God. Without that favor, the Democrats could only be wrong—and more than that, they could only be the one word that the totality of Gingrich's attack phrases pointed to but didn't directly state: they could only be *evil*.

This was a far cry from the language of devils and demons that had for decades been swirling through Evangelical and mainstream popular culture. There is, however, a key link between conspiratorial claims about Satan incarnate, *anti-* claims about liberal threats to the family, and slick, well-produced *pro-* claims about how much the Republican Party supports families (and children, and tradition, and America). Ultimately, these claims are the same claim about the destructiveness of liberals, which simultaneously positions liberal-fighting conservatives as America's savior. The intensity of pandemonic rhetoric in the 1990s is key to understanding how the New Right's ascendancy fueled the Republican Party's ascendancy.

The previous chapter argued that the conventional story of the New Right's origins gets something fundamentally wrong: it overlooks decades of demonological precedent. This chapter pushes that argument further. According to the conventional account, Evangelicals used biblically grounded beliefs, most importantly love for Jesus, to propel the Republican Party toward Evangelical positions on moral issues—and head-spinning electoral success.[14] The culture wars thesis, that there is a traditionalist-modernist divide within American religious traditions, and that traditionalism was essentially "standing its ground" in response to modernist encroachment, is said to be central to this outcome.[15] That's what motivated so many conservatives to fight to restore traditional values. That's what ultimately yielded the Republican Revolution of 1994.

The problem is that the three major assumptions that scaffold the conventional account—that God was the central motivator for conservative political activism, that the "family values" Republican platform that emerged in the 1990s reflected a grounded ideology, and that religious belief was the basis of that political playbook—simply don't line up with what actually happened. What the story of Republican-Evangelical fusing actually shows is that hatred of the devil was more politically expedient than love of Jesus; that what supported the Republican platform in the 1990s was demonology, not ideology; and that the playbook those leaders drew from wasn't the Bible, it was the shadow gospel. The resulting war over culture may have been hard-fought, but it did not begin with liberal advancement followed by conservative reaction. It began with conservative advancement followed by conservative reaction to its own satanic shadow.

SATAN IS ALIVE AND WELL ON PLANET EARTH

Placing Satan in the driver's seat might seem like a novel—and perhaps jarring—way to describe the development of the modern Republican Party, but such an approach echoes how many scholars of religion situate Satan within the Christian tradition more broadly. In separate studies, Neil Forsyth and Elaine Pagels both argue that if you want to understand who early Christians were, you have to understand the evils they were fighting,[16] particularly as their worldview placed moral value on inhabiting the subject position of an embattled minority. To be attacked by an evil other was to have one's Christian identity affirmed.[17]

Critically, those attacks, and the evils that underlay them, weren't set in stone. What early Christians faced was a *variable* bestiary and *situational* evil. That is the source of Satan's theological power: to exist in many forms while inhabiting "the essentially political figure of the cosmic rebel," as Pagels describes it.[18] Scripture reflects Satan's placeholder nature. Serpent-like and terrifying in the Book of Revelation, Satan has different demonic flavors across the different books of the Bible. Depending on the text one reads, he is a generalized adversary (in Numbers), God's main troll (in Job), the embodiment of Jesus's enemies (in Mark and Matthew), an animating force of darkness (in Luke), and Jesus's cosmic sparring partner (in John).[19] He plays other roles in apocryphal texts, including Neil Forsyth's observation that the Satan of the Book of Zechariah is "a J. Edgar Hoover or a CIA director who no longer clears his every move with the president."[20] The fact that Satan could be different things at different times—that he was, to revisit Raiswell, Brock, and Winter's insight, a figure of constant reiteration[21]—made him an always-expanding threat, helping to ensure believers' constant embattlement. Here, opposition wasn't just opposition. Opposition was a supernatural force[22] with the fate of the world always hanging in the balance.[23] One consequence was that evil was worldbuilding. The other consequence was that there was no room for compromise; why would anyone negotiate with the devil?[24]

As discussed in the book's introduction, there are many points of overlap between the liberal devil and the Christian devil, from the placeholder nature of evil to the degree to which the devil's opponents *need* evil to maintain their own identities.[25] There are also important differences. Within an anti-liberal framework, liberals aren't just *like* the Christian devil; they *are* the shadow devil, meaning that they are the devil stripped of theological specificity and connection to the Bible. Instead, they are suffused with demonology: a collection of threatening "liberal" things in the world that are incoherently collapsed together. Chapter 2 argues that this is what New

Evangelicals like Billy Graham brought to the shadow gospel party: a Satan shell that the anti-liberal amalgamation could be stuffed inside.

The animating political dynamic is that Satan is fast, God is slow. It is much easier to rally people around the devil than to encourage them to cultivate moral speech, action, and understanding within a pluralistic democratic system. And yet, relative to God and Jesus, the devil is barely discussed in the context of mainstream politics, reflecting the fact that Satan can be an awkward topic to broach.[26] He remains so even for religious studies scholars. "He is the weak place of the popular religion," Forsyth writes. "The vulnerable belly of the crocodile."[27]

This is quite an oversight. Through the 1970s and 1980s, Evangelicals aggressively spread the word about Satan, not as a down-the-road threat you would face on Judgment Day, but as an evil that was already here, hidden in malevolent secular influence. In making these claims, Evangelicals were also helping to spread a shadow conservatism in which the cosmic subject position of ultimate good was defined by and centered around the great redeemer: themselves. A demonological reframing of the culture wars thesis is therefore needed. The culture wars are not about honoring God and preserving tradition. The culture wars are about fighting Satan and inventing tradition. And so fighting Satan is where we will begin.

FEAR, FATALISM, AND SWEATY FASCINATION WITH THE IMPURE

At the end of the 1960s and into the 1970s, the apocalypse was having a moment. This wasn't a totally novel development; extreme focus on the figure of Satan and the apocalyptic showdown between good and evil had long existed in Christian fundamentalism.[28] The rise of the charismatic deliverance ministry movement overlapping with Pentecostalism in the 1960s helped push these narratives closer to the center of fundamentalist Protestant networks. Not only did the deliverance movement emphasize the casting out of demons, healing of sickness, and performance of other miracles; they disseminated an enormous amount of media and other communications material related to demonic influence.[29]

Jason Bivins situates these materials within what he calls the "religion of fear," a central characteristic of contemporary Evangelicalism born, first, of a "long tradition of evangelical darkness,"[30] and second, the sense of an increasingly threatening contemporary political climate. Religious historian Daniel G. Hummel similarly argues that end-times thinking focused on the Rapture is central to Evangelicalism as a resilient theological belief.[31] He further suggests that the apocalyptic undercurrent of Evangelicalism has significantly influenced the United States' cultural imagination.

As Bivins explains, Evangelicalism's religion of fear provides for believers "an affective template that posits demonological causes for political decline" and grants them a "coherent, unchanging place" within a good-versus-evil historical framework.[32] Unsurprisingly, the religion of fear is most basically about being and staying afraid. But as Bivins emphasizes, it also reflects a kind of eroticism, a "sweaty fascination with the impure"[33] and other cultural influences deemed sinful, evil, illicit, and carnal.[34]

One of the earliest and most striking articulations of the religion of fear can be found in the work of Jack Chick, whose "Chick Tracts" circulated extensively in the 1970s.[35] Chick's vision of America as a land of sinful filth, along with his militant opposition to secular culture, connected him to the long-standing Evangelical preoccupation with "youth at risk."[36] The resulting panic frames captured in his small, flip book–sized tracts are so overrun with demons and darkness that they can be considered a kind of "spiritual porn"[37] and Chick himself as a "cartographer of hell"[38] whose message about Jesus is, in a word, terrifying.

Though now regarded by many as religious kitsch, particularly his tracts on witchcraft, rock music, and the game Dungeons & Dragons, Chick presented a vision of Christianity that was fundamentally violent and preoccupied with revenge. Reverend Richard Lee, an Assembly of God preacher who knew Jack Chick and uses Chick Tracts in his ministry, affirms Chick's vision of the apocalypse, describing it as "Jesus coming back and killing everybody [in] very graphic and bloody detail . . . but it's good revenge because it's God doing it."[39] Chick was especially bombastic in how he presented this message—in one of his tracts, his representation of a bloodied Jesus resembles "hamburger on the cross"[40]—but his depictions of an America gripped by Satan's influence resonated widely.[41] Many fundamentalist and Evangelical Christians looked around and, like Chick, were convinced that the end was near, dovetailing with the belief that terrible evil within mainstream culture wasn't just threatening to drag America into hell; it had already made a hell out of America.

Although they arrived at similar conclusions about the imminence of the end times and its promise of Rapture (in which true Christians, living and dead, would be reunited with Jesus), fundamentalists and Evangelicals adopted very different plans of action.[42] Those who approached the apocalypse with fundamentalist insularity were, on the whole, inwardly focused, with their strongest energies directed at believers to prepare them for Jesus's return. The idea was to get right with God—and then patiently wait for his return. For those who approached the apocalypse with the outward-looking focus of Evangelicalism, waiting around wasn't a natural part of the communications strategy. Instead, like the New Evangelicals of the 1950s, 1970s Evangelicals used the language of apocalypse and all the terrors it promised to describe what was happening in the allegedly hellish world around them. This allowed Evangelicals to insert themselves into the cosmic battle and frame their version of Christianity as the only protection against hellfire. More on that self-centering soon.

Whichever apocalyptic path one followed, the end times indexed a complex set of beliefs. Daniel Wojcik highlights the key markers of premillennial dispensationalism, the most common end-times framework within Evangelicalism ("premillennialism" refers to the belief that Christ must return in an apocalyptic scenario and violently destroy all evil on Earth before a thousand-year period of peace can commence; "dispensationalism" refers to the process by which salvation is dispensed across distinct historical periods[43]). Set against the backdrop of a cosmic drama frame,[44] this belief system focuses on prophetic signs[45] and the appearance of an Antichrist[46] and is characterized by an abiding sense that the world is unrecuperably evil.[47] As described by Wojcik, fatalism is central to such beliefs and promotes the idea that "human beings are basically helpless against overpowering, sinister forces and that human effort is ineffectual in saving an increasingly evil and doomed world."[48] Reflecting the fatalist frame, the apocalypse isn't seen as something to prevent. The apocalypse is part of God's predetermined plan. That makes it, ultimately, *good*; it's how Jesus gets to come back to earth, resulting in a finally cleansed, finally redeemed, world free of evil and human suffering.[49]

HAL AND TIM

One of the superspreaders of apocalyptic belief during this time was Hal Lindsey, whose 1960s missionary work with Campus Crusade for Christ in California ultimately yielded a position as head of UCLA's campus ministry.[50] The author of bestselling books such as the *Late Great Planet*

Earth[51] and *Satan Is Alive and Well on Planet Earth*[52]—which by 1977 had already sold a combined total of fourteen million copies[53]—Lindsey hosted a news and call-in radio show, traveled on a nationwide lecture circuit, and greenlighted videotaped and filmed versions of his enormously popular writings.[54] Through these media, he helped shape the end-times narrative into what historian Scott Poole describes as "an exciting adventure/disaster novel format" marked by a "profound biblical illiteracy" that, while theologically suspect, also helped cultivate an appeal for those who had never attended church but liked the scary story he was telling.[55] This included Lindsey's gleeful discussion of how people's faces and eyes will be melted off during the Battle of Armageddon.[56]

Another key end-times prophesy proponent is Tim LaHaye, opening act for the John Birch Society recruitment video discussed in chapter 1. LaHaye was a California pastor who began his ministry in the 1950s, cofounded a network of 1970s Christian educational and activist institutions, and through the 2000s oversaw a multimedia empire of biblical prophecy.[57] He was also the husband of Beverly LaHaye, whose anti-feminist organization Concerned Women for America will be the focus of a later section. Together, the LaHayes made many prophetic claims, including that the United Nations and World Council of Churches could number among the satanic institutions predicted in the Book of Revelation.[58] For contemporary readers, LaHaye is probably best known as the coauthor of the global phenomenon *Left Behind* book series, which published new titles between 1995 and 2007 and chronicles in exuberantly gory detail the rapture of good Christians and punishment of everyone else.[59]

The prophecy media produced by figures like Lindsey and LaHaye fit into what Bivins calls a "vast and complicated" evangelical pop paraculture with roots extending back to the 1960s.[60] Bivins further explains that there was a great deal of thematic and narrative overlap between the kinds of books written by Lindsey and LaHaye and the apocalypse shock films "dripp[ing] with the viscera of fear"[61] shown to youth Bible study groups and camps (which would often be used as beta testing for wider-scale Evangelical media strategies).[62] The publishing companies that marketed Hal Lindsey's books—which, as Wojcik emphasizes, were kept affordable, distributed to national bookstores as well as Christian stores, and included cover art that looked like any other mass-market paperback[63]—may have been motivated to guide audiences down a righteous path, just as saving souls may have been the immediate objective of LaHaye's efforts to push his apocalyptic narratives across diverse networks and channels. What these media and their messengers also did was help create a market for the devil.

SELLING SATAN

The explosion in popularity of prophecy media in the 1970s corresponded with a similar explosion in popularity of satanic- and occult-themed media. Religious grifters known as "Satan sellers" hawked stories about their alleged experiences as satanic insiders (most of which were spectacularly debunked). Self-described "Number One Christian Comedian" Mike Warnke was arguably the most influential.[64] His 1972 book, *The Satan Seller*, was advertised thus: "A former satanist high priest reveals the demonic forces behind the fastest growing and most deadly occult religion in the world."[65] Warnke's work circulated widely within Evangelical networks; according to the authors of a *Cornerstone Magazine* exposé of Warnke's compounding lies, "a generation of Christians learned what they knew of Satanism and the occult from *The Satan Seller*."[66] His Satan-selling competition included John Todd, who passed along what he claimed were details about the inner workings of satanic cabals to Jack Chick, who integrated that insider (dis)info into his Chick Tracts.[67]

Interest in "satanic cults" mapped onto the broader "occult revival" of the early 1970s, in which fictionalized and often deliberately campy satanic references inundated popular media. The satanic trend fed into the growth of—and backlash to—New Age aesthetics and religious practices, which subsumed everything from tarot cards to "alternative" (i.e., non-Christian) religions to the "sexy fad" of suburban witches, who embraced what Poole calls "satanic chic."[68] And then there was the fact that Satan was simply in the news a lot during this time, connected to a series of crimes with apparent ritual elements.[69] Teenagers in particular embraced satanic-inflected criminality in order to make their crimes seem scarier—but also because some were genuinely disturbed.[70] Many serial killers—a category of violent criminal that seemed to emerge from nowhere in the 1970s—also employed satanic symbolism. Serial murderer Richard Ramirez, for example, drew a pentagram on his hand during his murder trial, which he flashed at cameras every chance he got.[71]

Conveniently, those who sold prophesies about Satan—its own form of occult titillation—could point to all this activity as concrete proof that the end was near. Noting that "nearly every respectable high school these days has its own witch,"[72] Hal Lindsey cited the rise in popularity of astrology, the existence of drug culture, the growth of "hippie cults," and college courses on witchcraft as signs of the impending apocalypse.[73] Billy Graham agreed, arguing in 1975 that the "apparent increase in satanic activity against people on the planet today may indicate that a Second Coming of Jesus Christ is close at hand. Certainly, the activity of Satan is evident on every side."[74] Pat Robertson, who would become one of the figureheads of the Christian Coalition, and whose Christian Broadcasting Network was, by 1975, beaming out via satellite to millions of viewers, also pushed end-times rhetoric. He regularly speculated about signs from Revelation and the rise of the Antichrist, and in a letter to station contributors in 1982, claimed that CBN was chosen by God to function as a ministry akin to John the Baptist, "to prepare the way for Jesus' second coming."[75]

The widespread fear among Evangelicals that the devil had infiltrated all aspects of American life[76] also fueled a burgeoning genre of straight-to-video satanic shock films.[77] Reflecting the "parallel institutionalism" of Evangelical media,[78] these videos circulated through church networks, a necessity born of the fact that in the 1970s, video stores didn't cater to Christian sensibilities. Pastors would therefore select or be given films that were most likely to appeal to their congregation, which church members could borrow or have screened at the church—a system that had the added bonus of keeping distribution costs low, in turn allowing more films to be made for less money.[79] Popular titles included *The Burning Hell*, which features a conventional slasher narrative set in hell; *Exposing the Satanic Web*, which posited a who's who of satanic conspiracy; and *Not Just Fun and Games*, which claims that kids' toys are vehicles for satanic influence by promoting ideals such as Hinduism and humanism.[80]

An underlying message of these films, like the underlying message of much end-times prophesying, is that pop culture lures youth to evil.[81] A series of panics thus ensued within Evangelical networks over the presumed satanic influence of children's cartoons, children's toys, Dungeons & Dragons, rock music and its allegedly backmasked satanic lyrics, and Halloween. For believers, satanic fear was pervasive—because the threats were everywhere.[82]

FROM SATAN TO SATANISTS

It's against this mass-mediated backdrop that the Satanic Panics of the 1980s and 1990s emerge. As we will see, these panics took many forms, but most shocking were the accusations of satanic ritual abuse that spread through mostly rural American communities. The sensational, graphic nature of these accusations—blood sacrifices; forced ingestion of urine, blood, semen, and excrement; depraved sexual violence; cannibalism, ritual murder of children; sexual abuse of children; forced sex between children; and violent infanticide[83]—prompted sociologist Jeffrey Victor to label them, broadly, as "atrocity stories."[84] Hundreds circulated during the 1980s; none were ever substantiated, even after criminal investigation.[85] And yet the satanic ritual accusations continued to fly, resulting in scores of criminal trials, most famously of daycare workers accused of ritual molestation.

As Victor explains, satanic atrocity stories were an amalgamation of many sources. Traditional folklore about black magic, witches, and devils fused with tropes from occult and horror movies, as well as details taken from the books and speeches of self-proclaimed satanic ritual abuse survivors.[86] Satan sellers hawking accounts of their occult misadventures also provided narrative fodder.[87] Once told, the stories circulated widely, traveling across networks of mental health professionals, particularly those within the "Christian therapy movement"; social workers, child welfare advocates, and other victim advocates inclined to believe the women and children's stories, particularly, again, when they came from Evangelical backgrounds; and law enforcement officers focused on occult crimes colloquially known as "cult cops," most of whom were Evangelical, and some of whom drew from Chick Tracts as part of their "recon."[88]

Mass media, notably cable talk shows, also helped amplify the stories. One of the first programs to address the "national crisis" of devil worship was *20/20*'s "The Devil Worshippers." Introducing the story with grave seriousness, host Hugh Downs runs through a litany of the terrors allegedly on the rise. "Perverse, hideous acts that defy belief," he states. "Suicides, murders, and ritualistic slaughter of children and animals."[89] Later, expert guests are brought on to help make sense of the trend. One was "Number One Christian Comedian" and former satanic priest Mike Warnke. The other was a Christian psychologist who believed in demonic possession. Both pushed narratives of Satan, here and now, on earth.[90]

The dubious honor of hosting the most infamous cable news special on satanism, however, goes to Geraldo Rivera, whose episode "Satan Underground" spliced together clips from horror films, described gruesome cases of ritual murder, touted Charles Manson's satanic connections, and lamented the evil influences of heavy metal music.[91] Rivera later wrote the foreword to *The Edge of Evil*, a book written by Evangelical traveling preacher Jerry Johnston, who ran an ostensibly secular arm of his ministry offering lectures around the country on teenage satanism to public schools. Rivera praised Johnston's "research." One representative case in Johnston's book describes a pregnant eighteen-year-old satanist who claims to have conjured a demon because she wanted to physically hurt someone and needed the demon to teach her how to fight. The demon obliged. He would also semi-possess her before a scuffle, allowing the young woman to, as she explains, "physically pick up people a lot heavier than me and throw them around."[92]

Within this context, stories about Satan incarnate, that is to say, "actual" demonic evil, could be woven into local rumors about satanic influence. But as the stories jumped from fundamentalist networks to more secular networks, particularly when filtered through mainstream mass media, worries about the risks of Satan—a supernatural being—to one's soul were supplanted by worries about the risks of *satanists*—non-supernatural deviants—to one's children, family, or community.

THE DEVIL'S IN THE DEVIANCE

When reflecting on the legacy of the Satanic Panics, many scholars and critics focus on those impacted by the various preschool trials, the most high profile of which, the McMartin trial in Los Angeles County, concluded in 1990. This makes sense; the trials are the most conspicuous and excessive outcrop of the panics. But there is another underexplored consequence: what happens as the charges of *actual* satanic influence, that is to say, evil incarnate, fuse with panic over threats to the family.

The fuzzy relationship between evil and deviance is present even in the campiest pop culture articulations of the panics. For example, in the "devil is in the machine" cycle of satanic horror films produced in the 1980s—in which some satanic element or another lurks within video games and other new technologies—the narratives ultimately loop back to the evils that are invited into one's home when technology is allowed to erode traditional family norms and structures.[93]

Religious organizations made the connection between deviance and evil explicit. Fighting deviance and therefore Satan was the stated objective of the secular-sounding American Family Association, run by Reverend Donald Wildman. Pushing for "biblical ethics of decency" in school curricula, the American Family Association coordinated with its 500 local chapters and other conservative Christian organizations to "fight against Satanism" in schoolbooks and thereby promote traditional American family values.[94] It was this overlap, Victor argues, that helps explain why satanic atrocity stories resonated so strongly with fundamentalists and Evangelicals. Not only did the stories affirm a good-versus-evil Christian cosmology; they affirmed conspiratorial beliefs about the erosion of traditional values and subsequent undermining of Christianity.[95] Sociologist David Bromley speaks to a similar point when he notes that "Satanism constitutes a metaphorical construction of a widely experienced sense of vulnerability and danger by American families."[96]

The anti-rock panic of the 1980s and 1990s epitomized the fusing of *anti-* frame satanic worry and *pro-* frame family values worry. These worries far transcended specifically Christian concerns about children's souls. Rock was linked with sex, crime, suicide, homicide, and disrespecting one's parents. These were the issues raised by the PMRC (which, as a reminder, stands for the Parents Music Resource Center), secular as the day was long, even if, behind the scenes, many of the wives and mothers railing against rock were deeply embedded within Evangelical networks (Susan Baker, for instance, one of the PMRC's "Washington Wives" mentioned in the book's introduction and who sat on Focus on the Family's board of directors, was profiled in a 1985 *Washington Post* article that described her Christian faith as her defining characteristic[97]).

The heavy metal musicians accused of being in league with the devil—or at least in league with eroding family values—were overwhelmingly white. Black hip-hop and rap artists, seen as stand-ins for Blackness generally, were subject to their own satanic and decidedly racist chains of signification.[98] Attacks against rap unfolded against the backdrop of persistent claims of "moral poverty" that Republicans—and the Democrats who cosigned the most demonological elements of the "Contract with America"[99]—heaped onto the "inner city," a term that was less about a specific point on a map and more about the Black and brown people who lived there.

As Poole explains, an entire vocabulary of evil was used to construct this urban enemy. Ronald Reagan did his part; many other politicians and media figures did as well.[100] Claims about "crackheads" and "welfare queens" living within "ghettos" emphasized that poor Black and brown people were unreachable, socially alien, hostile, and feral, with Black men in particular framed as "demonic predators" (we will return to the racist "superpredator" trope in a later chapter).[101] The role of police, at least as it was sold to white America, was thus to "crusade against evil, to slay monsters and demons,"[102] a position that aligned with Evangelical leaders' simultaneous insistence that "good" Christians were called to "engage in an unrelenting war on the forces of darkness threatening their homes, children, churches, and communities."[103]

To this end, rap music was sometimes explicitly roped into discourses of darkness and evil.[104] More often, Jason Bivins argues, rap—and the obscenity said to be its hallmark—was framed in terms of threats to social order.[105] In the context of rap and the "inner city" more broadly, white people's stated concerns about the family, education, and crime allowed them to vocalize fears about the dilution of whiteness without ever having to talk directly about race.[106] A person didn't need to; the demonization came through regardless.

SATAN'S LONG TAIL

Euphemism—and not just of the racist variety—is central to the Satanic Panic story. "Satan," both the word and figure, simply wasn't necessary to promote a worldview of cosmic good versus evil centering on threats to hearth and home. In fact, not saying the word "Satan" helped make the battle seem more reasonable to more people.[107]

This secularized, euphemistic, Satan-less Satanic Panic is what catalyzed the ascendancy of Gingrich's Republican Party—*not* the so-called culture wars, which posits tread-upon conservatives reacting to aggressive liberals encroaching on traditional values. Instead, what gave the Republicans and Evangelicals the upper hand was the demonological crusade to, first, define evil and, second, to present the false traditionalism of a very particular kind of white conservative Christianity as the only protection against that evil. In other words, we get to say who the devil is, and we're Jesus.

THE BATTLE FOR THE MIND

Decades before the phrase "culture wars" was internalized as Barthian myth, Evangelicals in the 1970s were articulating an early version of the culture wars thesis: that the "permanent religious truth" of a "pure" Christian America was on the retreat, ruthlessly pursued by a mainstream culture that wanted to destroy it.[108]

Tim LaHaye was particularly vocal about the threats posed to "pure" Christianity by secular humanism, a term that implicated socialism, feminism, sexual permissiveness, divorce, coed college dorms, and a litany of other allegedly corrosive elements that LaHaye attributes to "liberalized" state and federal policies.[109] ("Secular humanism" circulated widely within rightwing networks in the 1970s and 1980s, though ultimately proved to be less satanic—in terms of linguistic reiteration—and therefore less durable than "liberal"). For LaHaye, the demonology was literal, connected to Satan's unfolding schemes, a framing he also used to promote a profound and virulent homophobia that explicitly linked queerness with the devil.[110] Secular humanism and its offshoots thus created what LaHaye described as "the world's greatest evil"[111] that "destroys everything it touches."[112] And there was no escape. For LaHaye, every arena of American life was a contest between Christianity and secular humanist values,[113] with the general idea, imbued in the various organizations he founded, that secular humanism represented "deviations from a historic path of national righteousness."[114]

According to LaHaye, humanism wreaks havoc through four vehicles of mind control: education (which teaches evolution and relativism), media (especially television and its promotion of humanist views), organizations like the ACLU and other groups that advocate "situational ethics" (an ethics that takes context into account and focuses on the consequences of actions), and government (including government funding of education, which erodes "traditional freedoms" such as a biblical basis of classroom instruction). Secular humanists, he argues, aren't "real" Americans because they don't put Americans first and because they don't think like a "pro-moral American."[115] As a result, secular humanists shouldn't be allowed to educate children or hold government office.[116] They are, as LaHaye bluntly states, the mortal enemy to "pro-Americans."[117]

LaHaye focused on the evils of the secular world. However, he, like other Evangelicals, completed claims such as "this is a sinful world and feminism creates a stronghold for satanic influence" with the warning that the end was near; Judgment Day was coming. We will soon explore what happened when biblical apocalypticism gave way to a secularized Revelation-lite; but for LaHaye and others like him, the shadow gospel's fiery amalgamation was served in one hand and a promise of the Battle of Armageddon was served in the other.

"YOU GOT SATANIC PANICKING IN MY ERA FIGHT! YOU GOT ERA FIGHT IN MY SATANIC PANICKING!"

A central tenet propping up attacks against secular humanism was the need to preserve the traditional role of women. The belief wasn't just that gender traditionalism upheld family values; it was that it scaffolded the nation's soul.[118] Conversely, women who deviated from falsely traditionalist expectations were associated with evil.[119] As the second-wave feminist movement explicitly challenged traditional gender norms and patriarchal control, it became the Great Satan for many conservative women.

The conflict between "traditional" gender roles and feminism animated the Equal Rights Amendment (ERA) fight, which pushed to enshrine gender and sexual equity in the constitution. The ERA had been drafted in the early twentieth century but was updated and reintroduced to Congress in 1971. For the amendment to pass, it needed to be ratified by thirty-eight states, with a ratification deadline initially set for 1979 and later extended to 1982. Unsurprisingly, the feminist movement pushed for passage, tethered to other progressive causes such as abortion access and gay rights. Equally unsurprisingly, conservative women fought (ultimately successfully) against passage, fueled by well-organized anti-ERA activism but also by a so-called pro-family agenda, which in addition to opposing the ERA and its feminist backers, rallied against abortion, queerness, childcare, sex education in schools, pornography, gun control, welfare spending, and Communism.[120]

Two of the most prominent conservative women in the anti-ERA and associated "pro-family" fight were Beverly LaHaye, wife of Tim LaHaye and founder of Concerned Women for America, and Phyllis Schlafly, founder of STOP-ERA (whose unofficial motto was "stop taking our privileges," i.e., stop forcing women to have agency[121]) as well as the staunchly anticommunist Eagle Forum.

Beverly LaHaye was especially pointed in her religious—and specifically satanic—framings of the ERA, which she, similar to her husband, accused of threatening to destroy the sanctity of the Christian home.[122] "The forces of darkness are becoming darker," she proclaimed of feminism, the push for ERA, and its alleged broader objectives of lesbianism, Marxism, and extreme social change.[123] By taking a stand against the "never-ending attack on the family by the feminist/socialist/humanist coalition,"[124] women in the Concerned Women for America orbit had, according to LaHaye, "made a choice to oppose evil."[125] This was, in short, *war*. LaHaye was very clear about what kind. "The Word of God tells us that we're not really fighting against flesh and blood. We're not really in a battle against spiritual leaders. We're engaged in a struggle against the spiritual forces of darkness that control these individuals."[126] The takeaway from Beverly LaHaye's writing is clear: these are dark, evil days, and righteous women are called to defeat the devil and bring glory to God.[127]

On the surface, Beverly LaHaye seemed to be running a very different kind of organization than Schlafly's Eagle Forum. Concerned Women of America was grassroots, fueled by the volunteer activism of "kitchen table lobbyists," and focused much of its energies on "religious freedom" legal cases, including those highlighting alleged occult influences in classroom textbooks.[128] Concerned Women of America also had via Tim LaHaye closer ties to religious organizations within the New Right, with Beverly LaHaye admitting in a 1985 *LA Times* article that a primary distinction between Concerned Women of America and the Eagle Forum was that her group had "quicker access to church women."[129] The Eagle Forum helmed by Schlafly, in contrast, was more confrontational, more professionalized and centered on network organization, and more focused on legislative intervention in Washington, DC.[130] And yet, Susan Marshall argues, beneath the stylistic differences, "both organizations address[ed] the same issues in very similar ways."[131]

Thus Satan, or at least the threat of spiritual evil, was never too far from the messaging mark of even the secular-presenting Eagle Forum. Rosemary Thompson, for example, one of the STOP-ERA state coordinators appointed by Schlafly, circulated a leaflet titled "A Christian View of the Equal Rights Amendment." Of the amendment, Thompson wrote, "Jesus cautioned us about wolves in sheep's clothing . . . of Satan coming as an angel of light so even the elect will be deceived."[132] An audiocassette mass distributed to Eagle Forum members made similarly direct claims about spiritual evil. Produced to push back against 1975's International Women's Year conference, a federally funded national rally designed to generate support for ERA, the recording called on "traditional Christian women" to resist "evil that is inherent within the so-called women's liberation movement" and show "how as Christians we must do good as the Lord commands by opposing this evil."[133]

Schlafly herself didn't make direct appeals to Satan's influence. She did, however, frame feminism as an "enemy within that threatened the traditional order of a Christian-based society,"[134] argued that the pro-ERA International Women's Year conference was "a front for radicals and lesbians,"[135] and actively aligned herself with the chains of demonological signification that, as cultural theorist Linda Kintz states, "was capable only of dealing with cosmic wars of good and evil,"[136] where ambiguity of any kind contained the mark of the satanic, the Communist, and the perverse.[137]

FOCUSING ON THE FAMILY

The fact that so many Evangelical messages about creeping cultural evil traveled so far beyond church networks was, to an extent, a reflection of how many messengers there were—and how hard Evangelicals worked to spread the word. Among Evangelical leaders and media figures, there was also an active effort to flash the pro-family side of the Satanic Panicking coin to a wider secular audience. These messages didn't just sand down the figure of Satan; they sanded down the presence of religion entirely, repackaging demonology as American Pie.

THE CONTRACT WITH AMERICAN DEMONOLOGY

The Christian Coalition's expansion pack on Gingrich's "Contract with America" exemplifies the savvy secularization of Christian messaging using seemingly unassailable *pro-* frames. Titled the "Contract with the American Family," this Contract with America 2.0 was unveiled in a speech by Christian Coalition executive director Ralph Reed.[138] Gingrich, who had vowed to use his House Speakership to support the Christian Coalition's efforts,[139] sat in the audience. Echoing Gingrich, Reed emphasized in his speech that their contract wasn't about Republicans or Democrats; it was about reasonable, mainstream common sense. He reiterates this point in the preface to the published Contract, which sets up the Coalition's litany of policy goals designed to protect the American family:

- Restoring religious equality
- Local control of education

- Promoting school choice
- Protecting parental rights
- Family-friendly tax relief
- Restoring respect for human life
- Encouraging support of private charities
- Restricting pornography
- Privatizing the arts
- Punishing criminals, not victims.

As quoted in chapter 1, Paul Matzko mused, "Scratch the surface of any right-wing archive from the 1960s and religion oozes out."[140] The same basic observation applies to family values discussions, with a satanic twist. Scratch any pro-family conversation in the 1980s and early 1990s and anti-liberal demonology oozes out.

Here, the Contract's discussion of each point—which strongly echoes and in some cases directly cribs language from the Republicans' "Contract with America"—helps fill in the reasonable-sounding blanks of what exactly is being attacked and who exactly is guilty of attacking it: the various people, policies, and attitudes that, through decades of demonology (and more recent linguistic control efforts of figures like Newt Gingrich) had been subsumed under the collapsed concepts of liberals, leftism, and Democrats. It also makes clear that the "values" enshrined in "family values" are of a very specific kind: those of the white conservative framed as the unwavering, time-immemorial, moral center of "pure" Christian America. The following is a demonological translation—based on the explanations offered within the Contract itself—of what the Christian Coalition is actually asserting:

- Restoring religious equality: Christians' free speech is under attack by liberals who want to minimize Christian influence and open the public sphere to religious and sexual minorities.
- Local control of education: Traditional values taught in the home are under attack by liberals in government and teachers' unions that support teaching gay rights and sex ed in the classroom.
- Promoting school choice: Parents who teach traditional values are under attack by a liberal education bureaucracy that tries to suppress free market capitalism and impose politically correct curricula.
- Protecting parental rights: Traditionalist parents' control over their children's education, medical care, discipline, and religious teaching is under

attack by a liberal state that promotes secular humanist values and collectivist childrearing.

- Family-friendly tax relief: The stabilizing force of the traditional family is under attack by a liberal tax code that undermines family together time, forces women to work outside the home, and leaves teens unsupervised.
- Restoring respect for human life: Unborn children are under attack by a liberal state apparatus that is looking for "cheap fixes" to problems, like pregnancy out of wedlock, that are caused by the erosion of traditional values.
- Encouraging support of private charities: The social fabric is under attack by a liberal welfare system that undermines traditional values by not conditioning financial assistance on "good" behavior.
- Restricting pornography: America's standard of decency is under attack by a liberal media and mainstream society filled with foul influences that constantly bombard families with sexually suggestive and obscene messages.
- Privatizing the arts: Traditional religious beliefs are under attack by publicly funded liberal artists, academics, and legal advocates who promote a secular humanist agenda, including tolerance for homosexuality, critiques of Western culture, and divorce.
- Punishing criminals, not victims: Our streets are under attack by criminals whose lack of moral restraint stems from the breakdown of the family unit and liberal policies focused on the causes of crime rather than the punishment of criminals.

The Christian Coalition's religious affiliation doesn't account for the antiliberalism at the heart of its "Contract with the American Family." The word "God" and references to religion *do not appear in the document* except as quotes from outside sources—and even those are scant, no more prominent than in the ostensibly secular "Contract with America." Even the religious organizations cited by the "Contract with the American Family" are Christ-washed; direct acknowledgment of their religious orientation is sidestepped in favor of the descriptor that they are privately owned (as opposed to federally funded or linked to the state). For a Christian organization that makes Christian faith and advocacy an explicit part of its mission,[141] God is conspicuously missing from their "Contract with the American Family."

RESONANT EVIL

Other staunchly religious networks heading into the 1990s also down-played obvious references to God. The focus was on the family, not on Christianity—even if, just beneath that scratchable surface, a particular sort of Christianity was a precondition of "pure" American values. The most on-the-nose example was James Dobson's Focus on the Family organiza-tion, which would produce content with deliberately diluted Evangelical messages to compete with secular media and hail audiences who weren't especially crazy for Jesus but certainly hated feminism, gay rights, and wel-fare[142] (with "welfare" serving a similar euphemistically racist function as discourses around "crime"[143]). It was even common for Focus on the Fam-ily to distribute two versions of the same films, one that was intended for Christian audiences and the other that would minimize references to Jesus and scripture, which it would then distribute to institutions that were meant to remain religiously unaffiliated, like schools.[144] Pat Robertson's Christian Broadcasting Network embraced a similar branding strategy when, in 1981, it was renamed the Family Channel and began foreground-ing the family as its central programming metaphor.[145]

Linda Kintz's discussion of resonance helps explain how secular-sounding messages about the family ultimately run parallel to claims about a walking, talking Satan made by the likes of Hal Lindsay and Billy Graham. According to Kintz, resonance reflects an intense political passion "aroused and organized to saturate the most public, even global, issues."[146] The pas-sionate exaltation of a narrowly defined family over all other things, the unquestioning embrace of an equally narrow moral culture, and the instant delegitimization of anyone who stands outside these narrow definitions is the resonance unifying the 1990s Christian right.[147]

This resonance runs deep, Kintz argues, so deep that it is almost inartic-ulable: felt but not described with any critical distance, and maybe without conscious awareness. It is also imbued with a particular sort of apocalypti-cism. Whether described as liberalism or secular humanism (with the terms functioning as synonyms through robust chains of demonological signifi-cation), the wicked forces threatening to pull the family asunder are pit against those who don't just take up arms in the cosmic drama, but believe they are destined to win, reflecting the underlying Christian belief that, eventually, good will triumph over evil.[148]

Leaders who embrace the demonological cleaving benefit in a host of ways. Controlling what and who counts as evil allows these leaders to shift resources extremely quickly to new issues and ideas. It also allows them to shift away from other sets of issues and ideas as needed, encapsulated in what Michael Rogin describes as the "disembodied self" of Ronald Reagan,[149] whose capricious *pro-* sounding policies were always undergirded with an aggressive *anti-*. Speed of messaging and speed of pivoting are therefore privileged over the slow, quieter process of finding faith and cultivating a relationship with God. Going to church takes time, reading the Bible takes time, becoming a good and moral person takes time. Actual religious belief, belonging, and behavior develop over a lifetime; it's a process. But hating and mobilizing against Satan, metaphorical or literal, that's a reflex—and it works.

A HOLY-ISH WAR

In addition to asserting conservative defensiveness in response to alleged liberal encroachment, the culture wars thesis posits an ideological crusade about key issues, notably abortion, traditional gender roles, and traditional morality.[150] But the culture wars are not actually ideological; they are demonological, meaning not set in stone but shapeshifting, not calibrated toward good-faith argument but instead toward efficacy, not reflective of a stable conservative identity but instead one derived from the things that the conservative faithful hate.

Given the energies involved, not to mention the fervor and fury of the fights, it is still fair to describe anti-liberal mobilization in terms of a holy war. But they're based on a religion of communications strategy centered around Satan's evil rather than God's grace, which invents the enemies and picks the battlegrounds so that only one side, that of "pure" Christian America, can possibly win. To this end, reliance on false traditionalism is key; it's what allows anti-liberal demonologists to link so-called culture war issues to religious values, bestowing an easy legitimacy onto vacillating or downright cynical policy positions that can be used as both sword and shield against the perceived liberal threat.

AN OCEAN OF TINY PLASTIC BABIES

The abortion fight in the United States, framed as *the* culture wars issue, is in fact the ultimate example of the shadow gospel's demonological shapeshifting.

Contrary to the now set-in-stone belief that abortion has always been a rightwing cause célèbre, the abortion issue didn't begin as a partisan flashpoint. Initially, it aligned with New Deal attitudes about the federal government's responsibility to protect its citizens—including from the very moment they were conceived—dovetailing with beliefs, most vigorously embraced by Catholics, about the divinely bestowed right to life.[151] To be sure, there had been a strong gendered and racial conservatism running through the early anti-abortion movement, particularly around birth control and pornography. But this conservatism was bipartisan; some was embraced by Democrats and some was embraced by Republicans.[152] There had even been some left-leaning elements in the anti-abortion movement, mapped onto human rights, labor concerns, and anti-war sentiment. As fetal rights came more directly into conflict with other social justice concerns, particularly women's rights in the 1970s, what left-leaning elements had been present in the movement began to wane.[153] Following 1973's landmark *Roe v. Wade* Supreme Court ruling, the Democratic Party also began to realign behind choice.

Before this shift, Protestants opposed abortion in meager numbers, but they tended to be mainline Episcopalians, Methodists, and Lutherans. Up to the late 1960s, very few Evangelicals joined the anti-abortion cause, starkly undercutting subsequent Evangelical claims that Christians on the whole have opposed abortion "through the centuries."[154] The Evangelicals who were actively anti-abortion tended not to be very conservative,[155] aligning themselves with the progressive offshoots of the issue. Evangelicals at that time were much more concerned with anticommunism and perceived attacks against the moral order, including via the sexual revolution;[156] so to the extent that most cared about abortion, it was as a form of birth control that allowed women to have premarital sex.

The lack of Evangelical fervor stemmed from the fact that there wasn't much theological grounding within Protestantism to push abortion front and center. Limited biblical guidance meant that Evangelical leaders simply couldn't make a strong anti-abortion case.[157] Protestantism thus stood in stark contrast to Catholicism, whose theological opposition to abortion ran deep.[158] In 1968, Sherwood Wirt, Billy Graham's friend and collaborator,

highlighted this difference. "Evangelical opinion may differ from the official Roman view in placing more emphasis on the health and well-being of
the mother than on the survival of the fetus," he wrote, emphasizing the
need for "open discussion of the matter."[159] For Wirt, abortion was neither
an evil nor a fight, unlike the "evils of tobacco," which according to Wirt
had been a losing battle for churches for "350 years."[160]

Reflecting Protestants' differing moral positions on the issue,[161] there
was even some support among Evangelical leaders, including Billy Graham,
for abortion in certain cases, including rape, incest, and the health of the
mother, that Catholics at the time condemned.[162] Tellingly, in response
to *Roe* in 1973, the NAE criticized the Supreme Court's decision and its
providing, as they claimed, "abortion on demand," that is, unrestricted
abortion in the first trimester. Yet they still acknowledged the need for
therapeutic abortions and abortions in extreme circumstances.

The anti-abortion landscape began to shift in the mid-1970s, as white
Evangelicals were increasingly hailed into the fight through underlying
concerns over "moral disorder," including threats of women's sexuality to
the nuclear family.[163] Also galvanizing to Evangelicals was the claim that
legalized abortion aligned with the interests of a malevolent, immoral, secular state.[164] Significant behind the scenes anti-abortion activism stoked these
fires,[165] as did the stark uptick in fear-based anti-abortion media. Particularly effective were widely circulated videos and images featuring fetuses,[166]
including the grotesque visual of thousands of little plastic dolls floating in
the Dead Sea. Evangelical magazines, television programs, and radio broadcasts also flooded anti-abortion messaging into Evangelical lives.[167]

That abortion didn't have much biblically based religious content for
Evangelicals to latch onto wasn't a bug of the anti-abortion movement,
it was a feature—because keeping it in the realm of demonology rather
than theology allowed the issue to be politically mobilized with astonish-
ing speed. By the time Ronald Reagan delivered his "Evil Empire" speech
in 1983, the demonstrably false claim that Evangelicals had always been
the defenders of the unborn had been internalized as unshakable Barthian
myth. The demonological undercurrent of anti-abortion activism also
helped facilitate the purging within Evangelicalism of alleged liberals who
took a more moderate stance on the issue, as well as those inclined toward
fundamentalism, who resisted the activist call and argued that Jesus was
more important than the ballot box.

Another demonological bonus was that abortion could, via its extreme politicization, support broader claims about Satan's earthly influence. Choice was lumped in with gay rights and teaching evolution in schools and a host of other "secular humanist" sins that people like Tim LaHaye could accuse of being "filled with the Devil."[168]

Not incidentally, the linkage between abortion and evil emerged alongside the most extreme elements of the Satanic Panics, which explicitly and in gruesome detail focused on satanists' alleged baby killing and even eating. For example, one account included in Mike Warnke's ex-satanist/Christian comedy road show featured a story about the mutilation and murder of a young girl. *Cornerstone* investigative reporters Mike Hertenstein and Jon Trott sat in the audience as Warnke explained that the Satanists he once associated with "took this little girl and they killed her by cutting her sexual organs out while she was still alive. And after she was dead they cut her chest open, took out her heart, and cut it up into little pieces and took communion on it."[169] Take the term "Satanist" away from this and other atrocity stories and what remains is "abortionist." The demonological logic is the same either way. Both Satanists and abortionists are evil; both leave behind piles of dead babies for Evangelicals to embrace as objects of terror—and of political mobilization.

As it turned out, all this terror was great for the Evangelical brand. Disconnected from history and context, the demonological messaging that pushed abortion to the center of rightwing politics allowed anti-abortion activists to integrate the issue of reproductive choice into their broader messianic claim that they, and only they, could save the nation from moral destruction.[170] The alleged evil of those who were pro-choice, or at least not anti-choice enough, provided a helpful narrative boost. The more "liberals" there were calling for expanded abortion access (or simply for lower tones of voice), the better things were for anti-choice activists, whose self-proclaimed status as national savior *needed* a baby-killing Satan to crusade against.

SINNERS IN THE HANDS OF AN ANGRY SHADOW GOSPEL

In his book on the cultural significance of Satan, Scott Poole argues that the figure of Satan functions as an easy shorthand that pushes off more serious conversations about the problem of evil in favor of the overly simplistic framework not that the devil made *me* do it, but that the devil made *them* do it. Evil is out there, working through the people one hates.[171] The trick of the shadow gospel is that it allows a comparatively small group of people to define the devil for everyone else, then obscures its creation—born of minority interests and concerns—by hiding behind another creation, that of an enduring religious truth, ascribed to themselves by themselves, which despite claiming universality is born of a narrow set of interests and values. Those who end up demonized are cast into a special kind of hell that might be an invention but still torments, particularly when the sins they're accused of committing aren't sins at all but are just what another group of people has decided they don't like. Rather than recognizing this as intolerance or arbitrary personal preference, the devil-conjurers see God in a reflection of themselves, as the shadow gospel, that great deceiver, whispers: *it has always been this way.*

RELIGION WITHOUT RELIGION

Pat Buchanan may have wished he had won the 1992 Republican presidential nomination, but he was still thunderous in his enthusiasm for incumbent Republican president George H. W. Bush's reelection. At least, he was thunderous in his enthusiasm for the defeat of Bush's opponents, "Clinton & Clinton," as if Bill and Hillary were a singular leftist appendage, and "Prince Albert" Gore, who Buchanan derided for being an "environmental extremist" who he said put the interests of "birds and rats and insects" ahead of families, workers, jobs, and freedom.[1]

The Democrats had just nominated Clinton and Gore at their convention, which Buchanan described as "the greatest single exhibition of cross-dressing in American political history."[2] These people weren't moderates or centrists as they claimed, Buchanan scoffed; they were liberals and radicals, 20,000 strong, with the Clintons at the helm. Unlike Bush, who Buchanan extolled as "a champion of the Judeo-Christian values and beliefs upon which America was founded,"[3] the Clintons were calling for changes that couldn't be abided in a nation still called God's country. Hillary Clinton in particular was a radical feminist who believed that children had rights and said disparaging things about marriage. The agenda that she and her husband promoted—which Buchanan said included unrestricted abortion on demand, recognition of gays and lesbians as equal under the law, and discrimination against religious schools—was part of a full-on assault against the "conservatives of the heart" who were suffering silently all across the country as the victims of liberal failings, including the "raw sewage of pornography" polluting popular culture.

Buchanan did not mince words. This was nothing less than "a religious war, a cultural war"[4] for the soul of America. The Clintons and their liberal radicals were on one side; Bush and his conservatives of the heart were on the other. To illustrate this point, Buchanan pivoted to the riots that had just rocked Los Angeles following the acquittal of four LAPD officers who had been caught on film beating an unarmed Black man named Rodney King. The battle for Los Angeles reflected the battle for the soul of America, Buchanan said, a story he told through the eyes of several young federalized troopers sent to restore order. (Although the rioters' race wasn't stated, the strong implication was that they were Black.) Buchanan claimed that the soldiers had beat back the mob with "force, rooted in justice, and backed by moral courage."[5] Just as these soldiers had done, block by block, "we must take back our cities, and take back our culture, and take back our country," Buchanan implored. "God bless you," he concluded. "And God bless America."[6]

In 1992, Buchanan represented something new in Republican politics, described by Nicole Hemmer as a "pessimistic, media-savvy, revolution-minded conservatism"[7] driven by an "unpopular populism" that still managed to win power even if it never won majorities.[8] Buchanan's claims about a "culture war" was a prime example, as the fringe position he expressed during his RNC speech would soon be channeled by Newt Gingrich and the newly emboldened congressional Republicans in their Contract with America two years later.[9] In that short timeframe, the call to take up arms against the values-trampling liberal mob had transformed into retroactive historical fact, as if the culture wars—and strongly partisan, multidirectional sense of "liberal"—had always been a unifying principle of American politics.

The 1990s are thus a pivotal moment in our story and challenge yet another conventional narrative about U.S. politics: how the Republican and Democratic Parties realigned. Building on the previous chapter's argument that the central character of the culture wars discourse is Satan, not God, this chapter argues that the 1990s shadow gospel, not the Evangelical church gospel, was what ultimately fused the Republican Party and Evangelical voters. It did so through its great strength: adaptability coupled with a shapeshifting pandemonic rhetoric that could appeal to many different people by taking many different forms, from Pat Buchanan's borderline conspiratorial (or at least deeply *anti-*) invectives to Republican activists' polished communications about "common sense" pro-family policies to Evangelical leaders' end-times prophesying.

The widespread success of the shadow gospel during the 1990s had an ironic consequence: increased secularization of its most prominent messages and messengers, even as the notion of liberal apocalypse intensified among the faithful. This, however, was a very particular kind of apocalypse that had nothing to do with Jesus or the promise of redemption. It was where the shadow gospel established itself as a religion without religion: a religion, instead, of demonology.

To contextualize the shadow gospel's 1990s shift, the following section focuses on the 1970s Republican and Evangelical activists who, driven by a dominionist impulse to "cover the earth," expanded rightwing networks and media operations. The chapter then considers the media environment itself and how regulatory and other informational changes uniquely benefited the rightwing, facilitating an even more intense amalgamation of even more intensely circulating conservative media during the 1980s and early 1990s. Religious details—most basically, the presence of Jesus—were simply crushed by the density of the shadow gospel's expanding anti-liberal center. Finally, the chapter explores how the shadow gospel, guided by the hand of Rupert Murdoch in the mid-1990s, was able to contort itself to the needs of cable television. Heading into the new millennium, a strange truth rang out: as the standard-bearer of shadow gospel messages *and* the institutional Republican Party, Evangelicalism was dead; long live the Church of Fox News.

SETTING THE STAGE

The shadow gospel's secularization starts with a handful of people, mostly men, who are credited with fusing Republican Party machinery and conservative Christian networks in the 1970s.[10] We first mentioned this story in the book's introduction. One key figure is Republican strategist Paul Weyrich, who in the late 1960s set out to build a network that linked conservative political and religious organizations. In particular, he worked to connect Washington, DC, operatives and leaders within the Southern Baptist Convention, whose shift rightward in the 1970s and 1980s—one that increasingly brought them into the Evangelical fold—made them a perfect ally in the push for establishing a "Moral Majority," a name Weyrich attached to his nascent movement and later to the formal coalition lead by Southern Baptist preacher Jerry Falwell.[11] Richard Viguerie, a close associate of Weyrich, was another influential Republican activist. Viguerie began his career working for the fundamentalist and rabidly anticommunist preacher Billy James Hargis. He parlayed his experience promoting Hargis's anticommunism—and later, Barry Goldwater's—into marketing the

Moral Majority, particularly through sophisticated direct mail campaigns targeting Evangelicals.[12]

Other players include Evangelical leaders such as Pat Robertson, Tim LaHaye, and Ralph Reed, later of the Christian Coalition, who were eager to team up with Republicans like Weyrich and Viguerie. The Republicans wanted an electoral advantage, and the Evangelicals wanted to influence policy. To woo the Evangelical voter base, the Republican Party thus positioned itself as an ally in the battle to beat back what was framed as aggressive liberal encroachment. Evangelicals who may have been inclined to vote for fellow Evangelical Jimmy Carter were warned of Carter's liberalism and broke for Reagan instead.[13]

Feeding into the alliance between Republican and Evangelical activists was the racial realignment in party politics. Through the mid-1970s, white Southerners with conservative positions on race had been a reliable voting bloc for Democrats—hence President Kennedy's concern, discussed in chapter 3, that if he failed to tamp down the influence of rightwing radio in the early 1960s, their support of more extremist candidates like Barry Goldwater or George Wallace might siphon off votes from segregationist Democrats.[14] Seeing an opportunity to realize Kennedy's worst fears and split the Democratic Party down racial lines, Republican operatives and politicians began pushing a "Southern Strategy" in the mid-1960s. The objective was to court Democrats through aggressive outreach that highlighted conservative talking points on race and morality issues.[15] The kinds of direct mail campaigns that Richard Viguerie helped develop for Billy James Hargis made this possible. So did the leftward shift of the Democratic Party, which through the 1960s strengthened its platform on social and racial justice issues. More and more conservative Democrats, especially those who were Evangelical,[16] began defecting into the Republican fold.

The effects of racial realignment were profound. After the 1970s, the demographic makeup of the Republican and Democratic Parties was very different from where it had been ten years earlier. And there's no question that men like Weyrich and Viguerie, along with their Evangelical allies, established robust networks between conservative religious leaders and political activists. They did a great deal to facilitate the infrastructural rise of the New Right.

But as discussed in the introduction, this story generates some complications. In its conventional telling, the Republican/Evangelical fusing was the natural outcome of an ongoing and equally waged culture war between left and right.[17] Chapter 4 undercuts that assumption by showing how the culture wars thesis emerged through conservative advancement, false traditionalism, and self-reaction set against a satanic backdrop. In other words, the thing so confidently cited as the catalyst for the Republican/Evangelical fusing wasn't *real*. It was made to feel real as Barthian myth, but during the 1960s and 1970s, there was no marauding horde of aggressive, conspiratorial leftists scheming to deliver the final death blow to traditional conservative values (chapter 6 will present a much more accurate picture of what "the left," to the extent that such a label even makes sense to use as a broad political catchall, was actually doing during this time).

Additionally, in terms of electoral outcomes, the conventional realignment story is less straightforward than it seems. Even after the elite-level fusing between Evangelical and Republican leaders in the 1970s, Evangelical and Republican *voters* didn't start walking in lockstep until the 1990s. In Oklahoma, for example, Democrats controlled the governorship, state legislature, and a majority of House districts until 1994,[18] when Evangelicals mobilized by the Christian Coalition ushered in Republican success—a role the coalition would play many times throughout the decade.[19] A similar dynamic unfolded in South Carolina in 1994, when Democrats lost the governorship to a born-again Southern Baptist.[20] Put simply, the 1990s was when Evangelicals began voting at higher rates than other groups, with consistently strong support for Republican candidates.[21]

The twenty-year delay between when Republican and Evangelical elites fused in the 1970s and when Evangelical voters actually began turning out en masse for the Republican Party in the 1990s is counterintuitive. So is the fact that, even during the 1980s ascendancy of the New Right, Evangelicalism did not experience any growth as a religious tradition.[22] Evangelicals clearly had cultural and political power, but the country was not becoming more Evangelical measured by increasing church attendance or increasing rates of Evangelical self-identification. It was going to take something other than what these activists were doing to yield the fruit they are credited with growing.

A ONE-SIDED CULTURE WAR

Although Republican and Evangelical activists weren't as initially successful *electorally* as one might expect, there was a great deal of activity, particularly within Evangelical networks, to ready the troops for the culture war. This was not a two-sided front. But echoing the previous chapter, the fight was real, pursued through the active, even aggressive, effort to affect social change through political channels. These Evangelicals didn't want to preserve tradition, as the "traditionalist" side of the traditionalist/ modernist divide implies. They wanted to progress into a future that made them the center of everything.

A RAINBOW OF APOCALYPTICISM

In her 1984 antifeminist victory lap following the ERA's defeat, Beverly LaHaye exemplified this battle strategy. She railed against what she described as "Churchianity," the refusal by many Christian women to mobilize their faith to make a difference in the world.[23] She admitted that she once shied away from "the secular world and its problems."[24] But then she realized what God was imploring: he wanted Christians to "Wake up from your ignorance and apathy about the world around you. Get up and get to work exposing the works of darkness around you! Use every opportunity to defeat the devil and bring glory to God!"[25] She was very consciously a soldier for God, and other Christians needed to be as well.[26]

Tim LaHaye also criticized those Christians who were "unwilling to raise their voices or vote." In so doing, they had "resigned themselves to tribulation."[27] For Tim LaHaye, such a stance was downright unscriptural. Quoting Ephesians, he declared, "We are commanded to resist the devil and to put on the whole armor of God, that we may be able to withstand in the evil day."[28] Yes, the end times were coming. But the worldly chaos that would result from allowing "liberal humanists" to take control of the government was not predestined. It would come to pass, however, "unless Christians are willing to become much more assertive in defense of morality and decency than they have been during the past three decades."[29]

Up to a point, LaHaye's claims about the end times align him with what Daniel Wojcik describes as *non-avertive apocalypticism*, a theological stance best summarized as no way out—a deterministic view in which the world is believed to be inevitably doomed and impossible to save through human effort.[30] At the same time, LaHaye's language about the need to fight the liberal devil in order to forestall tribulation aligns him with *avertive apocalypticism*, which as Wojcik explains, is characterized by the belief that "spiritual or ritual actions" can delay or even prevent the end times, resulting in "collective or worldly salvation."[31] But even avertive apocalypticism doesn't quite capture it. Liberals within LaHaye's framework *are* the devil. In his screeds against humanism (and all his other *anti-* targets) LaHaye isn't suggesting that the Antichrist and demons *will*—future tense—roam the earth for a set number of years before Rapture occurs, one of the articulations of end-times beliefs that Wojcik discusses.[32] What LaHaye is arguing instead is that fully human, non-supernatural liberals *have already* made our world a living hell. It's an apocalypse unfolding in the here and now. Those who take up arms—not against the Great Serpent but against the everywhere-all-the-time liberal devil—become the redeemers of the nation.

Tim and Beverly LaHaye weren't the only Evangelicals in the 1980s who began to promote a quasi-avertive and, as Linda Kintz describes, "modernized" apocalyptic interpretation.[33] Increasingly common was a vision of apocalypse that maintained a deterministic outlook, advocated for avertive actions, and also took for granted—even if implicitly—that the cosmic clash with the liberal devil was presently underway and that an even bloodier battle would ensue if Christians didn't go on the offensive. Pat Robertson straddled this line during his 1988 presidential campaign. Kintz notes that his previously stark fatalism shifted to an increasingly utopian stance, one in which victory against the devil was at hand. At the same time, "in less publicized statements . . . he [continued] to warn of an apocalyptic end if conservative believers [did] not determine the course of American politics."[34]

Anti-liberal apocalypticism, in which the end-times battle with liberals was already happening, aligned with dominion theology: the push to "bring all life under God's rule"[35] and belief that Christians had a spiritual duty to attack and undermine the godless state and other institutions said to be overrun by humanists and liberals. As a theological position, dominionism emerged parallel to the fundamentalist turn of the Southern Baptist Convention, the goal of which was to establish something like a theocracy in the United States with the Bible as the source of U.S. law. It aligned with the fundamentalist-driven segregation movement of the 1950s as well, which sought to challenge the power of the federal government with local councils that had strong ties to white Southern Baptist Churches.[36]

Dominionism also had a demonological—rather than strictly theological—articulation that foregrounded future *and* present-tense apocalypse, with the latter mapping onto the here-and-now liberal devil. Rapture-happy

Hal Lindsey embraced such a stance in his book *Countdown to Armageddon*.[37]
In it, he pinned the "crisis of internal decay" weakening the United States
onto citizens' doubts about capitalism, the rise of the welfare system, government bureaucracy, and "socialist thinking."[38] By advocating for rightwing political pushback, he demonstrated how theological dominionism
could give way to a more shadowy articulation. For Christians who sought
to enshrine the Bible in U.S. law, dominionism was a grounding influence,
a specific structural goal: to change laws and institutions so they would be
more Christian. But dominionism in the theological sense was also restrictive. It wasn't just that it required adherents to practice what they preached.
It required adherents to know what biblical principles they were preaching.
A demonological approach to dominionism was much more expedient. It
also lacked biblical literacy requirements. In Lindsey's case, when he
encouraged his Christian readers to "get involved in preserving this country"[39] by helping to drive back the pervasive, world-destroying moral decay
said to be caused by secular and occultic influences, his call for "biblical
morality" wasn't about the specifics of governance. It was about fighting
the liberal devil. The fight *was* the goal.

THE ANITA BRYANT STORY

Evangelical activist Anita Bryant described her efforts to keep gay people
out of K-12 classrooms in similar demonological dominionist terms. After
quoting from Revelation to denounce the churches that had not joined her
cause and, indeed, had rejected her fervent homophobia, Bryant declared in
her autobiography that the only way to turn the tide of moral decay was to
"rise up and defend the moral principles we believe in."[40] For Bryant, this
meant heeding what she believed was God's command to dive headlong
into politics.[41]

Bryant's story began in Dade County, Florida, in 1977. The city of
Miami had just passed an ordinance that protected gays and lesbians from
job discrimination. Bryant, who in addition to being a born-again Christian, had a successful singing career and was known by many as the spokesperson for Florida orange juice ("A day without orange juice is like a day
without sunshine!" she sings in one commercial, rubbing her hand over
an orange and transforming it into a bird[42]). She therefore had a built-in
public platform when she found out about the ordinance from a sermon
delivered by her pastor. Bryant was particularly appalled at the prospect
of gay classroom teachers, which Bryant claimed would simultaneously

undermine her "healthy, decent community" and threaten her rights as a Christian.[43]

To counter the threat, Bryant formed an organization called Save Our Children Inc. and started to gather signatures to have the ordinance repealed. Her argument that "homosexuals can't reproduce so they must recruit" was an early articulation of the New Right battle cry against the "gay agenda," which was eventually codified in the 1990s by a series of videos called, predictably, *The Gay Agenda*, the first of which was released in 1992; *The Gay Agenda in Public Education* was released in 1993.[44]

As Bryant spread her gospel, other high-profile Evangelicals learned of her efforts, yielding invitations to appear on major Christian televangelist programs including Pat Robertson's *The 700 Club* and Jerry Falwell's *Old-Time Gospel Hour*. Falwell—who in a 1981 fundraising letter echoed Bryant's language and provided further rhetorical scaffolding for claims about a "gay agenda" when he declared, "Please remember, homosexuals don't reproduce! They recruit! And they are out after my children and your children"[45]—took his promotion of Bryant one step further. After taping the episode of his show, Falwell flew with Bryant back to Florida to hold a rally for 10,000 people protesting the ordinance and gay rights more broadly. Shortly thereafter, the Miami ordinance was repealed.[46]

Of course, not everyone in Miami celebrated this outcome; Bryant lambasted the pushback she received from news reporters who she claimed misrepresented her message. In one instance she was quoted as saying that if she allowed her children and other people's children to be exposed to gay people, she "might as well feed them garbage." Journalists had interpreted this to mean that she believed gay people *were* garbage. Bryant insisted that she said no such thing, but didn't clarify how the message was any less homophobic than reported. "I'll leave it to the reader to interpret as you wish," she concluded.[47]

Having told her side of the story, Bryant reflected on what her crusade against gay rights had taught her. "As a silent majority we are ineffectual," she stated, echoing Beverly LaHaye's lamentation against "Churchianity." But, she continued, "if we pool our efforts and resources as Christians and as morally concerned Americans to proclaim what we know and believe to be right, we can reverse the trend that militant homosexuals and others are working to force upon us."[48] By "protecting" America's children, Bryant and other anti-gay activists were doing righteous battle with the beast of their invented Apocalypse.

AND GOD BLESSED THEM

Whether rightwing activists specifically prescribed to dominionism or simply felt compelled to reclaim their cities, their culture, and their country block by block, they were well positioned to take action in the 1970s, 1980s, and 1990s thanks to a number of structural, organizational, and rhetorical advantages that uniquely benefited the conservative cause. Whatever story the culture wars thesis might tell about a beleaguered conservatism beaten back by ruthless liberal encroachment, what the New Right enjoyed instead was the wind at its back.

THE CHANGING REGULATORY ENVIRONMENT BENEFITED THE RIGHTWING

It is important, Paul Matzko says, to reflect on the rising demand for rightwing ideas in the 1970s. But the shift in the *supply* of those ideas is equally significant.[49] During the 1970s, changes in the regulatory environment translated to a supply-side bonanza for the right, with radio an especially powerful stronghold for Christian broadcasters.[50]

Ironically, it was Democratic president Jimmy Carter's FCC that initiated these changes. The agency simply stopped enforcing the Fairness Doctrine, though it wouldn't be abolished formally until 1987 under Reagan.[51] The result was that rightwing talk radio—which had been highly constrained by the doctrine—had newfound freedom to grow and develop an assertive approach to direct political advocacy (leftwing radio still faced roadblocks, to be discussed in the following chapter). The demonologically centered conservatism that subsequently established itself across the AM and FM radio dial allowed rightwing radio, and especially Christian radio, to "colonize the dial" and create an "invisible empire of the air"[52] that simultaneously harnessed the rightwing energies that had long circulated *and* whetted audience appetites for the kinds of policy goals that would later be outlined in Gingrich's Contract with America.[53]

NEW TECHNOLOGIES BENEFITED THE RIGHTWING

Cable television also proved to be a huge boon for the rightwing, with regulatory changes again playing a pivotal role. In the late 1970s, Carter's deregulation-inclined FCC removed expensive and onerous bureaucratic hurdles for cable network startups. It also reduced the red tape around non-competition restrictions, which had prevented cable television employees from sharing institutional knowledge with their next employer.[54]

Under the new FCC rules, the bar of entry for starting a cable station was suddenly much lower—an opportunity that Evangelicals, who had developed a sixth sense for harnessing emerging media, were quick to recognize and fully embrace. As they did, they were able to operate as production light craft: rather than being weighed down by the demands of large teams of reporters, fact checkers, and standards and practices divisions, upstart Christian networks had no internalized ideals around the public role of journalism and no established editorial norms. That simply wasn't part of their news culture. Further, given these producers' visceral opposition to mainstream media, they had zero interest in modeling themselves after the existing networks. They had their own agenda, which was to carve out as much market share as possible.[55]

Pat Robertson and Jerry Falwell were especially savvy in navigating the newly accessible cable landscape. They represented the growing push within Christian circles to embrace a "vertical integration" approach to media, most perfectly distilled in the decision to buy a television network so you didn't need to buy airtime. You *were* the airtime. Christian broadcasters also brokered various denominational mergers to keep overhead low and production high.[56]

Christian broadcasters were, in short, quick to adjust to market, regulatory, and technological change.[57] As they did, they adopted an overarching branding strategy that, as Jason Bivins explains, authorized conspiratorial thinking and denounced "neutrality or accountability to multiple constituencies as burdensome or even hostile to Christian faith."[58] For instance, Pat Robertson framed *The 700 Club* as revealing hidden truths that *they*, the mainstream media and liberal politicians, didn't want his viewers to know. At the same time, Robertson, along with Falwell and others, presented conservative talking points as objective truth.[59] They also actively nationalized local stories that reinforced their arguments about creeping mainstream threats, helping to signal-boost the salience of conservative issues and figures such as Anita Bryant.

SOUNDBITE CULTURE BENEFITED THE RIGHTWING

Writing in the late 1990s, Linda Kintz and Julia Lesage argue that mainstream media culture is characterized by "the simplicity of the sound bite and the instant message."[60] Rightwing figures had long harnessed this dynamic, a reflection of the sharp professionalization and keen focus on public communications within many rightwing media networks.[61] Beyond these figures' media training, the "rhetoric of simplification" that distinguished conservative messages was simply a good fit with what the mainstream media landscape rewarded and incentivized.[62]

Kintz spotlights Phyllis Schlafly and Beverly LaHaye as embodiments and direct beneficiaries of the rhetoric of simplification. We would also add Anita Bryant to the list. Though each woman embraced different communication styles, with LaHaye the least combative of the lot, each was driven by the conviction that "the right-wing position is an inherent part of humanity's authentic, true identity."[63] Such a claim is the essence of false traditionalism, but it is also extremely clear and compelling to those who agree. As Kintz argues, "complexity invites simplicity as a form of self-defense,"[64] and Schlafly was particularly skilled in her ability to sidestep complex arguments in favor of easy to digest moral binaries predicated on "false versus real American values."[65]

The straightforwardness of this binary allowed it to be applied in many different contexts with little need for adjustment. It also easily mapped onto the equally clear-cut binary of good versus evil.[66] In the process, it helped make contradictory claims seem coherent, for instance, Schlafly's persistent argument that the United States is the greatest country in the history of human civilization and that it has simultaneously been destroyed by liberals,[67] a point that aligned with Ronald Reagan's "Evil Empire" framing that Evangelicals are both the perennial guardians of enduring moral traditionalism and the scrappy upstarts who must rekindle the traditionalist fires. Anita Bryant played a similar rhetorical trick when she insisted that she absolutely did not call gay people garbage and then invited readers to decide if she did. A rhetoric of simplification shrugs its shoulders when asked to reconcile two opposing ideas; they are both true, so they are both true.

If the rhetoric of simplification were not so aligned with a media culture that loves a horse race, ten-second soundbite, and conflict, then perhaps that media culture would push back against people like Schlafly, LaHaye, and Bryant. As it was, these women could give reporters a horse race, a soundbite, and perhaps most important of all, conflict. Focusing on the anti-ERA fight, Donald Critchlow highlights how feminists, seemingly unaware of this dynamic, would try to goad Schlafly into an angry response. For the poised and well-trained Schlafly, these efforts didn't just backfire but were good for her brand. As long as feminists were screaming at her, reporters had every reason to keep their cameras pointed at her.[68] Schlafly, along with LaHaye, Bryant, and other prominent rightwing figures, were skilled communicators in their own right. Mainstream media helped make them celebrities, giving them every reason to keep doing what they were doing, since everything they were doing was so good for everyone's business.

TIGHT NETWORKS BENEFITED THE RIGHTWING
(AND SO DID KEEPING A LOW PROFILE)

Previous chapters have explored the overlap between rightwing corporate and grassroots activism, particularly the corporate sponsorship of Evangelicalism in the 1960s and 1970s. Heading into the 1980s, this already intense dynamic was further strengthened by the proliferation of conservative think tanks like the American Enterprise Institute, Hoover Institution, and Heritage Foundation, which developed a top-down approach to information delivery.[69] Rightwing institutes and foundations would develop messages—for instance, opposing gay rights—and those messages would be adopted by organizations like the Christian Coalition as they undertook their own national and local outreach efforts.[70] The result was a rightwing "ideas industry," yet another vertically integrated system in which a small number of people controlled programming, marketing, and distribution of rightwing messages.[71] Loose confederations of conservatives, including rightwing media audiences, could then work off the same sets of talking points.[72]

There were also many conservative people and groups actively communicating and sharing resources in the 1980s. Religious organizations were especially well-connected through networks of conservative political power such as the Council for National Policy, founded in 1981 by familiar names such as Tim LaHaye and H. L. Hunt. As Anne Nelson explains, the CNP was chartered as a think tank but functioned as a resource and networking hub for leading religious and political conservatives.[73] The hyperconnection that resulted is exemplified in the Christian Coalition's "Contract with the American Family." In addition to demonstrating very little separation between parachurch and state—the "Contract with the American Family" was essentially a companion piece to the "Contract with America"—the

closing pages of the Christian Coalition's Contract include a list of affiliated organizations, such as James Dobson's Focus on the Family, Beverly
LaHaye's Concerned Women for America, Phyllis Schlafly's Eagle Forum,
and the Heritage Foundation, among others.[74] To be a rightwing activist at
the time was to never be too far from other rightwing activists.

Equally valuable to the existence of those networks, however, was their
opacity, a result of various "covert actions" designed to obscure the origins
of conservative messaging.[75]

In the pursuit of opacity, Newt Gingrich would speak bombastically
to an empty chamber using key terms to disparage his liberal opposition.
He knew that after the press reported his statements and they entered public consciousness, people wouldn't necessarily know or care to learn where
the ideas came from.[76] Evangelicals embraced similarly evasive communication maneuvers, particularly to cast off explicitly religious-sounding
language. They also operated behind deliberately secular-sounding front
groups to create what Nelson describes as a "matrix of interlocking (but
seemingly independent) organizations" that surreptitiously worked with a
high degree of coordination.[77] Obscured origins—of networks, messages,
and shared objectives—afforded conservatives significant cultural and rhetorical power. They could point to the messaging swirl that they created,
day by day, campaign by campaign, and act as if they arrived at the same
conclusions because their claims were correct. In reality, they were all just
saying slightly different versions of the same thing.

SANDING THE EDGES OFF JESUS

The amalgamation that unified conservative messages and groups helped
to bring more ideas and more people into the shadowy fold. This intensified the shadow gospel's gravitational pull. It also resulted in something
very strange: the Second Coming part of the end-times story started to
disappear.

Traditional end-times narratives characterized by unwavering fatalism and belief in imminent apocalypse and the return of Jesus remained
prominent in fundamentalist circles. Tim LaHaye's *Left Behind* series kept
selling, and in 1998 even added a kids' line (*Left Behind: The Kids*) marketed to ten- to fourteen-year-olds.[78] A thriving 1990s subculture of Hell
Houses—spaces fashioned after haunted houses, but filled instead with

sweaty impurity and allegedly sinful deeds like premarital sex, abortion, and queerness—also affirmed that the religion of fear and its violently apocalyptic message was doing just fine.[79] So did many Evangelicals' vocal, sustained, and highly coordinated campaign against the magic-focused *Harry Potter* series in the early 2000s—resulting in "big business" for Potter opponents[80]—on the grounds that the series was satanic and, to quote from a Potter-themed Chick Tract, "opened a doorway that led untold millions of kids into hell."[81] And hardcore theological dominionism remained strong within some networks, frequently dovetailing with the White Power and paramilitary movements; as Kathleen Belew highlights, apocalyptic rhetoric worked as a "bridge issue" between groups.[82]

In these contexts, the biblically grounded account of end times in the Book of Revelation aligned with the trajectory of premillennial dispensationalism as described by Wojcik: it reflected a cosmic drama frame, was centered on prophecy, pointed to an antichrist figure, pushed the belief that the world is fundamentally evil, maintained to varying degrees that humans are helpless to do anything to intervene (and it might be blasphemous to try), and celebrated the destruction of the world as a necessary step toward redemption, at least for the select.[83]

When panic over threats to the family and traditional American values was disconnected from even the most tenuous connections to God and Jesus, however, a very different sort of apocalypticism emerged. Appeals to prophesy shifted to claims of anti-conservative bias. The figure of the antichrist transformed into the malevolent liberal. The abiding belief wasn't that the entire world was unrecuperably evil; it was just liberalism. Most significantly, believers stopped telling what had previously been the most important part of the apocalyptic story: that the annihilation of society would result in its glorious transformation, which in a Christian context refers to Christ returning to earth. That part, hitherto the narrative climax, quietly fell away. The promise of Christ's second coming or even a story where the biblical figure of Christ mattered very much gave way to a never-ending anti-liberal tribulation.

RUSHING TOWARD THE APOCALYPSE

So, while the Book of Revelation speaks ominously of the Horsemen of the Apocalypse, Revelation Lite speaks ominously of "Communists, Socialists, Environmentalist Wackos, Feminazis, Liberal Democrats, Militant

Vegetarians, Animal Rights Extremists, Liberal Elitists," to quote the preface of rightwing radio star Rush Limbaugh's *The Way Things Ought to Be*, the Book of Revelation Lite if there ever was one.[84]

By the time the book was published in 1992, Limbaugh had become, as Nicole Hemmer explains, "an inescapable presence in American life."[85] Brashly anti-liberal, Limbaugh casually and even jovially injected sexism, racism, and homophobia into his radio show *The Rush Limbaugh Show*—though he was careful to shroud his antagonisms under various forms of plausible deniability.[86]

The Way Things Ought to Be distills Limbaugh's greatest hits, from chapters on feminists (who Limbaugh claims are "at war with traditional American values and fundamental institutions such as marriage and the American family"[87]) to multiculturalism (which Limbaugh insists is a tool used by Black people to maintain their own alienation and which harms children by teaching them to hate America[88]). Thirty years of apocalyptic Evangelical messages simmer in its pages. And yet the end-times narrative is strikingly secular. In his chapter "Religion and America: They *Do* Go Together," the most Limbaugh can say about actual Christian belief is that "man is a spiritual being."[89] Otherwise, discussions of Christianity are opportunities to push the argument that liberals are trying to destroy religion and replace faith in God with "a belief in alphabet soup agencies, faceless bureaucrats, and government giveaways."[90]

Pat Buchanan, whom Limbaugh endorsed for president in 1992, also managed to keep Christ mostly out of his extolling of Christianity. Like Limbaugh, Buchanan bellowed about the liberal threats to God's country. Like Limbaugh, he was not claiming that we need to remake society so that Jesus can return.

What Buchanan and Limbaugh and Gingrich and even the Christian Coalition's (equally) strikingly secular Contract with the American Family were saying, instead, is that we need to remake society *so that we can be Jesus*, and from that exalted position, dictate that our interests, values, and families are the only ones that count. Limbaugh's book title, *The Way Things Ought to Be*, encapsulates the sentiment. Always lurking in the background is the liberal devil who has either taken or is planning to take—under a logic of simplification both things are true—everything that *we*, the real Americans, hold dear. But the story has no end. It's just perpetual clash, perpetual threat, no redemption, no Jesus, no hope for renewal. Fighting and only fighting; fighting because it's fun, fighting because it's the brand, fighting because fighting liberals is what a shadow conservative does. *This* is the cause of the partisan alignment between Evangelicals and Republicans. The power that Evangelicals amassed as a result did not go toward growing the church. It went toward selling Revelation Lite. It also made the shadowy realm of liberal devils and conservative redeemers an unmissable business opportunity for one Rupert Murdoch.

FOX AND FRIENDS

Fox News was, up to a point, a product of its times. The regulatory changes and technological advancements in the 1970s and 1980s—many of which we have already covered, critically the demise of the Fairness Doctrine and deregulation of the airwaves—contributed to an increasingly fragmented media landscape that allowed for, and indeed incentivized, increasingly partisan, increasingly niche cable television programming. As media scholar Reece Peck explains, Fox News benefited enormously from those changes; without them, there could have been no Fox.[91] However, the same could be said for CNN and MSNBC. What Fox News had was a special combination of conservative foundations, sensationalist and populist style, and a blistering anti-liberal demonology that primed the network to overtake Evangelicalism as the shadow gospel messaging hub.

The ongoing saga of the Family Channel, introduced in the previous chapter, foreshadows Fox News' ascendancy. The Family Channel had originally been Pat Robertson's Christian Broadcasting Network before it rebranded in 1988 to ride the wave of family-focused culture warrioring. News Corp. acquired the Family Channel in 1997,[92] which it bundled into the Fox Family Channel, complete with *700 Club* airings. The channel was later renamed ABC Family in 2001 when Fox Family was bought by the Walt Disney Company (also with *700 Club* episodes included).[93] Just as it metabolized the Family Channel, Fox News would metabolize Evangelical messaging. The liberal devil that emerged from Fox's Times Square studio continued affirming conservative identity, lending cosmic significance to political conflict, and constantly teeing up the here-and-now apocalypse. What it added to demonology was flair. This devil was also a good television character.

WHO RAN THE SHIP

The biographies and skillsets of Fox's primary driving figures played a significant role in Fox's early success.[94] Specifically, News Corporation founder Rupert Murdoch, Fox News CEO Roger Ailes, and early on-air talent like Bill O'Reilly and Sean Hannity were steeped in tabloid-style journalism and brought a great deal of knowledge from their previous projects—spanning print media to "infotainment" television to straight-up entertainment media—that they parlayed into successful visual formats and discursive registers (namely, antagonistic) that made for compelling TV.[95]

Rupert Murdoch was heir to an Australian media company that he grew into his successful and tabloid-centric News Corporation. He subsequently moved to the United Kingdom and acquired several papers there with the goal of going "downmarket," meaning that he would sidestep the elite market in order to court a broader working-class audience.[96] The hard-right slant of his *News of the World* and the *Sun*, coupled with their free-wheeling titillation, earned Murdoch the reputation, simultaneously, as the "Aussie tit-and-bum king"[97] and as a major force facilitating the "authoritarian populism" of the British right.[98] News Corporation began expanding into U.S. markets in the early 1970s with the acquisition of two San Antonio papers, the national tabloid *Star* magazine, and the *New York Post* before moving into television, including the cable television channel Fox in the mid-1980s.

In the United States, Murdoch continued his support of rightwing politics and developed close ties with powerful New York Republican politicians such as New York City mayor Rudy Giuliani. Murdoch was more than happy to leverage these connections to help expand News Corporation's reach, and also more than happy to provide his friends in high places with endorsements and other positive coverage in the *New York Post*.[99] Reflecting his downmarket aspirations, Murdoch also continued embracing what journalists and politicians alike derided as the "tabloidization" of culture.[100] He was singled out as a, if not the, major offender at the time because of his helming of sensationalist tabloids and the highly partisan *New York Post* and also his overseeing of the Fox network, which aired racy, irreverent shows like *The Simpsons* and *Married . . . with Children*. Altogether, Murdoch's media portfolio earned him the reputation in the 1980s as "the Anti-Christ of Professional Journalism."[101]

Fox News CEO Roger Ailes's background dovetailed with Murdoch's in three significant ways. First, Ailes hailed from entertainment media. At the age of twenty-six, he became the executive producer of *The Mike Douglas Show*, a 1960s variety television program that, according to journalist Gabriel Sherman, crystalized in Ailes the idea of politics as entertainment.[102] Second, Ailes had strong Republican ties, including with Rudy Giuliani and other New York Republicans.[103] These party loyalties went back decades. Ailes served as television consultant for Richard Nixon and was an "eager propagandist" in Nixon's war on the media, having determined during the 1968 campaign that journalists were the enemy.[104] Third, like Murdoch, who stated in 1984 on a panel hosted by a rightwing think tank that U.S. journalism disregards "the traditional values of the great masses,"[105] Ailes was focused on reaching the "flyover states," which he sometimes described as the "NASCAR audience."[106] His affiliation with this audience stemmed from his own working-class background; throughout his career, Ailes drew from that background to perpetually paint himself as an outsider.[107]

Ailes was also staunchly anti-liberal. "Roger sees the networks as genuinely left-wing and full of rotten people," his friend John LeBoutillier, former Long Island GOP congressional representative and author of the book *Harvard Hates America*, told reporter David Brock in a 1997 *New York Magazine* profile.[108] He made his animus known around the Fox News office. "I'm not going to have some fucking liberal tell me how to program my network," Ailes once barked about a News Corporation board member who had programming suggestions.[109] Echoing a claim that permeated Christian broadcasting, whose very existence was predicated on the critique that mainstream media were anti-Christian,[110] Ailes similarly rankled at how Christianity was portrayed in the news. As he explained to a *New York Times* reporter in 1996, "It's always a story that beats up on Jesus. They call him a cult figure of his time, some kind of crazy fool, and it's as if they go out and try to find evidence to trash him," with "they" in that sentence referring to the journalists Ailes believed were overwhelmingly liberal.[111] To help realize his vision for Fox News, Ailes thus brought on lieutenants who were conservative or who didn't care about politics.[112] In Brock's 1997 profile, former Fox producer Emily Rooney summarized what that vision was all about. "He wants to tap into that anger, the shouting-at-your-tv-types."[113]

ARE YOU ENTERTAINED?

From the outset of Fox News' programming launch on October 7, 1996, the network centered on putting on a good show—a prospect that was often overwhelming to the producers hired to do news who had never worked in news. "We were entertainment people," one founding producer told Gabriel Sherman. "I can't tell you how many people were on Xanax, trying to adapt."[114] To make sure they hooked viewers, Fox' creative team developed eye-catching graphics "that would light up the screen like a video game,"[115] prompting early critics to complain that Fox was too flashy, too fast, and too youthful.[116]

All the while, Ailes was actively promoting Fox as a serious news network. The reality was that its newsgathering capabilities were miniscule compared with competing news networks like CNN.[117] What Ailes was after, ultimately, wasn't hard news; he found stories like the NATO military campaign in Kosovo "expensive and boring."[118] Instead, he focused on the fusing of politics and entertainment, where stories could be distilled down into easy binaries. "Roger understands you must simplify, simplify, *simplify*," *New York Post* reporter and Ailes associate Lucianne Goldberg mused.[119] Reflecting on the talk show culture that Ailes cultivated within the network, one Fox producer explained to Sherman that every segment needed to have a "payoff"; something to reward the audience for watching.[120]

Confrontation was key. David Carr of the *New York Times* explained the dynamic. "People tune in for the warfare. They're not interested in the fruits of peace. It's bad television."[121] Carr was worried about the implications. Family values politicians were too. None other than Newt Gingrich complained about the trashiness, fast pace, and shouting that dominated cable television. While attempting—and failing—to drum up interest in his cable show on another network (more on that in a moment), Gingrich touted his production approach as the "antidote to sensational television coverage." In particular, he played up his show's "non-confrontational mode."[122]

Fox News host Bill O'Reilly, on the other hand, understood that his show's success hinged on well-produced warfare, noting, "My confrontational style is what people want."[123] Fox News producers kept the confrontation coming. Through these production choices, Fox aligned itself with centuries-old tropes of sensationalism. As media historians Amanda Frisken and Gretchen Soderlund explain, sensationalism "operates on a logic of exposure and visibility"[124] and functions to draw attention to specific causes, topics, or people by employing hyperbole and excess, presenting engaging and controversial content in attention-grabbing packages, and reveling in lurid and idiosyncratic details.[125] Within sensationalist media, recognizable characters, especially in the form of victims and villains, are set against repetitive storylines and reinforce the same messages over and over, making the messages difficult to refute.[126]

The recognizable characters of sensationalism thus translate into *good characters* for audiences. What makes a character *good* in a sensationalist context often makes them bad or evil by the audiences' existing moral standards. Simply put, they are compelling monsters. And yet sensationalism can move in many directions. Friskin and Soderlund emphasize its truth-telling potential and the fact that it has been harnessed by various progressive activists pushing for social and racial justice.[127] It just as easily dovetails into demonology, the very existence of which centers on the pursuit of monsters.

TRUST YOUR GUT

Early Fox News programming focused on one kind of monster in particular: elites. Its entire news brand was predicated on claims of elitism and bias at CNN and MSNBC; Fox positioned itself as the remedy.[128] It did so in part by telling a basic lie about itself: that it, an elite corporate product of the coasts, represented the "real" America that wasn't literally and geographically grounded (it was a national network; its viewers lived in every state) but was demonologically ungrounded in the myth of an America that was more pure, and more real, and more moral. The authenticity of this America was what Fox News centered its *pro-* frames around.

These stances—being pro-America, pro-heartland, pro-regular guy—was what allowed Fox to sidestep partisan identification.[129] In fact, the network very pointedly framed itself as nonpartisan. This was a rhetorically savvy decision; *pro-* frames are the most difficult to counter and they appeal to the widest possible swath of people. Fox's nonpartisan stance also likely stemmed from the failures of four previous rightwing television channels. The National Empowerment Television (NET), which was founded by none other than Paul Wyrich and funded by conservative businessmen, ran from 1993 to 2000 and was the most successful of the doomed ventures. This was the network that hosted Newt Gingrich's deliberately nonconfrontational and therefore boring talking-head show. Two others, the Republican Exchange Satellite Network (RESN) and the RNC-produced

GOP-TV, made it for two and three years, respectively, while a fourth, the Conservative Television Network, didn't survive the funding stage.[130] Each of these channels explicitly branded itself as conservative. Each focused on policy. This was hardly the formula for exciting television, a point reflected in contemporaneous news coverage. For instance, a 1994 *Sacramento Bee* article called the Republican Exchange Satellite Network's "electronic town hall" format "Wayne's World for policy nerds."[131]

In contrast, early Fox News embraced populism rather than partisan politics, an argument Reece Peck lays out in his aptly titled book *Fox Populism*.[132] For Fox, populism was a mode of representation, a style. Deviating significantly from the organizational and comparatively highbrow populism embraced by the likes of Paul Weyrich, Fox's populism favored the subjective over the institutional, the affective over the rational, and was more interested in getting its point across than building consensus.[133] It emerged just as "trash" television, the term ascribed to television talk shows like the punch-drunk *Jerry Springer Show*, was reaching a cultural zenith. In her study of 1990s trash TV, sociologist Laura Grindstaff emphasizes the extent to which television producers would go to meet their audience's expectations not just to be entertained but to *feel*.[134] Conflict, aggression, and the pursuit of "don't-change-that-dial" moments communicating shock, anger, and other intense bodily responses—"the money shot," as Grindstaff describes it[135]—became a production necessity for talk shows, and Fox News fit right into that loud, fast, and ultimately sensationalist milieu, even as it celebrated traditional values and Christian morals.[136] Fox News may not have been trash TV per se, but it was a form of tabloid journalism.[137]

As such it fed into intensely appealing *anti-* frames. Fox's rhetoric centered on "real" America and celebrated its viewers not just as "the people" but as the mainstream and the country's "authentic moral core."[138] Always, though, *pro-* contained *anti-*. As a form of brand positioning, in which one brand, or in this case, one audience, is defined in opposition to another,[139] Fox's "real" America was always set in contrast to the morally bankrupt, less American places where the cultural elites lived, even if that happened to be next door. The binary may have been framed geographically as red/rural versus blue/urban, but the ultimate distinction was between the *us* that aligned with Fox's litany of *pro-* frames and the *them* who were presumed to thumb their noses at everything Fox's real American audience loved and stood for—including Fox News itself.[140] Fox had a vested interest in ensuring that its audience felt maximally minimized. The more alienating it could make the other networks seem, the more Fox could position itself as a safe haven.

A related element of Fox's early populism—and its cultivation of notions of "real" America—was how it related to experts and expertise. On the surface, Fox hosts derided the very notion of expertise, a premise built into its early tagline, "We Report, You Decide." What "We Report, You Decide" communicated, according to the Republican advertising consultants that came up with the slogan, is that "it was up to you to decide if we're fakers or if we're telling the truth."[141] Viewers were thus made the ultimate arbiters of facts, an idea that in one direction devalued those who had expertise (who are *they* to tell *you* what you think is true), and in the other direction lauded the audience for having good instincts and ultimately good taste. Several years later, Stephen Colbert, then of *The Daily Show* and dressed in Bill O'Reilly drag, would send up Fox's tagline and associated ethos by introducing the concept of "truthiness," which asserts that truth comes from one's gut, not from facts or experts.[142]

Still, Fox's relationship to expertise could be nuanced. Reece Peck emphasizes that the "trust your gut" ethos of the network allowed for some experts, and even some academics, to speak to current events.[143] However, these experts and academics were of a particular kind. They were "friendly" experts, experts who aligned with the ideals of "real" America that Fox cultivated. Fox had no qualms citing them, because it wasn't the expertise itself that was the problem. It was who was claiming it.

Fox reinforced their rejection of (certain) expertise, which was ultimately a rejection of (alleged) elitism, through the "everyguy blue collar" stylization of the network's hosts, notably Bill O'Reilly, Sean Hannity, and Shepherd Smith. Each played up elements of their biography that aligned with the "NASCAR audience" and geographic imaginary (a heartland that didn't need to be located anywhere in particular) that Ailes wanted to reach[144] and quietly ignored the elements that didn't quite line up with the story Ailes was selling, for example, the fact that they all lived in New York City and by just about every measure qualified as "elite" themselves.[145]

Fox did all of this while maintaining its "fair and balanced"—another of its early taglines—neutral political stance. Up to a point this was a farce. Anyone who knew anything about Rupert Murdoch and Roger Ailes knew that they were explicitly partisan and that Fox could hardly be considered an apolitical media property. As an example, as the network headed toward its programming launch in 1996, Fox producers were on the hunt for high-profile guests. When one Fox executive asked newly elected President Bill Clinton's senior advisor George Stephanopoulos if Clinton would consider appearing on-air, Stephanopoulos started laughing; no, of course he wouldn't. The executive asked why not, since Clinton had appeared on rival network MSNBC. "Well, for one thing," Stephanopoulos told the executive, "MSNBC's not owned by Rupert Murdoch and run by Roger Ailes."[146] Fox's neutrality was also belied by its boosters, notably, Roger Ailes's close friend Rush Limbaugh, who offered support for and actively promoted Fox News' launch on his radio show.[147]

How Fox politically aligned itself (or not) wasn't the point. The network simply didn't need to. Positioning itself as pro-America, pro-heartland, and pro-regular guy did all the rhetorical work. *Pro-* meant *anti-*. Audiences who identified with America, the heartland (even if they lived in Manhattan), and regular guys knew who the devils were. Still, Fox's populist style had a key effect, explained by Reese Peck. "Fox News' flashy graphics, leg-revealing women pundits, and partisan emotionality has worked to execute . . . a populist-intellectual sleight of hand, which encourages its critics to underappreciate the network's role in promoting conservative intellectual culture."[148] And a fundamental part of that culture—indeed, for audiences, a very *fun* part of that culture—was to perpetually fight with liberals.

GOOD CHARACTERS

Fox didn't invent this fight. It had inherited from the realm of shadow conservatism and shadow Christianity a template for family-first satanic panicking that didn't need to talk about devils to communicate that "real" Americans were already in hell.

That said, some of Fox's anti-liberal messages still walked an actually satanic line. In one such segment, Billy Graham was brought on to comment on the mass school shooting at Columbine High School in 1997. Graham claimed that the shooters had been possessed by Satan,[149] an extreme articulation of the widespread and by then bipartisan claim that violent video games and other seedy elements of pop culture had infected the minds of vulnerable youth. Similarly, in a segment called "Children at Risk," Bill O'Reilly linked shock rocker Marilyn Manson to Satan—a connection that, to be fair, Manson actively encouraged by playing into every satanic cliché imaginable. For O'Reilly, Manson's explicit embrace of anti-Christian themes and visuals was proof positive of the secular threat to America's youth, a direct echo of Evangelical-filtered demonology.[150]

But the last vestiges of the Satanic Panics suffused a variety of media; Fox certainly wasn't the only network clutching its pearls over Marilyn Manson's late 1990s performative satanism. More than that, the Christian figure of Satan—Satan as such—wasn't where Fox's demonology was pointing. Instead, it directed its cameras and writers to where the ratings were: good characters. Writing in 1997, David Brock summarized the approach. "Fox prefers to focus on people who are doing bad," he explained, "especially if they're Democrats, or environmentalists, a particular Murdoch peeve."[151]

Fox's skill for telling compelling stories about people who were doing bad—all the better when those people were Democrats—ran parallel with a broader mainstreaming push within the network. Segments would feature controversial guests whose shouted or extreme arguments would give the hosts a chance to seem reasonable or respectably neutral, like when Bill O'Reilly, whose criticisms of Bill Clinton were endless, brought Jerry Falwell onto his show and proceeded to browbeat him for continually attacking Bill Clinton ("You guys wanted him out since Day One. Don't care that he's been a good president. How do you answer *that*?").[152]

The dynamic of "editorializing by proxy," in which hosts would bring on guests with controversial perspectives or otherwise would explain that "some people" believed extreme claims, served a similar purpose; doing so amplified the statements while allowing the hosts to take the moral high ground.[153] For example in one 2001 episode of *Hannity & Colmes*, Sean Hannity and Alan Colmes interviewed radio shock jock Mancow Muller, who in between jabs at various liberals called Hillary Clinton a lesbian and Bill Clinton a rapist. The hosts jumped in and tried to wrangle their wayward guest, a move that simultaneously affirmed their status as responsible adults while also ensuring a below-the-belt double Clinton attack.[154] To maximize segment drama, Ailes's producers also frequently reached out to those whose very presence could start a partisan fight.[155] David Brock's profile of Ailes, written as the network was launched, thus rang prescient. "It may be that Murdoch wants to fight the culture wars more than he wants a strong news product," Brock speculated.[156]

As in the Falwell interview, some of Fox's most bombastic guests would be rightwingers. When they weren't physically in-studio, these figures could still end up as topics of on-air conversion. In a dizzying segment with Sean Hannity on partisanship in the media, for example, O'Reilly criticized Rush Limbaugh for calling liberals Communists—never mind the fact that a year before that segment aired, O'Reilly had hosted a guest that questioned whether Hillary Clinton had ties to the Communist Party.[157] Other "good characters" would be entertaining pop culture punching bags, like when O'Reilly interviewed members of the "horrorcore" face-painted white rap duo the Insane Clown Posse and showed clips of its members telling kids to "go home and smoke something." In the segment introduction, O'Reilly cranked up the scorn. "What they advocate makes some of the Black rappers look like Shirley Temple," he stated.[158]

So, Fox diversified. But the network's most contentious "good character" exchanges were with liberals making their case on cultural and political issues. The Fox host could shoot down the guest for not aligning with the ideals of "real" America—also described in terms of "America's heartland" or "blue-collar America"—or simply for not being reasonable. As they lobbed this critique, hosts positioned themselves, and by extension Fox News and its viewers, squarely within "real" America (or the heartland, or blue-collar America), and certainly within its realm of reasonableness. Here too, Bill O'Reilly mastered the art of policing the boundaries of "real" America while making himself seem like the most even-keeled, common-sense person on the soundstage.

O'Reilly's 2001 book *The No Spin Zone* is a masterclass example, opening with the declaration that his show is for anyone who believes in "truth, common sense, and decency."[159] One of the chapters includes the transcript of an interview with Dr. Joycelyn Brothers (described in the book as "an avowed and outspoken liberal"[160]), who, as U.S. Surgeon General from 1993 to 1994, had been fired by Bill Clinton after making controversial remarks about masturbation and sex ed curricula. O'Reilly opens the interview by saying that Brothers must have known a firestorm was coming after her masturbation remarks. Brothers asks why. "Come on," O'Reilly responds. "This is America!" He follows up by insisting that "Parents don't want it taught in school." Brothers clarifies that the call wasn't to teach children how to masturbate, it was to dispel disinformation about what would happen if they did (for instance, that their hair would fall out).[161] In the interview, O'Reilly is unmoved. He knows what America is, and he knows what American parents think. The "real" ones, anyway.

THE CLINTON GLOBAL INITIATIVE

Fox's breathless coverage of President Bill Clinton's affair with White House intern Monica Lewinsky exemplifies the network's strategy of making good television out of bad liberals. It also exemplifies how reliant the shadow gospel is on its devils.

Fox wasn't the only cable network to benefit from the scandal, which exploded onto the political stage in 1998. But the story's labyrinthine ins and outs, not to mention all the good characters it introduced—Linda Tripp, the backstabbing best friend; Kenneth Starr, the "deeply Christian"[162] bloodhound prosecutor (who, despite his public moralizing, privately admitted of the sex affair, "I love the narrative!"[163]); and of course Monica Lewinsky, the lovestruck intern—gave Fox a target perfectly calibrated to its branding strengths.

Unsurprisingly, Fox producers eagerly pounced on the most tawdry elements of the scandal: cigars, soiled dresses, and fellatio in the Oval Office. The chyrons wrote themselves. But they didn't stop at the sex talk; the network also made news out of nothing. On quiet days, Fox, and especially Brit Hume's show *Special Report*, would lead with footage of Kenneth Starr taking out the trash.[164] As the Lewinsky story became a full-time beat, Fox News was out in front, breaking many of the scandal's biggest moments and ensuring that it remained maximally painful for the Clinton administration and maximally entertaining for audiences.

An added storytelling bonus for Fox was the fact that Hillary Clinton was reviled by Fox's audience. Not only was she a Democrat, she was a feminist, and for years within rightwing circles had been framed, sometimes quite literally, as a demon; in a notebook she'd kept during her time at the 1992 RNC, Susan Faludi recorded the various conspiracy theories she'd heard lobbed against Clinton, including claims that she was a member of a satanic cult and that she had orchestrated multiple murders.[165] And Roger Ailes *hated* her. Over two decades of vitriolic coverage, he ensured that Clinton would become "one of the longest-running villains on TV."[166]

Drawing from the Whitewater panoply of scandals that had dogged the Clintons for years in Little Rock, Arkansas, Fox pushed an equally aggressive populist angle to their Bad Clintons soap opera. Whitewater allowed the network to expand their cast of good characters to include the media and political elites said to be covering up for "their good-times president."[167] Fox's self-crowning as the "anti-Clinton News Network" was a product of this narrative framing; an undercurrent of their coverage was that cable news competitors were covering for Clinton.[168] They were not. But describing CNN as the Clinton News Network was part of the story Fox was telling.

And what a story it was; it had something for every demonologist. Outright conspiracists could focus on the alleged plots the Clintons were said to be spearheading; the *anti-* crowd could focus on the fundamental immorality of liberals (never mind how much they, like Ken Starr, actually loved the narrative); and *pro-* viewers could focus on the family and all the moral centrality that went with it. Recognizing the pandemonic (and ratings) potential, Fox hosts went broad with their coverage. They framed themselves, self-styled champions of flyover country, as protectors against a litany of culture war horsemen the Clintons were said to represent: uncontrolled sexuality, establishment media, gay rights activists, environmentalism, political correctness, and other go-to harbingers of the Revelation Lite end times.[169] All of it reflected the same sweaty fascination with the impure that characterized Evangelical apocalypse media, but rather than compelling audiences to cower in fear over the devil at their doorstep, it invited them to reach for a bowl of popcorn and enjoy the show.

The result of Fox's turn as the "anti-Clinton News Network" was, first, a ratings windfall; primetime viewership jumped 400 percent. CNN and MSNBC also benefited from the story, but ratings increased only by 40 percent for CNN and 53 percent for MSNBC. Ailes's magic branding formula simply allowed Fox News to tell the story better. But it wasn't just ratings that Fox was gifted by the Clintons. Through the ongoing melodrama, Fox News came into its own. As one former senior Fox executive explained, "when Bill [O'Reilly] started wagging his finger at the president and raising his voice, that was the genesis of the modern Fox News."[170]

THE GOSPEL ACCORDING TO FOX

What the modern Fox News proved to be was the new hub of the shadow gospel, supplanting Evangelicalism as the driver of messages about "real" America beset by a radical, values-corroding left. Just as Christianity needs

Satan, Revelation Lite needs a devil to fight. Fox's version was no different. But echoing the network's special demonological flavor, the liberal devils they spotlighted were also the key to the demo, their economic salvation.

Fox's ratings slump following the end of the Lewinsky scandal evidenced its need for a steady supply of bad liberals to wag fingers at. And then came the 2000 presidential election, which pit Republican George W. Bush against Democrat Al Gore. The final vote was too close to call, chaos reigned for thirty-three days, and Fox News was back in its happy place, airing segments on what a sore loser Gore was being and how the Democrats were trying to steal the election from Republicans.[171] Ultimately, the Supreme Court gave Bush the victory, which could have proven problematic for a network best calibrated for loathing a Democratic president. Then came a sunny Tuesday in September.

Post-9/11 Fox News thrived,[172] fighting the Wars on Terror and Christmas with equal verve. Regarding the latter, even when they filed story after story about the "reason for the season," the focus was liberal godlessness and perfidy, not Jesus's love or grace. And it was good television. So good that after the network was supercharged by hatred for Democratic president Barack Obama and subsequently adopted as an unofficial branch of Donald Trump's Republican White House Press Office, as Evangelicals flocked to Fox's good news,[173] they became increasingly unreachable by their increasingly baffled pastors who could not understand how the sermons coming from their cable televisions had more power over them than the sermons coming from their churches. But that is a story for the book's conclusion.

THE LEFT HATES AMERICA

Following the September 11, 2001, terrorist attacks against the United States, Attorney General John Ashcroft set out to develop new legislation designed to give FBI agents and U.S. prosecutors bulked-out powers and minimal oversight to pursue suspected terrorists. The hastily written law was called the Provide Appropriate Tools Required to Intercept and Obstruct Terrorism (PATRIOT) Act. The executive director of the ACLU along with several rightwing House Republicans on the Judiciary Committee attempted to work with Ashcroft to make the bill more palatable; many of its provisions would have been sweeping and, as they warned in a letter sent to Ashcroft, "unacceptable as written" in terms of its risks to citizens' civil liberties.[1]

Despite an intense bill negotiation process, what passed the Senate 98–1 and then the House 337–79 reflected almost total concession to Ashcroft. Wisconsin Democratic senator Russ Feingold, the one dissenting vote, had attempted to amend the bill with stronger civil liberty protections.[2] Democratic House Majority Leader Tom Daschle responded with a "chilly lecture" about not having time for diversions—the country was, in essence, at war—and scuttled Feingold's efforts.[3] Following the bill's passage, staffers at the ACLU called staffers on the Hill "screaming about a betrayal." When members of Congress were contacted directly with the ACLU's grave concerns about the severity of the bill and how quickly it had been jammed through, the response was stark: the ACLU didn't know what the atmosphere in Washington was like. People were afraid.[4]

To an extent, the fear that swirled the Capitol was a function of the *actual* terrorist threat level, the *actual* domestic risks. The attacks on September 11 had been terrible, unspeakable, almost incomprehensible; maybe there would be other targets. But the post-9/11 political atmosphere became thick with much more shadowy fear, one that would intensify as the months passed and the country declared war in Afghanistan and Iraq. That was the fear of being called unpatriotic and therefore un-American.[5]

The fight—or perhaps more appropriately, the acquiescence—over the PATRIOT Act proved to be the opening salvo in a years-long political contest to prove just how much one loved one's country, measured by one's support for President George W. Bush, enthusiasm for the wars (described in a popular country song by Toby Keith as "Putting a boot in [the vague terrorist enemy's] ass, it's the American Way"[6]), and frequency of wearing an American flag lapel pin. Refusing to do so carried significant political risks, underscored by George Bush's stark 2001 declaration that "You are either with us or you are against us in the fight against terror."[7]

Republican politicians took the president's demonological decree to heart, often to grimly absurdist extremes. The jingoistic fervor they affixed to the attacks was echoed in many Evangelical churches, which began integrating props like massive screens projecting digital images of American flags "swaying gently in the wind" during service.[8] Congress had its own props. For instance, in the symbolic effort to punish the French for not joining the United States in its preemptive war in Iraq, two Republican congressmen proposed renaming "French fries" "Freedom fries." Soon, "Freedom fries" were being sold in all House office buildings.[9] Many Democrats in Congress also embraced post-9/11 chest-thumping, with their American flag lapel pins serving as a visual marker of their support for the troops and boots in asses and the American way. Bush still declared that congressional Democrats were "not interested in the security of the American people."[10]

Previous chapters explored how anti-liberal conservatives have embraced and benefited from shadow gospel messages. This chapter focuses on liberals: those who actively self-identify as such and those who have ended up conscripted in the army of liberal darkness through constant demonological encoding and decoding, a concept to which we will soon return. White conservative women have always been at the vanguard of liberal encoding/decoding efforts, ensuring through their dual roles as field officers and war correspondents that the shadow gospel would continue growing, shaping public discourse, and stockpiling enemies.

Democrats—especially Democratic politicians—during the 1990s and 2000s aided in the anti-liberal war efforts as well. Sometimes they did so inadvertently by amplifying shadow gospel messages through pushback and criticism. But they also spread the messages by actively choosing to spread them. Highlighting all the groups that have helped, deliberately or not, cohere the liberal enemy is the only way to push back against the shadow gospel's two great sources of power: its disconnection (from ideology, theology, and basic details of history) and its ability to hide in rhetoric that sounds positive—like loving America.

LEFTISM, LIBERALS, AND GROUNDED HISTORY

For years, Rush Limbaugh touted his imaginary "Institute for Advanced Conservative Studies," framed as a training ground for contemporary conservatives.[11] In 2017 he opted for a rebrand; it would now be called the "Institute for Advanced Anti-Leftist Studies." His reasoning was that "it's not enough just to espouse conservatism and explain it, teach it, define it. There's a missing component. It has to be presented simultaneously with anti-leftist studies as a contrast rather than as a stand-alone."[12] Limbaugh had been circling this argument for years. Nicole Hemmer explains that he had never been too immersed in conservative ideology or policy; he was always more focused on "liberal hypocrisy and Democratic excesses." His show was, as a result, "less about articulating a fully developed conservative vision than ridiculing the left."[13] For Limbaugh, conservative identity wasn't really about conservatism. It was about opposing liberals.

Cold War housewife populists had been guided by the same instinct. Michelle Nickerson highlights how anticommunist wives and mothers defined their identities not in terms of what they believed, but in contrast to what they hated.[14] The "progressive school administrator, the guileless bridge-playing housewife, and the duped liberal PTA member," as well as members of civil rights groups, numbered among the threatening people through which these wives and mothers configured their sense of "the left" and, thus, their own subjectivities.[15] However, reflecting the fact that modern political terminology was still very much in flux—the category of "conservative" was still a decade away from widespread adoption—the so-called housewife populists Nickerson studied did not always use the term "left."

What marked the boundaries of their great if poorly defined enemy was "guilt by association" within an "inchoate political force" that was not connected organizationally and focused on very different issues yet was believed to have a shared goal of destroying American freedoms.[16] The amalgamation was thus subject to imprecise descriptors such as "communist-type" or "pro-communist" and was broadly framed as a "masculine predatory force that exploited the trusting."[17] Overwhelmed by this vague sense of personal threat, anticommunists transformed the fact that there were never very *many* Communists, and that they never had significant political power in the United States, into the myth of a Communist under every bed.[18] Objectively strange bedfellows resulted. Romantic and sexual attraction to members of the same gender, for example, is not in itself a political position. It certainly has nothing to do with economic ideology. And yet thanks to a logic of guilt by association predicated on shadowy notions of "subversion," queer people were placed in the same maligned category as actual Communist Party members.[19]

"Liberal" and "liberalism" were also unlikely additions. Those ideas were just so *specific*. Chapter 1 emphasized that during and after the Great Depression, "liberal" was linked to New Deal policies; if a person supported those policies, they were a liberal, regardless of the other political positions they might hold.[20] Chapter 2 explored how liberalism as a concept mapped onto the modernist/traditionalist divide within mid-century American Christianity. To be a liberal was to focus on social outreach and to try and make the world a better place.[21] Chapter 3 discussed the "vital center" of 1950s and 1960s liberalism that aligned with the news media's claims of objectivity, universities' claims of neutrality, and government's claims of technocracy. Much to the agitation of rightwing activists, liberals advocated for what the rightwingers saw as a nonpartisan, nonconfrontational, nonideological middle ground.[22]

When "liberal" was used in these specific historical contexts, the conversations (and criticisms) could be ideological or theological; they could be grounded. But once the discourses were sucked into the shadow gospel's black hole, they grafted onto a Satan of increasing reiteration, ensuring that the concept of liberal overlapping with an aggressive, unified left would seem enduring, omnipresent, and increasingly dangerous.

At the same time, actual leftist strongholds in the United States were being dismantled. Organized labor was all but gutted by the 1970s thanks in large part to the right-to-work movement that originated within an Evangelical parachurch organization.[23] Billy Graham was particularly critical of the labor movement. He hadn't always been. Initially, he supported organized labor and claimed that it aligned with Christian ideals.[24] Ultimately, Graham's vigorous support of Big Business prevailed, prompting him to equate union dues and labor leaders with snakes in the Garden of Eden.[25] For the next several decades, Evangelicals campaigned aggressively on behalf of corporate interests, helping to erode mass support for unions.[26] Hollywood was also subject to an anti-leftist purge. Terrified of red baiting, studios and actors in the 1950s clamored to cut ties with anything that could remotely be perceived as Communist, including labor unions, but also New Deal liberalism more broadly.[27] Broad liberal ideals may have persisted through the 1950s—Jennifer A. Delton highlights how, perhaps surprisingly, the decade saw significant government redistribution of wealth, taxation of the rich, corporate regulation, and expanding public works projects[28]—but liberal activist causes and organizations did not.[29]

The next generation of leftist activists—known as the "New Left"—didn't fare too much better.[30] Radical, intellectual, and centered on college campuses, the New Left was not uniformly focused on "Old Left" issues of economic equality, poverty, and labor.[31] While it adopted some elements of late 1950s to early 1960s civil rights activism, the religious roots of the civil rights movement weren't the easiest fit with the secular leftism that flourished on college campuses. Neither was the institutionalism of traditional liberalism the easiest fit with New Left activists inclined toward fast and dirty revolution. Neither was the persistent segregation in the Democratic Party the easiest fit with the New Left's anti-segregationism.[32]

The New Left, in other words, couldn't be cleanly equated—not in the moment and not retroactively—with previous liberal and leftist groups or with the Democratic Party. And yet Evangelical and conservative groups adopted the figure of the radical, revolutionary student activist as the stand-in for all leftism and liberalism. Never mind the fact that the New Left student movement didn't enjoy anything close to the resource- and network-sharing with national leftist activists and organizations as did conservative campus groups with national rightwing activists and organizations.[33] Never mind the fact that, unlike conservative campus groups, whose influence on party politics persisted for decades, New Left student groups were not absorbed by Democratic Party machinery.[34] Never mind the fact that conservative campus organizations like Campus Crusade for Christ preceded the existence of New Left organizations like Students for a Democratic Society by ten years, undermining sweeping claims that rightwing campus activism was a reaction to leftwing campus activism. Never mind the fact that the New Left had collapsed by the early 1970s.[35]

None of that mattered. What did was that the pot-smoking, free-loving, war-protesting, long-haired, dirty hippie leftist fit perfectly into the shadow gospel's threat narrative. It allowed demonologists in the 1970s to push the anti-liberal message that all these radicals had shown up, unified and marauding, to threaten everything "classic" America held dear. They were a clear and present moral enemy of America. What the country needed was a clear and present moral solution—and conveniently, shadow gospel conservatives had just the thing: themselves.

SUBVERSIVES, SUBVERSIVES EVERYWHERE

To wage this battle, demonologists needed a process for detecting the enemy—a particularly important step when no one was actually attacking. Beverly LaHaye's 1984 *Who But a Woman? Concerned Women Can Make a Difference* exemplifies how that army was raised in order to be fought. Lesbians, Marxists, people who call for extreme social change, gay men, people who are permissive, people who support the state, conscious agents of Communism, seculars, people who encourage disrespect and disobedience toward parents, sinners, and those who seek to destroy the sanctity of the home[36]—all interchangeable villains for LaHaye—were not unified ideologically or theologically. But they were amalgamated demonologically.

LaHaye acknowledges the unwieldiness of her classification system, explaining that "they may call themselves feminists or humanists. The label makes little difference, because many of them are seeking the destruction of morality and human freedom."[37] Not having clearly demarcated labels naturally invites an expanding—or at the very least shapeshifting—pile of suspected subversives. It also strengthens one's own demonological identity. The worse they are, the more of them they are, the more critical it is to contrast their degeneracy with our truth-telling, child-protecting, God-defending, and America-saving.

As always, these *pro-* frames point to the *anti-* of the liberal or leftist or whatever-someone-might-call-it enemy. Four shadow gospel truths unify their threats. *They* censor conservatives, *they* endanger children, *they* are anti-Christian, and *they* hate America. The specific criteria for these truths ultimately reflect a form of demonological encoding and decoding, a framework introduced by cultural theorist Stuart Hall to describe the process by which media producers use coded symbols—things with existing cultural meaning—to communicate ideas to an audience, which the audience then interprets as a form of translation.[38]

First, where there is, or seems to be, attacks on conservatives, endangerment of children, godlessness, or anti-Americanism, the people responsible are encoded as a particular kind of world-threatening evil by producers of shadow gospel messages. For demonological audiences, the subsequent decoding process is seamless; the intended meaning "here be monsters" is successfully communicated and successfully translated. Everybody agrees on what things mean, even if they aren't using exactly the same words to do it.

The decoding process looks very different when message producers and message audiences are not demonologically aligned. Conservative attacks against "political correctness" are one example. Political correctness initially emerged as an inside joke within leftist circles in the 1980s; people used the term to playfully engage with the acceptable limits of progressive politics.[39] By the 1990s, rightwing foundations and media figures had seized on the idea of a leftist "thought police" targeting conservative speech. "PC fascism," as it was sometimes called, was said to be especially pernicious on college campuses, where conservative students were allegedly being bludgeoned by "tenured radicals indoctrinating [students] with leftist propaganda."[40] Rightwing media figures like Rush Limbaugh railed against PC culture, suggesting that anyone who took issue with anything he said was nothing more than an overreacting liberal.[41]

The encoding/decoding process here is asymmetric. Any expressed sensitivity around language or call for diversity, equity, and inclusion—or simply a rejection of identity-based cruelty—was decoded by conservatives as a strategic, deliberate, *coordinated* attack against conservative thought. Had Limbaugh asked any of these accused liberals if they were members of the "PC police," they likely would have laughed nervously. Maybe they would have tried to explain the difference between censorship and cultivating a value of inclusiveness, which does mean taking a stand against racist, sexist, and homophobic speech but isn't an inherently anti-conservative position. What would have been clear is that the accused liberals were not operating under the same logic as those doing the accusing.

Demonological decoding doesn't happen spontaneously. Like the FBI's stealth anticommunist propaganda efforts, which, as Carol Stabile argues, educated audiences in detecting red presence,[42] the shadow gospel educates its audiences to detect liberal/leftist presence—and, by default, liberal/ leftist malevolence. The evils exist in the eye of the conservative beholder trained to see the signs, helping explain how the accusation of liberalism/ leftism gets affixed to things that are nonpartisan or are aligned with mainstream institutions. The standard is not whether those things regard themselves as liberal or leftist. The standard is that they are decoded as posing particular kinds of threats to "classic" Christian Americans.

CHILD ABUSE IN THE CLASSROOM

The 1980s fights over "parents' rights" in public schools—an uncanny, almost verbatim precursor for school board fights of the Trump era— demonstrate how the four shadow gospel truths create demonological decoding frameworks, such that amalgamated threats aren't just identified but are searched for.

Central to these fights was the Protection of Pupil Rights Amendment, with Phyllis Schlafly and her Eagle Forum once again serving as battalion leaders. The PPRA was enacted in 1978 and was developed to help protect students' privacy, particularly related to sensitive personal information. It stipulates, first, that parents have the right to inspect new and experimental curricular materials and, second, that students can't be subject to psychological experimentation or treatment without parental approval. The law hadn't been controversial when it passed. But when conservative parents began to complain to the U.S. Department of Education, arguing that public school curricula violated the PPRA, they realized that there was no formal enforcement mechanism nor a satisfactory process for filing complaints.

Schlafly explains the nature of these complaints in a book unsubtly titled *Child Abuse in the Classroom*.[43] Parents, at least those affiliated with the Eagle Forum, claimed that the "humanistic" curriculum in public schools was a form of experimental therapy, and therefore was in violation of PPRA. The argument was that it encouraged students to discuss their feelings and experiences, in the process revealing what the parents argued was sensitive information like details about their family's faith and political affiliation. These parents also claimed that a "humanistic" curriculum was a form of behavioral modification in that it "confused students about life, about standards of behavior, about moral choices, about religious loyalties, and about relationships with parents and with peers."[44] In other words: it threatened to change the students' values, which is what made it "therapy" rather than education. Because these parents had not been provided the "therapeutic" materials to inspect, they argued that schools were in double violation of the PPRA.

Child Abuse in the Classroom isn't just Schlafly's take on the issue; it's a collation of the testimonies of hundreds of parents who traveled to seven different Department of Education hearings on proposed regulations to PPRA. Across the testimonies, which Schlafly admits were edited and condensed, with context on the pedagogical theories behind the curriculum deliberately omitted to foreground "first-hand proof of child abuse in the classroom,"[45] concerned parents painted a grim picture. "Therapy education," as they called it, required engagement with violent and disturbing media content, including literature "that is mostly negative and depressing";[46] exploration of difficult topics such as abortion, divorce, and suicide; games that "invade the private thoughts of the child";[47] and role-playing exercises that address mortality, sex education, and what the parents argued was "a deliberate attempt to make the child reject the values of his parents and his religion."[48]

The worries these parents were pointing to weren't new, and neither was the drumbeat of "parents' rights" they foregrounded; both echoed the decades-old concerns of anticommunist mothers in the 1950s who campaigned against the progressive education movement, which these parents claimed borrowed "psychological tools from their social scientist comrades" to brainwash children into having Communist sympathies.[49] For similar reasons as PPRA crusaders, Cold War anticommunist mothers attacked the growing mental health movement on the grounds that, armed with emerging social-scientific research, schoolteachers and counselors were "invading the home" by administering questionnaires and presenting frank discussions of health, including sexual health, to students.[50]

Another parallel between the "parents' rights" fights of the 1950s and 1980s was how the classroom enemy was described: as a totally unwieldy linguistic amalgamation. Schlafly focuses in particular on the "national disease" spread from state to state by "the Typhoid Marys of federal funding."[51] Symptoms of this disease included "high rates of teenage suicide, loneliness, premarital sex, and pregnancies,"[52] emotional and moral confusion, rebellion toward parents, alienation from the Ten Commandments, situational approaches to ethics, and humanism.[53] The parents who submitted testimony to the Department of Education hearings were more specific in their denunciations. Evil ones included secular humanists (said to helm a "religion of humanism," borrowing from Tim LaHaye's framing in *Battle for the Mind*), promoters of birth control, those who were immodest, moral relativists, those with liberal attitudes toward divorce, those who used socialist language, those who undermined traditional gender roles, and those who encouraged autonomy in children.[54]

The shadow gospel's four interconnected truths cohered these accusations. As Eagle Forum parents described it, "therapy education" silenced conservative parents and their traditional American values.[55] Its undermining of God was a given, with different parents lamenting how teachers were destroying their children's faith as well as obedience to God (and to them).[56] Others complained that school curricula programmed students to "accept a new global perspective"[57] and, in the process, undermined their love of country[58] and alienated them from "our American heritage."[59] School administrators, counselors, and classroom teachers were accused of brainwashing, indoctrinating, discriminating against, harassing, manipulating, and traumatizing children. For Schlafly, only one word fit what was happening: abuse.[60]

Schlafly admits, however, that unless parents knew what they were looking for, they would not find it on their own. She *explicitly* describes her book's collection of parents' testimonies as a decoder tool. Parents who read her book, she explains, emerge with a framework and set of linguistic terms they can use to interrogate their children about what goes on in their classrooms. Unsurprisingly, when they ask the right questions in the right ways, these parents "find that their children have been subject to the violation of [the Pupil Rights Amendment] for years, but that fact had been concealed from parents who did not suspect that classroom time was devoted to psychological 'therapy' instead of to traditional basics."[61] They did not suspect, because they did not know what they needed to be looking for—until Phyllis Schlafly and the Eagle Forum told them.

Armed with an inchoate yet deeply resonant litany of offenders—a list that grew with each demonological decoding—the "classic" conservative *us* at the center of the PPRA case and other cases like it became increasingly unified in their oppositional identities. They also became, in their own minds, increasingly necessary as saviors against the depraved if amorphous *them*. So long as the shadow gospel remained filtered through

Evangelicalism, as was the case throughout the PPRA fight, the messianic impulse at least gestured toward a cosmic battle between good and evil. Its Revelation may have been euphemistic, but it remained steeped in religious symbology. As the hub of the shadow gospel shifted to the sensationalist, populist Church of Fox News, however, the satanic amalgamation that had ultimately settled on "liberal" overlapping with "leftist" and "Democrat" opened up to a whole new set of good characters—and a whole new mode of delivery for its highest-profile evangelists.

GODLESS

Conservative pundit Ann Coulter exemplifies the Fox News expansion of the anti-liberal demon realm. Coulter, who began her career as a corporate lawyer, was hired as a congressional aide in 1994 following the Republican Revolution. Tall, blonde, and conventionally attractive, she started appearing on cable news in 1996, where she would make outrageous and incendiary claims, particularly about Democrats. Initially, this was a liability. During Bill Clinton's impeachment trial it became an asset. She published a book, *High Crimes and Misdemeanors*, that pored over each of Clinton's impeachment charges and helped her become a staple of what a *Washington Post* profile from 1998 describes as the "shout show circuit."[62]

Over the years, Coulter's appearances on Fox News were regular enough that even Fox employees assumed she was a hired contributor.[63] Coulter claimed, however, that she had only ever been formally hired by MSNBC—who continually fired and rehired her, as she was a "good character" in her own right, one that liberal audiences loved to hate.[64] In a 2003 *Guardian* profile titled "An Appalling Magic,"[65] her communication style was described thus: "she flits from one rightwing prejudice to another, taking not so much as a gasp for oxygen. In a couple of sentences, she can play with overt racism, soften it with a line so provocative she could only be kidding, then round off the performance with a sweeping smear of the liberal enemy."

Coulter was, in short, a troll. But not of the equal-opportunity variety; her focus wasn't generating strong negative reactions across the board. Her trolling style was pointedly anti-liberal. She said everything she could to make the libs mad, and if the libs weren't listening, she said everything she could to rile up her anti-liberal audience, the volume of whose applause matched the level of Coulter's meanness. Thus if Rush Limbaugh's 1992

The Way Things Ought to Be is the Book of Revelation Lite, Coulter's 2006 *Godless: The Church of Liberalism*[66] is the Book of the Church of Fox News.

In chapters with titles such as "On the Seventh Day, God Rested and Liberals Schemed" and "The Liberal Priesthood: Spare the Rod, Spoil the Teacher," Coulter expands the definition of "liberal" to the point of self-satire, a reflection of the continual ante-upping necessitated by the fusing of sensationalism and populism. Pundits like Coulter had to keep generating increasingly creative ways to troll the libs; audiences would get bored if she said the same insults every time. So, the usual, predictable liberal targets—socialism, humanism, secularism—were augmented with criteria like going camping, eating organic foods, opposing toilets that use too much water, following the rules in smoking sections, forcing people to give up SUVs and snowmobiles, divorcing sex from procreation, fixating on youth and idealized beauty, supporting laws against sexual harassment, and not knowing Bible passages.[67] And while she doesn't make a specific statistical claim that all public school teachers are liberals, Coulter does argue that public school teachers, broadly described as "taxpayer-supported parasites . . . inculcating students in the precepts of the Socialist Party of America," are the priesthood of liberalism[68]—a priesthood that, she casually claims, is corrupted by a "teacher child-molestation problem."[69]

Just like Beverly LaHaye's and Phyllis Schlafly's unwieldy litanies, Coulter's shadow realm definition of liberalism is cohered through the four shadow gospel truths. As she explains, liberals threaten conservatives by forcing them to accept "liberal orthodoxy." Liberals threaten children with their constant indoctrination efforts, particularly in schools. Liberals threaten God by prohibiting the existence of Christianity and Judaism (curiously, Coulter specifies that when she uses the term "Christian" throughout her book, she is also referring to Jews, since both groups "subscribe to the Bible and God of Abraham"[70]). And liberals threaten America simply by living here, given what Coulter describes as their drive "to preside over our state-managed descent into hell."[71]

This is extreme language. It is also a product of extreme demonological encoding. Many of the examples of liberalism that Coulter provides would barely inconvenience conservatives, let alone threaten them. It's that conservatives—at least, the conservatives that Coulter represents—don't like the idea of them, which is enough to make them liberal. What the shadow gospel truths do is reframe dislike, discomfort, or simple inconvenience into an existential threat.

MOTHERS OF MASSIVE LIBERAL RESISTANCE

Coulter's rhetoric is unique in that it reflects a new hub of shadow gospel messages that push the liberal devil to absurdism, shadow gospel evangelists to trolldom, and demonological encoding/decoding to delirium. But beneath Coulter's bombast is the same pandemonic argument that had been swirling around the rightwing ecosystem for decades. Coulter's role in promoting the Foxified shadow gospel also speaks to the unique role that white women have played in spreading demonology.

Shadow gospel conservatives have long understood—and long exploited—white women's role as conservative messengers. Within New Right networks in the 1980s and 1990s, white women who embodied traditional values were seen as having special, almost messianic qualities, with their love for their children framed as the strongest possible bulwark against the fill-in-the-blank amalgamated threat.[72] The same was true throughout the Cold War's hearth-and-home domestic policy of sexual containment. Producing and raising white middle-class Christian American babies steeped in traditional values was heralded by anticommunists as a patriotic and even salvational act.[73] The title of Beverly LaHaye's book *Who But a Woman? Concerned Women Can Make a Difference* summarizes this argument, and she elaborates on the sentiment in the book's conclusion:

> I believe, as I have stated before, that we Christian women were asleep for too long. We focused solely on our families and church activities while the rest of our society was sliding into moral chaos. We ignored our schools, our government, our entertainment industry, our news media, and we've been paying a terrible price for our ignorance and apathy. . . .
>
> But the times are changing. We are here to keep the traditional women of America informed about the threats to the family. . . . As the salt of the earth, we are here to heal the wounds of those who have been victimized by the purveyors of moral filth and permissiveness. . . . If we are truly committed to Jesus Christ, we have no other alternative but to wage warfare against those who would destroy our children, our families, our religious liberties. There is no other option.[74]

LaHaye published these words in 1984, just as the ERA was being defeated by overlapping networks of conservative women, some more and some less explicitly religious, but all committed to slaying the Beast of the Apocalypse known as moral filth and permissiveness. Ten years earlier, Anita Bryant led the crusade against gay rights in Miami, buoyed by the spiritual support of her women's prayer group[75] and the organizational support of the Dade County Federation of Women's Clubs, which Bryant boasted had over 10,000 members. These clubs had lobbied the mayor, city commissioners, and the two organizations with whom Bryant had an advertising contract—the Florida Citrus Association and First Federal Savings & Loan Association of Miami—to support Bryant's cause.[76]

Twenty years earlier than that, housewife populists led national boycotts against companies deemed inadequately Americanist, ran interconnected rightwing bookstores, and pushed immeasurable volumes of anticommunist messages.[77] Anticommunist women's groups overlapped with a tangle of other women-driven grassroots networks, notably pro-segregation networks.[78] Elizabeth McRae highlights the "eternal vigilance" these women demonstrated regarding "subversive" materials in classrooms.[79] There was often no daylight between what the anticommunist and segregationist women were railing against; both groups sought to remove classroom content said to promote socialism, un-Americanism, and atheism, and both groups argued that their traditional values and families were under threat by the state. Separated by a generation of rightwing activism, segregationist women working behind the scenes following the 1954 *Brown v. Board of Education* Supreme Court decision even echoed the specific verbiage of 1980s Eagle Forum mothers, claiming that that their children had been subject to "insult and mistreatment"[80] and that their rights as parents were being threatened.[81]

When she burst onto the political scene, Ann Coulter was described as "something special," as an otherwise critical profile described her.[82] She may have seemed like a new kind of conservative star, but ultimately she was a slightly warped facsimile of a particular kind of conservative woman reinforcing the resonance of a particular kind of conservative message. Linda Kintz describes this resonance as a form of family worship, an intense focus on a narrowly defined moral culture, and immediate othering of anyone who falls short.[83] Coulter sang that same old hymn, one whose chorus about liberal depravity reflected a decades-long accumulation of enemies.

They censor the truth; we are the truth. They erode family values; we are family values. They destroy Christianity; we are Christianity. They hate America; we are America.

However they may have performed the song, conservative women were in a unique position to sing. Ironically, this was due to widespread sexism among journalists and other cultural critics—adding to the litany of structural dynamics that uniquely benefited the right. When Phyllis Schlafly received mainstream attention, for example, it was typically in the context of feminist attack and ridicule. All that conflict and clash helped make her a media star.[84] Kintz explains that despite the attention she received, Schlafly was also trivialized, particularly by those inclined to relegate "emotions, religion, and the family,"[85] realms historically associated with women, as something that existed outside "real" politics—not realizing just how serious and how professionalized Schlafly's politics and political organizing actually were.[86]

Schlafly, along with other rightwing activist women like Beverly LaHaye, recognized an additional benefit to trivialization: it could be cited as proof of contempt for Christian wives and mothers, thus serving as an effective recruitment tool for the conservative movement.[87] The takeaway, Kintz argues, is that the trivialization of white conservative women's interest and activism "actually worked to their advantage,"[88] not just by providing a cover of invisibility at the time but by ensuring that the pervasiveness and often serious sophistication of their activities would escape scholarly attention for years, even decades, a point Paul Matzko emphasizes in his study of anticommunist housewife populists[89] and which Elizabeth McRae also highlights in her study of segregationist women.[90]

At the height of her popularity (and infamy), Ann Coulter enjoyed the same trivialization; her conventional attractiveness and willingness to bill herself as another "blond right-wing pundit" who doesn't mind acknowledging that "sex sells"[91] translated into fetishized, even sweatily fascinated profiles that focused on her looks, including a *Time* magazine cover photo that consisted almost entirely of her legs.[92] Buried in those profiles— mentioned in passing, if at all—was the extent to which Coulter had been embedded in rightwing networks, including connections to figures and organizations discussed in previous chapters, including the *National Review*, Regnery Publishing,[93] and the Young Americans for Freedom-affiliated National Journalism Center, a conservative political organization founded by Stanton Evans,[94] whose 1961 *Revolt on the Campus* was profiled in chapter 3 (with Evans also serving as a mentor to Coulter).[95] Billing her as a "saucy siren" or "The Conservative Pin-Up Girl" or "Ms. Right"[96] allowed supporters and critics alike to falsely present her as an upstart solo artist rather than a highly tuned voice in a well-established choir.

WITH FRIENDS LIKE THESE

Sexism is an unexpected source of rightwing structural advantage. There is another source that is even more unexpected: people who describe themselves as liberal. In particular, Democratic politicians and other media figures have inadvertently fed into anti-liberal demonology at three different levels: overcompensatory parroting, frame-replicating, and not recognizing their role in the shadow gospel game.

THE LOONY LEFT LOVES PREEMPTIVE WAR TOO

In the post-9/11 landscape, Democratic politicians at the local, state, and national levels contorted themselves to prove just how much they loved America.[97] Congressional Democrats did so most conspicuously and most disastrously by lining up behind Bush in the runup to the Afghanistan and Iraq Wars. Only one dissenter in both chambers of Congress, House Democrat Barbara Lee of California, voted against the Afghanistan war resolution. The reaction was "furious,"[98] with outlets like the *Wall Street Journal* calling her a "clueless liberal" and questioning her Americanness.[99] Letters poured into her office condemning her choice, accusing her of being a traitor, and threatening her life.[100] There were more dissenters for the Iraq War resolution; the final vote in the Senate was 77–23 (one Republican and one Independent voted against; the other dissenters were Democrats),[101] and in the House, 296–133 (6 Republicans and 1 Independent voted against while the rest were Democrats).[102] Still, overwhelming numbers of Democrats supported Bush wherever he and his cabinet steered the country.

Five years after the vote, a *Politico* survey revealed that half of the Democratic senators who cast a yes vote to authorize war in Iraq regretted their decision.[103] Some claim to have been duped by the Bush administration; they believed that Iraq president Saddam Hussein had been a threat, but only later realized that the intelligence regarding the "weapons of mass destruction" he was purported to have and intended to use on the United

States was faulty.[104] Numbering among those who have come see their votes as profound mistakes, Hillary Clinton has described her yes vote as New York's senator her "greatest regret."[105]

However, Democrats who opposed the resolution from the outset challenge that view, as they were shown the same intelligence and came to very different conclusions. That didn't make the decision any easier. Senator Patty Murray, Democrat from Washington, described what had been an intense "emotional pressure" to vote yes (Murray ultimately voted no), with other congressional representatives similarly emphasizing the outraged criticism they knew they would receive if they voted against the administration.[106] The risk—and it was a risk Barbara Lee knew was very real—was that they would be accused of lacking toughness, patriotism, and basic loyalty to the country, reflecting what historian Gerald Webster describes as a "banal nationalism" colliding with "collective amnesia" that significantly weakened opposition to the war.[107]

The political landscape of September 12, 2001, wasn't the first and wouldn't be the last time that Democrats would cosign shadow gospel messaging; nor was it the first or last time that their votes were guided by a collision of false traditionalism and fear of what the public backlash would be if they took unpopular positions on hot button cultural issues.

As First Lady and senator, Hillary Clinton found herself on the shadow gospel side of the fence more than once. Perhaps most infamous was her support for the 1994 Violent Crime Control and Law Enforcement Act, also known as the Crime Bill, which rode the wave of early 1990s "tough on crime" rhetoric. Whether or not Clinton was aware of it at the time—she never acknowledged it in public—her stance on crime had deep roots in the anti-crime advocacies of Evangelicals. Although their efforts were often masked as a desire to reform criminals,[108] Evangelicals firmly established the link between crime and sin during the 1950s and 1960s, which helped pave the wave for aggressive fear mongering and demonization of criminals, simultaneously justifying punishment of them and vigilance against them.[109]

Echoing both positions, Clinton doubled down on her rhetoric in 1996. She delivered a speech in which she emphasized the need to "take back our streets from crime, gangs, and drugs."[110] In addition to touting the Crime Bill's accomplishments, she described criminal offenders with connections to the drug trade who she claimed lacked a conscience and empathy as "superpredators."

This was a racist dog whistle. The term "superpredator" became affixed to Black youth six months earlier after a conservative political commentator named John Dilulio—then a professor at Princeton University—published a 1995 essay with upstart rightwing newspaper the *Weekly Standard*.[111] Dilulio focused his argument on what he claimed were predominantly Black "chronic offenders" that threatened the safety of inner cities, the suburbs, and even rural areas. In other words: white people beware.[112] Echoing language from the Contract with America, he argued that these youth were products of "moral poverty . . . the poverty of being without loving, capable, responsible adults who teach you right from wrong." Dilulio, described as a "clever popularizer," was also embedded within the rightwing think tank circuit, which helped facilitate the term's spread.[113] Language from another of Dilulio's writings that laments the influence of "liberal elites" and "secularized" conservatives[114] was picked up in the Christian Coalition's Contract with the American Family to justify advocacy for harsh criminal punishment to stem the tide of rising crime.[115]

And yet Dilulio's underlying claims were not strictly partisan. "Unless we do something about that cadre of young people—tens of thousands of them born out of wedlock, without parents, without supervision, without any structure, without any conscience developing—because they literally have not been socialized, they literally have not had an opportunity . . . we should focus on them now," one politician implored in 1993, speaking on the Senate floor in support of the Crime Bill. "If we don't, they will—or a portion of them will—become the predators 15 years from now."[116] That politician? Democratic senator from Delaware and future U.S. president Joe Biden.

Hillary Clinton has since called some parts of the Crime Bill a "mistake"[117] and in 2016 while running for president repudiated her use of the term "superpredator." "I shouldn't have used those words, and I wouldn't use them today," she said.[118] But she did use them, because at that time, speaking about crime and protecting the family—and a whole host of other issues centering on morality—was what savvy politicians did, serving as a stark reminder that shadow gospel messages are not inherently Republican messages. They are anti-liberal messages. Democrats who parrot them may not be framing their positions as anti-liberal as such, but one doesn't need to know that they are taking a demonological stance in order to do it. It happens any time there's reinforcement of "real" America and its traditional values set upon by some encoded liberal threat. The effect is to promote the demonological logic that you can't *not* vote for the war because that would make you a bad and unpatriotic American (or at least look like one to voters), or you can't *not* endeavor to keep our streets, or our families, or our institution of marriage safe, because if you didn't, that would make you a family hater. Or at least look like one to voters.

DON'T THINK OF AN ELEPHANT

Democrats and liberals can reinforce shadow gospel messaging even when they aren't trying to keep up with the demonological Joneses. The reason is both simple and complex: the shadow gospel and its asserted truths about liberals—they hate conservatives, families, God, America—are extremely powerful frames.

Frames are, in essence, cultural grammars, ways of understanding and describing the world that, according to sociologist Erving Goffman, help people answer the question, "What's going on here?"[119] In addition to providing cognitive shortcuts, frames often guide how people respond to things. A positive frame lends itself to positive responses; a negative frame lends itself to negative responses. George Lakoff builds on these ideas by exploring how the negation of frames still reinforces the frame.[120] As an example, he points to the imperative "don't think of an elephant." When you tell a person not to think of an elephant, the first thing they do is think of an elephant. In the same way, if an issue is framed in a particular way, for example, by using highly charged emotional language, even criticizing the issue highlights and indeed foregrounds that emotional charge.

Lakoff's argument about frames emerged from his analysis of the Republicans' 1994 Contract with America. As he explains, he didn't understand how Republican positions on tax cuts connected to their social positions on "family values" until he began articulating the frames that distinguished conservative and progressive worldviews.[121] Lakoff's reflections yielded his 2004 book, *Don't Think of an Elephant!*, in which he explains Republican successes in selling policies that otherwise were out of step with majority public opinion. Over forty years, he argues, rightwing politicians, working closely with conservative think tanks and corporate donors, and evangelized by rightwing media working off the same set of talking points, had developed a sophisticated communications strategy that reframed key issues in such a way that the debate was slanted by virtue of the frame. For instance, by describing tax cuts for corporations as "tax relief for middle-class families," anyone who opposed a Republican tax plan could be attacked for opposing middle-class relief.[122]

In the introduction to *Don't Think of an Elephant!*, progressive activist Don Hazen sums up the successes of Republican communications. "Even our allies were using language invented by the conservatives," he explains, "shooting themselves in the foot every time."[123] Democrats and liberals—at least, "liberals" as defined by the shadow gospel—enact this dynamic whenever they deny or attempt to preempt any of the four shadow gospel truths.

Barack Obama's fraught relationship with the American flag lapel pin illustrates how attempts to contradict a shadow gospel frame help reinforce that frame. In 2007, then-candidate Obama discussed his reasoning for retiring his flag pin. He admitted to a reporter that he wore it immediately following the 9/11 attacks but grew disillusioned by the politics surrounding the pin and the fact that it became, in his estimation, a substitute for true patriotism. "I decided I won't wear that pin on my chest," Obama explained. "Instead I'm going to try to tell the American people what I believe what will make this country great and hopefully that will be a testimony to my patriotism."[124]

Echoing rightwing rumors that Obama didn't place his hand on his heart during the Pledge of Allegiance and that he generally lacked patriotism, Fox News pounced on Obama's statement about flag pins.[125] An October 5, 2007, episode of Fox News Live captured the tenor of the coverage.[126] Co-host E. D. Hill discussed the flag pin controversy with Fox legal analyst Andrew Napolitano and Fox News Radio co-host Brian Kilmeade, with claims such as, Obama is "anti–Betsy Ross" (Kilmeade), that Obama was disrespecting the flag in order to appeal to "hard-left voters" (Napolitano), and that Obama's assertion that he didn't wear the flag pin was similar to Bill Clinton's assertion of Monica Lewinsky that "I did not have sex with that woman" (Hill). Obama's top Democratic rivals issued statements in response to the controversy. Hillary Clinton explained that wearing a flag pin, flying the flag, pledging allegiance to the flag, and talking about American values were among the many ways a person could demonstrate patriotism. Joe Biden's spokesperson announced that Biden usually wore a flag pin. Dennis Kucinich's spokesperson didn't mention the pin but stated that the senator carried a miniature copy of the Constitution around in his pocket.[127]

That April, Obama was photographed wearing a flag pin in Pittsburgh, prompting a question about the pin and patriotism at a televised ABC debate the following week.[128] Obama called the controversy a manufac-tured issue. For the remainder of the campaign, he continued sometimes wearing his pin and continually facing criticism about it from Republicans. When those Republicans would be asked why they weren't wearing flag pins (and they often weren't),[129] their answers reflected an implicit truth: as Republicans, they didn't have to.

In contrast, Democrats who thrashed against challenges to their patri-otism by wearing flag pins or touting American values or throwing their mini-Constitutions at reporters during interviews weren't likely to con-vince even casual demonologists of their patriotism. The same is true for any (accused) liberal who responds to a demonological claim by insisting how much they respect opposing perspectives, how safe and decent they are around children, or how they actually do have a moral compass. What these performances are much more likely to do is reinforce the underlying frame that these are qualities naturally lacking in liberals, and which there-fore need to be proven.

ALL PUSHBACK IS GOOD PUSHBACK

Democrats and other accused liberals have many reasons for wanting to push back against shadow gospel messages. Anti-liberal demonology is predicated on falsehood; everything it touches is misinformation. As the last several years of American chaos highlight, rampant misinformation can be devastating to public health, public safety, and civic engagement, and it undercuts social justice and pluralism more broadly when demonolog-ical falsehoods threaten the speech, bodily autonomy, or lives of targeted groups. It can feel—and may objectively be—irresponsible, cowardly, or downright cruel to say nothing, to let toxic falsehoods simmer. *And*, attacks against the shadow gospel by "liberals," whatever that term might mean, strengthens the shadow gospel. Laughter—for many, a reflexive response to the "baroque strangeness" that so often emerges from the shadow gos-pel's excesses[130]—is an especially powerful amplifier.

The shadow gospel backlash effect has a long history. In the 1950s and 1960s, many social scientists and political historians regarded the white anticommunist family as an incubator of racism, with anticommunism increasingly described as a mental disorder. These researchers worried about the children raised in such environments and for the country as a whole if it absorbed a generation of fascist ducklings.[131] Michelle Nickerson emphasizes that studies focusing on and attempting to push back against political toxicity in the white family had a profoundly galvanizing effect on anticommunist mothers. These mothers quickly took up activist arms against a "mental health establishment" they claimed was a stronghold of Communist subversion and which was said to include psychologists, therapists, school guidance counselors, and even government bureaucrats administering state mental health services. Anticommunism *was* fascist. It was also white supremacist. Both things undermine democracy. And yet by saying so, researchers created a new category of enemy for anticommunists to rail against and reinforced their existing mistrust of the state.[132]

This is the problem with demonology; it is quite literally defined against its opposition. The stronger the opposition, the stronger the belief in one's own cause and, indeed, in one's basic sense of self. Rupert Murdoch was well aware of this dynamic from the inception of Fox News. He recognized that negative pushback from established networks—and from "elites" generally—was an "added benefit" to the Fox brand.[133] Fox subsequently built its populist, sensationalist, demonological style around an outsider identity tethered to the idea that liberals think you, the Fox News viewers, are stupid, which is what unites us as "real" Americans.[134] Giving its audience a reason to feel mocked and disrespected was a basic part of Fox's communications strategy. It was good for the network whenever Fox, any of its hosts, or any of the media and entertainment figures Fox claimed as their own, were in fact sneered at or seemed like they were being sneered at. That only proved elite antagonism and bias.[135] All the more reason to keep watching Fox News.

Fox's embrace, defense, and simultaneous attacks on behalf of Samuel Wurzelbacher during the 2008 presidential election exemplify this dynamic.[136] Wurzelbacher, a plumber, had asked then-candidate Barack Obama a question about Obama's proposed tax policy during a campaign stop. Republican candidate John McCain later referred to Wurzelbacher as "Joe the Plumber" during a televised debate with Obama, and suddenly Wurzelbacher was a political star. Fox News quickly adopted Wurzelbacher as the face of working-class America and began highlighting what they claimed was sustained mockery of Wurzelbacher by Democrats.

In a representative October 2008 episode of *Hannity & Colmes*, Sean Hannity declared that Wurzelbacher had been "criticized about everything" by the news media and Democrats (including the fact that the head of the plumber's union in Toledo, Ohio, where Wurzelbacher worked, revealed that "Joe the Plumber" didn't have his plumber's license, an assertion that Wurzelbacher eventually confirmed).[137] Hannity even teed up a clip of Obama and Joe Biden reflecting on "Joe's" reportedly high annual salary and laughing about McCain's choice to parade Wurzelbacher around as a campaign prop. Hannity framed this as an attack on working-class Americans everywhere. "Let's watch as Biden and Obama mock him, and listen to the laughing in the crowd as we play this," Hannity states.[138]

By playing a clip of "liberal" laughter ostensibly directed at "real" America, Hannity and his show's producers were exploiting a central dynamic of the shadow gospel: that liberal pushback, and especially liberal laughter, reinforces the need for a unified and hyperdefensive oppositional identity. Whether those attacks are merely demonologically decoded or are actually directed at conservatives, pushback feeds into the shadow gospel myth of the beleaguered, censored conservative. The truth is that no amount of "liberal" pushback has ever come close to matching the preemptive, progressive, highly strategic efforts undertaken by the anti-liberal right to wage war and colonize culture. What the shadow gospel does best is obscure that asymmetry.

NOT-SO-BELEAGUERED CONSERVATIVES

In particular, the shadow gospel avoids telling stories that show how significantly the activist left—that is to say, actual leftist political advocacy—has been disadvantaged by the same dynamics that have benefited the right. For instance, while the left had a foothold on AM radio as those networks first flourished, leftwing radio was stymied by competition from National Public Radio (NPR), which was subsidized by the government and had better sound quality and reach. Upstart leftwing radio wasn't able to colonize the dial in the way that rightwing radio could.[139]

The activist left was also much more unwieldy in their messaging, preventing them from harnessing the messaging power of the "rhetoric of simplification"[140] successfully embraced by rightwing activists like Phyllis Schlafly and Beverly LaHaye as they pushed to block passage of the ERA. Feminists promoting the ERA were torn between competing visions of how radically and confrontationally to undertake the fight and how strongly to push for gay rights and abortion rights as part of an overall feminist agenda. There was no messaging lockstep; therefore, there was no consistent, wraparound messages.[141]

That there was no message convergence on the left speaks to another important distinction. As the New Right ascended, leftist activists did not have a comparable network infrastructure or even awareness of the extent to which the rightwing was entangled with itself.[142] One basic reason was that progressive thought tended to be produced within and tended to remain confined to the comparatively closed university system; these were the kinds of experts that had, as Reece Peck explains, "high degrees of intellectual autonomy but low degrees of public engagement."[143] In contrast—and often because they felt or chose to be alienated from universities—many rightwing intellectuals gravitated toward public communications–focused think tanks, whose interconnected networks were facilitated by generous corporate endowments. Funding that, needless to say, was not extended to those on the left. Progressive and centrist intellectuals did just as much work as their conservative counterparts. And yet the rightwing was able to monopolize the ideas industry and, indeed, could have been mistaken as the only group who had any ideas, because those were the only ideas the American public was regularly encountering.[144]

YES WE CAN?

The rise of social media, mapped onto the Obama era, gave the right yet another boost. This is not what conservatives tend to say about social media; rather, the focus is on claims of censorship by Big Tech, denounced as a liberal bastion walking in lockstep with the Democratic Party. Conservatives aren't the only group with an alternative narrative. The dominant story of social media—told by many journalists, academics, activists, and even the platforms themselves—is of democratization and the boosting of progressive movements.

In her study of digital activists across the political spectrum, Jen Schradie acknowledges that some leftwing causes and groups have unquestionably benefited from digital organizing. However, rather than being a great political equalizer and allowing for truly democratized participation, social media and the activism it facilitates inherently favors conservatives. Network structures simply benefit the kind of activism that has long been established on the right.[145]

Schradie's analysis of the Tea Party demonstrates how digital organizing favors the rightwing. Ostensibly focused on economic issues and the push for small government reforms, the Tea Party emerged as Barack Obama took office in 2009. He had inherited a mess. The country was spiraling into financial catastrophe, necessitating massive bailouts of the auto industry and banking sector. Sidestepping the fact that it was President George W. Bush who initiated the bailouts, conservatives around the country rallied under the Tea Party banner, which provided a forum for participants to express what they saw as "authentic patriotism." Theda Skocpol and Vanessa Williamson explain that this "patriotism" aligned with the implicit (and often explicit) demand, "I want my country back!"[146] Tea Partiers also railed against Obama's plans for the Affordable Care Act, dubbed "Obamacare," which they immediately denounced as socialist.

In comparing the rise of the Tea Party with less successful leftwing causes and groups, Schradie found that economic class played a particularly important differentiating role. Individual rightwing activists may not have been wealthy, but they had access to a sprawling network of well-funded conservative think tanks and political advocacy organizations, including the Koch Brothers' Americans for Prosperity, that provided logistic support and political and technological trainings for Tea Party members.[147] A second factor driving the activist gap was organization. Previous chapters have emphasized the extent to which conservative groups have developed a political culture of organization, with top-down management structures and teams of people dedicated to common goals. As Schradie emphasizes, "digital activism takes work, and work takes organization,"[148] and this was something that the right had that the left did not.

The final characteristic that separated right and leftwing activism in the late 2000s was what Schradie describes as ideology—and which we would reframe as demonology. Rightwing groups affiliated with the Tea Party had a unified mission of evangelizing positive truths around freedom (theirs, anyway) and negative truths around the people accused of trying to take those freedoms away (liberals in media and government). These efforts took a strong reformist stance: the point of the activism was to influence the influencers in order to change laws and reshape the political environment to be more favorable to conservative values and causes.[149] Mimicking the feminists' disadvantage during the 1970s ERA fight, leftwing groups were always more fractured in their messaging and, critically, did not embrace the role of cultural evangelist so uniformly.[150] Given all this, of course the Tea Party thrived; it had, quite literally, every advantage.

DEMOCRATS ARE GOING TO KILL YOU

With the winds once again at their backs, Republicans, fueled by the Tea Party movement, dominated the 2012 midterms. But the Tea Party wasn't exclusively a product of digital organizing. It simultaneously fueled and was fueled by the energies of Fox News, particularly as Fox shifted its branding strategy away from attacking the cable news competition and toward attacking the Obama administration, a cause Roger Ailes actively embraced.[151] Indeed, throughout Obama's first term, as the Tea Party went, so too did Fox News. By promoting and sympathetically covering Tea Party events, "Fox News fans morphed into activists, and the activists became marketing vehicles for Fox News," Reece Peck explains.[152] Fox also helped amplify a seemingly endless series of anti-Obama stories that augmented its long-established populist sensationalism with populist conspiracism.[153]

One such story was the "death panel" controversy promoted by Sarah Palin in 2009. A year earlier, Palin, then governor of Alaska, had been tapped by Republican presidential candidate John McCain to be his running mate. As a political unknown outside her home state, Palin was the perfect person to carry the "real American" populist mantle. She also proved to be the perfect person to evangelize the shadow gospel's increasingly trollish articulation of anti-liberal demonology. Palin's incendiary attacks against Obama, liberals, and the "lame-stream media"[154] made her an instant celebrity. When Fox's spotlight swiveled to Obama's alleged association with college radical Bill Ayers, with whom Obama had a casual acquaintanceship, Palin went for the folksy jugular, claiming that Obama "pals around with terrorists,"[155] a statement with double resonance for a Fox News audience regularly warned that Obama was a "secret Muslim" and maybe not even an American.[156]

Palin never made it to the White House, but she knew how to keep herself in the news. Death panels were a shadow gospel no-brainer. The controversy stemmed from a provision in the Affordable Care Act that would have provided government subsidies for doctors' appointments in which patients discussed living wills and other end-of-life issues. A conservative commentator falsely claimed that this provision included a euthanasia directive for seniors, which Palin further distorted into the accusation that Democrats planned to haul senior citizens and people with disabilities in front of panels of government bureaucrats so that they could decide who would be euthanized. "Such a system is downright evil," Palin declared in a Facebook post.[157] Fox News ran with the death panels story[158] and later offered Palin a $1 million contract as a Fox News contributor.[159] The deeply demonological implication was that Democrats were so depraved that they would kill your grandmother, or kill *you*, if they were given the chance.

The initial narrative twisting of the ACA provision was already egregious. Palin warped it beyond recognition—and in so doing, exemplified how unmoored the shadow gospel had become. A supercharge of a supercharge of a supercharge now loosed on social media and incentivized by an algorithmically driven attention economy, the shadow gospel had even more networks to inundate with its messages, even more potential to take things out of context, even more opportunity to obscure its messages' origins. The egregiousness of its falsehoods grew, including the racist Birther conspiracy theory that rejected Obama's U.S. citizenship on the grounds that the president was Black (alleged foreign birth was cited, but Obama's Blackness, reframed as an inherent un-Americanness, was ultimately the issue). There was ample proof that Obama was a citizen. That proof was publicized. It didn't matter. Nothing offered up by a liberal could be trusted; everything they did strengthened the conspiracy theory. Donald Trump smelled an opportunity. So did Fox News, as the latter gave the former constant airtime to promote Birtherism[160] and wink to the audience about "just asking questions."

How Democratic politicians and other alleged and self-identifying liberals tried to placate, fact check, and push back against these kinds of claims would have been just fine if the debates had been ideological, centered on one set of policies pit against another set of policies. But they were not ideological; they were demonological and increasingly deranged, built upon decades of historically disconnected myth, enveloped within a realm of shadowy bizarre that unified all enemies as "liberals," and animated by the transformation of the apocalypse into a push for clicks. All the things one would typically do in politics—from coordinated attacks to coordinated compromise—just ended up feeding the shadow gospel beast. And it was about to get hungrier.

CONCLUSION: THE DEVIL YOU KNOW

Crouched down, intense and wild-eyed in the shadows, the figure of the Roman god Saturn in Francisco Goya's painting *Saturn Devouring His Son* grips the decapitated torso of one of his children.[1] The violence is recent; he is eating. But Saturn's movement, for the moment, seems frozen, as if suddenly discovered. His child's arm dangles from the black hole of his mouth. Was this the son prophesied to overthrow him? Even if it wasn't, would he have let him live? Saturn's eyes answer emptily: no. The threat of a threat is still a threat.

Just like Saturn, the shadow gospel has no loyalty. Its cannibalistic, even filicidal, impulse is most visible in its attacks on its most conservative and devout offspring. The same groups of people who helped institutionalize anti-liberal demonology, who tried to harness it for electoral or personal gain, or who simply humored it, have found themselves subject to precisely the same anti-liberal attacks that didn't seem so bad when they were directed at *real* liberals. The shadow gospel's Saturn will turn on anyone who questions its myths. But it is a particular kind of monster that will murder its own children.

SATURN COMES FOR THE REPUBLICAN PARTY

In 2013, a contingent of Freedom Caucus House Republicans—those who translated Tea Party energies into electoral success during the 2010 midterms, giving Republicans control of the House and John Boehner the title of Speaker—attempted to hitch debt ceiling negotiations to repealing Obamacare. This was a dangerous game of chicken. Not raising the debt ceiling, a vote that takes place in Congress annually, would mean that the United States couldn't pay its debts. A national default would almost certainly result in a pummeling recession. Thus by threatening a no vote, Freedom Caucus members and their ringleader Senator Ted Cruz of Texas, who directed the House charge despite his seat in the opposite chamber, were essentially saying: *Obamacare goes or the economy goes.* Caucus members were willing to take such a risk for two basic reasons. First, they hated Obamacare. Second, they hated Obama. Destroying the administration's signature piece of legislation would have been a victory on both fronts.

Speaker Boehner went along with the plan, pushing the Freedom Caucus's demands in front of every television camera he could find. In response, the Freedom Caucus hailed him as a hero and a "true conservative."[2] In his 2021 memoir *On the House*, Boehner admits that he thought the Freedom Caucus's plan was "insanity" and yet another example of the "kamikaze stunts" the Freedom Caucus, described by Boehner as the "chaos caucus," was constantly trying to pull.[3] This wasn't conservatism, Boehner argues; there was no guiding ideology, no consistency. They just wanted to fight, but who exactly they were fighting against wasn't clear. The Establishment? That's what they said, but Boehner admits that he never knew what that meant—and doesn't think they did either. He also admits that he didn't understand why they said he was a "true conservative" for supporting such a terrible, dangerous idea.[4]

Yet he continued his support. As leader of the Republican House conference, it was his job to advocate for his members. This was, in addition, a nice change of pace. From the very moment he was sworn in as Speaker, the Freedom Caucus hadn't just *not* embraced him as a true conservative, they had attacked him mercilessly for being an "Establishment asshole"[5] and, worse, as some kind of liberal because he . . . was seen in public talking with President Obama? Because he affirmed that Obama was a U.S. citizen? It was, Boehner explains, "bizarre."[6] He had spent his career proving his conservative bona fides, including his enthusiastic signing of the Contract with America in 1994; he was a Reagan Republican through and through. But thanks to the chaos caucus and its incessant effort to kneecap the opposition (which apparently included other Republicans) and secure prime-time cable news slots to stoke even more outrage, Boehner found himself constantly on the defensive "as if I were a hippie with flip flops and beads plotting a socialist takeover of America. I didn't get it," he states.[7]

Boehner was similarly baffled during the 2013 debt ceiling fight as Ted Cruz and his House allies lashed out at Republican dissenters on the grounds that they weren't "pure" conservatives—suggesting that agreeing with Ted Cruz was the litmus test for whether someone was a true conservative. Having laid out the full 2013 story, including the last-minute aversion of disaster when the rest of the Republican conference rallied to overrule the Freedom Caucus, Boehner states with an almost audible sigh, "If reading this story now doesn't make sense to you, congratulations—I didn't understand it either. I still don't."[8]

Boehner's experience with the Freedom Caucus demonstrates that Democrats—and others described as "liberal"—weren't the only ones knocked off center by the shadow gospel. The former Speaker wouldn't be the last Republican to fall. By the time Donald Trump was sworn in as president in 2016, the shadow gospel had trained its cannibalistic sights on even more Republicans, including President George W. Bush, who Boehner muses is now "generally considered a liberal failure" by many of the same politicians who had forced Boehner to field "one batshit idea after another" when he was Speaker.[9] The so-called Never Trumpers, media figures and politicians who had resisted Trump's candidacy from the start, paid an especially high price. For holding an anti-Trump line, they were exiled from the Republican Party and received enormous amounts of harassment,[10] including death threats from Trump's Make America Great Again faithful.[11]

While many Democrats were more than happy to roll out the red carpet for the Never Trumpers, critics cautioned against giving these Republicans too much credit, as they had been active participants in the same rightwing media ecosystem that ultimately selected for a President Trump.[12] In short, before Saturn started feeding on them, they had spent years, even decades, feeding red meat to Saturn.

Tim Miller, a former GOP strategist who had traveled in John Boehner's orbit, began his career doing exactly that, which he describes with unusual candor in *Why We Did It: A Travelogue from the Republican Road to Hell*.[13] The purpose of writing the book, Miller explains, was to wrestle with Saturn directly; to understand why so many of his friends—former colleagues, pundits, politicians—allowed themselves to be drawn so fully into something that was "so unambiguously monstrous"; and, more than that, to understand "why they continued to do so once the monster became uncontrollable."[14] He offers up some answers—demonization of the left and the fun of the fight are recurring themes—but what he does most effectively is explain what it feels like to have been chewed up by the monster that you helped raise.

However sympathetically one might be inclined to view the Never Trumpers' plight (Saturn, incidentally, is the planetary ruler of karma in esoteric circles), the MAGA purity test intensified following Trump's two impeachments; the majority of those who voted to convict retired from politics or were pushed out by pro-Trump primary voters.[15] Many were forced to exit public life entirely, as conservative Trump critic Jonah Goldberg lamented.[16] Senator Mitt Romney from Utah, the sole Republican who voted to convict Donald Trump in 2020 on impeachment charges of abuse of power and one of seven Republicans who voted to convict in 2021 on charges of inciting an insurrection, was one of the exiled.[17] By 2023, he was spending $5,000 per day in security for his family.[18] Speaking to biographer McKay Coppins about his experiences following the January 6 insurrection, Romney offered an explanation of the party's chaotic turn by way of a Lord Tennyson quote: "This madness has come on us for our sins."[19]

The madness certainly came for Liz Cheney, representative from Wyoming and, at one point, Republican conference chairperson. Cheney had not been a Never Trumper in 2016. She had supported Trump in his bid for the presidency. She continued supporting him after he was elected.[20] As a congressional representative, she voted consistently with Trump's political agenda (93 percent of the time by one estimate[21]), and as a citizen, she voted for a second Trump term in the 2020 election.[22] None of this was out of political character. Cheney had considered joining the House Freedom Caucus[23] and during the Obama era had harnessed precisely the grievance-based politics that placed her squarely on the side of the shadow gospel.[24]

But when Trump lost the presidential election in 2020 but insisted that he'd won, Cheney pushed back, factually stating the outcome of the election and refusing to entertain what became known as Trump's Big Lie. Following the January 6, 2021, attack on the U.S. Capitol, she voted to impeach Trump on charges of incitement of insurrection. She then agreed to co-chair the House Select Committee that would investigate the Capitol attack and Trump's role in promoting it.[25] Unsurprisingly, Cheney received ferocious pushback from pro-Trump politicians, particularly from the Freedom Caucus, which among other invectives accused her and Adam Kinzinger, the other Republican on the January 6 committee, of being "spies" for the Democrats.[26] Her Republican colleagues stripped her of her leadership position.[27] Her constituents voted her out of office.[28] Saturn had come for Liz Cheney.

Saturn is also, it seems, coming for Fox News. After the network correctly called Arizona for Joe Biden during the 2020 presidential vote count, Fox faced a deluge of criticism from its viewers and from Donald Trump. Text messages exchanged between Fox hosts and producers reveal that Fox employees were well aware of the blowback from audiences in real time.[29] They also reveal that Fox's most prominent hosts, including Tucker Carlson, were well aware that the election hadn't been stolen.[30] But they needed to support Trump and his Big Lie or their audience would make the network pay by flocking to even more pro-Trump networks like Newsmax or One America News. So in the months leading up to Biden's inauguration, they pushed Trump's lie and all the conspiracy theories that went along with it. Carlson even concluded his show monologue the night of the January 6 attack by insisting that it wasn't Trump supporters' fault that the attack happened. It was *their* fault, the liberals' fault, for not taking conservative grievances seriously—a statement he'd prefaced with the warning that Democrats would use January 6 to take away conservatives' rights.[31]

Fox paid a high price for their MAGA fan service. Their false claims about rigged voting machines yielded two major defamation suits, the discovery for which was what unearthed Fox hosts' damning post-election texts. Just as one of the suits was about to go to trial in March 2023, Fox paid a nearly $800 million settlement to the plaintiff, Dominion Voting Systems. As of this writing, Fox's other election disinformation suit, filed by electronic voting system company Smartmatic, is pending.[32]

Despite Fox's willingness to acquiesce to their audience and keep playing the anti-liberal hits, Trump has neither forgiven nor forgotten what he sees as its ultimate disloyalty. He continually slings invectives at the network[33]—which his spokesperson suggested was "controlled opposition,"[34] that is, a puppet for the libs—from Truth Social, the microblogging platform Trump founded after he was banned from Twitter following the insurrection. Fox's once-loyal MAGA audience also wavered after Tucker Carlson was fired from the network the same week the $800 million settlement was reached.[35] Many viewers opted instead, as Fox hosts had feared, for Newsmax or One America News or any of the other alternative channels, including the show Carlson began hosting on X, the social platform previously known as Twitter.

It might seem surprising that people as conservative as John Boehner, Mitt Romney, Liz Cheney, and Never Trump Republicans—to say nothing of the temple mount of the shadow gospel known as Fox News—would end up in the belly of the shadow gospel beast. Where there is anti-liberal demonology, however, there is great unwieldiness—and great potential for cannibalism. After half a century of growth, the shadow gospel has become so effective at demonizing the left that even the *right* becomes the left when those on the right fail to do "right" right—which could simply mean disagreeing with Ted Cruz.

Those unconvinced by the shadow gospel frame might be inclined to brush aside much of this book's argument as "politics as usual." Of course Republicans demonize Democrats; demonizing the opponent is what you *do*, that's how you win elections—by making the other side look as bad as possible. The rampant cannibalization within the Republican Party undercuts that line of critique. Republicans devouring other Republicans runs counter to expected ideological patterns, speaking instead to what are, objectively, deeply weird cross-partisan pressures. Our established political frameworks can't account for these pressures. A shadow gospel frame predicts them.

SATURN COMES FOR THE EVANGELICAL CHURCH

A similar cannibalization has been unfolding within Evangelicalism. Years of tensions over COVID lockdowns, vaccines, and various conspiracy theories like the satanic panicked QAnon theory—a narrative initially tethered to Donald Trump's presidency that has spun out into increasingly vague claims about alleged pedophilic and sex trafficking schemes coordinated by Democrats—have threatened to tear local congregations apart, as many pastors scramble to understand why God is being used to justify political violence, continued false belief in a stolen 2020 election, and outrageous claims about satanic sexual abuse.[36] "You need to know how crazy this is," one pastor lamented to a QAnon-believing, January 6–supporting parishioner.[37] "Losing a congregation to QAnon" has become a common framing in news articles describing the trend, which many of the pastors interviewed connect to the COVID-19 pandemic and the increased circulation during lockdown of antistatist satanic conspiracy theorizing.[38]

But it's what happened to the pastors who resisted these beliefs, who affirmed the outcome of the 2020 election and supported COVID mitigation measures, that is most indicative of Saturn's appetites. In a March 2022 survey of Protestant pastors, 42 percent said they were considering leaving their congregations; the top two reasons cited were the immense stress of the job and current political divisions.[39] Specifically, rampant Trumpism.[40] As one Evangelical leadership coach explained, the decision to leave ultimately boils down to "a matter of conscience and mental health."[41] And that's when the pastor has the choice. Others have been forced out of their positions for attempting to debunk pro-Trump conspiracy theories or for speaking out against the January 6 insurrection.[42] Reflecting on his decision to leave his congregation and indeed to leave the United States entirely, a young pastor mused, "What do you do when your God loses?"[43]

For those Evangelicals who find themselves alienated from their congregations and even the denomination writ large, the fact that contemporary Evangelical Christianity has less and less room for anything that deviates from hardline rightwing politics is unquestionably jarring, distressing, and disappointing. But given Evangelicalism's history it is not surprising. As it coalesced in the 1950s, New Evangelicalism actively cannibalized American Christianity. It may have painted itself as the middle-road alternative between modernism and fundamentalism, but it embodied instead the most extreme versions of each: it was extremely progressive in its communication strategy and extremely demonological in its approach to theology. Through both channels, Evangelicalism found more devils than any other denomination and did more to fight them, including among the ranks of fellow Christians.

As an example, there had been a growing Evangelical leftwing movement in the 1970s motivated by opposition to the Vietnam War, support for civil rights, and concern about global hunger. Left-leaning Evangelicals tried to rally other Evangelicals to these causes.[44] But by the 1980s, actual Evangelical liberals had been driven away by a combatively conservative Evangelicalism. As this book chronicles, the 1970s purge hadn't been the first. Chapter 2 focused on the New Evangelical effort to weed out suspected liberals in their own ranks—with "liberal" vaguely mapping onto "modern," which was only a problem when it was used toward ends not supported by the New Evangelicals. Chapter 2 also considered the New Evangelicals' anti-liberal efforts across U.S. society as a whole. Leaders like Billy Graham undertook a sustained, coordinated campaign to identify, declare as satanic, and do righteous battle with all the "liberal" elements claimed to make the United States a hell on earth.

So of course contemporary establishment Evangelicals would be attacked for aligning with or being liberals. What else could these figures be accused of being? What could possibly be *worse* to accuse them of being? When considering the strange case of former vice president Mike Pence, whose entire political identity centers on his conservative Evangelicalism, one could try to argue that something other than an endemic anti-liberal demonology is the reason for his being booed at the 2023 Family Leadership Summit, an Evangelical Christian conference, or for the accusation, lobbed by the Summit host Tucker Carlson, that Pence wasn't anti-anti-Christian enough.[45] However one would be hard-pressed to come up with an alternative explanation for the fact that, within many Evangelical churches, parishioners have started complaining to their pastors that the teachings of Jesus Christ—which preach forgiveness, acceptance of difference, and compassion toward the poor—are "liberal talking points."[46]

SATURN COMES FOR SECULARS

The distress, exhaustion, and even panic palpable in the statements of so many Evangelical leaders reflect how disorienting it is, and indeed how *scary* it is, to suddenly realize that one's arm is being chewed off—especially for those who did not realize they were making a deal with such a devil. Shadow gospel Saturn doesn't just cannibalize from within the church, however. For decades he has frightened people *away* from the church and from religion generally.

Beginning in the 1990s, the rising influence of the Religious Right and their "family values" crusading alienated many left-leaning American Christians, prompting them to re-identify as secularists or "nones."[47] Mainline Protestantism, a religious tradition with much more moderate and modernist roots (hence the wrath of the New Evangelicals in the 1950s), was most impacted by the rising rates of spiritual attrition. As Mainline numbers diminished, the power of Evangelical Christianity grew. Or to frame the dynamic another way, the size of the Evangelical Jesus fish stayed the same; what changed was the size of the pond, reflecting the overall shrinking number of American Christians.

As the dominant religious voice, Evangelicalism—for decades the central hub of shadow gospel messages about an America transformed into a liberal hellscape—became the face of American Christianity, defining the shape and scope of American morality and even what it meant to be a religious person. Ask any of the tens of millions of Americans, mostly Mainline Protestants, who have left religion in the last thirty years to describe what they think of American religion, and the answer will very likely be rooted in Evangelical Christianity.

But Evangelical Christianity is not *the* Christianity; it's *a* Christianity built on shadows that has successfully positioned itself as the American standard-bearer through decades of intense anti-liberal messaging. As more Christians have become more estranged from the moral narrowness of these messages, the pond has shrunk even further. Compounding the liberal Christian exodus, many Americans who are not Christian, and who mistake Evangelicalism for Christianity writ large, have developed increasing resistance and even hostility to the idea of Christianity. Indeed, at present, Evangelicals are viewed extremely negatively, mapping onto sharp partisan divisions; 47 percent of Democrats view Evangelical Christians negatively, an even higher percentage than how Republicans view Muslims or atheists.[48] Rising animosity toward Evangelical Christians, in turn, feeds into anti-Christian grievance narratives—narratives that are ultimately useful for bolstering the myth of the beleaguered, censored, just-about-to-be-canceled implicitly Christian conservative.

There is much to critique in the moral apocalypticism and associated moral narrowness that so many Evangelicals have embraced. What we contend is that what secularists—and other disaffected Christians—are often reacting to isn't Christianity as such. Christianity as such warrants grounded theological discussion, debate, and critique in its own right. But what tends to be discussed, debated, and critiqued in the United States instead is an anti-liberalism fine-tuned over decades to resist compromise, coexistence, and the willingness to extend grace to different others. In fashioning itself as the only true American Christianity, Evangelicalism has made Christianity in the United States smaller. And the less Christianity there is, the more the shadow gospel can parade around in its skin. Journalist Tim Alberta—a practicing Christian and pastor's son—gestures toward this tension in his exploration of the crisis within Evangelicalism, though he identifies the problem as too many parishioners turning away from the unseen realm of the spirit and focusing instead on secular, worldly concerns.[49] We contend that many of the parishioners Alberta describes likely *are* focused on an unseen realm. It's that the spirit they turned to is a black hole.

MONSTER HUNTING

Whether it's biting the hands that enable it or scaring away the moderates that could temper its influence, the consequences of the shadow gospel do not stay confined to conservative and religious circles. Millions of others feel those teeth, which is why literacy around shadow gospel messages is so important. You can't fight a monster if you don't know where to find it.

OUTRIGHT CONSPIRACISM

Sensational, lurid, and at times downright satanic conspiracy theories are the most conspicuous outcropping of shadow gospel messages. At this rhetorical level, Donald Trump's position as MAGA messiah is also most conspicuous. Reporters and other cultural critics discuss Trump's religious hold over his followers—and the bombast of his proclamations—with grave concern or simple befuddlement, particularly when reflecting on why such an obviously irreligious man would appeal so intensely to Evangelical voters.[50] For their part, Trump's supporters have adopted him as their savior unabashedly, even gleefully, a role that Trump actively embraced in the lead-up to the 2024 Iowa caucuses when he released a campaign ad declaring himself chosen by God to be the "caretaker" of the nation.[51]

However Trump's exalted position is presented, the conspiratorial din over which he presides makes pointed accusations against specific groups of nefarious liberals. It also singles out individual liberal masterminds; frequent targets have included the former head of the National Institute of Allergy and Infectious Diseases Dr. Anthony Fauci, billionaire philanthropist George Soros, and pop star Taylor Swift.

There is, without question, a *wildness* to these kinds of accusations. But they can't accurately be described as extreme, as this form of pro-Trump conspiracism has been actively embraced within the institutional Republican Party and, further, is built on decades of mainstreamed ideas about the danger and perfidy of liberals. The swirl of conspiratorial falsehoods about January 6 is a case in point. Following a short-lived bipartisan consensus about the chaos and terror of the day as well as Trump's complicity in fomenting it,[52] the Republican Party, rightwing media lead by Fox News, and networks of funders returned to promoting falsehoods about the 2020 election. They quickly began reframing the Capitol attack as "legitimate political discourse"[53] or as explicitly positive, with some claiming that the insurrection was actually a "false flag"[54] operation perpetuated by radical leftists in antifa or the Black Lives Matter movement who were posing as Trump supporters to make the former president look guilty.

In these instances, the damaging consequences of flash-bang conspiracy theories might seem straightforward. In some ways they are; particularly in the context of January 6, they justify and promote violence and are devastating to public discourse. But in other ways, the flash-bang is a distraction. It is all too easy to lose the demonology for the conspiracy, to point and perhaps laugh at off-the-wall claims about satanic Democrats or Taylor Swift rigging the Superbowl as part of a Pentagon psyop[55] and assume that it is self-contained *craziness*, something that only die-hard Trump fans believe. The conspiracism might be flash-bang, but the demonology is institutional. Excessive focus on the former obscures the pervasiveness of the latter among those who are *not* MAGA diehards. Literacy is most needed when fringe positions have mainstream foundations.

THE *ANTI-* FRAME

If the shadow gospel's conspiratorial frame is a cacophonous clatter, its *anti-* frame is a steady drumbeat against corrosive liberal influences in society. Conservative discourse around January 6 that doesn't specifically posit a Democratic conspiracy highlights this distinction. There are, Anthony Nadler and Doron Taussig emphasize, many conservatives who reject the violence of the day and generally accept the 2020 election results yet still feel attacked and blamed by what they see as a mainstream liberal culture that condemns all conservatives as guilty by MAGA association. As punishment for the crime of being themselves, these conservatives feel that they are being pushed from public life by liberals—an outcrop of the identity-shaping deep story that Nadler and Taussig describe as The Shunning.[56]

The Shunning is the anti-liberal backdrop for conservative worry over being silenced and disenfranchised. It can take many forms, some of which are spotlight-grabbing sensationalist or "we mean what we say but are also having fun with this" trollish. One especially antagonistic outcrop is the rightwing fight against "woke capitalism," a derisive term for companies that invest in or publicly embrace social, racial, and environmental justice efforts. Pizza Hut, for instance, was threatened with boycotts in 2022 after it recommended LGBTQ-themed books in its Book It! book club for pre-kindergarten through sixth grade readers.[57] Target faced enormous backlash in 2023—including physical threats to their employers—when it unveiled a Pride Month collection of merchandise.[58] And Anheuser-Busch Inbev, the company that produces Bud Light, caused an uproar in 2023 (and saw sales numbers plunge) when the company publicized sending a can of beer to trans social media influencer Dylan Mulvaney.[59] One conservative nonprofit organization even developed a "woke-o-meter" to assess which companies posed the greatest risk of "going woke." On Fox News, the organization's president encouraged readers to print out their report, take a copy to the suspect business, ask to speak to the manager, and say, in the president's words, "Why are you doing this? Are you going to cancel me?" The goal of these efforts isn't merely to boycott this or that offending consumer product. It's to create a "parallel economy"[60] in which demonologists can, in all facets of their life, avoid "liberals" and the discomfort or inconvenience they might cause.

The *anti-* frame is also central to the Trump era parents' rights movement, a loosely coordinated grassroots network of parents, mostly mothers, who initially coalesced in opposition to masking and other COVID mitigation efforts.[61] Their direct action efforts have included hijacking school board meetings, attempting to remove "liberal" school board members and librarians, running for school board, and harassing other parents.[62] Parents' rights advocates rely on anti-woke,[63] anti–critical race theory,[64] and anti-groomer[65] frames to push back against and pathologize what is seen as liberal indoctrination in K-12 classrooms. What *specifically* the parents' rights advocates are railing against is amorphous, as "woke" boils down to "thing in culture I don't like," "critical race theory" boils down to "discussion of whiteness I don't like," and "groomer" boils down to "queer person whose existence I don't like." Ultimately it all boils down to "liberal I don't like."

True to shadow gospel form, strategic communications are central to these activists' efforts. So is creating a devil in order to fight it. Republican senator John Kennedy of Louisiana provided a striking example of both in 2023 when, during a congressional hearing on book bans, he read into the congressional record sexually explicit passages from two books focused on queer identity and sexuality.[66] Both books had been frequent targets of book banning efforts. Failing to note that one of the passages was describing sexual abuse, Kennedy read lines about blow jobs, dildos, oral sex, and the mechanics of the sex act. Kennedy also failed to note that, contrary to his assertion that these books were being given to kids, neither of the books were shelved in the children's section.

Both omissions served to further the claim that liberals were actively and deliberately exposing children to sexually explicit content (which is not too far from the claim that these children were being "groomed" by pedophilic teachers and librarians). They also set a rhetorical trap: those who critiqued the book bans could be attacked for supporting "porn for kids." Illinois secretary of state Alexi Giannoulias, who had been called to testify in opposition to book bans, attempted to redirect the conversation, emphasizing that no one was advocating for children to read porn; the argument was that one group of parents shouldn't have the ability to impose their own standards onto other parents. But it was Kennedy's delivery of the passages that went viral; Fox News delighted in his ability to make "Dems squirm," as if he had revealed a hidden truth about the liberal agenda.[67] Kennedy underlined this point in a statement made following his viral turn. "Those demonizing parents for trying to protect the innocence of their children ought to be ashamed for defending explicitly sexual images and scenes in books that 10 year olds have access to," he wrote. "Parents aren't concerned about *The Catcher in the Rye*—they're worried that their children are being indoctrinated by radicals who think that exposing young students to pornographic material is what's best for their kids."[68]

Ostensibly, the point of parents' rights efforts is to provide parents with more oversight of their children's education, echoing Phyllis Schlafly's Protection of Pupil Rights Amendment fight of the 1980s; and ostensibly, the point of attacks against "woke capitalism" is to expose liberal corporate bias. The underlying concern, however, takes an eighty-year-old page out of the shadow gospel playbook: to push back against what is seen as the coordinated effort to erode traditional values, pathologize conservatism, and make children less likely to believe what their parents believe. The *anti*-frame, in short, is an extinction narrative—and liberals are the meteor.

However, because the claims aren't explicitly conspiratorial—at this level, believers are pointing to liberals as a broadly corrosive force, not telling stories about specific actors or ringleaders—their assertions are easily mistaken for policy-based arguments and, further, as part of an ongoing culture war in which a presumably coherent conservative ideology is pushing back against a presumably coherent liberal ideology. This is where rhetorical literacy is needed. The shadow gospel's *anti*- claims aren't about

policy and aren't grounded in ideology, reflected most basically in the neb-
ulousness of terms like "woke," "critical race theory," and "groomer."
These words don't mean anything consistent, other than "I don't like it."
Even the term "liberal" is untethered. When describing the liberal threat,
the respondents that Nadler and Taussig interviewed didn't cite specific sets
of policy positions. Instead, they described a style of mind: liberals' "contempt for what [the conservatives] viewed as traditional American culture
generally and conservatives specifically."[69] Trying to respond with counter-
arguments or counterproposals doesn't just miss the demonological point.
It *proves* the point of the demonologist: here comes a liberal, ready to shun.

THE *PRO-* FRAME

The shadow gospel is most effective, however—and not just with the
shadow faithful but with the broader population—when it is least conspiratorial, least negative, and most seemingly positive, even commonsensical.
The Republican Party gave a masterclass in shadow gospel *pro-* framings
with their 1994 Contract with America and the Christian Coalition's fol-
low-up Contract with the American Family. Chapter 4 showcased how,
beneath the surface of the pro-family agenda, there was a litany of anti-
liberal assertions that didn't directly veer into outright conspiracism but
easily dovetailed into parallel discourses about, for example, the "gay
agenda" said to be infiltrating culture and threatening children during the
1990s, a much uglier stance that the pro-family agenda helped obscure.

The pro–free speech position embraced by many on the right reflects a
similar sleight of hand. As they long have been, college campuses are particular hotbeds for these kinds of fights, where student activists and their
off-campus backers rally behind calls for "free speech" as a smokescreen
to pursue an anti-liberal agenda. One example is Turning Point USA, a
national organization of campus conservatives whose mission is to "identify, educate, train, and organize students to promote freedom," a statement offset on its website with an image of founder Charlie Kirk giving the
thumbs-up and double-captioned with a flashing banner that reads in part,
"We Believe in Freedom."[70] TPUSA also has a dedicated "Free Speech"
section on its website and a high school outreach program called "Free the
First" focused on promoting free speech ideals (activities include collating
a "cancel culture burn book," an unclear reference to the book used to col-
lect insults and gossip in the 2004 film *Mean Girls*, and encouraging student

members to film their classmates as they answer questions about free speech and censorship).[71]

TPUSA's positive framings of speech are balanced out by a growing database of alleged "radical professors" via its Professor Watchlist.[72] These professors are said to discriminate against conservative students and promote leftist propaganda, an abstract concept that includes research focusing on diversity and inclusion. Professors are publicly searchable by name; the site's profile of accused professors includes their photographs, descriptions of their work, and links to their university profiles, most of which list faculty emails, phone numbers, and the physical location of their offices on campus. Campus Reform is another conservative publication (its *pro-* frame raison d'être: "Leadership") with a dedicated "Free Speech Zone" section on its website. By foregrounding speech issues on campuses, it chronicles instances of what it calls "liberal bias and abuse,"[73] as well as "woke" teaching and research focusing on "race, equity, multiculturalism," and similar subjects.[74]

Of course, not chronicled by such organizations are the threats to free speech posed by demonological calls for "free speech." The full extent of self-censorship on college campuses—born of worry that one will come under fire for not seeming pro-conservative, pro-family, pro-religion, or pro-America enough—can be difficult to measure. Professors experiencing chilling effects, who would rather adjust course content to be less controversial or cancel courses entirely,[75] tend not to publicly advertise; that would defeat the entire purpose of trying to stay beneath the anti-woke radar. And yet this is the persistent, uneasy reality among a wide spectrum of faculty, particularly among adjunct and untenured faculty, women faculty, queer and trans faculty, faculty of color (especially those who study issues that could be denounced as "woke"), and faculty in states where legislators have taken aim at curricula focused on race and other social justice issues.[76]

The reality of *pro-* frames that must be emphasized is that, first, they always have a demonological shadow side and, second, they actually do the opposite of whatever they purport to advocate. This is where the minoritarianism of the shadow gospel is most insidious. Spoken by a demonologist, a pro–free speech stance, or a pro-family stance, or a pro-children stance isn't about protecting speech generally, or families generally, or children generally. It's about protecting *my* speech (or people saying the same things as me), *my* family (or families that resemble mine), *my* children (or children who act like mine do), and ultimately *my* comfort (or the comfort of people who are like me), regardless of what preserving a perfectly unperturbed, unfettered life might do to everyone else. And yet that *pro-*frame is the side that shines through. It sounds good and optimistic, even unassailable as a value. More compelling than that, most people would do just about anything to avoid the accusation that they are anti-speech, anti-family, anti-children—the list goes on—so shut their mouths and go along with the demonological program, not stopping to ask: *Whose* speech, *whose* families, *whose* children are actually under discussion here and, more important, whose are not?

SHADOW GOSPEL MIXOLOGY

Shadow gospel messages aren't always so cleanly parsed. Sometimes, outright conspiracism jumbles up with *anti-* and *pro-* framings. Such was the case in Donald Trump's now-infamous January 6, 2021, speech at the Ellipse, a park just south of the White House and two miles down the road from the U.S. Capitol.[77] Trump spoke as the 2020 election vote was being certified by Congress. Following the speech, members of the riled-up crowd made their way to the Capitol building. Chaos, destruction, and violence ensued, and the text of Trump's speech was later included in his second impeachment trial and the federal grand jury indictment over charges related to 2020 election subversion.

Unsurprisingly, Trump's most conspiratorial claims were also his most incendiary. He lobbed rapid-fire accusations against specific Democratic politicians, election workers, and other groups said to be aligned with Democrats, including local and state officials he accused of election fraud. He claimed that the media helped steal the election. He claimed that Big Tech rigged the election because Trump surprised them by winning in 2016. He rattled off so many detailed descriptions of the election's "explosions of bullshit" ("Bullshit! Bullshit!" the crowd chanted in response) that he implored the crowd not to get bored listening to him ("don't get bored, don't get angry with me because you're going to get bored because it's so much," he whined).

Trump augmented his conspiratorial grievances with a litany of corrosive people and things: his *anti-* list. He railed against ruthless "radical-left Democrats," the fake news media that suppresses thought and speech and is the "biggest problem we have in this country," Big Tech, the "radical left that tries to blacklist you" on social media, "weak Republicans," teachers attempting to indoctrinate your children, the "Liz Cheneys of the world," and a nebulous group that tears down monuments, heroes, and culture. Woven among his *anti-* list were all the things Trump said he loved: history, culture, the "real people" who built the nation, safety, the economy, the military, democracy, the Constitution, children, patriots, elections, and America.[78]

When these three framings fuse together in the same speech, it's easy to see how *pro-* frames are the other side of *anti-* frames, and how *anti-* frames are abstract versions of outright conspiracy theories. In Trump's January 6 speech, each frame feeds into the same objective: not just to overturn the election results and install Trump as president, and certainly not to establish a Christian theocracy. Instead, the ultimate goal is to fight the liberal devil. That is Trump's advocacy. That is what makes him such an effective shadow messiah. "We will not let them silence your voices. We're not going to let it happen, I'm not going to let it happen," Trump bellowed during the speech, to which the audience responded by chanting, "Fight for Trump! Fight for Trump!"—because he's the best at fighting the libs.

In everyday life, the connection between *pro-* frames, *anti-* frames, and outright conspiracism isn't always so clear. Being aware of the different forms the shadow gospel can take and, further, how all of its messages are fueled by the same demonological energy allows for keener discernment of what is actually being argued (or not argued) by a shadow gospel evangelist. This is an especially important literacy skill to develop in the absence of outright conspiracism, when attacks against teachers, trans kids, or the Liz Cheneys of the world are presented as ideological, or when statements about Jesus, the Bible, or flags and crosses are presented as theological. Or, most deceptively of all, when positions on the family, traditional values, or protecting children are presented as apolitical common sense.

It is July 2024 as we finalize edits on this book. Joe Biden is out as the Democratic nominee for President; Kamala Harris is in. Donald Trump survived an assassination attempt and then picked Senator JD Vance, an ambitious shadow gospel proselytizer, as his running mate. Despite a brief flirtation with "unity" messages following the shooting, Trump has been leaning hard into outright conspiracism and a demonology that doesn't even bother trying to hide behind euphemism; following Harris's ascension to the top of the Democratic ticket, Trump explicitly described her as "evil" and "sick," which he attributed to her radical liberalism.[79] Trump's outbursts directed at Harris are new, but they fit into an overall messaging strategy centered on anti-liberal demagoguing. For example—and there are many to choose from, particularly given his ongoing legal troubles and multiple felony convictions—Trump declared during his February 2024 Conservative Political Action Committee (CPAC) speech that "A vote for Trump is your ticket back to freedom, it's your passport out of tyranny and it's your only escape from Joe Biden and his gang's fast track to hell. And in many ways, we're living in hell right now." Trump also warned that, under a second Biden term, law enforcement would begin "hunting" for conservatives and people of faith. November 5 would therefore be "judgment day" for the "liars and cheaters and fraudsters and censors and imposters who have commandeered our government."[80]

But not everything in Trump's orbit is so demonologically noisy. The Trump-boosting Heritage Foundation is actively publicizing its plans to "institutionalize Trumpism" through its Project 2025 initiative, which seeks to reverse what it claims is institutional bias against conservatives—and to root out those who might resist.[81] Regardless of the 2024 election outcome, the push to translate shadow gospel bombast into bureaucracy is a long-term policy goal for conservative demonologists. Recognizing the three levels of pandemonic rhetoric will be a critical skill given the only certainty that can be stated about the election and its aftermath: more shadows are coming.

THE FUTURE OF THE SHADOW GOSPEL IS LIBERAL?

An intensifying shadow gospel would be damaging enough if it were confined to MAGA networks. But MAGA isn't the only demonological stronghold, thanks in part to a media landscape that facilitates messaging wraparound, obscures the origins of information (and sources of funding), and amalgamates content more intensely than in any previous era. Within such a hospitable communications environment, the seeds of anti-liberal demonology are cast into expected and unexpected places—including among networks of people who would describe themselves as liberal or would be placed, accurately or not, on the political left.

In the previous chapter, we discussed how self-identifying liberals, and particularly Democratic politicians, have fed into the shadow gospel's messages by embracing demonological *pro-* frames. Wearing American flag lapel pins, making sure the camera is rolling when saying the God part of the Pledge of Allegiance, carrying around pocket-sized Constitutions to flash at reporters, the list goes on—these kinds of behaviors reinforce the idea that, as a liberal Democrat, one's patriotism and overall morality is in question. In recent years, self-identifying liberals and leftists have also embraced demonological *anti-* frames—or at the very least, end up making some of the same *anti-* arguments using the same words as anti-liberals.

One example can be found in Jacob Nelson and Seth Lewis's study of audience trust in the news media during the height of the COVID-19 crisis.[82] In qualitative interviews with an ideologically diverse sample of news consumers, Nelson and Lewis found that, across the political spectrum, respondents adopted an anti-journalism stance; they described the news as inherently biased and therefore untrustworthy. Because of this perceived bias, many respondents, including self-described liberals, indicated that they did their own fact checks of news reports—which they characterized to the researchers as a point of identity and even pride. Nelson and Lewis contend that the respondents' lack of trust in journalism wasn't a function of specific news articles, that is, the news itself; rather, it appeared to emerge from respondents' folk theories about journalism. Defined as beliefs about the news that help people make sense of the news, such theories are informed by many sources, including a person's community, their broader social networks, and the rhetoric of elites, including politicians.[83]

The consistency of the respondents' folk theories around media bias and the call to do one's own research, both hallmarks of rightwing critiques of mainstream journalism, makes little sense when considered through a traditional polarization frame. That frame would predict, instead, that the extent to which people on the right reject something, people on the left would be inclined to support it. Accordingly, they should have different folk theories about the news, particularly given the years and years Donald Trump has spent railing against journalists as enemies of the people and the years and years liberals have spent railing against Donald Trump. In contrast, and echoing the previous discussion of Republican cannibalization, a shadow gospel frame both accounts for and predicts the overlap of news audiences' folk theories. Its myths are diffuse and enduring. So is its influence. Distressingly, the shadow gospel frame also predicts that cross-partisan demonology is likely to become more intense (and more confusing) with time; as Nelson and Lewis emphasize, journalism is far from the only institution that has experienced a nosedive in public trust. Institutional mistrust is a growth industry—and we would argue, is tethered to a thriving and increasingly stealthy shadow gospel.

This is not to suggest that all critiques of institutions—including science, government, and higher education—should be seen as demonological or harmful. Institutions need oversight and critique; and very often they require structural reform to better serve the goals of equity and justice. There is, however, an important difference between directing an ideologically focused, historically grounded critical eye to certain institutions (and the people who run them) and firing off placeholder evil attacks against an amorphous institutional enemy underwritten by the logic of simplification inherent to demonological thinking: the assertion, in no way confined to the right, that institutions are fundamentally threatening while remaining vague on the specifics. Institutions are imperfect, but democracy needs them to function. A pandemonic shadow gospel threatens to erode them from all sides.

THE LONG ROAD TO RESISTANCE

The potential of an increasingly unwieldy shadow gospel underscores the need to recognize, decode, and resist demonological messages wherever they might crop up. Not being beholden to anyone or anything, these messages can be weaponized against anyone and anything. Including *you*, regardless of your politics or religious identity. The messages can certainly be weaponized against meaningful civic discourse, the central requirement of deliberative democracy.

ANTI-LIBERAL OBSTRUCTIONS

Resisting the shadow gospel is not easy to do. The most basic reason is the depth of its demonology. If you are someone steeped in an anti-liberal worldview, to encounter a liberal isn't just to run into someone who thinks differently about the world; it's to be confronted by an enemy who holds a basic contempt for your existence and wants to make your life worse in every imaginable way.

Liberal presence thus functions as an *emergency claim* for anti-liberal demonologists. Visual culture scholar Ariella Azoulay introduces this concept to describe the rhetorical impact of violent or otherwise distressing photography; but the two interconnected assertions that constitute an emergency within Azoulay's schema are applicable to much more than violent imagery.[84] The first assertion is that *this terrible [something] is unacceptable and does not line up with the kind of society we want.* The second assertion is that *we must do something to stop it.*[85] To trigger an emergency claim for the demonologist, a liberal—whatever that term might mean in the moment—doesn't need to do much to feel like a threat. The dangers liberals pose are decoded through demonological chains of signification.

When the demonologist subsequently lashes out, whether in person or online with maybe wild, maybe more tempered accusations about what is being destroyed by the liberal enemy, people who are aligned with institutional consensus—that is to say, with the standards of evidence, expertise, and empirical truth that emerge from the norms of mainstream journalism, government, and academia[86]—are primed to respond with their own emergency claim.

In the case of Big Lie–believing Trump supporters (with the Big Lie about a stolen 2020 election serving as its own emergency claim for believers), those within the institutional consensus say with alarm, *Look at these crazy conservatives brainwashed by rightwing disinformation; this is unacceptable and does not line up with the kind of society we want. We must do something to stop it.* Efforts to do exactly that by fact-checking 2020 election conspiracy theories or lobbying for stronger moderation on social networking platforms fuels an equally forceful conservative emergency claim: *This [censorship] is unacceptable and does not line up with the society we [conservatives] want. We [conservatives] must do something to stop [the liberal attacks against us].* The result is a politics of dueling emergency claims, each reinforcing the intensity of the other.

Admittedly, this schema is complicated when the dueling emergency claims are traded between those aligned with institutional consensus and those who are described as leftist or adopt the mantle of leftism—not just because there is often a fine, or at least obscured, line between ideological and demonological critique of institutions (particularly on social media, where the demonological churns alongside the ideological), but because designations of "leftism" are very often shadow gospel mirages. But that is a conundrum for another research project.

However the emergency claims arise, sounding the alarm about specific shadow gospel messages can have the unfortunate effect of strengthening the perceived need to return fire. That's not the only shadow gospel trap. Unwittingly buying into the version of history that the shadow gospel says exists is similarly risky. The decision by Florida and Oklahoma's state education departments to establish formal use agreements with PragerU Kids, a K-12 offshoot of the rightwing video series PragerU,[87] provides an example—but perhaps not for the reasons that one might expect. Like its adult counterpoint, PragerU Kids claims to be the "pro-America" antidote to the "woke agendas" being taught in schools.[88] Oklahoma superintendent of public instruction Ryan Waters emphasized PragerU's *anti-* scaffolding when he praised the company for "challenging the left's domination of academia" and arguing that "[i]t is of the utmost importance that we're able to correct this leftist bend of history, get this radicalism out, and go back to teaching true history to our kids."[89] For PragerU Kids, "true history" includes minimizing the negative consequences of slavery and colonialism and playing up the heroism of white Christian Americans,[90] reflecting what Waters describes as "a war for the soul of our kids."[91]

Many of the people aligned with institutional consensus who condemned Oklahoma's and Florida's formal use announcements still reinforced the demonological frame by describing the controversy in terms of the culture wars. News coverage of the controversy was especially quick to play up the "culture wars" angle, which either was included directly in the headline or was prominently featured in the article, even in stories that gleefully highlighted the overall electoral failures of similar parents' rights initiatives.[92] A culture war frame might seem like the natural and necessary way to describe these kinds of fights. And yet whenever a "culture wars" setup is used, it strengthens the shadow gospel's pull by reinforcing the idea of a two-sided, equally waged war: that of conservative traditionalism, steady and stable through time, under attack from encroaching liberal influence. A "culture wars" setup also reinforces the false claim that efforts to teach American history accurately is *partisan*, further expanding what qualifies as "the left" and increasing the overall surface area of the liberal devil.

FINDING A WAY

Whether it prompts an emergency claim or feeds into the feeling of could-not-be-otherwise, the shadow gospel has an incredibly powerful center of gravity. It is very difficult not to get sucked in. But in the realm of culture and politics, gravity isn't the same as inevitability.

Understanding how its shadows developed and what kinds of apocalyptic claims its gospel has normalized can help communicators craft messages and conduct outreach efforts that are less likely to feed directly into anti-liberal counterpunching (or emergency-claiming). Some demonologists may never be reachable. The dark enchantment of a world teeming with custom-made evil may be too emotionally compelling, or simply too much fun. But maybe some people, under the right conditions, remain open to other perspectives. These kinds of interventions will not be top-down, especially not if the information is being communicated by mistrusted institutions. They must instead be grassroots, brokered by trusted community members who understand their neighbors' or their coworkers' or their clients' context and how the liberal threat for them is encoded and decoded. By laying out the history of pandemonic roadblocks, this book can help readers scout alternative routes through their own personal networks.

A related strategy—echoing George Lakoff—is to offer up different frames for describing what is happening in our politics. As discussed in chapter 6, the frames we use structure our understanding of reality.[93] Our understanding of reality, in turn, shapes our assessment of appropriate action. If our frames distort our understanding of reality, we cannot expect that our actions will be reliably appropriate to the situation.

The need to rethink the value, efficacy, and basic coherence of the words "liberal" and "left" is especially pressing. The issue isn't just the specific words that are used; it's the worlds those words sustain and the emergency claims they trigger. For demonological conservatives, the word "liberal" describes a person who threatens them and sustains a world where one must always fight back. As previously emphasized, sometimes that threat is totally imagined; what the "liberals" are accused of doing simply isn't happening. Sometimes it is happening; sometimes the demonologists are actually being shouted at or mocked. Real conflict transforms into shadowboxing when the people doing the shouting or mocking are subsequently held up as the universal representatives of "the left." This is a form of demonological synecdoche, a figure of speech in which a part of something is presented as the whole (for example, saying "wheels" when describing a car). The anti-liberal version goes: the person who I feel is threatening me *is* the left, helping elevate a small sliver of an otherwise heterogenous group—particularly when that sliver aligns with a generations-old caricature of the left as radical and wild-eyed—as the ultimate destructive force in U.S. politics.

But the words demonologists use—and the worlds those words sustain—are only one source of shadow gospel energy. Ideological conservatives and even self-described liberals also feed into demonological synecdoche when they uncritically flatten vastly divergent groups into the category of "liberal/left" or otherwise reflexively affix a leftist label to groups that align with something—an aspect of identity, an economic outlook, an aesthetic or rhetorical style—that at some point found its way into the shadows. By approaching the liberal amalgamation as totalizing and linguistically stable, people who hate liberals, people who disagree with liberals, and people who call themselves liberals reinforce the presumption of liberal encroachment. They make the culture wars feel real.

As a replacement for "liberal," the word "pluralist" can help create a different world by casting itself against a true and grounded opposite. Pluralism posits a distinction between those who affirm diversity and the balancing of various interests, choices, and lifestyles, and those who are minoritarian: who, in stark opposition to pluralists, reject diversity and are only willing to make space for interests, choices, and lifestyles that align with their own.

Focusing on the value of pluralism and the harms of minoritarianism in a democratic society helps avoid demonological synecdoche in cases when a person or group pegged as leftist is advocating for minoritarian outcomes. A left/right polarization frame focuses the critique—and subsequent emergency claims—on the (alleged) leftism itself, which of course is a boon for the shadow gospel, especially when the leftism emerged from the shadows. In contrast, a pluralism/minoritarianism frame focuses the critique on who is excluded from a space or conversation, for what reasons, and to what consequences. The more grounded the details about the concern, the less energizing they are to the shadow gospel.

Adopting a pluralism frame could also help engage conservatives who may not be full-blown demonologists but who are still primed to expect liberal attack. It's easy to pick a side when a fight—for example, the clash around parents' rights—is described as a culture war crusade between left and right. When a fight is framed, instead, as a clash between people trying to make space for a variety of experiences and perspectives and people trying to make space only for themselves, different kinds of conversations may be possible. Most basically, the conservatives—some of them anyway—might not automatically feel implicated in the critique and therefore might not automatically feel compelled to cast the first emergency claim.

A linguistic shift from a vaguely defined liberalism to grounded-in-specificity pluralism, and related shift from a left/right polarization frame to a minoritarian/pluralist frame, isn't going to pacify a deeply agitated nation. But solutions will remain elusive if how we frame the problem is part of the problem. We need to think differently about how we talk about the electorate and draw distinctions within the electorate. We need to think differently about how we understand ourselves and others. We cannot continue allowing the shadow gospel to do that work for us.

TRUMP TOWN USA

There is a traditional brick church at the center of town in Boones Mill, Virginia.[94] At least, there had been a church. Built in 1920 and converted in 2020 into a Trump-themed store called Trump Town USA, MAGA banners hang on the entrance façade. A thirty-foot-tall portrait of Trump giving a double thumbs-up sign, the image slightly warped, stands to the right of the church doors. More images of Trump peer out from the lunette above the door and from the arch moldings. Inside, Trump 2024 and Confederate flags hang along the walls. The store's range of anti-Biden merchandise— from euphemistic "Let's Go Brandon" bumper stickers, shirts, and hats to its more direct "Fuck Biden" line—are nestled on the shelves alongside other Trump items, "Faith over Fear" bumper stickers, "Biden Sucks" yard signs, and sparklers. Anti-Harris offerings are, undoubtedly, in production.

Heading into the 2024 election, it might be tempting to focus on the specter of Donald Trump, whose grip on the Republican Party remains white-knuckled. But that is the wrong place to look. The final strategy for pushing back against the shadow gospel is to not mistake the messiah for the realm. The shadow messiah, like the shadow devil, is just a placeholder. The realm is what endures.

Those of us who reject the shadows must contend with the fact that our dysfunctional politics is not the converted church that Trump built. Our dysfunctional politics is the converted church that the shadow gospel built. Trump has his display racks set up for now. Eventually, because he dies, or because some fill-in-the-blank surprise catapults the country into the terrible unknown, again, Trump will no longer be the face peering out from the lunette. Some other face will replace it, some other line of Fuck This Person merchandise will be piled atop the shelves, as some other set of Republicans dangle from Saturn's mouth. While there is time, we must show what this gutted church is: how it was built, what it preaches, who it harms. And we must show what the church is not: not ideology, not theology, just anti-liberal invective, just stacks of Fuck This Person bumper stickers. So long as the country is guided by the possessing spirit of the shadow gospel, the pluralist *we*, the pro-democracy *we*, will be trapped in political hell.

NOTES

INTRODUCING THE SHADOW GOSPEL

1. John Gibson, *The War on Christmas: How the Liberal Plot to Ban the Sacred Christian Holiday Is Worse than You Thought* (New York: Sentinel, 2005); Liam Stack, "How the War on Christmas Got Started," *New York Times*, December 19, 2016, https://www.nytimes.com/2016/12/19/us/war-on-christmas-controversy.html.

2. Parker Mollow, "A War on Christmas Story: How Fox News Built America's Dumbest Part of the Culture War," Media Matters for America, December 23, 2019, https://www.mediamatters.org/war-christmas/war-christmas-story-how-fox-news-built-dumbest-part-americas-culture-war.

3. Daniel Denvir, "A Short History of the War on Christmas," *Politico Magazine*, December 16, 2013, https://www.politico.com/magazine/story/2013/12/war-on-christmas-short-history-101222/; Richard Shiffman, "Rush Limbaugh's War on Christmas," *Huffington Post*, December 21, 2012, https://www.huffpost.com/entry/rush-limbaughs-war-on-christmas_b_2329505.

4. Mike Ives, "Fox News Replaces Christmas Tree That Went Up in Flames in Manhattan," *New York Times*, December 8, 2021, https://www.nytimes.com/2021/12/08/nyregion/fox-christmas-tree-fire.html.

5. Gerrard Kaonga, "Fox News Contributor Compares Christmas Tree Fire to Pearl Harbor," *Newsweek*, December 10, 2021, https://www.newsweek.com/fox-news-christmas-tree-rev-jacques-degraff-compared-pearl-harbor-1658054.

6. Michelle Goldberg, "How the Secular Humanist Grinch Didn't Steal Christmas," *Salon*, November 21, 2005, https://www.salon.com/2005/11/21/christmas_6/.

7. David Emery, "A History of the 'War on Christmas,'" *Snopes*, November 29, 2017, https://www.snopes.com/news/2017/11/29/the-war-on-christmas/. As of August 2022, Brimelow's 2000 post was accessible via the Internet Archive, however, the link was broken as of March 2023 and as of March 2024 the post was not searchable.

8. Susan M. Shaw, "Don't Succumb to Criticism of 'Happy Holidays,' It Can Be an Expression of God's Inclusive Embrace," *Baptist News Global*, December 6, 2019, https://baptistnews.com/article/dont-succumb-to-criticism-of-happy-holidays-it-can-be-an-expression-of-gods-inclusive-embrace/#.YbjZT55Kg0p.

9. Alan Cooperman, "Evangelicals Use Courts to Fight Restrictions on Christmas Tidings," *Washington Post*, December 20, 2004, https://www.washingtonpost.com/archive/politics/2004/12/20/evangelicals-use-courts-to-fight-restrictions-on-christmas-tidings/8b4450d5-733d-4531-8726-0db807cd07a9/.

10. Justin Ariel Bailey, "Pagans, Puritans, and Putting Christ Back in Christmas," *Banner*, December 2, 2019, https://www.thebanner.org/features/2019/12/pagans-puritans-and-putting-christ-back-in-christmas.

11. "All across Long Island, Movement Is on to 'Keep Christ in Christmas,'" CBS New York, December 16, 2013, https://www.cbsnews.com/newyork/news/all-across-long-island-movement-is-on-to-keep-christ-in-christmas/.

12. Zach Schonefeld, "Parental Advisory Forever: An Oral History of the PMRC's War on Dirty Lyrics," *Newsweek*, September 19, 2015, https://www.newsweek.com/2015/10/09/oral-history-tipper-gores-war-explicit-rock-lyrics-dee-snider-373103.html.

13. Eric Nuzum, *Parental Advisory: Music Censorship in America* (New York: Harper, 2001), 17–18.

14. "How Heavy Metal and Satan Gave Us This Sticker," Vox, 2020, https://www.youtube.com/watch?v=v9gLmBgUTV4&t=25s.

15. Amy Binder, "Constructing Racial Rhetoric: Media Depictions of Harm in Heavy Metal and Rap Music," *American Sociological Review* 58, no. 6 (1993): 753–767, https://doi.org/10.2307/2095949.

16. Tipper Gore, *Raising PG Kids in an X-Rated Society* (Nashville, TN: Parthenon Press, 1987), 33.

17. Nuzum, *Parental Advisory*, 19.

18. Richard Cromelin, "Parents Get the Message from Video," *Los Angeles Times*, August 22, 1987, https://www.latimes.com/archives/la-xpm-1987-08-22-ca-1103-story.html; Dave Marsh and Phyllis Pollack, "Wanted for Attitude: The FBI Hates This Band," *The Village Voice*, October 10, 1989, https://www.villagevoice.com/2020/09/02/crackdown-on-culture-the-fbi-hates-this-band/.

19. Laura Sessions Stepp, "The Empire Built on Family Faith," *Washington Post*, August 8, 1990, https://www.washingtonpost.com/archive/lifestyle/1990/08/08/the-empire-built-on-family-faith/a2b300eb-25f8-4925-af24-ce076c620f51/.

20. Gavin Baddeley, *Lucifer Rising: Sin, Devil Worship, and Rock & Roll* (London: Plexus, 2016), 117; Lisa Ladouceur, "The Filthy 15: When Venom and King Diamond Met the Washington Wives," in *Satanic Panic: Pop-Cultural Paranoia in the 1980s*, ed. Kier-La Janisse and Paul Corupe (Surry: FAB Press, 2015), 158–172, 169; John Brackett, "Satan, Subliminals, and Suicide: The Formation and Development of an Anti-Rock in the United States during the 1980s," *American Music* 36, no. 3 (2018): 271–302.

21. Brackett, "Satan, Subliminals, and Suicide," 273.

22. thefivecount, "The Peters Brothers—Truth about Rock," YouTube, 2012, https://www.youtube.com/watch?v=RIRZ97wqOZ4.

23. Bracket, "Satan, Subliminals, and Suicide," 287.

24. J. D. Considine, "Sound and Attitude PMRC Still Keeps a Close Ear on the Message of Rock Lyrics," *Baltimore Sun*, October 6, 1992, https://www.baltimore sun.com/news/bs-xpm-1992-10-07-1992281110-story.html; Baddeley, *Lucifer Rising*, 117.

25. Marsh and Pollack, "Wanted for Attitude."

26. Ed Kilgore, "What If Republicans Were Anti-Lockdown, Anti-Mask, and Pro-Vaxx?," *New York Magazine Intelligencer*, July 21, 2012, https://nymag.com /intelligencer/2021/07/what-if-republicans-hated-lockdowns-masks-but-not -vaccine.html.

27. Jamelle Bouie, "Do Republicans Actually Want the Pandemic to End?," *New York Times*, August 31, 2021, https://www.nytimes.com/2021/08/31/opinion /republicans-anti-vax-covid.html.

28. Michael D. Shear and Noah Weiland, "Biden Calls for Door-to-Door Vaccine Push; Experts Say More Is Needed," *New York Times*, July 6, 2012, https://www .nytimes.com/2021/07/06/us/politics/biden-vaccines.html.

29. "Right-Wing Media Deems Vaccine Resistance a Badge of Honor," *Don Lemon Tonight*, CNN, July 10, 2021, https://www.cnn.com/videos/media/2021/07/10 /vaccine-rejection-rhetoric-right-wing-media-republicans-stelter-dlt-vpx.cnn.

30. Dean Obeidallah, "Fox News' Alarming Vaccine Disinformation Is a Danger to America," CNN, July 20, 2021, https://www.cnn.com/2021/07/18/opinions /vaccine-disniformation-fox-news-obeidallah/index.html.

31. Caleb Ecarma, "Fox News' Anti-Vax Mandate Messaging Is Out of Step with Its Own Strict Policies," *Vanity Fair*, October 7, 2021, https://www.vanityfair .com/news/2021/10/fox-news-anti-vax-messaging-policies.

32. Rob Savillo and Tyler Monroe, "Fox's Efforts to Undermine Vaccines Has Only Worsened," Media Matters for America, August 19, 2021, https://www .mediamatters.org/fox-news/foxs-effort-undermine-vaccines-has-only-worsened.

33. Gustaf Kilander, "Only 62% of Fox Viewers Are Vaccinated Compared to 83% for CNN and MSNBC, Poll Shows," *Independent*, July 27, 2021, https://www .independent.co.uk/news/world/americas/vaccinated-viewers-fox-cnn-msnbc -b1891460.html.

34. Jake Lahut, "Newsmax Readers Are Nearly Twice as Likely to Refuse the Vaccine than Fox News Watchers, New Poll Finds," *Business Insider*, July 12, 2021, https://www.businessinsider.com/newsmax-fox-news-vaccine-hesitancy-poll -oann-2021-7.

35. For an example, see the Heritage Foundation event, "Religion Is Essential: COVID Lockdowns and Unjust Religious Discrimination," co-hosted by the National Review Institute, February 1, 2021, https://www.heritage.org/religious -liberty/event/demand-religion-essential-covid-lockdowns-and-unjust-religious.

36. Molly Jong-Fast, "My Body My Choice? The Paradox of Republican Anti-Vaxxers," *Vogue*, July 14, 2021, https://www.vogue.com/article/my-body-my -choice-the-paradox-of-republican-anti-vaxxers.

37. "Tucker Carlson: Christianity Is Dying and Being Replaced by Cult of Coronavirus," Fox News, September 28, 2021, https://www.foxnews.com/opinion /tucker-carlson-christianity-dying-replaced-cult-coronavirus.

38. Martin Pingelly, "Tucker Carlson Claims US Military Vaccine Mandate a 'Purity Test' for 'Men with High Testosterone,'" *Guardian*, September 21, 2021, https://www.theguardian.com/media/2021/sep/21/tucker-carlson-fox-news-us -military-vaccine-mandate.

39. For an example, see "A Christian Perspective on the Covid Vaccine," part of the NAE's Covid Vaccines Resource Hub, accessed March 2023, https://www.nae .org/covid-vaccines/.

40. Mark Kreidler, "No Major Religious Denomination Opposes Vaccinations, but Religious Exemptions May Still Complicate Mandates," CNN, September 9, 2021, https://www.cnn.com/2021/09/09/health/covid-vaccine-religious-exemp tions-khn/index.html; "Pope Urges People to Receive Covid-19 Vaccine," *Vatican News*, August 2021, https://www.vaticannews.va/en/pope/news/2021-08/pope -francis-appeal-covid-19-vaccines-act-of-love.html.

41. Stephanie Martin, "Edmund Burke Wouldn't Recognize Evangelicals' Vaccine Resistance as Conservatism," *Religion News Service*, October 7, 2021, https:// religionnews.com/2021/10/07/evangelical-christians-turned-individual-freedom -into-vaccine-resistance/.

42. Colleen Long and Andrew Demillo, "As Covid-19 Vaccinations Rise, Religious Exemptions Grow," AP News, September 15, 2021, https://apnews.com /article/joe-biden-health-religion-los-angeles-arkansas-3ba53f2f00e1ab7105d7 d128f2b1e65d.

43. The shadow gospel and its anti-liberal messages are not restricted to the United States and warrant investigation in other parts of the world, especially considering the global rise of Christian-inflected authoritarianism. We are focused on the United States for this study because the origin of the shadow gospel is tied to mid-century American Evangelical and rightwing media networks.

44. Geoffrey Layman, *The Great Divide: Religious and Cultural Conflict in American Party Politics* (New York: Columbia University Press, 2001), 20; Andrew Hartman, *A War for the Soul of America: A History of the Culture Wars* (Chicago: University of Chicago Press, 2019), 86, 98–99; Frances FitzGerald, *The Evangelicals: The*

Struggle to Shape America (New York: Simon and Schuster, 2017); Darren Dochuk, *From Bible Belt to Sunbelt: Plain-Folk Religion, Grassroots Politics, and the Rise of Evangelical Conservatism* (New York: W. W. Norton, 2010); Brian Steensland and Eric L. Wright, "American Evangelicals and Conservative Politics: Past, Present, and Future," *Sociology Compass* 8, no. 6 (2014): 705–717.

45. Andrew Busch, *Reagan's Victory: The Presidential Election of 1980 and the Rise of the Right* (Lawrence: University Press of Kansas, 2005), 23, 107; Clyde Wilcox, "Evangelicals and the Moral Majority," *Journal for the Scientific Study of Religion* 28, no. 4 (1989): 400–414.

46. Clyde Wilcox, "America's Radical Right Revisited: A Comparison of the Activists in Christian Right Organizations from the 1960s and the 1980s," *Sociological Analysis* 48, no. 1 (1987): 46–57; Daniel K. Williams, *God's Own Party: The Making of the Christian Right* (New York: Oxford University Press, 2012), 187–212.

47. Laura R. Olson and Adam L. Warber, "Belonging, Behaving, and Believing: Assessing the Role of Religion on Presidential Approval," *Political Research Quarterly* 61, no. 2 (2008): 192–204; Robert D. Putnam and David E. Campbell, *American Grace: How Religion Divides and Unites Us* (New York: Simon and Schuster, 2012), 7.

48. For an account of how January 6 tapped into a decade of "meme wars" and helped unify disparate factions of the political right behind Trump and the MAGA movement, see Joan Donovan, Emily Dreyfuss, and Brian Friedberg, *Meme Wars: The Untold Story of the Online Battles Upending Democracy in America* (New York: Bloomsbury Publishing, 2022).

49. This work focused on trolling subculture centering around 4chan's infamous /b/ board from 2008 to 2014. See Whitney Phillips, *This Is Why We Can't Have Nice Things: Mapping the Relationship between Online Trolling and Mainstream Culture* (Cambridge, MA: MIT Press, 2015).

50. Ryan P. Burge, "Evangelicals Show No Decline, despite Trump and Nones," *Christianity Today*, March 21, 2019, https://www.christianitytoday.com/news/2019/march/evangelical-nones-mainline-us-general-social-survey-gss.html.

51. For measures of the percentage of the population identified as Evangelical using data from the General Social Survey, see Ryan Burge, "American Religion in 2030," *Religion in Public*, October 24, 2019, https://religioninpublic.blog/2019/10/24/american-religion-in-2030/.

52. Ryan Burge, "How Has Partisanship and Theology Shifted in America's Religious Traditions?," *Religion in Public*, May 22, 2017, https://religioninpublic.blog/2017/05/22/how-has-partisanship-and-theology-shifted-in-americas-religious-traditions/.

53. Travis Mitchell, "In U.S., Decline of Christianity Continues at Rapid Pace," Pew Research Center's Religion & Public Life Project, October 17, 2019, https://

www.pewresearch.org/religion/2019/10/17/in-u-s-decline-of-christianity-continues
-at-rapid-pace/.

54. Gregory A. Smith, "More White Americans Adopted than Shed Evangelical Label during Trump Presidency, Especially His Supporters," Pew Research Center, September 15, 2021, https://www.pewresearch.org/fact-tank/2021/09/15/more -white-americans-adopted-than-shed-evangelical-label-during-trump-presidency -especially-his-supporters/; "Faith after the Pandemic: How COVID-19 Changed American Religion," American Enterprise Institute, January 5, 2023, https:// www.aei.org/research-products/report/faith-after-the-pandemic-how-covid-19 -changed-american-religion/.

55. Ryan Burge, "44 Years of Religion and Politics in One Graph," *Religion in Public*, May 11, 2017, https://religioninpublic.blog/2017/05/11/44-years-of-religion -and-politics-in-one-graph/. See also Putnam and Campbell, *American Grace*, 373– 374, which shows key inflection points in the 1990s.

56. Axel R. Schäfer, *American Evangelicals and the 1960s* (Madison: University of Wisconsin Press, 2013), 3.

57. See Wilcox, "America's Radical Right Revisited." Also see Wilcox's comparison between the Christian Anti-Communism Crusade and the John Birch Society, Clyde Wilcox, "Sources of Support for the Old Right: A Comparison of the John Birch Society and the Christian Anti-Communism Crusade," *Social Science History* 12, no. 4 (1988): 429–449.

58. In this book, we argue that what looks like "church gospel" Evangelicalism is often the shadow gospel in disguise. However, when we highlight that overlap, we are focused on the shadows, not on the church, that is to say, the grounded elements of the religious tradition manifesting as the beliefs, behaviors, and sense of belonging of Evangelical adherents. For that reason, we are not wading directly into theological debates and thick descriptive accounts of "church gospel" Evangelicalism. There is an enormous corpus of scholarship that does. For some key texts, see Randall Balmer, *Evangelicalism in America* (Waco, TX: Baylor University Press, 2016) and *The Making of Evangelicalism: From Revivalism to Politics and Beyond* (Waco, TX: Baylor University Press, 2010); Barry Hankins, *American Evangelicals: A Contemporary History of a Mainstream Religious Movement* (Lanham, MD: Rowman & Littlefield, 2008); and Harriet A. Harris, *Fundamentalism and Evangelicals* (Oxford: Clarendon Press, 1998).

59. Vera Bergengruen, "Why a Group of Christians Is Fighting the Growing Threat of Christian Nationalism," *Time*, December 30, 2022, https://time.com /6242260/christians-against-christian-nationalism-violence/.

60. Nik Popli, "How the Great Replacement Theory Has Fueled Racist Attacks," *Time*, May 16, 2022, https://time.com/6177282/great-replacement-theory-buffalo -racist-attacks/.

61. Shannon Bond, "How Tucker Carlson Took Fringe Conspiracy Theories to a Mass Audience," *Morning Edition*, NPR, April 25, 2023, https://www.npr.org/2023/04/25/1171800317/how-tucker-carlsons-extremist-narratives-shaped-fox-news-and-conservative-politi.

62. Studies that use survey-based analyses and interviews to uncover white Christian nationalism in the general public and in Evangelicalism include Eric L. McDaniel, Irfan Nooruddin, and Allyson F. Shortle, *The Everyday Crusade: Christian Nationalism in American Politics* (Cambridge: Cambridge University Press, 2022); Pamela Cooper-White, *The Psychology of Christian Nationalism: Why People Are Drawn in and How to Talk across the Divide* (Minneapolis: Augsburg Fortress, 2022); Angela Denker, *Red State Christians: A Journey into White Christian Nationalism and the Wreckage It Leaves Behind* (Minneapolis: Augsburg Fortress, 2022). Many also focus on the historical and racist roots of white Christian nationalism, including Bradley Onishi, *Preparing for War: The Extremist History of White Christian Nationalism—And What Comes Next* (Minneapolis: Broadleaf Books, 2023); and John Fanestil, *American Heresy: The Roots and Reach of White Christian Nationalism* (Minneapolis: Augsburg Fortress, 2023). Other volumes make calls for immediate action and revival of democracy and pluralism, including Carter Heyward, *The Seven Deadly Sins of White Christian Nationalism: A Call to Action* (Lanham, MD: Rowman & Littlefield, 2022), and Andrew L. Whitehead, *American Idolatry: How Christian Nationalism Betrays the Gospel and Threatens the Church* (Grand Rapids, MI: Brazos Press, 2023), which is written to other Christians. Many explicitly focus on nationalism, populism, and white supremacy, including Carol M. Swain, *The New White Nationalism in America: Its Challenge to Integration* (Cambridge: Cambridge University Press, 2002); Atalia Omer and Joshua Lupo, *Religion, Populism, and Modernity: Confronting White Christian Nationalism and Racism* (Notre Dame, IN: University of Notre Dame Press, 2023); Leonard Zeskind, *Blood and Politics: The History of the White Nationalist Movement from the Margins to the Mainstream* (New York: Farrar, Straus and Giroux, 2009); and Lerone A. Martin, *The Gospel of J. Edgar Hoover: How the FBI Aided and Abetted the Rise of White Christian Nationalism* (Princeton, NJ: Princeton University Press, 2023).

63. Philip Gorski and Samuel Perry, *The Flag and the Cross: White Christian Nationalism and Its Threat to American Democracy* (New York: Oxford University Press, 2022).

64. The questions Gorski and Perry rely on to measure Christian nationalism have come under scrutiny by Nicholas T. Davis, who suggests, using dimensional analysis, that the questions do not reflect a single underlying concept. This statistical analysis broadly calls into question survey research that relies on these kinds of survey questions to make claims about Christian nationalist beliefs. One possible explanation for the slipperiness of the scale is that the underlying concept is not Christian nationalism at all. See Nicholas T. Davis, "The Psychometric Properties of the Christian Nationalism Scale," *Politics and Religion* 16, no. 1 (2023): 1–26.

65. Gorski and Perry, *The Flag and the Cross*, 15–16.

66. Richard Hofstadter, *The Paranoid Style in American Politics, and Other Essays* (Chicago: University of Chicago Press, 1979), xi.

67. Hofstadter, *The Paranoid Style*, 74.

68. Hofstadter, *The Paranoid Style*, 72–73.

69. See Raymond E. Wolfinger et al., "America's Radical Right: Politics and Ideology," in *Ideology and Discontent*, ed. David Apter (New York: Free Press, 1964), 267–269.

70. Tim Alberta makes an impassioned argument about the takeover of Evangelicalism by Christian nationalism and Trumpism in his book *The Kingdom, the Power, and the Glory: American Evangelicals in an Age of Extremism* (New York: HarperCollins, 2023). He emphasizes that Evangelical churches across the country have been impacted. We agree with the symptoms Alberta describes but posit a different cause. We will revisit Alberta's work in the conclusion.

71. Joel Kovel, *Red Hunting in the Promised Land: Anticommunism and the Making of America* (New York: Basic Books, 1994), xii, 8–9.

72. Lawrence Grossberg, *Cultural Studies in the Future Tense* (Durham, NC: Duke University Press, 2010), 40–43; Jeremy Gilbert, "This Conjuncture: For Stuart Hall," *New Formations* 96, no. 1 (2019): 5–37, http://dx.doi.org.uoregon.idm.oclc .org/10.3898/NEWF:96/97.EDITORIAL.2019.

73. Phillip Stephens Jr., "The Demonology of Satanism," in *The Satanism Scare*, ed. James T. Richardson, Joel Best, and David G. Bromley (New York: Routledge, 1991), 21.

74. Tom De Luca and John Buell, *Liars! Cheaters! Evildoers! Demonization and the End of Civil Debate in American Politics* (New York: New York University Press, 2005), 2–7; see also S. Jonathon O'Donnell, *Passing Orders: Demonology and Sovereignty in American Spiritual Warfare* (New York: Fordham University Press, 2020), 3–4, for a link between demonology and demonization.

75. De Luca and Buell, *Liars!*, 7.

76. Jason C. Bivins, *The Fracture of Good Order: Christian Antiliberalism and the Challenge to American Politics* (Chapel Hill: University of North Carolina Press, 2004), 3.

77. Gibson, *The War on Christmas*, xxi, xxiv.

78. Jessica Johnson, "White Terror and the Great Replacement," paper presented at "SPAWN 2022: White Supremacy, Misogyny, and the 'New' Terrorism," June 25, 2022.

79. Jake Lahut, "'Beyond Tragic': Fox & Friends Hosts Say the Christmas-Tree Fire outside Their Studio Is Proof of 'the Crime Surge in This Country,'" *Business*

Insider, December 8, 2021, https://news.yahoo.com/beyond-tragic-fox-friends-hosts-172920238.html.

80. Bobby Lewis, @revrrlewis, clip from December 8, 2021, *Fox and Friends* show, Twitter, December 8, 2021, https://twitter.com/revrrlewis/status/14686016943 59625732?s=20.

81. Elaine Pagels, *The Origin of Satan: How Christians Demonized Jews, Pagans, and Heretics* (New York: Vintage, 1996), xxiii, 179. She describes this dynamic in more detail in the context of Jews and pagans, 110–114, and heretics, 49, 150.

82. Pagels, *The Origin of Satan*, 13.

83. Pagels, *The Origin of Satan*, 179.

84. Richard Raiswell, Michelle D. Brock, and David R. Winter, "Introduction: Giving the Devil His Due," in *The Routledge History of the Devil in the Western Tradition*, ed. Richard Raiswell, Michelle D. Brock, and David R. Winter (New York: Routledge, 2025).

85. Raiswell, Brock, and Winter, "Introduction."

86. Raiswell, Brock, and Winter, "Introduction."

87. Michael Rogin, *Ronald Reagan: The Movie* (Berkeley: University of California Press, 1988), 4–5, 19.

88. Rogin, *Ronald Reagan*, xiii–xv, viii, 19, 272–275; Diane Winston, *Righting the American Dream: How the Media Mainstreamed Reagan's Evangelical Vision* (Chicago: University of Chicago Press, 2023), 5–8.

89. Pagels, *The Origin of Satan*, 19, 38, 83–84, 88, 139, 165, 179, 184.

90. Pagels, *The Origin of Satan*, 13, 123.

91. Pagels, *The Origin of Satan*, 60, 74, 82–83, 111.

92. Pagels, *The Origin of Satan*, 12.

93. Daniel Wojcik, *The End of the World as We Know It: Faith, Fatalism, and Apocalypse in America* (New York: New York University Press, 1997), 11, 33–35.

94. Pagels, *The Origin of Satan*, 181.

95. Stephens and Giberson, *The Anointed*, 150–151.

96. Daniel Wojcik, "Modern Mythology, Visionary Art, and Techno-Reenchantment," Keynote presentation for the conference "New Approaches to 'Re-enchanted' Central and Eastern Europe," Institute for Theoretical Studies of the Moholy-Nagy University of Art and Design of Budapest, April 7, 2022. In his study of Satan in the twenty-first century, Robert Ivie similarly argues that, for many, the figure of Satan breaks the secular spell of disenchantment, helping to re-enchant the world. See Ivie, "Into the 21st Century," in *The Routledge History of the*

Devil in the Western Tradition, ed. Richard Raiswell, Michelle D. Brock, and David R. Winter (New York: Routledge, 2025).

97. Wojcik, *End of the World*, 33, 144–145.

98. See Corey Robin, *The Reactionary Mind: Conservatism from Edmund Burke to Sarah Palin* (New York: Oxford University Press, 2011), 4; Matthew McManus, *The Rise of Post-Modern Conservatism: Neoliberalism, Post-Modern Culture, and Reactionary Politics* (New York: Palgrave Macmillan, 2019), 16–17, 47.

99. Katherine J. Cramer, *The Politics of Resentment: Rural Consciousness in Wisconsin and the Rise of Scott Walker* (Chicago: University of Chicago Press, 2016), 7–9; Arlie Russel Hochschild, *Strangers in Their Own Land: Anger and Mourning on the American Right* (New York: New Press, 2018). See also Dochuk, *From Bible Belt to Sunbelt*, for an account of the effect of Southern migration on the rise of Evangelical conservatism in urban Southern California.

100. Jeremy Engels, *The Politics of Resentment: A Genealogy* (University Park: Penn State University Press, 2015), 5, 11.

101. James Davison Hunter, *Culture Wars: The Struggle to Control the Family, Art, Education, Law, and Politics in America* (New York: Basic Books, 1991), 4, 14, 17.

102. In his study of the international circulation of rightwing memes, Uygar Başpehlivan similarly emphasizes the need to foreground enjoyment—particularly enjoyment in fighting the enemy—as a significant driver of rightwing communications and antagonisms. See his article "Cucktales: Race, Sex, and Enjoyment in the Reactionary Memescape," *International Political Sociology* 18, no. 3 (2024): olae026, https://doi.org/10.1093/ips/olae026.

103. As an example, former Trump advisor and rightwing media figure Steve Bannon has frequently described Democrats as demonic and satanic. See Payton Armstrong, "Steve Bannon Is Using Right-Wing Religious Rhetoric about 'Spiritual Warfare' against 'Demonic' Democrats," *Media Matters for America*, January 24, 2024, https://www.mediamatters.org/steve-bannon/steve-bannon-using-right -wing-religious-rhetoric-about-spiritual-warfare-against; see also Bannon's 2023 speech at Turning Point USA's annual AmericaFest conference in which he describes liberals as demons and working for Lucifer, "Steve Bannon Full America-Fest Speech," Amfest, December 17, 2023, https://www.amfest.com/steve-bannon -amfest2023-full-speech.

104. Roland Barthes, *Mythologies* (New York: Farrar, Straus and Giroux, 1972). Barthes's conception of myth is, ultimately, secular, which differentiates it—and therefore our usage of the term—from more traditional accounts of myth that emphasize sacred origins. In *Hunt the Devil: Demonology in U.S. War Culture* (Tuscaloosa: University of Alabama Press, 2015), Robert L. Ivie and Oscar Giner come close to that usage, describing political myths as "foundational narratives with sacred origins and secular uses" (4). However, as we are focused on the role that

mass media play in perpetuating seemingly natural and necessary beliefs, it would be more accurate to say that for us, myths are foundational narratives with secular origins and semi-sacred uses.

105. Hyrum Lewis and Verlan Lewis, *The Myth of Left and Right: How the Political Spectrum Misleads and Harms America* (New York: Oxford University Press, 2023), 2.

106. Lewis and Lewis, *The Myth of Left and Right*, 4.

107. See Başpehlivan, "Cucktails." He uses this term when describing enjoyment as a structuring condition of reactionary politics.

108. Kovel, *Red Hunting in the Promised Land*, 208–219; also see Ivie and Giner, *Hunt the Devil*, for an analysis of how American Puritans and, later, westward colonizers, projected images of the devil onto Indigenous people.

109. Kelly J. Baker, *Gospel According to the Klan: The KKK's Appeal to Protestant America, 1915–1930* (Lawrence: University Press of Kansas, 2017), 34.

110. Anthea Butler, *White Evangelical Racism: The Politics of Morality in America* (Chapel Hill: University of North Carolina Press, 2021), 23–30.

CHAPTER 1

1. Episode 1332, *Bannon's War Room*, October 13, 2021, https://rumble.com /vnp4k1-episode-1332-congress-is-proving-to-be-out-of-control.html.

2. Aila Slisko, "Marjorie Taylor Greene Says Bernie Sanders, Democrats 'Swore' College Oath to Communism," *Newsweek*, October 13, 2021, https://www.news week.com/marjorie-taylor-greene-says-bernie-sanders-democrats-swore-college -oath-communism-1638789.

3. Larry Felton Johnson, "Marjorie Taylor Green Says Communists Took away Her Twitter," *Cobb County Courier*, January 3, 2022, https://cobbcountycourier .com/2022/01/marjorie-taylor-greene-says-communists-took-away-her-twitter/.

4. Senator Scott Weiner, @Scott_Wiener, Twitter, November 23, 2022, https:// twitter.com/Scott_Wiener/status/1595443181591891969; Dustin Gardiner, "Rep. Marjorie Taylor Greene Calls Senator Scott Weiner a 'Communist Groomer' after He Tweets about Hate Speech," *San Francisco Chronicle*, November 23, 2022, https://www.sfchronicle.com/politics/article/Rep-Marjorie-Taylor-Greene-calls -Sen-Scott-17606923.php.

5. Ed Kilgore, "Do Republicans Know What Communism Is?," *New York Magazine*, March 6, 2022, https://nymag.com/intelligencer/article/do-republicans -know-what-communism-is.html.

6. For a discussion of how opposition to New Deal politics dovetailed with opposition to worry about "creeping socialism," see Nicole Hemmer, *Messengers of the*

Right: Conservative Media and the Transformation of American Politics (Philadelphia: University of Pennsylvania Press, 2016), 14–15, 52–53.

7. Sara Diamond, *Roads to Dominion: Right-Wing Movements and Political Power in the United States* (New York: Guilford Press, 1995), 39.

8. Carol Stabile, *The Broadcast 41: Women and the Anti-Communist Blacklist* (Cambridge, MA: MIT Press, 2018), 62.

9. Stabile, *Broadcast 41*, 62–63; David Caute, *The Great Fear: The Anti-Communist Purge under Truman and Eisenhower* (New York: Simon and Schuster, 1978), 185.

10. Kathryn Olmstead, *Real Enemies: Conspiracy Theories and American Democracy, World War I to 9/11* (Oxford: Oxford University Press, 2009), 84–85.

11. See Daniel Wojcik, *The End of the World as We Know It: Faith, Fatalism, and Apocalypse in America* (New York: New York University Press, 1999), for an analysis of religious and secular Cold War apocalypticism centering on the threat of nuclear war during the Cold War and in the post–Cold War era.

12. Joel Kovel, *Red Hunting in the Promised Land: Anticommunism and the Making of America* (New York: Basic Books, 1994), 5. Kovel's description of anticommunism as "the realm of the shadowy bizarre," quoted in chapter 1, is the inspiration for the chapter title. See *Red Hunting*, xii, 8–9.

13. Kovel, *Red Hunting*, 9. Kovel uses the term "ideological furnace," but we would suggest that such a dynamic is not ideological, it's demonological, to denote exactly the black hole fusionist qualities that Kovel is describing.

14. Diamond, *Roads to Dominion*, 4; Stabile, *Broadcast 41*, 8, 15, 94.

15. Kovel, *Red Hunting*; Diamond, *Roads to Dominion*, 9.

16. Robbie Lieberman, *The Strangest Dream: Communism, Anticommunism, and the U.S. Peace Movement, 1945–1963* (Syracuse, NY: Syracuse University Press, 2000), 58; Hyrum Lewis and Verlan Lewis, *The Myth of Left and Right: How the Political Spectrum Misleads and Harms America* (New York: Oxford University Press, 2023), 22–23.

17. Lewis and Lewis, *The Myth of Left and Right*, 24.

18. Lewis and Lewis, *The Myth of Left and Right*, 24–25.

19. Caute, *The Great Fear*, 540; Olmstead, *Real Enemies*, 94.

20. Cedric Belfrage, *The American Inquisition: 1945–1960* (Indianapolis: Bobbs-Merrill, 1973), 70, 174, 11; Caute, *The Great Fear*, 350, 351, 503; Stabile, *Broadcast 41*, 12; Kathleen Belew, "Veterans and White Supremacy," *New York Times*, April 16, 2014, https://www.nytimes.com/2014/04/16/opinion/veterans-and-white-supremacy.html.

21. Diamond, *Roads to Dominion*, 55, 51.

22. Michelle Nickerson, *Mothers of Conservatism: Women and the Postwar Right* (Princeton, NJ: Princeton University Press, 2012); Paul Matzko, *The Radio Right: How a Band of Broadcasters Took on the Federal Government and Built the Modern Conservative Movement* (New York: Oxford University Press, 2020), 42, 45, 38.

23. Kovel, *Red Hunting*, 112; Stabile, *Broadcast 41*, 137, 143, 109.

24. Liebman quoted in Diamond, *Roads to Dominion*, 43.

25. Caute, *The Great Fear*, 54.

26. Diamond, *Roads to Dominion*, 9; Kovel, *Red Hunting*, 104, 118.

27. Reagan quoted in Kovel, *Red Hunting*, 134.

28. Hoover quoted in Kovel, *Red Hunting*, 99.

29. Kovel, *Red Hunting*, 19; Stabile, *Broadcast 41*, 147, 60, 75, 83–86, 140; Caute, *The Great Fear*, 166.

30. Belfrage, *The American Inquisition*, 12.

31. Diamond, *Roads to Dominion*, 79.

32. Frederick Simonelli, *American Fuehrer: George Lincoln Rockwell and the American Nazi Party* (Urbana: University of Illinois Press, 1999), 75.

33. Diamond, *Roads to Dominion*, 86; Claire Connor, *Wrapped in the Flag: A Personal History of America's Radical Right* (Boston: Beacon Press, 2013), 110.

34. Diamond, *Roads to Dominion*, 20, 56, 58.

35. John Sbardellati, *J. Edgar Hoover Goes to the Movies: The FBI and the Origins of Hollywood's Cold War* (Ithaca, NY: Cornell University Press, 2012), 171.

36. Elaine Tyler May, *Homeward Bound: American Families in the Cold War Era*, 2nd ed. (New York: Basic Books, 2008), 10.

37. Stabile, *Broadcast 41*, 26.

38. Hemmer, *Messengers of the Right*, 116.

39. Diamond, *Roads to Dominion*, 21–22; Kovel, *Red Hunting*, 25–26.

40. Edward S. Shapiro, "The Approach of War: Congressional Isolationism and Anti-Semitism, 1939–1941," *American Jewish History* 74, no. 1 (1984): 45–65.

41. Paul Moses, "Old Anti-Semitism, New Audience," *LaCroix International*, November 12, 2022, https://international.la-croix.com/news/politics/old-antisemitism-new-audience/16885.

42. Diamond, *Roads to Dominion*, 22, 93.

43. Talcott Parsons, "Postscript to 'The Sociology of Modern Anti-Semitism,'" *Contemporary Jewry* 5 (1980): 31–38.

44. Stabile, *Broadcast 41*, 74–75.

45. Stabile, *Broadcast 41*, 15.

46. Many studies have explored this link in contemporary and historical contexts. To name just a few, Kathleen Belew demonstrates the overlap between white supremacist and anti-Semitic thought in her extensive study of the White Power and paramilitary movements in the United States; see *Bring the War Home: The White Power Movement and Paramilitary America* (Cambridge, MA: Harvard University Press, 2018). Kathleen Blee explores the racist and anti-Semitic underpinnings of modern racism using interviews with women involved in the hate movement; see *Inside Organized Racism: Women in the Hate Movement* (Berkeley: University of California Press, 2003). And Jessie Daniels chronicles how white supremacist discourses constructed a dehumanized category of "Jew"; see *White Lies* (New York: Routledge, 1997).

47. Howard Suber, "Politics and Popular Culture: Hollywood at Bay, 1933–1953," *American Jewish History* 68, no. 4 (1979): 517–533; Belfrage, *The American Inquisition*, 75; Caute, *The Great Fear*, 466–470.

48. Raymond A. Mohl, *South of the South: Jewish Activists and the Civil Rights Movement in Miami, 1945–1960* (Gainesville: University Press of Florida, 2004); Shana Bernstein, "From Civic Defense to Civil Rights: The Growth of Jewish American Interracial Civil Rights Activism in Los Angeles," in *A Cultural History of Jews in California: The Jewish Role in American Life*, ed. Bruce Zuckerman, William Deverell, and Lisa Ansell (West Lafayette, IN: Purdue University Press, 2009), 55–80; Anita Grossman, "Shadows of War and Holocaust: Jews, German Jews, and the Sixties in the United States, Reflections and Memories," *Journal of Modern Jewish Studies* 13, no. 1 (2014): 99–114.

49. Caute, *The Great Fear*, 475.

50. Peter Jan Margry, "Envisioning and Exploring Mary's Theatre of War," in *Cold War Mary: Ideologies, Politics, and Marian Devotional Culture*, ed. Peter Jan Margry (Leuven: Leuven University Press, 2020), 8. This chapter introduces an interdisciplinary collection of studies exploring how the Virgin Mary was marshaled by Catholics around the globe to promote anticommunism.

51. Jennifer M. Miller and Udi Greenberg, "From Mental Slavery to Brainwashing: Anti-Catholic Legacies in Anti-Communist Polemics," in *Defending the Faith: Global Histories of Apologetics and Politics in the Twentieth Century*, ed. Todd Weir and Hugh McLeod (Oxford: Oxford University Press, 2021), 119–140; Caute, *The Great Fear*, 437, 108.

52. Nickerson, *Mothers of Conservatism*, xx, xxi, 31.

53. Kovel, *Red Hunting*, 106; May, *Homeward Bound*, 92, 71, 140.

54. May, *Homeward Bound*, 97.

55. May, *Homeward Bound*, 94; Kovel, *Red Hunting*, 107, 101.

56. Belfrage, *The American Inquisition*, 286.

57. Kovel, *Red Hunting*, 101, 106–107; May, *Homeward Bound*, 95–96.

58. May, *Homeward Bound*, 73, 93.

59. Belfrage, *The American Inquisition*, 149, 195, 131; May, *Homeward Bound*, 208; Caute, *The Great Fear*, 296, 177; Nickerson, *Mothers of Conservatism*, 7, 8.

60. Kovel, *Red Hunting*, 134, 198.

61. Dianne Kirby, "Religion and the Cold War—An Introduction," in *Religion and the Cold War*, ed. Dianne Kirby (New York: Palgrave Macmillan, 2003), 1.

62. Nickerson, *Mothers of Conservatism*, 47.

63. Heather Hendershot, *What's Fair on the Air: Cold War Right-Wing Broadcasting and the Public Interest* (Chicago: University of Chicago Press, 2011), 12.

64. Matzko, *The Radio Right*, 19.

65. Diamond, *Roads to Dominion*, 94.

66. Diamond, *Roads to Dominion*, 97.

67. Hendershot, *What's Fair on the Air*, 9.

68. Diamond, *Roads to Dominion*, 13, 95.

69. D. J. Mulloy, *The World of the John Birch Society: Conspiracy, Conservatism, and the Cold War* (Nashville, TN: Vanderbilt University, 2014), 2–3.

70. Mulloy, *The World of the John Birch Society*, 2–3.

71. Matzko, *Radio Right*, 19.

72. Nickerson, *Mothers of Conservatism*, 140.

73. Hendershot, *What's Fair on the Air*, 2.

74. Diamond, *Roads to Dominion*, 103.

75. Conner, *Wrapped in the Flag*, 34.

76. Hendershot, *What's Fair on the Air*, 13.

77. Diamond, *Roads to Dominion*, 101.

78. Eric C. Groce, Tina Heafner, and Elizabeth Bellows, "'Under God' and the Pledge of Allegiance: Examining a 1954 Sermon and Its Meaning," *Social Education* 77, no. 4 (2013): 186; Lee Canipe, "Under God and Anti-Communist: How the Pledge of Allegiance Got Religion in Cold War America," *Journal of Church and State* 45, no. 2 (Spring 2003): 318.

79. Brooks quoted in Kovel, *Red Hunting*, 158.

80. Kovel, *Red Hunting*, 82.

81. The most fevered articulations of anticommunism were not restricted to the rightwing; the bipartisan nature of Cold War anticommunism is highlighted in

Caute, *The Great Fear*, 20–28, which also argues that many self-identifying liberals adopted this stance out of fear of being attacked and possibly punished for not being anticommunist enough.

82. Kovel, *Red Hunting*, 78; Caute, *The Great Fear*, 21.

83. Kovel, *Red Hunting*, 68.

84. John M. Mulder, "The Moral World of John Foster Dulles," *Journal of Presbyterian History* 49, no. 2 (Summer 1971): 157–182.

85. Kovel, *Red Hunting*, 69.

86. John Foster Dulles, *War or Peace* (New York: Macmillan, 1950), 259, 261.

87. Belfrage, *The American Inquisition*, 58.

88. Peter Knight, "Introduction: A Nation of Conspiracy Theorists," in *Conspiracy Nation: The Politics of Paranoia in Postwar America*, ed. Peter Knight (New York: New York University Press 2002), 7.

89. Kovel, *Red Hunting*, 176.

90. Bill Ellis, *Raising the Devil: Satanism, New Religions, and the Media* (Lexington: University of Kentucky Press, 2000), 132–133.

91. Ellis, *Raising the Devil*, 128–131.

92. Ellis, *Raising the Devil*, quoting Welch, 132.

93. Ellis, *Raising the Devil*, quoting Welch, 125.

94. Michelle Nickerson, *Mothers of Conservatism*, 124.

95. Nickerson, *Mothers of Conservatism*, 114–116.

96. Nickerson, *Mothers of Conservatism*, 118–119.

97. Nickerson, *Mothers of Conservatism*, 107.

98. Nickerson, *Mothers of Conservatism*, 110–111.

99. Nickerson, *Mothers of Conservatism*, 109, 120.

100. Hendershot, *What's Fair on the Air*, 7.

101. Robert Greene II, "National Review and Civil Rights Memory," in *News on the Right: Studying Conservative News Cultures*, ed. Anthony Nadler and A. J. Bauer (New York: Oxford University Press, 2020), 177–178. In his chapter, Greene traces the magazine's attitudes toward segregation and civil rights. Following the passage of major civil rights legislation in 1964 and 1965, the *National Review* shifted from explicit white supremacy to a more implicit foregrounding of the dangers of government overreach, and by century's end emphasized a "color blind" ideology that also required a whitewashing of civil rights memory.

102. Nickerson, *Mothers of Conservatism*, 131.

103. Buckley first articulated the dangers of secularist, collectivist, liberal ideology in *God and Man at Yale* (Chicago: Henry Regnery, 1951), which catapulted him to the firmament of the conservative media world.

104. Hemmer, *Messengers of the Right*, xii, 130, 132; Julie B. Lane, "Cultivating Mistrust of the Mainstream Media," in *News on the Right: Studying Conservative News Cultures*, ed. Anthony Nadler and A. J. Bauer (New York: Oxford University Press, 2020), 169. For an account of accusations of liberalism directed at Republican Nelson Rockefeller by other Republicans, Rockefeller's efforts to avoid the liberal label, and the category of New Deal-supporting "Rockefeller Republicans" more generally, see Marsha E. Barrett, "Defining Rockefeller Republicanism: Promise and Peril at the Edge of Liberal Consensus, 1958–1975," *Journal of Political History* 36, no. 2 (2022): 336–370, https://doi.org/10.1017/S0898030622000100.

105. Lane, "Cultivating Mistrust,"166–171.

106. *National Review* editor Frank Meyer quoted by Lane, "Cultivating Mistrust," 166.

107. Lane, "Cultivating Mistrust," 168–169.

108. Stephen Asma, "Possessing Demons and Witches," in *On Monsters: An Unnatural History of Our Worst Fears* (Oxford: Oxford University Press, 2009), 103–123.

109. *Masters of Deceit* was ghostwritten by staff members of the FBI's public relations arm; see Stabile, *Broadcast 41*, 80.

110. Kovel, *Red Hunting*, 186.

111. Pegler quoted in Stabile, *Broadcast 41*, 144.

112. Harry Schwartz, "U.S. Communists Survey a Weakened Party," *New York Times*, December 13, 1959; "U.S. Communists Mark 39th Year," *New York Times*, September 27, 1959; Schwartz, "Drop in Numbers Is Noted by Reds," *New York Times*, November 15, 1959.

113. Belfrage, *The American Inquisition*, 275.

114. Belfrage, *The American Inquisition*, 195.

115. Quoted in Caute, *The Great Fear*, 215; Samuel Stouffer, *Communism, Conformity, and Civil Liberties: A Cross Section of the Nation Speaks Its Mind* (New Brunswick, NJ: Transaction, [1955] 1992), 43, 176–177.

116. Kovel, *Red Hunting*, 12, 121, 179; for methodological discussions and an overview of critiques of Stouffer's work, see Mark Peffley and Lee Sigelman, "Intolerance of Communists during the McCarthy Era: A General Model," *Political Research Quarterly* 43, no. 1 (1990): 93–111.

117. John Kennedy Toole, *Confederacy of Dunces* (Baton Rouge: Louisiana State University Press, 1980), 5–7.

118. Belfrage, *The American Inquisition*, 119.

119. For more on Senator Joseph McCarthy and the history of the House Un-American Activities Committee (HUAC), which was formed at the outset of World War II and during the height of the Red Scare pumped out several editions of its *Guide to Subversive Organizations and Publications*, see Belfrage, *The American Inquisition*; Caute, *The Great Fear*; and Kovel, *Red Hunting*. For a study of HUAC and its relationship to both the Hollywood Blacklist and the FBI, see Sbardellati, *J. Edgar Hoover Goes to the Movies*. For more details on the imperative to hunt and punish those deemed subversive, including those listed in the FBI-spinoff *Counterattack* newsletter, see Stabile, *Broadcast 41*. For the history and consequences of the Loyalty Program created under President Truman and other forms of "bureaucratic oppression," see Caute, *The Great Fear*, and Olmstead, *Real Enemies*. For the history of the "informer racket" spearheaded by former FBI agents, see Caute, *The Great Fear*, and Stabile, *Broadcast 41*. For an overview of aggressive anticommunist propaganda efforts in the military and corporate sphere and the general push to "scare the hell out of the American people," see Kovel, *Red Hunting*, 105; Diamond, *Roads to Dominion*; and Matzko, *Radio Right*. For the history of redbaiting journalists and the anticommunist efforts of ultra-right Hollywood, including figures such as John Wayne and Walt Disney, see Donald T. Critchlow, *When Hollywood Was Right: How Movie Stars, Studio Moguls, and Big Business Remade American Politics* (Cambridge: Cambridge University Press, 2013).

120. Citing a range of Cold War–era media, Belfrage in *The American Inquisition* outlines how Americans were frightened into orthodoxy and the consequences of "subversion" coming to mean just about anything; Caute in *The Great Fear* focuses on the Red Scare's chilling effects on speech as well as its effects on the scientific community and labor movement; Kovel in *Red Hunting* and Caute in *The Great Fear* explore the widespread effects on educators, whom Caute emphasizes were disproportionately Jewish; and Stabile in *Broadcast 41* offers detailed studies of the women whose careers and in some cases entire lives were destroyed by the blacklist.

121. Stephanie Coontz, *The Way We Never Were: American Families and the Nostalgia Trap* (New York: Basic Books, 2016), 129–130.

122. Coontz, *The Way We Never Were*, 96.

123. Coontz, *The Way We Never Were*, 180; May, *Homeward Bound*, 49–54.

124. Coontz, *The Way We Never Were*, xxvii.

125. May, *Homeward Bound*, 132.

126. Coontz, *The Way We Never Were*, 29; May, *Homeward Bound*, 158–159.

127. May, *Homeward Bound*, 104.

128. May, *Homeward Bound*, 98, 13.

129. May, *Homeward Bound*, 133.

130. Stabile, *Broadcast 41*, 51.

131. May, *Homeward Bound*, 68, 164, 165, 132, 133.

132. J. E. Smyth, "Organisation Women and Belle Rebels: Hollywood's Working Women in the 1930s," in *Hollywood and the Great Depression: American Film, Politics, and Society in the 1930s*, ed. Iwan Morgan and Philip John Davies (Edinburgh: Edinburgh University Press, 2016), 66.

133. May, *Homeward Bound*, 42–46, 133–135; Coontz, *The Way We Never Were*, 28.

134. Beverly Gage, *G-Man: J. Edgar Hoover and the Making of the American Century* (New York: Penguin Books, 2022), xiv.

135. Stabile, *Broadcast 41*, 19–26.

136. Stabile, *Broadcast 41*, 32, 83.

137. Stabile, *Broadcast 41*, 80.

138. Kovel, *Red Hunting*, 92, 181; Stabile, *Broadcast 41*, 73–74, reference to "copaganda" on 176.

139. Gage, *G-Man*.

140. Stabile, *Broadcast 41*, 80–81.

141. Powers quoted by Stabile, *Broadcast 41*, 82.

142. In their edited volume *The Ghost Reader: Recovering Women's Contributions to Media Studies* (London: Goldsmiths Press, 2023), Elena D. Hristova, Aimee-Marie Dorsten, and Carol A. Stabile provide a sustained case study of what ideas weren't circulated due to the stifling confines of anticommunism. They resist this erasure by foregrounding the theoretical contributions of diverse women scholars who worked on the edges of the burgeoning fields of media studies, cultural studies, and communication studies from the 1930s to 1950s but whose intersectional work was lost to history and to the disciplinary canon.

143. Stabile, *Broadcast 41*, 41.

144. Coontz, *The Way We Never Were*, 31.

145. Nickerson, *Mothers of Conservatism*, xvii.

146. Stabile, *Broadcast 41*, 83–85.

CHAPTER 2

1. David Harrington Watt, "The Private Hopes of American Fundamentalists and Evangelicals, 1925–1975," *Religion and American Culture* 1, no. 2 (1991): 155–175, https://doi.org/10.1525/rac.1991.1.2.03a00020; Daniel Silliman, "An Evangelical Is Anyone Who Likes Billy Graham: Defining Evangelicalism with Carl Henry and Networks of Trust," *Church History* 90, no. 3 (September 2021): 621–643, https://doi.org/10.1017/S000964072100216X.

2. "Billy Graham: A New Kind of Evangelist," *Time*, October 25, 1954, https://content.time.com/time/subscriber/article/0,33009,823597-1,00.html.

3. Grant Wacker, *America's Pastor: Billy Graham and the Shaping of a Nation* (Cambridge, MA: Harvard University Press, 2014).

4. Interview with Merrill Dunlop (1979), Tape 3, Collection 50, Billy Graham Center Archives, Wheaton College, accessed March 2023, https://www2.wheaton.edu/bgc/archives/exhibits/YFC%201945/02%20background%2010.html. Merrill Dunlop was a Youth for Christ musician and in this interview reflects on his experiences performing at early Youth for Christ rallies.

5. Evans et al., "A Politics of Conversion: Billy Graham's Political and Social Vision," in *Billy Graham: American Pilgrim*, ed. Andrew Finstuen, Grant Wacker, and Anne Blue Wills (New York: Oxford University Press, 2017), https://doi.org/10.1093/acprof:oso/9780190683528.003.0007.

6. For an account of a biblically based fundamentalist conception of Satan, see George M. Marsden, *Fundamentalism and American Culture* (Oxford: Oxford University Press, 2006), 30, 49.

7. Frances Fitzgerald, "How Billy Graham Mainstreamed Evangelicals," *Daily Beast*, June 11, 2017, https://www.thedailybeast.com/how-billy-graham-conquered-america.

8. "Protestants: Boycotting Billy," *Time*, March 18, 1966, https://content.time.com/time/subscriber/article/0,33009,941981,00.html. Jones was addressing Graham's propensity to reach out to liberal Protestant denominations and not convert liberal Protestants to fundamentalist denominations, opting instead to send them back to their own denominations.

9. Joel A. Carpenter, "Fundamentalist Institutions and the Rise of Evangelical Protestantism, 1929–1942," *Church History* 49, no. 1 (March 1980): 62–75, https://doi.org/10.2307/3164640.

10. Michael Lienesch, *In the Beginning: Fundamentalism, the Scopes Trial, and the Making of the Antievolution Movement* (Chapel Hill: University of North Carolina Press, 2007).

11. Bradley J. Gundlach, "The Fundamentalist-Modernist Controversy," in *The Oxford Handbook of Presbyterianism* (New York: Oxford University Press, 2019), 97–115, https://doi.org/10.1093/oxfordhb/9780190608392.013.11.

12. Gundlach, "The Fundamentalist-Modernist Controversy."

13. Gundlach, "The Fundamentalist-Modernist Controversy."

14. Tona J. Hangen, *Redeeming the Dial: Radio, Religion, and Popular Culture in America* (Chapel Hill: University of North Carolina Press, 2003).

15. Hangen, *Redeeming the Dial*, 17.

16. Michael E. Pohlman, *Broadcasting the Faith: Protestant Religious Radio and Theology in America, 1920–50* (Eugene: Wipf and Stock, 2021), 3, 12, 26.

17. Thomas C. Berg, "'Proclaiming Together'? Convergence and Divergence in Mainline and Evangelical Evangelism, 1945–1967," *Religion and American Culture: A Journal of Interpretation* 5, no. 1 (1995): 49–76.

18. Charles E. Harvey, "John D. Rockefeller, Jr., and the Interchurch Movement of 1919–1920: A Different Angle on the Ecumenical Movement," *Church History* 51, no. 2 (June 1982): 198–209.

19. George M. Marsden, *Reforming Fundamentalism: Fuller Seminary and the New Evangelicalism* (Grand Rapids, MI: William B. Eerdmans, 1995), 3.

20. For a discussion of the proposed reaction to the isolationism of fundamentalism and the need for outreach, see Carl F. H. Henry, *The Uneasy Conscience of Modern Fundamentalism*, 2nd ed. (Grand Rapids, MI: William B. Eerdmans, 2003), 5–15.

21. Duane Murray Oldfield, *The Right and the Righteous: The Christian Right Confronts the Republican Party* (Lanham, MD: Rowman & Littlefield, 1996), 22.

22. Fundamentalism's relationship with the corporeal influence of Satan is based primarily around the ability of worldly desires to tempt people into sin. This temptation must be resisted on the personal level, particularly by enhancing one's own spirituality and insulating oneself from tempting influences. See Charles B. Strozier, *Apocalypse: On the Psychology of Fundamentalism in America* (Eugene, OR: Wipf and Stock, [1994] 2002), 87, 105.

23. See Richard Kyle, *Evangelicalism: An Americanized Christianity* (New York: Routledge, 2017), 103, for an overview of evangelist Billy Sunday's description of hell and heaven. An early work on the shift of the meaning of hell is found in George Wolfe Shinn, "What Has Become of Hell?," *North American Review* 170, no. 523 (1900): 837–849. For an excellent discussion of the evolution of the idea of hell through fundamentalism and Evangelicalism, see Joshua David Wright, "'The Devil Hates That Doctrine': Hell in American Fundamentalism and Evangelicalism, 1900–2015," MA thesis, University of Colorado at Boulder, 2016, https://scholar.colorado.edu/concern/graduate_thesis_or_dissertations/th83kz71s.

24. Wright, "The Devil Hates That Doctrine," 45–46.

25. "Billy Sunday 'Booze' sermon (1910)," in Barry Hankins, *Evangelicalism and Fundamentalism: A Documentary Reader* (New York: New York University Press, 2008), 118. In this famous sermon, evangelist Billy Sunday describes the evils of liquor.

26. W. Scott Poole, *Satan in America: The Devil We Know* (Lanham, MD: Rowman & Littlefield, 2009), 113–115; Stanley High, *Billy Graham: The Personal Story of the Man, His Message, and His Mission* (New York: McGraw-Hill, 1956), 64.

27. William D. Apel, "The Lost World of Billy Graham," *Review of Religious Research* 20, no. 2 (1979): 138–149.

28. Mary Beth Mathews, "The History of Black Evangelicals and American Politics," African American Historical Perspectives, March 30, 2017, https://www.aaihs.org/the-history-of-black-evangelicals-and-american-politics/.

29. "Graham Urges Restraint in Sit-Ins," *New York Times*, April 18, 1963, https://timesmachine.nytimes.com/timesmachine/1963/04/18/82057349.pdf?pdf_redirect=true&ip=0.

30. Martin Luther King Jr., *Letter from Birmingham Jail* (London: Penguin Classics, [1963] 2018).

31. For more on the relationship between New Evangelicals and Black Protestants, see Anthea Butler, *White Evangelical Racism: The Politics of Morality in America* (Chapel Hill: University of North Carolina Press, 2021), 35.

32. The SBC's position in the fundamentalist-modernist divide somewhat mirrored that of the NAE, as they took a slightly more moderate position between fundamentalism and modernism and would not label themselves fundamentalists. However, their focus on segregation and race had the effect of insulating them from other religious denominations and society as a whole. See Barry Hankins, *Uneasy in Babylon: Southern Baptist Conservatives and American Culture* (Tuscaloosa: University of Alabama Press, 2002).

33. Mary Beth Swetnam Mathews, *Doctrine and Race: African American Evangelicals and Fundamentalism between the Wars* (Tuscaloosa: University of Alabama Press, 2017), 2.

34. James Innell Packer and Thomas C. Oden, *One Faith: The Evangelical Consensus* (Downer's Grove, IL: InterVarsity Press, 2004), 23; David Buckelew Hunsicker, "The Rise of the Parachurch Movement in American Protestant Christianity during the 1930s and 1940s: A Detailed Study of the Beginnings of the Navigators, Young Life and Youth for Christ International," PhD dissertation, Trinity Evangelical Divinity School, 1998, https://philpapers.org/rec/HUNTRO-10; Paul Matzko, "Radio Politics, Origin Myths, and the Creation of New Evangelicalism," *Fides et Historia* 48, no. 1 (Winter/Spring 2016): 61–90.

35. Matzko, "Radio Politics," 61.

36. Hangen, *Redeeming the Dial*, 15, 16.

37. Carpenter, "Fundamentalist Institutions."

38. Quentin J. Schultze, "Evangelical Radio and the Rise of the Electronic Church, 1921–1948," *Journal of Broadcasting & Electronic Media* 32, no. 3 (Summer 1988): 289–306, https://doi.org/10.1080/08838158809386703.

39. Michele Rosenthal, "Introduction: The Triumph of Televangelism and the Decline of Mainline Religious Broadcasting," in *American Protestants and TV in*

the 1950s: Responses to a New Medium, ed. Michele Rosenthal (New York: Palgrave Macmillan US, 2007), 1–5, https://doi.org/10.1057/9780230609211_1.

40. Pohlman, *Broadcasting the Faith*, 3, 26.

41. Connor S. Kenaston, "Broadcasting the Gospel of Tolerance: Media, Capitalism, and Religion in Twentieth-Century America," Issue Lab, September 5, 2019, https://mediaimpact.issuelab.org/resource/broadcasting-the-gospel-of-tolerance-media-capitalism-and-religion-in-twentieth-century-america.html.

42. Harry Emerson Fosdick, *The Living of These Days: An Autobiography* (New York: Harper, 1956).

43. Robert Moats Miller, *Harry Emerson Fosdick: Preacher, Pastor, Prophet* (New York: Oxford University Press, 1985).

44. Hangen, *Redeeming the Dial*, 34, 96.

45. Hangen, *Redeeming the Dial*, 68, 96. For an example of this type of program, see *Old Fashioned Revival Hour* (1940s), "Christ Our Peace" (1-6-1952 Full Broadcast)—The Old Fashioned Revival Hour," YouTube, August 12, 2021, accessed March 2023, https://www.youtube.com/watch?v=7vvjkYJU5mU.

46. Paul Matzko, *The Radio Right: How a Band of Broadcasters Took on the Federal Government and Built the Modern Conservative Movement* (New York: Oxford University Press, 2020), 5.

47. Hangen, *Redeeming the Dial*, 27, 73.

48. Mark Ward, *Air of Salvation: The Story of Christian Broadcasting* (Grand Rapids, MI: Baker Books, 1994).

49. Hangen, *Redeeming the Dial*, 105.

50. Schultze, "Evangelical Radio."

51. National Religious Broadcasters, "Our History," accessed March 2023, https://nrb.org/who-we-are/our-history/.

52. Matzko, "Radio Politics," 61.

53. Lowell Sperry Saunders, "The National Religious Broadcasters and the Availability of Commercial Radio Time," PhD dissertation, University of Illinois at Urbana-Champaign, 1968.

54. Hangen, *Redeeming the Dial*, 17.

55. Hangen, *Redeeming the Dial*, 113–114.

56. Hangen, *Redeeming the Dial*, 125.

57. Clarence Bouma, "The Cancer of Liberalism," Calvin University Digital Commons, 1945, https://digitalcommons.calvin.edu/cgi/viewcontent.cgi?article=1109&context=calvin_forum.

58. Arlin C. Migliazzo, "Henrietta Mears, the Improbable Evangelical Leader," *Christianity Today*, December 13, 2021, https://www.christianitytoday.com/ct/2022/january-february/henrietta-mears-improbable-leader-teacher-migliazzo.html; Ethel May Baldwin and David V. Benson, *Henrietta Mears and How She Did It!* (Raleigh, NC: Regal Books, 1966).

59. Bruce L. Shelley, "The Rise of Evangelical Youth Movements," *Fides et Historia* 18, no. 1 (1986): 47–63.

60. Mark Senter, "The Youth for Christ Movement as an Educational Agency and Its Impact upon Protestant Churches, 1931–1979," PhD dissertation, Loyola University Chicago, 1989, 405, https://ecommons.luc.edu/luc_diss/2698/.

61. Randall J. Stephens, *The Devil's Music: How Christians Inspired, Condemned, and Embraced Rock 'n' Roll* (Cambridge, MA: Harvard University Press, 2018).

62. William Ward Ayer, "Jungle Madness in American Music," 1956, 19–21, accessed March 2023, http://archive.org/details/JMMMc. Includes the reprint from *Baptist Standard* magazine as well as related Youth for Christ material reprinted in the *Sunday School Times*.

63. *Life Lines* 10, no. 147 (1968), https://jstor.org/stable/community.28146299.

64. Rev. David A. Noebel, "Communism, Hypnotism and the Beatles," 1965, accessed February 2023, http://archive.org/details/CommunismHypnotismAndTheBeatles.

65. David R. Swartz, "Chicago 1945: Youth for Christ and World War II," in *Facing West: American Evangelicals in an Age of World Christianity*, ed. David R. Swartz (New York: Oxford University Press, 2020), 13–34, https://doi.org/10.1093/oso/9780190250805.003.0002.

66. Shelley, "The Rise of Evangelical Youth Movements"; Hunsicker, "The Rise of the Parachurch Movement"; "Pamphlets from Chicagoland Youth for Christ. Chicagoland—Memorial Day Rally—Soldier Field," 1945, accessed February 2023, http://archive.org/details/chicagoland-memorial-day-rally.

67. "[Pamphlets Published by Youth for Christ]," (Chicago: Youth for Christ International), accessed March 2023, http://archive.org/details/pamphletspublish00unse.

68. "Background—The Greatest Youth Gathering: Billy Graham and the 1949 Los Angeles Campaign," exhibit of the Billy Graham Center Archives, Wheaton College, accessed December 13, 2022, https://www2.wheaton.edu/bgc/archives/exhibits/YFC%201945/02%20background.html.

69. Rosenthal, "The Triumph of Televangelism," 12.

70. Michael S. Hamilton, "From Desire to Decision: The Evangelistic Preaching of Billy Graham," in *Billy Graham: American Pilgrim*, ed. Andrew Finstuen, Grant Wacker, and Anne Blue Wills (New York: Oxford University Press, 2017), 43–63, https://doi.org/10.1093/acprof:oso/9780190683528.003.0003.

71. See Billy Graham Evangelistic Association, "Billy Graham's 1957 New York Crusade Sermon at Yankee Stadium," YouTube, July 21, 2017, accessed March 2023, https://www.youtube.com/watch?v=1aZoqIwHsdM.

72. See songs from Fuller's *Old Fashioned Revival Hour Songs*, accessed March 2023, https://digitalcommons.gardner-webb.edu/cgi/viewcontent.cgi?article=1020& context=round-note-collection.

73. Fuller sermon, accessed March 2023, https://ia600201.us.archive.org/1/items /SERMONINDEX_SID12481/SID12481.mp3.

74. Douglas T. Miller, "Popular Religion of the 1950's: Norman Vincent Peale and Billy Graham," *Journal of Popular Culture* 9, no. 1 (Summer 1975): 66.

75. Pamphlets Published by Youth for Christ, accessed December 15, 2022, http://archive.org/details/pamphletspublish00unse.

76. Anti-liquor advertisements of the time often conjured demonic imagery and temptation, for example, the "Devil's Toboggan Slide," accessed March 2023, https://ohiomemory.org/digital/collection/p267401coll32/id/21796/; see also Ralph G. Giordano, *Satan in the Dance Hall: Reverend John Roach Straton, Social Dancing, and Morality in 1920s New York City* (Lanham, MD: Scarecrow Press, 2008).

77. Matthew Avery Sutton, *American Apocalypse: A History of Modern Evangelicalism* (Cambridge, MA: Harvard University Press, 2014), 25. Many sermons and pamphlets of New Evangelicals point out the link between liberal religion and Satan. For an overview, see W. Scott Poole, *Satan in America: The Devil We Know* (Lanham, MD: Rowman & Littlefield, 2009), and James DeForest Murch, *Cooperation without Compromise: A History of the National Association of Evangelicals* (Grand Rapids, MI: William B. Eerdmans, 1956), 64.

78. Joel A. Carpenter, *A New Evangelical Coalition: Early Documents of the National Association of Evangelicals* (New York: Garland, 1988), 74.

79. Ockenga quoted in Carpenter, *A New Evangelical Coalition*, 33.

80. Poole, *Satan in America*, 2009.

81. Anna Nekola, "'More than Just a Music': Conservative Christian Anti-Rock Discourse and the U.S. Culture Wars," *Popular Music* 32, no. 3 (2013): 407–426; Stephens, *The Devil's Music*; Hunsicker, "The Rise of the Parachurch Movement."

82. Pamphlets Published by Youth for Christ (Chicago: Youth for Christ International), accessed December 15, 2022, http://archive.org/details/pamphlets publish00unse.

83. Billy Graham, "The World's Darkest Hour," Billy Graham Evangelical Association, June 27, 2019, https://billygraham.org/video/the-worlds-darkest-hour-2/. Sermon delivered in 1958.

84. Graham, "The World's Darkest Hour."

85. Milton J. Coalter et al., *Vital Signs: The Promise of Mainstream Protestantism* (Grand Haven, MI: FaithWalk, 2002), 10–12.

86. Harriet A. Harris. *Fundamentalism and Evangelicals* (Oxford: Clarendon Press, 1998), 58.

87. Ockenga quoted in Carpenter, *A New Evangelical Coalition*, 33.

88. See Thomas Aiello, "Constructing 'Godless Communism': Religion, Politics, and Popular Culture, 1954–1960," *Americana* 4, no. 1 (Spring 2005), https://american popularculture.com/journal/articles/spring_2005/aiello.htm; Clyde Wilcox and Ted Jelen, "Evangelicals and Political Tolerance," *American Politics Quarterly* 18, no. 1 (1990): 25–46; Angela M. Lahr, *Millennial Dreams and Apocalyptic Nightmares: The Cold War Origins of Political Evangelicalism* (New York: Oxford University Press, 2007); Stephen Bates, "'Godless Communism' and Its Legacies," *Society* 41, no. 3 (2004): 29–33.

89. Billy Graham, "Satan's Religion," *American Mercury*, August 1954.

90. Graham, "Satan's Religion."

91. Melissa M. Deckman, *School Board Battles: The Christian Right in Local Politics* (Washington, DC: Georgetown University Press, 2004).

92. Natalia Mehlman, "Sex Ed . . . and the Reds? Reconsidering the Anaheim Battle over Sex Education, 1962–1969," *History of Education Quarterly* 47, no. 2 (2007): 203–232.

93. United States Congress Committee on Un-American Activities, "100 Things You Should Know about Communism Series" (Washington, DC, 1949), 42, accessed March 2023, http://archive.org/details/100thingsyoushou1949unit.

94. "Is There a Pink Fringe in the Methodist Church? If so, What Shall We Do about It? A Report to Methodists," Committee for the Preservation of Methodism (Houston, 1951), accessed March 2023, http://archive.org/details/isthere pinkfring0000comm.

95. W. H. Locke Anderson, "Red Hunting in the Promised Land," *Monthly Review* 46, no. 1 (May 1994): 54–61.

96. Lerone A. Martin, *The Gospel of J. Edgar Hoover: How the FBI Aided and Abetted the Rise of White Christian Nationalism* (Princeton, NJ: Princeton University Press, 2023).

97. Curtis J. Evans, "White Evangelical Protestant Responses to the Civil Rights Movement," *Harvard Theological Review* 102, no. 2 (2009): 245–273.

98. Butler, *White Evangelical Racism*, 54.

99. Nancy Gibbs and Michael Duffy, *The Preacher and the Presidents: Billy Graham in the White House* (New York: Center Street, 2007).

100. Evans et al., "A Politics of Conversion."

101. Jack Cargill Jr., *The American Far Right: A Case Study of Billy James Hargis and Christian Crusade* (Grand Rapids, MI: William B. Eerdmans, 1969).

102. Heather Hendershot, "God's Angriest Man: Carl McIntire, Cold War Fundamentalism, and Right-Wing Broadcasting," *American Quarterly* 59, no. 2 (2007): 373–396.

CHAPTER 3

1. "Ronald Reagan, 'Evil Empire' Speech (March 8, 1983)," Voices of Democracy, accessed February 2023, https://voicesofdemocracy.umd.edu/reagan-evil-empire-speech-text/.

2. Reagan, "Evil Empire," paragraph 47.

3. Diane Winston, *Righting the American Dream: How the Media Mainstreamed Reagan's Evangelical Vision* (Chicago: University of Chicago Press, 2023), 113.

4. Thomas G. Paterson, *Meeting the Communist Threat: Truman to Reagan* (New York: Oxford University Press, 1988), xi, 47.

5. Nicole Hemmer, *Messengers of the Right: Conservative Media and the Transformation of American Politics* (Philadelphia: University of Pennsylvania Press 2016), xii.

6. Hemmer, *Messengers of the Right*, xii.

7. Donald T. Critchlow, *When Hollywood Was Right: How Movie Stars, Studio Moguls, and Big Business Remade American Politics* (Cambridge: Cambridge University Press, 2013), 8–10, 15, 30.

8. Sara Diamond, *Roads to Dominion: Right-Wing Movements and Political Power in the United States* (New York: Guilford Press, 1995), 17–18, 24.

9. Diamond, *Roads to Dominion*, 24.

10. Critchlow, *When Hollywood Was Right*, 34.

11. Diamond, *Roads to Dominion*, 24.

12. Diamond, *Roads to Dominion*, 24.

13. Critchlow, *When Hollywood Was Right*, 38.

14. Hemmer, *Messengers of the Right*, 21.

15. Hemmer, *Messengers of the Right*, 20–21.

16. Hemmer, *Messengers of the Right*, 32–33.

17. Critchlow, *When Hollywood Was Right*, 39.

18. Michelle M. Nickerson, *Mothers of Conservatism: Women and the Postwar Right* (Princeton, NJ: Princeton University Press, 2012), xvi, 32.

19. Diamond, *Roads to Dominion*, 30; Julie B. Lane, "Cultivating Mistrust of the Mainstream Media," in *News on the Right: Studying Conservative News Cultures*, ed.

Anthony Nadler and A. J. Bauer (New York: Oxford University Press, 2020), 160.

20. Nickerson, *Mothers of Conservatism*, 32.

21. Mary C. Brennan, *Wives, Mothers, and the Red Menace: Conservative Women and the Crusade against Communism* (Boulder: University Press of Colorado, 2008), 4–5.

22. Hemmer, *Messengers of the Right*, 124.

23. Paul Matzko, *The Radio Right: How a Band of Broadcasters Took on the Federal Government and Built the Modern Conservative Movement* (New York: Oxford University Press, 2020), 22.

24. Hemmer, *Messengers of the Right*, 22, 51.

25. Hemmer, *Messengers of the Right*, 51.

26. Hemmer, *Messengers of the Right*, 52.

27. Hemmer, *Messengers of the Right*, 42–43; Matzko, *Radio Right*, 30; Nickerson, *Mothers of Conservatism*, 30.

28. Hemmer, *Messengers of the Right*, 5, 24–25.

29. Hemmer, *Messengers of the Right*, 30.

30. Hemmer, *Messengers of the Right*, 22–23; Diamond, *Roads to Dominion*, 30.

31. Nickerson, *Mothers of Conservatism*, xvii, 32.

32. Lane, "Cultivating Mistrust," 161.

33. Hemmer, *Messengers of the Right*, 130, 161; Lane, "Cultivating Mistrust," 162–163.

34. Hemmer, *Messengers of the Right*, 40.

35. Lane, "Cultivating Mistrust," 170.

36. Hemmer, *Messengers of the Right*, 82.

37. Hemmer, *Messengers of the Right*, 29.

38. Buckley quoted in Hemmer, *Messengers of the Right*, 42.

39. Hemmer, *Messengers of the Right*, 43.

40. Hemmer, *Messengers of the Right*, xiii.

41. Manion quoted in Hemmer, *Messengers of the Right*, 130.

42. Hemmer, *Messengers of the Right*, 55.

43. D. J. Mulloy, *The World of the John Birch Society: Conspiracy, Conservatism, and the Cold War* (Nashville, TN: Vanderbilt University, 2014), 27.

44. Mulloy, *World of John Birch*, 15–22.

45. Diamond, *Roads to Dominion*, 64–65; Heather Hendershot, *What's Fair on the Air: Cold War Right-Wing Broadcasting and the Public Interest* (Chicago: University of Chicago Press, 2011), 7.

46. Hemmer, *Messengers of the Right*, 109; Mulloy, *World of John Birch*, 21; Critchlow, *When Hollywood Was Right*, 155, 187.

47. Nickerson, *Mothers of Conservatism*, xviii.

48. Mulloy, *World of John Birch*, 29.

49. Mulloy, *World of John Birch*, 28.

50. Matzko, *Radio Right*, 115.

51. Matzko, *Radio Right*, 73.

52. Matzko, *Radio Right*, 101–102.

53. Hendershot, *What's Fair on the Air*, 17.

54. Hemmer, *Messengers of the Right*, 116.

55. Matzko, *Radio Right*, 117.

56. Hemmer, *Messengers of the Right*, 116.

57. Hemmer, *Messengers of the Right*, 109.

58. Hemmer, *Messengers of the Right*, 117.

59. Hemmer, *Messengers of the Right*, 32.

60. Hemmer, *Messengers of the Right*, 117.

61. Matzko, *Radio Right*, 108–109.

62. Matzko, *Radio Right*, 93, 102, 132; Hendershot, *What's Fair on the Air*, 17.

63. Matzko, *Radio Right*, 133.

64. Matzko, *Radio Right*, 191.

65. Matzko, *Radio Right*, 66.

66. Matzko, *Radio Right*, 206, 191.

67. Matzko, *Radio Right*, 196.

68. Matzko, *Radio Right*, 181.

69. Matzko, *Radio Right*, 194; Hemmer, *Messengers of the Right*, 119, 123–124.

70. Matzko, *Radio Right*, 206–207.

71. Matzko, *Radio Right*, 224.

72. John Durham Peters, *Speaking into the Air: A History of the Idea of Communication* (Chicago: University of Chicago Press, 2001), 52.

73. Kate Starbird, "Information Wars: A Window into the Alternative Media Ecosystem," *Medium*, March 14, 2017, https://medium.com/hci-design-at-uw

/information-wars-a-window-into-the-alternative-media-ecosystem-a1347
f32fd8f; Kate Starbird et al., "Eco-System or Echo-System? Exploring Content
Sharing across Alternative Media Domains," *Proceedings of the Twelfth International
AAAI Conference on Web and Social Media* 12, no. 1 (2018), https://doi.org/10.1609
/icwsm.v12i1.15009.

74. Hemmer, *Messengers of the Right*, 45–48.

75. Kim Phillips-Fein, *Invisible Hands: The Businessmen's Crusade against the New
Deal* (New York: W.W. Norton, 2010), 83–84.

76. Matzko, *Radio Right*, 10; Mary C. Brennan, *Turning Right in the 60s: The Conservative Capture of the GOP* (Chapel Hill: University of North Carolina Press,
1995), 13, 145n18.

77. Sara Diamond in *Roads to Dominion* explains that funding for anti-union efforts
were especially high, 52; Phillips-Fein in *Invisible Hands* explains how panic over
wealth distribution motivated corporate largesse, 84; Hemmer in *Messengers of the
Right* discusses Hunt and the various rightwing causes he supported, 52, 111.

78. Phillips-Fein, *Invisible Hands*, 70–71, 77.

79. Darren E. Grem, "'Christianity Today,' J. Howard Pew, and the Business of Conservative Evangelicalism," *Enterprise & Society* 15, no. 2 (June 2014):
353–354.

80. Phillips-Fein, *Invisible Hands*, 71.

81. John G. Turner, *Bill Bright's Campus Crusade for Christ: The Renewal of Evangelicalism in Postwar America* (Chapel Hill: University of North Carolina Press, 2008),
92–93; Linda Kintz, *Between Jesus and the Market: The Emotions That Matter in Right-
Wing America* (Durham, NC: Duke University Press, 1997), 24.

82. Grem, "Christianity Today," 341.

83. Nickerson, *Mothers of Conservatism*, 24.

84. Hemmer, *Messengers of the Right*, 113.

85. Matzko, *Radio Right*, 51.

86. Elizabeth Gillespie McRae, *Mothers of Massive Resistance: White Women and the
Politics of White Supremacy* (New York: Oxford University Press, 2018), 4, 9, 13, 16.

87. Matzko, *Radio Right*, 53.

88. Matzko, *Radio Right*, 34, 50.

89. Nickerson, *Mothers of Conservatism*, 40.

90. Nickerson, *Mothers of Conservatism*, xvii.

91. Nickerson, *Mothers of Conservatism*, 142–148.

92. Nickerson, *Mothers of Conservatism*, 148.

93. Dan Carter, *The Politics of Rage: George Wallace, the Origins of the New Conservatism, and the Transformation of American Politics*, 2nd ed. (Baton Rouge: Louisiana State University Press, [1995] 2000), 299.

94. Carter, *Politics of Rage*, 297.

95. Carter, *Politics of Rage*, 299. For more on Wallace's relationship to white Southern Baptists, see Anthony M. Orum, "Religion and the Rise of the Radical White: The Case of Southern Wallace Support in 1968," *Social Science Quarterly* 51, no. 3 (1970): 674–688.

96. Carter, *Politics of Rage*, 338–339.

97. Hemmer, *Messengers of the Right*, xiii; see also Randall J. Stephens and Karl W. Giberson, *The Anointed: Evangelical Truth in a Secular Age* (Cambridge, MA: Harvard University Press, 2011), 10.

98. Hemmer, *Messengers of the Right*, xiv.

99. Hendershot, *What's Fair on the Air*, 12.

100. Michelle Goldberg, "How the Secular Humanist Grinch Didn't Steal Christmas," *Salon*, November 21, 2005, https://www.salon.com/2005/11/21/christmas_6/.

101. Hemmer, *Messengers of the Right*, 22; Hendershot, *What's Fair on the Air*, 53, 120.

102. Nickerson, *Mothers of Conservatism*, 27.

103. McRae, *Mothers of Massive Resistance*, 13.

104. W. Stanford Reid, "Christians and the United Nations," *Christianity Today*, June 22, 1959, https://www.christianitytoday.com/ct/1959/june-22/christians-and-united-nations.html.

105. Grem, "'Christianity Today,'" 366.

106. Grem, "'Christianity Today,'" 354.

107. Hemmer, *Messengers of the Right*, 45; Anthony Nadler and A. J. Bauer, "Taking Conservative News Seriously," in *News on the Right*, ed. Nadler and Bauer, 3; Phillips-Fein, *Invisible Hands*, 85.

108. Matzko, *Radio Right*, 18.

109. Turner, *Bill Bright's Campus Crusade*, 111. As Turner highlights, Campus Crusade may have emphasized outreach and conversion, but was not enormously successful in its efforts to reach students who didn't already number among the Evangelical flock, 126–128.

110. Stanton Evans, *Revolt on the Campus* (Chicago: Henry Regnery, 1961), 47–56.

111. Evans, *Revolt on the Campus*, 51–53.

112. Evans, *Revolt on the Campus*, 54.

113. Evans, *Revolt on the Campus*, 184.

114. Diamond, *Roads to Dominion*, 30, 85; Caroline Rolland-Diamond, "Another Side of the Sixties: Festive Practices on College Campuses and the Making of a Conservative Youth Movement," *Revue Française d'études Américaines* 146, no. 1 (2016): 39–53, 40.

115. Turner, *Bill Bright's Campus Crusade*, 122; Evans, *Revolt on the Campus*, 46; Hemmer, *Messengers of the Right*, 83.

116. Turner, *Bill Bright's Campus Crusade*, 64, 108, 132.

117. Evans, *Revolt on the Campus*, 189.

118. Turner, *Bill Bright's Campus Crusade*, 108.

119. Bill Bright, "Come and Help Change the World," 1970, accessed March 2023, https://archive.org/details/comehelpchangewo00brig/mode/2up.

120. Carter, *Politics of Rage*, 336.

121. Turner, *Bill Bright's Campus Crusade*, 110.

122. For instance, Pew was connected with the political action groups Christian Citizen and the Christian Freedom Foundation, both of which were linked to Bill Bright, whose relationship to Sunbelt businessmen like Pew could only be described as *entangled*. See Turner, *Bill Bright's Campus Crusade*, 109–110, and Darren Dochuk's *Anointed in Oil: How Christianity and Crude Made Modern America* (New York: Basic Books, 2019), which describes how men like Pew helped fund the rise of Evangelicalism, as well as his article "The Other Brother Duo That Brought Us the Modern GOP," *Politico Magazine*, September 2, 2019, https://www.politico.com/magazine/story/2019/09/02/pew-brothers-politics-influence-wealth-227993/; for more on the extensive ties between Pew and various Evangelical organizations, see Carmen Celestini, "God, Country, and Christian Conservatives: The National Association of Manufacturers, the John Birch Society, and the Rise of the Christian Right," PhD dissertation, University of Waterloo, 2018.

123. Hemmer, *Messengers of the Right*, 83.

124. Diamond, *Roads to Dominion*, 30.

125. Hemmer, *Messengers of the Right*, 86.

126. Hemmer, *Messengers of the Right*, 89–90.

127. Hemmer, *Messengers of the Right*, 52.

128. Hemmer, *Messengers of the Right*, 58.

129. Rolland-Diamond, "Another Side of the Sixties."

130. Rolland-Diamond, "Another Side of the Sixties," 44.

131. Rolland-Diamond, "Another Side of the Sixties," 45, 48–49.

132. Rolland-Diamond, "Another Side of the Sixties," 50.

133. Rolland-Diamond, "Another Side of the Sixties," 52.

134. Evans, *Revolt on the Campus*, 51–52.

135. Diamond, *Roads to Dominion*, 29.

136. Diamond, *Roads to Dominion*, 127.

137. Diamond, *Roads to Dominion*, 127.

138. Diamond, *Roads to Dominion*, 98.

139. Matzko, *Radio Right*, 225.

140. Matzko, *Radio Right*, 223–224.

141. Hemmer, *Messengers of the Right*, 87.

142. Reagan, "Evil Empire," paragraph 53.

CHAPTER 4

1. House Republican Conference, *Contract with America: The Bold Plan by Rep. Newt Gingrich, Reps. Dick Armey, and the House Republicans to Change the Nation* (New York: Times Books, 1994).

2. Gingrich speech printed in *Contract*, 182.

3. David Mikkelson, "Newt Gingrich Auschwitz Quote," *Snopes*, November 17, 2011, https://www.snopes.com/fact-check/i-of-newt/; Maureen Dowd, "Who's the Con Man?," *New York Times*, September 14, 2010, https://www.nytimes.com/2010/09/15/opinion/15dowd.html.

4. Myra MacPherson, "Newt Gingrich, Point Man in a House Divided," *Washington Post*, June 12, 1989, https://www.washingtonpost.com/archive/lifestyle/1989/06/12/newt-gingrich-point-man-in-a-house-divided/b26c704a-e1f8-4705-b9cc-9c01eb93187d/.

5. James Salzer, "Gingrich's Language Set a New Course," *Atlanta Journal-Constitution*, July 5, 2016, https://www.ajc.com/news/local-govt--politics/gingrich-language-set-new-course/O5bgK6lY2wQ3KwEZsY.

6. "Gingrich 'Loony Left' 88," CSPAN, January 28, 2021, accessed June 2023, https://www.c-span.org/video/?c4941963/user-clip-16783633-fzpp-gingrich-loony-left-88.

7. Salzer, "Gingrich's Language," 2016; David Corn and Tim Murphy, "A Very Long List of Dumb Things Newt Gingrich Has Said and Done," *Mother Jones*, November 15, 2016, https://www.motherjones.com/politics/2016/11/very-long-list-dumb-and-awful-things-newt-gingrich-has-said-and-done/; Lawrence Simon,

"How the Republican Revolution Broke Congress," *Review*, January 16, 2019, https://virginiapolitics.org/online/2019/1/16/how-the-republican-revolution -broke-congress; Julian E. Zelizer, *Burning Down the House: Newt Gingrich, the Fall of a Speaker, and the Rise of the New Republican Party* (New York: Penguin, 2020).

8. Myra MacPherson, "Newt Gingrich, Point Man in a House Divided," *Washington Post*, June 11, 1989, https://www.washingtonpost.com/archive/lifestyle/1989 /06/12/newt-gingrich-point-man-in-a-house-divided/b26c704a-e1f8-4705-b9cc -9c01eb93187d/.

9. Salzer, "Gingrich's Language," 2016.

10. "Language: A Key Mechanism of Control," GOPAC, 1995, accessed May 2023, http://users.wfu.edu/zulick/454/gopac.html.

11. Salzer, "Gingrich's Language," 2016.

12. Republican Conference, *Contract*, 7.

13. Republican Conference, *Contract*, 7.

14. Geoffrey C. Layman, *The Great Divide: Religious and Cultural Conflict in American Party Politics* (New York: Columbia University Press, 2001), 44, 101, 239; J. Brooks Flippen, *Jimmy Carter, the Politics of Family, and the Rise of the Religious Right* (Athens: University of Georgia Press, 2011), 68, 198–200, 264; Matthew Levendusky, *The Partisan Sort: How Liberals Became Democrats and Conservatives Became Republicans* (Chicago: University of Chicago Press, 2009).

15. James Davison Hunter, *Culture Wars: The Struggle to Control the Family, Art, Education, Law, and Politics in America* (New York: Basic Books, 1991); Robert Wuthnow, *The Struggle for America's Soul: Evangelicals, Liberals, and Secularism* (Grand Rapids, MI: William B. Eerdmans, 1989).

16. Neil Forsyth, *The Old Enemy: Satan and the Combat Myth* (Princeton, NJ: Princeton University, 1987); Elaine Pagels, *The Origin of Satan* (New York: Vintage Books, 1995), 12, 60, 74, 82–83, 111.

17. Pagels, *Origin of Satan*, 13–14, 74.

18. Pagels, *Origin of Satan*, 146.

19. Pagels, *Origin of Satan*, 39–48, 102–103, 179.

20. Forsyth, *The Old Enemy*, 115; Pagels, *Origin of Satan*, 12, 39–41, 102.

21. Richard Raiswell, Michelle D. Brock, and David R. Winter, "Introduction: Giving the Devil His Due," in *The Routledge History of the Devil in the Western Tradition*, ed. Richard Raiswell, Michelle D. Brock, and David R. Winter (New York: Routledge, 2025).

22. Pagels, *Origin of Satan*, 19, 38, 83–84, 88, 139, 165, 179, 184.

23. Pagels, *Origin of Satan*, 13, 123.

24. Pagels, *Origin of Satan*, 28, 82, 91, 98, 114.

25. In *The Old Enemy*, Forsyth highlights the centrality of Satan within the Christian system with the simple proclamation "No Devil, no God," quoting John Wesley, 7–8; in *Origin of Satan*, Pagels emphasizes what is unique to the early Christians regarding their good versus evil cosmology, xxii, 130, 84.

26. One notable exception is *Hunt the Devil: Demonology in U.S. War Culture* (Tuscaloosa: University of Alabama Press, 2015) by Robert L. Ivie and Oscar Giner, which explores the figure of the devil in U.S. war discourse and other forms of political demonization.

27. Forsyth, quoting Percy Bysshe Shelley, *The Old Enemy*, xiii.

28. Jason C. Bivins, *Religion of Fear: The Politics of Horror in Conservative Evangelicalism* (Oxford: Oxford University Press, 2008), 10.

29. W. Scott Poole, *Satan in America: The Devil We Know* (Lanham, MD: Rowman and Littlefield, 2009), 158, 160; Bill Ellis, *Raising the Devil: Satanism, New Religions, and the Media* (Lexington: University of Kentucky Press, 2000), 11.

30. Bivins, *Religion of Fear*, 40.

31. Daniel G. Hummel, *The Rise and Fall of Dispensationalism: How the Evangelical Battle over the End Times Shaped a Nation* (Grand Rapids, MI: William B. Eerdmans, 2023). We agree with Hummel's overarching argument about the cultural influence of Evangelical apocalypticism, with a slight adjustment. It's not just that Evangelicalism's apocalypticism has influenced U.S. culture and politics. It's that the shadow gospel's apocalypticism has influenced Evangelicalism. For more on the history of how end-times narratives entered vernacular American discourse, see Donald Harman Akenson, *The Americanization of the Apocalypse: Creating America's Own Bible* (Oxford: Oxford University Press, 2023).

32. Bivins, *Religion of Fear*, 9.

33. Bivins, *Religion of Fear*, 19, 21, 37, 137.

34. Bivins, *Religion of Fear*, 17.

35. For a collection of Chick's work, see Kurt Kuersteiner, *The Unofficial Guide to the Art of Jack T. Chick: Chick Tracts, Crusader Comics, and Battle Cry Newspapers* (Atglen, PA: Schiffer Publications, 2004).

36. Bivins, *Religion of Fear*, 47.

37. Bivins, *Religion of Fear*, 49.

38. Bivins, *Religion of Fear*, 56.

39. Richard Lee quoted in Bivins, *Religion of Fear*, 84.

40. Bivins, *Religion of Fear*, 85.

41. Bivins, *Religion of Fear*, 85, 231, 233.

42. The line between what is called "fundamentalist" and what is called "Evangelical" can be fuzzy, with the terms unevenly applied across disciplines, scholars, and sometimes even within the same study. One can, however, make a broad *positional* claim (insular versus externally focused), which is how we are distinguishing the groups here.

43. Nancy T. Ammerman, "North American Protestant Fundamentalism," in *Media, Culture, and the Religious Right*, ed. Linda Kintz and Julia Lesage (Minneapolis: University of Minnesota Press, 1998), 62.

44. Daniel Wojcik, *The End of the World as We Know It: Faith, Fatalism, and Apocalypse in America* (New York: New York University Press, 1997), 144. For a succinct overview of apocalypticism across religious traditions, see Daniel Wojcik, "Apocalypticism and Millenarianism," in *Encyclopedia of New Religions: New Religious Movements, Sects, and Alternative Spiritualities*, ed. Christopher Partridge (Oxford: Lion Publishing, 2004), 388–395.

45. Wojcik, *The End of the World*, 32, 50–53.

46. Wojcik, *The End of the World*, 162–165.

47. Wojcik, *The End of the World*, 35–36, 56.

48. Wojcik, *The End of the World*, 141; see also Daniel Wojcik, "Fatalism," in *Encyclopedia of Millennialism and Millennial Movements*, ed. Richard Landes (New York: Routledge, 2000), 149–155.

49. Wojcik, *The End of the World*, 11, 14, 36, 56–58, 136.

50. Wojcik, *The End of the World*, 38.

51. Hal Lindsey with C. C. Carlson, *The Late Great Planet Earth* (Grand Rapids, MI: Zondervan Publishing House, 1970).

52. Hal Lindsey with C. C. Carlson, *Satan Is Alive and Well on Planet Earth* (Grand Rapids, MI: Zondervan Publishing House, 1972).

53. Jonathan Kirsch, "Interview with Hal Lindsey," *Publishers Weekly*, March 14, 1977. In this interview, Lindsey speaks to his appreciation for the finer things in life, including Porsche sports cars, prompting his interviewer to describe him as "the preacher in the Porsche jacket." Lindsey expresses agitation at how people have discussed his personal finances. "I've made my money legitimately," he snips (30, 32).

54. Wojcik, *The End of the World*, 48–49, 37. For an extended analysis of Lindsey's influence on apocalyptic belief in the United States, see Wojcik's chapter, "Signs of the End Times" in *The End of the World*, 37–59.

55. Poole, *Satan in America*, 190.

56. Lindsey, *Late Great Planet Earth*, 174–175.

57. Bivins, *Religion of Fear*, 182.

58. Wojcik, *The End of the World*, 47.

59. Bivins, *Religion of Fear*, 179.

60. Bivins, *Religion of Fear*, 37.

61. Bivins, *Religion of Fear*, 178.

62. Bivins, *Religion of Fear*, 178.

63. Wojcik, *The End of the World*, 48–49.

64. Mike Hertenstein and Jon Trott, authors of the *Cornerstone Magazine* exposé of Warnke, expanded their investigation into *Selling Satan: The Evangelical Media and the Mike Warnke Scandal* (Chicago: Cornerstone Press, 1993).

65. Mike Warnke, *The Satan Seller* (Plainfield, NJ: Logos International, 1972).

66. Poole, *Satan in America*, 172; Hertenstein and Trott elaborate on the Evangelical influence of Warnke in *Selling Satan*, xiii, 4, 14.

67. For more on Mike Warnke and John Todd, see Poole, *Satan in America*, 172. Jeffrey Victor provides a full account of Todd's relationship to Jack Chick in *Satanic Panic: The Creation of a Contemporary Legend* (Chicago: Open Court Press, 1993), 143, 168, 227–230.

68. Poole, *Satan in America*, 161.

69. Whitney Phillips and Ryan Milner, *You Are Here: A Field Guide for Navigating Polarized Speech, Conspiracy Theories, and Our Polluted Media Landscape* (Cambridge, MA: MIT Press, 2021, 24–30).

70. See generally Viktor, *Satanic Panic*, 133–152.

71. Phillips and Milner, *You Are Here*, 28.

72. Lindsey, *The Late Great Planet Earth*, 126.

73. Billy Graham, *Angels: God's Secret Agents* (Waco, TX: Word Books, 1975), 107, 120, 124, 126, 185–186.

74. Graham, *Angels*, 19.

75. Wojcik, *The End of the World*, 47; John Dart, "He Predicted Early Second Coming: Pat Robertson Remarks Deter Secular Believers," *Los Angeles Times*, March 4, 1988, https://www.latimes.com/archives/la-xpm-1988-03-04-mn-378 -story.html.

76. Wojcik, *The End of the World*, 45, 49, 58.

77. Razelle Frankl, "Transformation of Televangelism: Repackaging Christian Family Values," in *Media, Culture, and the Religious Right*, ed. Kintz and Lesage, 169.

78. Eithne Johnson, "The Emergence of Christian Video and the Cultivation of Videoangelism," in *Media, Culture, and the Religious Right*, ed. Kintz and Lesage, 191.

79. Wm Conley, "The Tracking of Evil: Home Video and the Proliferation of the Satanic Panic," in *Satanic Panic: Pop-Cultural Paranoia in the 1980s*, ed. Kier-La Janisse and Paul Corupe (Surrey: FAB Press, 2015), 243.

80. Conley, "Tracking of Evil," 236–239.

81. Bivins, *Religion of Fear*, 138, 140.

82. Joshua Benjamin Graham, "Masters of the Imagination: Fundamentalist Readings of the Occult in Cartoons of the 1980s," in *Satanic Panic: Pop-Cultural Paranoia in the 1980s*, ed. Janisse and Corupe, 83–96; Phil Phillips, *Turmoil in the Toy Box* (Lancaster: Starburst, 1990); Phil Phillips, *Saturday Morning Mind Control* (Nashville, TN: Oliver-Nelson Books, 1991); Daniel Martin and Gary Allen Fine, "Satanic Cultures, Satanic Play: Is Dungeons & Dragons a Breeding Ground for the Devil?," in *The Satanism Scare*, ed. James T. Richardson, Joel Best, and David G. Bromley (New York: Routledge, 1991), 107–126; Paul Corupe, "20-Sided Sins: How Jack Chick Was Drawn into the RPG War," in *Satanic Panic: Pop-Cultural Paranoia in the 1980s*, ed. Janisse and Corupe, 69–82; Phil Phillips and Joan Hake Robie, *Halloween and Satanism* (Lancaster: Starburst, 1987).

83. Victor, *Satanic Panic*, 16; Phillip Stevens Jr., "The Demonology of Satanism: An Anthropological View," in *The Satanism Scare*, ed. Richardson, Best, and Bromley, 24–33.

84. See generally Victor, *Satanic Panic*, 1993.

85. Sherrill Mulhern, "Satanism and Psychotherapy: A Rumor in Search of an Inquisition," in *The Satanism Scare*, ed. Richardson, Best, and Bromley, 155; Shawn Carlson and Gerald Larue, *Satanism in America: Final Report for the Committee for Scientific Examination of Religion* (El Cerrito, CA: Gaia Press, 1989).

86. One of the first published accounts can be found in Michelle Smith and Lawrence Pazder's *Michelle Remembers* (New York: Congdon and Lattes, 1980), which established a narrative template for subsequent ritual abuse accounts. For more on Smith and Pazder's role in perpetuating the panics, see Phillips and Milner, *You Are Here*, 29–33.

87. Victor, *Satanic Panic*, 83, 93.

88. Phillips and Milner, *You Are Here*, 32–33; Ben Crouch and Kelly Damphousse, "Law Enforcement and the Satanism-Crime Connection: A Survey of 'Cult Cops,'" in *The Satanism Scare*, ed. Richardson, Best, and Bromley, 191–204; Poole, *Satan in America*, 173.

89. "The Devil Worshippers," *20/20*, episode aired May 16, 1985.

90. Victor, *Satanic Panic*, 18, 230.

91. "Devil Worship: Exposing Satan's Underground," *The Geraldo Rivera Show*, episode aired October 22, 1988.

92. Victor, *Satanic Panic*, 230; Jerry Johnston, *The Edge of Evil: The Rise of Satanism in North America* (Dallas: Word Publishing, 1989), 26–27.

93. Kevin L. Ferguson, "Devil on the Line: Technology and the Satanic Film," in *Satanic Panic: Pop-Cultural Paranoia in the 1980s*, ed. Janisse and Corupe, 97.

94. Victor, *Satanic Panic*, 231.

95. Victor, *Satanic Panic*, 220.

96. David G. Bromley, "Satanism: The New Cult Scare," in *The Satanism Scare*, ed. Richardson, Best, and Bromley, 69.

97. Johnson, "Emergence of Christian Video," 192; "The Faith of Susan Baker," *Washington Post*, April 30, 1985, https://www.washingtonpost.com/archive/life style/1985/04/30/the-faith-of-susan-baker/73c011c8-f487-4587-9bf1-ff4df 343dc7b/.

98. We again borrow this phrase from Carol Stabile. See chapter 1 and its discussion of Stabile's work.

99. We will focus on these Democrats in chapter 6.

100. Diane Winston, *Righting the American Dream: How the Media Mainstreamed Reagan's Evangelical Vision* (Chicago: University of Chicago Press, 2023), 10–11, 178.

101. Poole, *Satan in America*, 174.

102. Poole, *Satan in America*, 175.

103. Poole, *Satan in America*, 175.

104. Bivins, *Religion of Fear*, 122.

105. Bivins, *Religion of Fear*, 20, 89–92, 116–118, 119–124, 164.

106. Julia Lesage, "Christian Coalition Leadership Training," in *Media, Culture, and the Religious Right*, ed. Kintz and Lesage, 320.

107. As an example of this dynamic, Debbie Nathan notes that the phrase "satanic ritual abuse" ultimately gave way to more euphemistic phrases like "ritual abuse," "sex rings," "multidimensional sex rings," or "multivictim, multioffender abuse" (Nathan, "Satanism and Child Molestation: Constructing the Ritual Abuse Scare," in *The Satanism Scare*, ed. Richardson, Best, and Bromley, 83). Either the child protection workers, state and federal prosecutors, and/or investigators who used these phrases were resistant to the religious tinge of the word "Satan" or they understood that secular juries and journalists would resist, if not outright laugh at, references to Satan incarnate, 82–85.

108. Bivins, *Religion of Fear*, 14.

109. Tim LaHaye, *The Battle for the Mind* (Old Tappan, NJ: Fleming H. Revell, 1980), 25, 64.

110. Poole, *Satan in America*, 192.

111. Tim LaHaye, *Battle*, 57.

112. Tim LaHaye, *Battle*, 43.

113. Bivins, *Religion of Fear*, 180.

114. Tim LaHaye, *Battle*, 181.

115. Tim LaHaye, *Battle*, 78.

116. Tim LaHaye, *Battle*, 42, 78.

117. Tim LaHaye, *Battle*, 187.

118. Bivins, *Religion of Fear*, 193–194.

119. Bivins, *Religion of Fear*, 194.

120. Susan E. Marshall, "Who Speaks for American Women? The Future of Anti-feminism," *Annals of the American Academy of Political and Social Science* 515 (1991): 50–62.

121. Donald T. Critchlow, *Phyllis Schlafly and Grassroots Conservatism* (Princeton, NJ: Princeton University Press, 2005), 219.

122. Beverly LaHaye, *Who But a Woman? Concerned Women Can Make a Difference* (Nashville, TN: Thomas Nelson, 1984), 29.

123. Beverly LaHaye, *Who But a Woman?*, 13.

124. Beverly LaHaye, *Who But a Woman?*, 43.

125. Beverly LaHaye, *Who But a Woman?*, 23.

126. Beverly LaHaye, *Who But a Woman?*, 68.

127. Beverly LaHaye, *Who But a Woman?*, 67.

128. Beverly LaHaye, *Who But a Woman?*, 92–93.

129. Betty Cuniberti, "Other Voices Crying Out against Feminists: Concerned Women for America at 2nd Convention Join Other Conservatives," *Los Angeles Times*, October 2, 1985, https://www.latimes.com/archives/la-xpm-1985-10-02-vw-16246-story.html.

130. Marshall, "Who Speaks for American Women?," 56–58.

131. Marshall, "Who Speaks for American Women?," 60.

132. Critchlow, *Schlafly and Grassroots Conservatism*, 236.

133. Critchlow, *Schlafly and Grassroots Conservatism*, 245.

134. Critchlow, *Schlafly and Grassroots Conservatism*, 272.

135. Critchlow, *Schlafly and Grassroots Conservatism*, 245.

136. Linda Kintz, "Clarity, Mothers, and the Mass-Mediated National Soul: A Defense of Ambiguity," in *Media, Culture, and the Religious Right*, ed. Kintz and Lesage, 136.

137. Kintz, "Clarity, Mothers," 137.

138. "Contract with the American Family," C-SPAN, May 17, 1995, accessed May 2023, https://www.c-span.org/video/?65156-1/contract-american-family.

139. Laurie Goodstein, "Gingrich Vows to Pursue Christian Coalition Agenda," *Washington Post*, May 18, 1995, https://www.washingtonpost.com/archive/politics /1995/05/18/gingrich-vows-to-pursue-christian-coalition-agenda/a747755d -0319-4ce2-a32c-5eed3e3f51b1/.

140. Paul Matzko, *The Radio Right: How a Band of Broadcasters Took on the Federal Government and Built the Modern Conservative Movement* (New York: Oxford University Press, 2020), 19.

141. *Contract with the American Family: A Bold Plan by the Christian Coalition to Strengthen the Family and Restore Common-Sense Values* (Nashville, TN: Moorings, 1995), 147.

142. Johnson, "Emergence of Christian Video," 204–205.

143. Lesage, "Christian Coalition Leadership," 320.

144. Johnson, "Emergence of Christian Video," 204–205.

145. Johnson, "Emergence of Christian Video," 181, 183.

146. Linda Kintz, *Between Jesus and the Market: The Emotions That Matter in Right-Wing America* (Durham, NC: Duke University Press, 1997), 6.

147. Kintz, *Between Jesus and the Market*, 7.

148. Pagels quoted by Kintz, *Between Jesus and the Market*, 9.

149. Michael Rogin, *Ronald Reagan: The Movie* (Berkeley: University of California Press, 1988), 4–5, 19.

150. Hunter, *Culture Wars*, xi.

151. Daniel K. Williams, "The Partisan Trajectory of the American Pro-Life Movement: How a Liberal Catholic Campaign Became a Conservative Evangelical Cause," *Religions* 6 (2015): 451–475.

152. Jennifer Holland, *Tiny You: A Western History of the Anti-Abortion Movement* (Berkeley: University of California Press, 2020), 24, 38.

153. Williams, "The Partisan Trajectory," 458.

154. Harold Lindsell, *The World, the Flesh, and the Devil* (Moscow, ID: Canon Press, 1973), 102.

155. Williams, "The Partisan Trajectory," 459.

156. Williams, "The Partisan Trajectory," 460.

157. Robert Booth Fowler, *A New Engagement: Evangelical Political Thought, 1966–1976* (Grand Rapids, MI: William B. Eerdmans, 1982), 182, 196.

158. Williams, "The Partisan Trajectory," 460.

159. Sherwood Eliot Wirt, *The Social Conscience of the Evangelical* (New York: Harper & Row, 1968), 141.

160. Wirt, *The Social Conscience of the Evangelical*, 146.

161. Robert Campbell, *New Morality or No Morality* (New York: Bruce Publishing, 1969).

162. Williams "The Partisan Trajectory," 461, 462.

163. Holland, *Tiny You*, 182.

164. Williams, "The Partisan Trajectory," 463.

165. Williams "The Partisan Trajectory," 464; Holland, *Tiny You*, 21–53; Anne Nelson, *The Shadow Network: Media, Money, and the Secret Hub of the Radical Right* (New York: Bloomsbury, 2019), 17–19.

166. Holland, *Tiny You*, 68–71.

167. Holland, *Tiny You*, 102–103.

168. Poole, *Satan in America*, 193.

169. Hertenstein and Trott, *Satan Seller*, 16.

170. Williams, "The Partisan Trajectory," 464.

171. Poole, *Satan in America*, xxi.

CHAPTER 5

1. "Patrick Joseph Buchanan, 'Culture Wars Speech: Address to the Republican National Convention' (17 August 1992)," Voices of Democracy, accessed August 10, 2023, https://voicesofdemocracy.umd.edu/buchanan-culture-war-speech-speech -text/.

2. Buchanan, "Culture Wars," paragraph 4.

3. Buchanan, "Culture Wars," paragraph 16.

4. Buchanan, "Culture Wars," paragraph 39.

5. Buchanan, "Culture Wars," paragraph 48.

6. Buchanan, "Culture Wars," paragraph 50.

7. Nicole Hemmer, "The Man Who Won the Republican Party before Trump Did," *New York Times*, September 8, 2022, https://www.nytimes.com/2022/09 /08/opinion/pat-buchanan-donald-trump.html.

8. Hemmer, "The Man Who Won the Republican Party."

9. Dan Carson, "How the 1992 RNC in Houston Started the 'Culture War' Politics We Know Now," *Chronicle of Higher Education*, December 25, 2022, https:// www.chron.com/politics/article/1992-rnc-houston-culture-war-17487677.php.

10. Geoffrey Layman, *The Great Divide: Religious and Cultural Conflict in American Party Politics* (New York: Columbia University Press, 2001), 20; Andrew Hartman, *A War for the Soul of America: A History of the Culture Wars* (Chicago: University of Chicago Press, 2019), 86, 98–99; Frances FitzGerald, *The Evangelicals: The Struggle to Shape America* (New York: Simon and Schuster, 2017); Darren Dochuk, *From Bible Belt to Sunbelt: Plain-Folk Religion, Grassroots Politics, and the Rise of Evangelical Conservatism* (New York, W. W. Norton, 2010); Gregory S. Pastor, Walter J. Stone, and Ronald B. Rapoport, "Candidate-Centered Sources of Party Change: The Case of Pat Robertson, 1988," *Journal of Politics* 61, no. 2 (May 1999): 423–444; Duane Murray Oldfield, *The Right and the Righteous: The Christian Right Confronts the Republican Party* (Lanham, MD: Rowman & Littlefield, 1996).

11. Anne Nelson, *Shadow Network: Media, Money, and the Secret Hub of the American Right* (New York: Bloomsbury, 2019), 12.

12. Nelson, *Shadow Network*, 24.

13. J. Brooks Flippen, *Jimmy Carter, the Politics of Family, and the Rise of the Religious Right* (Athens: University of Georgia Press, 2011), 12, 277; Andrew Busch, *Reagan's Victory: The Presidential Election of 1980 and the Rise of the Right* (Lawrence: University Press of Kansas, 2005), 35.

14. See also Matthew Levendusky, *The Partisan Sort: How Liberals Became Democrats and Conservatives Became Republicans* (Chicago: University of Chicago Press, 2009).

15. Edward G. Carmines and James A. Stimson, *Issue Evolution: Race and the Transformation of American Politics* (Princeton, NJ: Princeton University Press, 1989), 54, 104; Tod A. Baker, *Political Parties in the Southern States: Party Activists in Partisan Coalitions* (Westport, CT: Praeger, 1990); James L. Sundquist, *Dynamics of the Party System: Alignment and Realignment of Political Parties in the United States* (Washington, DC: Brookings Institution Press, 2011).

16. This also included Southern Baptists, who were becoming increasingly aligned with Evangelicals during this period. See generally James Leo Garrett, E. Glenn Hinson, and James E. Tull, *Are Southern Baptists "Evangelicals"?* (Macon, GA: Mercer University Press, 1983).

17. Andrew Hartman, *A War for the Soul of America: A History of the Culture Wars* (Chicago: University of Chicago Press, 2019), 86, 98–99; FitzGerald, *The Evangelicals*; Geoffrey C. Layman and John C. Green, "Wars and Rumours of Wars: The Contexts of Cultural Conflict in American Political Behaviour," *British Journal of Political Science* 36, no. 1 (2006): 61–89.

18. Nancy N. Bednar and Allen D. Hertzke, "The Christian Right and Republican Realignment in Oklahoma," *PS: Political Science & Politics* 28, no. 1 (2013): 11–15, https://doi.org/10.2307/420572.

19. Brett M. Clifton, "Romancing the GOP: Assessing the Strategies Used by the Christian Coalition to Influence the Republican Party," *Party Politics* 10, no. 5 (2004): 475–498, https://doi.org/10.1177/1354068804045384.

20. James L. Guth, "South Carolina: The Christian Right Wins One," *PS: Political Science & Politics* 28, no. 1 (1995): 8–11, https://doi.org/10.2307/420571.

21. Philip A. Klinkner, *Midterm: The Elections of 1994 in Context* (Boulder, CO: Westview Press, 1996).

22. Evangelicalism did not grow, as measured by the percentage of the population classified as Evangelical, from the mid-1980s until 2020. For measures of the percentage of the population identified as Evangelical using data from the General Social Survey, see Ryan Burge, "American Religion in 2030," *Religion in Public*, October 24, 2019, https://religioninpublic.blog/2019/10/24/american-religion-in-2030/; Ryan Burge, "How Has Partisanship and Theology Shifted in America's Religious Traditions?," *Religion in Public*, May 22, 2017, https://religioninpublic.blog/2017/05/22/how-has-partisanship-and-theology-shifted-in-americas-religious-traditions/.

23. Beverly LaHaye, *Who But a Woman? Concerned Women Can Make a Difference* (Nashville, TN: Thomas Nelson, 1984), 64.

24. Beverly LaHaye, *Who But a Woman?*, 68.

25. Beverly LaHaye, *Who But a Woman?*, 67.

26. Beverly LaHaye, *Who But a Woman?*, 68.

27. Tim LaHaye, *The Battle for the Mind: A Subtle Warfare* (Old Tappan, NJ: Fleming H. Revell, 1980), 217.

28. Tim LaHaye, *The Battle for the Mind*, 218.

29. Tim LaHaye, *The Battle for the Mind*, 218.

30. Daniel Wojcik, "Avertive Apocalypticism," in the *Oxford Handbook of Millennialism*, ed. Catherine Wessinger (Oxford: Oxford University Press, 2011), 66–89, 68.

31. Wojcik, "Avertive Apocalypticism," 66.

32. For an overview of the different flavors of apocalypticism, see Daniel Wojcik, *The End of the World as We Know It: Faith, Fatalism, and Apocalypse in America* (New York: New York University Press, 1997), 42.

33. Linda Kintz, *Between Jesus and the Market: The Emotions That Matter in Right-Wing America* (Durham, NC: Duke University Press, 1997), 9.

34. Kintz, *Between Jesus and the Market*, 9.

35. Nancy T. Ammerman, "North American Protestant Fundamentalism," in *Media, Culture, and the Religious Right*, ed. Linda Kintz and Julia Lesage (Minneapolis: University of Minnesota Press, 1998), 102.

36. For more on white Southern Baptists' heavy reliance on biblical and religious justifications for segregation, a stance that was a precursor to the contemporary

Christian nationalist push to structurally impose Christianity on U.S. culture, see Bronislaw Misztal and Anson Shupe, *Religion and Politics in Comparative Perspective: Revival of Religious Fundamentalism in East and West* (New York: Bloomsbury, 1992).

37. Hal Lindsey, *The 1980s: Countdown to Armageddon* (New York: Bantam, 1980). Lindsey's embrace of demonological dominionism is somewhat ironic given how vigorously he would come to thrash against theological dominionism ostensibly because he claimed it endangered the United States and Israel. It also competed with his fatalist prophecies and therefore market share. See Hal Lindsey, *The Road to Holocaust* (New York: Bantam Books, 1989).

38. Lindsey, *Countdown to Armageddon*, 141–144.

39. Lindsey, *Countdown to Armageddon*, 157. For Lindsey's reflections on occult influences in the United States, see 21–22.

40. Anita Bryant, *The Anita Bryant Story: The Survival of Our Nation's Families and the Threat of Militant Homosexuality* (Old Tappan, NJ: Fleming H. Revell, 1977), 105.

41. Bryant, *The Anita Bryant Story*, 94.

42. gladtobegaynet, "Anita Bryant Florida Orange Juice Ad," YouTube, April 3, 2010, accessed October 7, 2023, https://www.youtube.com/watch?v=3ld8 DQkC6po.

43. Bryant, *The Anita Bryant Story*, 15–16.

44. Kintz, *Between Jesus and the Market*, 71. For more on 1990s claims about the "gay agenda" and how it dovetailed into condemnation by demonologists of the "special rights" of gays and lesbians, see Laurie Schulze and Frances Guilfoyle, "Facts Don't Hate, They Just Are," in *Media, Culture, and the Religious Right*, ed. Kintz and Lesage, 327–344, as well as Ioannis Mookas, "Faultlines: Homophobic Innovation in Gay Rights/Special Rights," in the same volume, 345–362. Regarding the "gay agenda" video series, Kintz, *Between Jesus and the Market*, notes that the film "The Gay Agenda in Public Schools" included appearances from Trent Lott, who would be elected Senate Majority Leader in 1996, as well as the head of the so-called Traditional Values Coalition, 277n9.

45. Neil Miller, *Out of the Past: Gay and Lesbian History from 1869 to the Present* (New York: Vintage Books, 1995), 409.

46. Paul Matzko, *The Radio Right: How a Band of Broadcasters Took on the Federal Government and Built the Modern Conservative Movement* (New York: Oxford University Press, 2020), 228.

47. Bryant, *The Anita Bryant Story*, 27.

48. Bryant, *The Anita Bryant Story*, 138.

49. Matzko, *Radio Right*, 228.

50. Linda Kintz and Julia Lesage, "Religious Culture in the United States," in *Media, Culture, and the Religious Right*, ed. Kintz and Lesage, 53.

51. Matzko, *Radio Right*, 232.

52. Meryem Ersoz, "Gimmie That Old-Time Religion in a Postmodern Age: Semiotics of Christian Radio," in *Media, Culture, and the Religious Right*, ed. Kintz and Lesage, 212–214; Matzko, *Radio Right*, 233.

53. Ersoz, "Gimmie That Old-Time Religion," 213; Matzko, *Radio Right*, 233.

54. Matzko, *Radio Right*, 226.

55. Nelson, *Shadow Network*, 45.

56. Razelle Frankl, "Transformation of Televangelism: Repackaging Christian Family Values," in *Media, Culture, and the Religious Right*, ed. Kintz and Lesage, 166–167.

57. Frankl, "Transformation of Televangelism," 167–168.

58. Jason Bivins, "Tracing the Rise of Christian Media in American Political Discourse," *Pacific Standard*, May 30, 2018, https://psmag.com/news/the-rise-of -the-christian-media.

59. Nelson, *Shadow Network*, 45.

60. Kintz and Lesage, "Religious Culture in the United States," 53.

61. See generally Julia Lesage, "Christian Coalition Leadership Training," in *Media, Culture, and the Religious Right*, ed. Kintz and Lesage, 295–326.

62. Linda Kintz, "Clarity, Mothers, and the Mass-Mediated National Soul: A Defense of Ambiguity," in *Media, Culture, and the Religious Right*, ed. Kintz and Lesage, 133.

63. Kintz, "Clarity, Mothers," 115.

64. Kintz, "Clarity, Mothers," 116.

65. Kintz, "Clarity, Mothers," 122.

66. Kintz, "Clarity, Mothers," 126.

67. Kintz, "Clarity, Mothers," 127.

68. Donald T. Critchlow, *Phyllis Schlafly and Grassroots Conservatism: A Woman's Crusade* (Princeton, NJ: Princeton University Press, 2005), 218, 226–227.

69. Julia Lesage, "Christian Media," in *Media, Culture, and the Religious Right*, ed. Kintz and Lesage, 27.

70. Lesage, "Christian Media," 28.

71. Frankl, "Transformation of Televangelism," 173; Anna Williams, "Conservative Media Activism: The Free Congress Foundation and National Empowerment Television," in *Media, Culture, and the Religious Right*, ed. Kintz and Lesage, 275–276.

72. Lesage, "Christian Media," 27–28.

73. Nelson, *Shadow Network*, 29; Jason Bivins, *Religion of Fear: The Politics of Horror in Conservative Evangelicalism* (Oxford: Oxford University Press, 2008), 184.

74. *Contract with the American Family: A Bold Plan by the Christian Coalition to Strengthen the Family and Restore Common-Sense Values* (Nashville, TN: Moorings, 1995), 147.

75. Williams, "Conservative Media Activism," 286; Eithne Johnson, "The Emergence of Christian Video and the Cultivation of Videovangelism," in *Media, Culture, and the Religious Right*, ed. Kintz and Lesage, 204–206, 247–248.

76. James Salzer, "Gingrich's Language Set New Course," *Atlanta Journal-Constitution*, July 5, 2016, https://www.ajc.com/news/local-govt--politics/gingrich-language-set-new-course/O5bgK6lY2wQ3KwEZsYTBlO/.

77. Nelson, *Shadow Network*, 26.

78. Jerry B. Jenkins and Tim LaHaye, *Left Behind: The Kids* (Carol Stream, IL: Tyndale House, 1998–2001).

79. Bivins, *Religion of Fear*, 138–139.

80. Amanda Cockrell, "Harry Potter and the Witch Hunters: A Social Context for the Attacks on Harry Potter," *Journal of American Culture* 29, no. 1 (2006): 24–30, https://doi.org/10.1111/j.1542-734X.2006.00272.x.

81. Jack Chick, "The Nervous Witch," Chick.com, n.d., accessed June 26, 2024, https://www.chick.com/products/tract?stk=5012; "The Nervous Witch" was originally published in 2001.

82. Kathleen Belew, *Bring the War Home: The White Power Movement and Paramilitary America* (Cambridge, MA: Harvard University Press, 2018), 188.

83. Wojcik, *End of the World*, 11, 35–36, 146, 163.

84. Rush Limbaugh, *The Way Things Ought to Be* (New York: Simon & Schuster, 1992).

85. Nicole Hemmer, *Partisans: The Conservative Revolutionaries Who Remade American Politics in the 1990s* (New York: Basic Books, 2022), 96.

86. Hemmer, *Partisans*, 99–100.

87. Limbaugh, *The Way Things Ought to Be*, 187.

88. Limbaugh, *The Way Things Ought to Be*, 208–212.

89. Limbaugh, *The Way Things Ought to Be*, 281.

90. Limbaugh, *The Way Things Ought to Be*, 281.

91. Reece Peck, *Fox Populism: Branding Conservatism as Working Class* (Cambridge: Cambridge University Press, 2019), 82.

92. Mike Mills, "Murdoch to Buy Half of Family Channel," *Washington Post*, June 12, 1997, https://www.washingtonpost.com/archive/business/1997/06/12/murdoch-to-buy-half-of-family-channel/5eede35b-5463-4065-87fe-72181010c3ff/.

93. "Disney Buys Fox Family Channel," CBS News, July 23, 2001, https://www.cbsnews.com/news/disney-buys-fox-family-channel/.

94. Peck, *Fox Populism*, 82.

95. Peck, *Fox Populism*, 50–52.

96. Peck, *Fox Populism*, 41.

97. Jonathan Mahler, *Ladies and Gentlemen, the Bronx Is Burning: 1977, Baseball, Politics, and the Battle for the Soul of a City* (New York: Picador, 2006), 34.

98. Peck, *Fox Populism*, 68.

99. Gabriel Sherman, *The Loudest Voice in the Room: How the Brilliant, Bombastic Roger Ailes Built Fox News—and Divided a Country* (New York: Random House, 2014), 207.

100. Peck, *Fox Populism*, 71.

101. Kevin Glynn, *Tabloid Culture: Trash Taste, Popular Power, and the Transformation of American Television* (Durham, NC: Duke University Press, 2000), 28.

102. Sherman, *The Loudest Voice*, 30.

103. Sherman, *The Loudest Voice*, 207–209.

104. Sherman, *The Loudest Voice*, 72–73, 48.

105. Peck, *Fox Populism*, 51.

106. Peck, *Fox Populism*, 51.

107. Peck, *Fox Populism*, 51.

108. David Brock, "Roger Ailes Is Mad as Hell," *New York Magazine*, November 17, 1997, 32.

109. Sherman, *The Loudest Voice*, xvi.

110. Susan B. Ridgely, "Conservative Christianity and the Creation of Alternative News: An Analysis of Focus on the Family's Multimedia Empire," *Religion and American Culture* 30, no. 1 (January 2020): 1–25.

111. Lawrie Mifflin, "At the Fox News Channel, the Buzzword Is Fairness, Separating News from Bias," *New York Times*, October 7, 1996, https://www.nytimes.com/1996/10/07/business/at-the-new-fox-news-channel-the-buzzword-is-fairness-separating-news-from-bias.html; Sherman, *The Loudest Voice*, 192.

112. Sherman, *The Loudest Voice*, 214.

113. Brock, "Roger Ailes Is Mad as Hell," 32.

114. Sherman, *The Loudest Voice*, 194.

115. Sherman, *The Loudest Voice*, 200.

116. Peck, *Fox Populism*, 34.

117. Sherman, *The Loudest Voice*, 197.

118. Sherman, *The Loudest Voice*, 242.

119. Sherman, *The Loudest Voice*, 231.

120. Sherman, *The Loudest Voice*, 192.

121. "War of Words: Partisan Ranting Is 'Marketing of Fear,'" Ted Koppel reports, NBC News, September 20, 2012, https://www.nbcnews.com/news/amp -video/mmvo42570309659; Peck, *Fox Populism*, 59.

122. Peck, *Fox Populism*, 31–32.

123. O'Reilly interview of 1998 with the *St. Louis Post-Dispatch* quoted in Peck, *Fox Populism*, 52.

124. Amanda Frisken and Gretchen Soderlund, "Editors' Introduction: Sensationalism's Enduring Power," *Feminist Media Histories* 8, no. 4 (2022): 1–32, https://doi .org/10.1525/fmh.2022.8.4.1.

125. Frisken and Soderlund, "Sensationalism," 1, 17.

126. Frisken and Soderlund, "Sensationalism," 1.

127. Frisken and Soderlund, "Sensationalism," 7–8; in her book *Sex Trafficking, Scandal, and the Transformation of Journalism, 1885–1917* (Chicago: University of Chicago Press, 2013), Soderlund explores how the sex trafficking scandal of the late 1800s and early 1900s, spurred on by media sensationalism, functioned as a "surplus scandal" that resulted in important reforms, or at least discourses about the need for reform, regarding policing, journalism, and politics.

128. Peck, *Fox Populism*, 48.

129. Peck, *Fox Populism*, 48, 23, 35.

130. Peck, *Fox Populism*, 20–21, 28.

131. Archived news articles discussed in Peck, *Fox Populism*, 34.

132. Peck, *Fox Populism*, 2019.

133. Peck, *Fox Populism*, 43–44.

134. Laura Grindstaff, *The Money Shot: Trash, Class, and the Making of TV Talk Shows* (Chicago: University of Chicago Press, 2008).

135. Grindstaff, *The Money Shot*, 19.

136. Peck, *Fox Populism*, 34–35.

137. Peck, *Fox Populism*, 43–44.

138. Peck, *Fox Populism*, 86.

139. Peck, *Fox Populism*, 48.

140. Peck, *Fox Populism*, 53, 86.

141. Messner quoted in Sherman, *The Loudest Voice*, 199.

142. Ben Zimmer, "Truthiness," *New York Times Magazine*, October 13, 2010, https://www.nytimes.com/2010/10/17/magazine/17FOB-onlanguage-t.html.

143. See generally Peck, *Fox Populism*, 185–221.

144. Sherman, *The Loudest Voice*, 151.

145. Peck, *Fox Populism*, 146.

146. Stephanopoulos quoted in Sherman, *The Loudest Voice*, 226.

147. Kerwin Swint, *Dark Genius: The Influential Career of Legendary Political Operative and Fox News Founder Roger Ailes* (New York: Union Square Press, 2008), 138.

148. Peck, *Fox Populism*, 70.

149. Interview with Billy Graham, *The Crier Report*, April 30, 1999, Fox News Network.

150. "Children at Risk: Is Marilyn Manson Putting Children at-Risk?," *The O'Reilly Factor*, August 20, 2001, Fox News Network.

151. Brock, "Roger Ailes Is Mad as Hell," 35.

152. Sherman, *The Loudest Voice*, 234.

153. Whitney Phillips, *This Is Why We Can't Have Nice Things: Mapping the Relationship between Online Trolling and Mainstream Culture* (Cambridge, MA: MIT Press, 2015), 51.

154. "Mancow behind Bars," *Hannity & Colmes*, March 30, 2001, Fox News Network.

155. Sherman, *The Loudest Voice*, 214.

156. Brock, "Roger Ailes Is Mad as Hell," 129.

157. "Personal Stories: Partisanship in the Media," *The O'Reilly Factor*, November 29, 2000, Fox News Network; "Unresolved Problem: Hillary Rodham Clinton," *The O'Reilly Factor*, November 8, 1999, Fox News Network.

158. "Children at Risk: Insane Clown Posse," *The O'Reilly Factor*, August 16, 2001, Fox News Network.

159. Bill O'Reilly, *The No Spin Zone: Confrontations with the Powerful and Famous in America* (New York: Broadway Books), 1.

160. O'Reilly, *The No Spin Zone*, 20.

161. O'Reilly, *The No Spin Zone*, 21.

162. Marc Fisher, "Starr Warriors," *Washington Post*, February 3, 1998, https://www
.washingtonpost.com/wp-srv/politics/special/clinton/stories/starr020398.htm.

163. David Greenberg, "Ken Starr: The Man Who Created the Lewinsky Scandal," *Politico*, September 18, 2022, https://www.politico.com/news/magazine
/2022/09/18/ken-starr-lewinsky-scandal-00057381.

164. Sherman, *The Loudest Voice*, 232.

165. Susan Faludi, "How Hillary Clinton Met Satan," *New York Times*, October
29, 2016, https://www.nytimes.com/2016/10/30/opinion/sunday/how-hillary
-clinton-met-satan.html.

166. Amy Chozick, "Roger Ailes, Hillary Clinton, and Me," *New York Times*,
May 20, 2017, https://www.nytimes.com/2017/05/20/opinion/sunday/roger-ailes
-hillary-clinton-fox-news.html.

167. Sherman, *The Loudest Voice*, 225.

168. Sherman, *The Loudest Voice*, 225.

169. Sherman, *The Loudest Voice*, 225.

170. Sherman, *The Loudest Voice*, 225.

171. Sherman, *The Loudest Voice*, 251.

172. Lisa de Moraes, "In Monthly Ratings, Fox Stays on Top," *Washington Post*,
May 3, 2003, https://www.washingtonpost.com/archive/lifestyle/2003/05/03/in
-monthly-ratings-fox-news-stays-on-top/0a7e1b8e-b4fe-47b4-a7f9-d3f446447122/.

173. Ryan Burge, "Faith in Numbers: Fox News Is Must-Watch for White
Evangelicals, a Turnoff for Atheists . . . and Hindus, Muslims Really like CNN,"
Conversation, May 24, 2021, https://theconversation.com/faith-in-numbers-fox
-news-is-must-watch-for-white-evangelicals-a-turnoff-for-atheists-and-hindus
-muslims-really-like-cnn-161067.

CHAPTER 6

1. "After: How America Confronted the September 12th Era," *Newsweek*, March
9, 2003, https://www.newsweek.com/after-how-america-confronted-sept-12-era
-132547.

2. Amanda Terkel, "Watch the One Senator Who Voted against the Patriot Act
Warn What Would Happen (Video)," *Huffington Post*, June 7, 2013, https://www
.huffpost.com/entry/russ-feingold-patriot-act-speech_n_3402878.

3. Robin Toner and Neil A. Lewis, "A Nation Challenged: The Legislation; Bill
Greatly Expanding Surveillance Power in Terrorism Fight Clears the Senate,"
New York Times, October 12, 2001, https://www.nytimes.com/2001/10/12/us
/nation-challenged-legislation-bill-greatly-expanding-surveillance-power.html.

4. "How America Confronted."

5. For an overview of how this fear shaped entertainment media, see Nathalie Baptiste, "9/11: When Pop Culture Went into Patriotic Overdrive," *Mother Jones*, September 9, 2021, https://www.motherjones.com/politics/2021/09/9-11 -when-pop-culture-went-into-patriotic-overdrive/.

6. Toby Keith, "Courtesy of the Red, White, and Blue (the Angry American)," track 1 on Unleashed, DreamWorks Nashville, 2002.

7. "'You Are Either with Us or against Us,'" *CNN*, November 6, 2001, https:// edition.cnn.com/2001/US/11/06/gen.attack.on.terror/.

8. Anthony E. Cook, "Encountering the Other: Evangelicalism and Terrorism in a Post 911 World." *Journal of Law and Religion* 20, no. 1 (2004): 1–30, 1.

9. Timothy Bella, "'Freedom never tasted so good': How Walter Jones Helped Rename French Fries over the Iraq War," *Washington Post*, February 11, 2019, https://www.washingtonpost.com/nation/2019/02/11/freedom-never-tasted-so -good-how-walter-jones-helped-rename-french-fries-over-iraq-war/.

10. E. J. Dionne Jr., "Inevitably, the Politics of Terror: Fear Has Become Part of Washington's Power Struggle," *Brookings*, May 25, 2003, https://www.brookings .edu/articles/inevitably-the-politics-of-terror-fear-has-become-part-of-washing tons-power-struggle/.

11. We were made aware of this shift via Anthony Nadler in his article, "The Great Anti-Left Show," *Los Angeles Review of Books*, October 2, 2020, https:// lareviewofbooks.org/article/the-great-anti-left-show/.

12. "New Rush 24/7 Gift! The Limbaugh Institute for Advanced Anti-Leftist Studies Car Magnet," *The Rush Limbaugh Show*, May 30, 2017, https://www .rushlimbaugh.com/daily/2017/05/30/new-rush-247-premium-the-limbaugh -institute-for-advanced-anti-leftist-studies-car-magnet/.

13. Nicole Hemmer, *Partisans: The Conservative Revolutionaries Who Remade American Politics in the 1990s* (New York: Basic Books, 2022), 99.

14. Michelle Nickerson, *Mothers of Conservatism: Women and the Postwar Right* (Princeton, NJ: Princeton University Press, 2012), 32.

15. Nickerson, *Mothers of Conservatism*, 32, 54.

16. Nickerson, *Mothers of Conservatism*, 4, 54.

17. Nickerson, *Mothers of Conservatism*, 55.

18. Joel Kovel, *Red Hunting in the Promised Land* (New York: Basic Books, 1994), 5.

19. For a detailed history of the overlap between the red and lavender scares, see David K. Johnson, *The Lavender Scare: The Cold War Persecution of Gays and Lesbians in the Federal Government* (Chicago: University of Chicago Press, 2004).

20. Hyrum Lewis and Verlan Lewis, *The Myth of Left and Right: How the Political Spectrum Misleads and Harms America* (New York: Oxford University Press, 2023), 24.

21. See also Randall J. Stephens and Karl W. Giberson, *The Anointed: Evangelical Truth in a Secular Age* (Cambridge, MA: Harvard University Press, 2011), 3, 17, 182, for a discussion of Evangelicalism and liberalism.

22. Nicole Hemmer, *Messengers of the Right: Conservative Media and the Transformation of American Politics* (Philadelphia: University of Pennsylvania Press, 2016), xii.

23. Michael Pierce, "The Racist Origins of Right to Work," *Labor Notes*, August 3, 2017, https://labornotes.org/blogs/2017/08/racist-who-pioneered-right-work-laws.

24. Ken Estey, "WCP: Billy Graham and the Evangelical Origins of Organized Labor," Georgetown University, Kalmanovitz Initiative for Labor and the Working Poor, accessed June 2023, https://lwp.georgetown.edu/visitingscholars/wcp-billy-graham-and-the-evangelical-origins-of-organized-labor/.

25. Kevin M. Kruse, "A Christian Nation? Since When?," *New York Times*, March 14, 2015, https://www.nytimes.com/2015/03/15/opinion/sunday/a-christian-nation-since-when.html.

26. Darren E. Grem, *The Blessings of Business: How Corporations Shaped Conservative Christianity* (New York: Oxford University Press, 2016), 54.

27. Jeongsuk Joo, "The Hollywood Red Scare: An Attack on the Labor and Progressive Politics of Hollywood," *International Area Review* 13, no. 3 (2010): 125–143.

28. Jennifer A. Delton, *Rethinking the 1950s: How Anticommunism and the Cold War Made America Liberal* (Cambridge: Cambridge University Press, 2013).

29. H. W. Brands, *The Strange Death of American Liberalism* (New Haven, CT: Yale University Press, 2001), 67–98.

30. Brands, *Strange Death of American Liberalism*, 127–133.

31. John Bokina and Timothy J. Lukes, eds., *Marcuse: From the New Left to the Next Left* (Lawrence: University Press of Kansas, 1994), 5, 30, 33–34.

32. Sara Diamond, *Roads to Dominion: Right-Wing Movements and Political Power in the United States* (New York: Guilford Press, 1995), 72.

33. Gregory L. Schneider, *Cadres for Conservatism: Young Americans for Freedom and the Rise of the Contemporary Right* (New York: New York University Press, 1999), 39–40.

34. Schneider, *Cadres for Conservatism*, 40.

35. Cyril Levitt, "The New Left, the New Class and Socialism," *Higher Education* 8, no. 6 (1979): 641–655.

36. Beverly LaHaye, *Who But a Woman? Concerned Women Can Make a Difference* (Nashville, TN: Thomas Nelson, 1984), 13, 45, 23, 30, 62, 105, 98, 134, 29.

37. LaHaye, *Who But a Woman?*, 14.

38. Stuart Hall, "Encoding/Decoding," in *Culture, Media, Language: Working Papers in Cultural Studies 1972–1979*, ed. Stuart Hall, Dorothy Hobson, Andrew Love, and Paul Willis (London: Hutchinson, 1980), 128–138.

39. "How Cancel Culture Became Politicized—Just like Political Correctness," *All Things Considered*, NPR, July 26, 2021, https://www.npr.org/2021/07/09 /1014744289/cancel-culture-debate-has-early-90s-roots-political-correctness; John K. Wilson, *The Myth of Political Correctness: Conservative Attack on Political Correctness* (Durham, NC: Duke University Press, 1995).

40. Wilson, *Myth of Political Correctness*, xi.

41. Charles Sykes, "Rush Limbaugh: The Radio Voice Who Owned the Libs Long before Trump," *Politico*, December 27, 2021, https://www.politico.com /news/magazine/2021/12/27/2021-obituary-rush-limbaugh-520597.

42. Carol Stabile, *The Broadcast 41: Women and the Anti-Communist Blacklist* (Cambridge, MA: MIT Press, 2018), 104.

43. Phyllis Schlafly, *Child Abuse in the Classroom* (Alton, IL: Pere Marquette Press, 1984).

44. Schlafly, *Child Abuse*, 11.

45. Schlafly, *Child Abuse*, 18.

46. Schlafly, *Child Abuse*, 14.

47. Schlafly, *Child Abuse*, 14.

48. Schlafly, *Child Abuse*, 14.

49. Schlafly, *Child Abuse*, 105.

50. Nickerson, *Mothers of Conservatism*, 112.

51. Schlafly, *Child Abuse*, 17.

52. Schlafly, *Child Abuse*, 12.

53. Schlafly, *Child Abuse*, 12.

54. Schlafly, *Child Abuse*, 30, 41, 44, 47, 51, 55, 60, 69, 79, 86, 91, 109, 118.

55. Schlafly, *Child Abuse*, 119.

56. Schlafly, *Child Abuse*, 125, 130.

57. Schlafly, *Child Abuse*, 113.

58. Schlafly, *Child Abuse*, 129.

59. Schlafly, *Child Abuse*, 12.

60. Schlafly, *Child Abuse*, 49, 51, 46, 58, 91.

61. Schlafly, *Child Abuse*, 22.

62. Howard Kurtz, "The Blonde Flinging Bombshells at Bill Clinton," *Washington Post*, October 16, 1998, https://www.washingtonpost.com/wp-srv/politics/special /clinton/stories/coulter101698.htm.

63. Dorsey Shaw, "Even Fox News Employees Think Ann Coulter Works for Fox News," *BuzzFeed News*, January 8, 2014, https://www.buzzfeednews.com/article /dorsey/even-fox-news-employees-think-ann-coulter-works-for-fox-news.

64. "An Appalling Magic," *Guardian*, May 16, 2003, https://www.theguardian .com/media/2003/may/17/pressandpublishing.usnews.

65. "An Appalling Magic."

66. Ann Coulter, *Godless: The Church of Liberalism* (New York: Crown Forum, 2006).

67. Coulter, *Godless*, 1–22.

68. Coulter, *Godless*, 148.

69. Coulter, *Godless*, 150.

70. Coulter, *Godless*, 3.

71. Coulter, *Godless*, 6.

72. Linda Kintz, *Between Jesus and the Market: The Emotions That Matter in Right-Wing America* (Durham, NC: Duke University Press, 1997), 43.

73. Elaine Tyler May, *Homeward Bound: American Families in the Cold War Era* (New York: Basic Books, 2008), 10.

74. LaHaye, *Who But a Woman?*, 133–137.

75. Anita Bryant, *The Anita Bryant Story: The Survival of Our Nation's Families and the Threat of Militant Homosexuality* (Old Tappan, NJ: Fleming H. Revell, 1977), 93–94.

76. Bryant, *The Anita Bryant Story*, 44.

77. Matzko, *The Radio Right: How a Band of Broadcasters Took on the Federal Government and Built the Modern Conservative Movement* (New York: Oxford University Press, 2020); Hendershot, *What's Fair on the Air: Cold War Right-Wing Broadcasting and the Public Interest* (Chicago: University of Chicago Press, 2011); Nickerson, *Mothers of Conservatism*, 2012.

78. Elizabeth Gillespie McRae, *Mothers of Massive Resistance: White Women and the Politics of White Supremacy* (New York: Oxford University Press, 2020).

79. McRae, *Mothers of Massive Resistance*, 59.

80. Ogden quoted in McRae, *Mothers of Massive Resistance*, 237.

81. McRae, *Mothers of Massive Resistance*, 167.

82. "An Appalling Magic."

83. Kintz, *Between Jesus and the Market*, 7.

84. Donald T. Critchlow, *Phyllis Schlafly and Grassroots Conservatism: A Woman's Crusade* (Princeton, NJ: Princeton University Press, 2005), 227.

85. Kintz, *Between Jesus and the Market*, 2.

86. Kintz, *Between Jesus and the Market*, 2–3.

87. Kintz, *Between Jesus and the Market*, 28–29.

88. Kintz, *Between Jesus and the Market*, 3.

89. Matzko, *Radio Right*, 45.

90. McRae, *Mothers of Massive Resistance*, 4, 8, 18.

91. Kurtz, "Blonde Flinging Bombshells," 1998.

92. "Ann Coulter: Ms. Right," *Time*, April 25, 2005, https://content.time.com /time/covers/0,16641,20050425,00.html.

93. "Ann Coulter," Regnery Publishing, accessed June 2023, https://www.regnery .com/author/ann-coulter/.

94. "Ann Coulter: Saucy Siren of the Right," *Daily Record*, September 24, 2003, https://thedailyrecord.com/2003/09/24/ann-coulter-saucy-siren-of-the-right -sounds-off-in-her-latest-book/.

95. Steven F. Hayward, *M. Stanton Evans: Conservative Wit, Apostle of Freedom* (New York: Encounter Books, 2022). As of October 12, 2023, the YAF URL to Ann Coulter's National Journalism Center's alumni page, https://students.yaf.org /alumni/ann-coulter-njc-alumna-spring-1985/, redirects to its "Become a Member Page." This is perhaps due to a falling out Coulter had with YAF over a canceled 2017 speech at Berkeley; see David French, "Ann Coulter Needs to Stop Attacking the Young America's Foundation," *National Review*, April 28, 2017, https://www .nationalreview.com/corner/ann-coulter-needs-stop-attacking-young-americas -foundation-yaf/. But her connection to the group extends back many years, as she participated in speaker series associated with YAF's training sessions for college conservatives; see Boone W. Shear, "Gramsci, Intellectuals, and Academic Prac- tice Today," *Rethinking Marxism* 20, no. 1 (2008): 55–67, https://doi.org/10.1080 /08935690701739964.

96. "Ann Coulter: Saucy Siren"; Howard Kurtz, "The Conservative Pin-Up Girl," *Washington Post*, April 19, 2005, https://www.washingtonpost.com/archive /business/technology/2005/04/19/the-conservative-pin-up-girl/ce648cd2-7afa -4ea6-a7c7-8f88b8fd06f8/; "Ann Coulter: Ms. Right."

97. Dionne, "Inevitably, the Politics of Terror."

98. Gillian Brockell, "She Was the Only Member of Congress to Vote against War in Afghanistan. Some Called Her a Traitor," *Washington Post*, August 17, 2021, https://www.washingtonpost.com/history/2021/08/17/barbara-lee-afghanistan -vote/.

99. John Fund, "Who Is Barbara Lee?," *Wall Street Journal*, September 17, 2001, https://www.wsj.com/articles/SB122418640015141825.

100. Austin Wright, "How Barbara Lee Became an Army of One," *Politico Magazine*, July 30, 2017, https://www.politico.com/magazine/story/2017/07/30/how -barbara-lee-became-an-army-of-one-215434/.

101. "Senate Roll Call: Iraq Resolution," *Washington Post*, October 11, 2001, https://www.washingtonpost.com/wp-srv/onpolitics/transcripts/senaterollcall _iraq101002.htm.

102. Jim VandeHei and Juliet Eilperin, "House Passes Iraq War Resolution," *Washington Post*, October 11, 2002, https://www.washingtonpost.com/archive /politics/2002/10/11/house-passes-iraq-war-resolution/2fd97857-7d4d-4422-95cc -ce2debff2734/; "Roll Call 455 | Bill Number: H. J. Res. 114," Clerk, United States House of Representatives, accessed July 2023, https://clerk.house.gov /Votes/2002455.

103. Daniel D. Reilly and Carrie Budoff Brown, "Half of Democratic Senators Regret Iraq Vote," *Politico*, February 5, 2007, https://www.politico.com/story /2007/02/half-of-democratic-senators-regret-iraq-vote-002639.

104. "Senate Regrets the Vote to Enter Iraq," *ABC News*, January 4, 2007, https:// abcnews.go.com/GMA/Politics/story?id=2771519&page=1.

105. Mary Claire Jalonick, "Twenty Years on, Reflection and Regret on 2002 Iraq War Vote," Associated Press, March 26, 2023, https://apnews.com/article/2002 -iraq-war-vote-senate-authorization-reflection-60989b19ca76a2d9c2e2ff1bad 97dc5a.

106. Jalonick, "Twenty Years On."

107. Gerald R. Webster, "American Nationalism, the Flag, and the Invasion of Iraq," *Geographical Review* 101, no. 1 (2011): 1–18, http://www.jstor.org/stable /41303604. For a twenty-year retrospective, see Carroll Doherty and Jocelyn Kiley, "A Look Back at How Fear and False Beliefs Bolstered U.S. Public Support for War in Iraq," Pew Research Center, March 14, 2023, https://www.pewre search.org/politics/2023/03/14/a-look-back-at-how-fear-and-false-beliefs -bolstered-u-s-public-support-for-war-in-iraq/.

108. Aaron Griffith, *God's Law and Order* (Cambridge, MA: Harvard University Press, 2020), 54, 57–68.

109. Griffith, *God's Law and Order*, 81, 142; see also Joshua Dubler and Vincent W. Lloyd, "The Political Theology of Mass Incarceration," in *Break Every Yoke:*

Religion, Justice, and the Abolition of Prisons, ed. Joshua Dubler and Vincent W. Lloyd (New York: Oxford University Press, 2020), 65–104, 65–66.

110. "Mrs. Clinton Campaign Speech—Super-Predators," C-SPAN, uploaded November 6, 2015, https://www.c-span.org/video/?c4558907/user-clip-mrs-clinton -campaign-speech-super-predators.

111. John DiIulio, "The Coming of the Super-Predators," *Washington Examiner*, November 27, 1995, https://www.washingtonexaminer.com/weekly-standard /the-coming-of-the-super-predators.

112. Carroll Bogert and LynNell Hancock, "How the Media Created a 'Super-predator' Myth That Harmed a Generation of Black Youth," *NBC News*, November 20, 2020, https://www.nbcnews.com/news/us-news/analysis-how-media-created -superpredator-myth-harmed-generation-black-youth-n1248101.

113. Bogert and Hancock, "How the Media Created a 'Superpredator' Myth."

114. John DiIulio Jr., "The Crime of Not Punishing: A History of U.S. Justice," *Washington Times*, September 12, 1993, B8.

115. Griffith, *God's Law and Order*, 251.

116. "Joe Biden in 1993 Speech Warned of 'Predators on Our Streets,'" CNN, March 5, 2019, https://www.cnn.com/videos/politics/2019/03/05/joe-biden-tough -on-crime-speech.cnn.

117. Matthew Nussbaum, "Clinton Calls Parts of 1994 Crime Bill 'a Mistake,'" *Politico*, March 6, 2016, https://www.politico.com/blogs/2016-dem-primary-live -updates-and-results/2016/03/hillary-clinton-1994-crime-bill-220344.

118. Jonathan Capehart, "Hillary Clinton on 'Superpredator' Remarks: 'I Shouldn't Have Used Those Words,'" *Washington Post*, February 25, 2016, https:// www.washingtonpost.com/blogs/post-partisan/wp/2016/02/25/hillary-clinton -responds-to-activist-who-demanded-apology-for-superpredator-remarks/.

119. Erving Goffman, *Frame Analysis: An Essay on the Organization of Experience* (Boston: Northeastern University Press, 1986). We were introduced to the concept of "cultural grammars" by Bill Ellis, who used the term to describe how satanic subversion myths functioned to frame experiences for believers. See Ellis, *Raising the Devil: Satanism, New Religions, and the Media* (Lexington: University of Kentucky Press, 2000).

120. George Lakoff, *Don't Think of an Elephant! Know Your Values and Frame the Debate* (White River Junction, VT: Chelsea Green, 2004).

121. Lakoff, *Don't Think of an Elephant!*, 4–14.

122. Lakoff, *Don't Think of an Elephant!*, 3.

123. Don Hazen, "Introduction," in Lakoff, *Don't Think of an Elephant!*, xii.

124. "Obama Dropped Flag Pin in War Statement," ABC News, February 18, 2009, https://abcnews.go.com/Politics/story?id=3690000&page=1.

125. John Whitesides, "Obama Fights Back against Questions on Patriotism," *Reuters*, June 30, 2008, https://www.reuters.com/article/us-usa-politics/obama-fights-back-against-questions-on-patriotism-idUSN3041349420080701; "Barack Obama Captured on Tape Not Putting His Hand over His Heart during the National Anthem," Fox News, October 24, 2007, https://www.foxnews.com/story/barack-obama-captured-on-tape-not-putting-his-hand-over-his-heart-during-the-national-anthem; "Opinion: Breaking News: Obama Caves! Flag Pin Returns to His Coat Lapel," *Los Angeles Times*, April 16, 2008, https://www.latimes.com/archives/blogs/top-of-the-ticket/story/2008-04-16/opinion-breaking-news-obama-caves-flag-pin-returns-to-his-coat-lapel; "Was Barack Obama Shunning the American Flag?," Fox News, October 5, 2007, https://www.foxnews.com/story/was-barack-obama-shunning-the-american-flag.

126. Adam Shah, "Fox News' Hill on Obama: "'I won't wear that [flag] pin" . . . reminded me of the "I didn't have sex with that woman,""" Media Matters for America, October 5, 2007, https://www.mediamatters.org/fox-news/fox-news-hill-obama-i-wont-wear-flag-pin-reminded-me-i-didnt-have-sex-woman.

127. "Candidates Have Their Say on Obama's Decision Not to Wear Flag Pin," Fox News, October 6, 2007, https://www.foxnews.com/story/candidates-have-their-say-on-obamas-decision-not-to-wear-flag-pin.

128. Jay Newton Small, "Obama's Flag Pin Flip-Flop?," *Time*, May 14, 2008, https://content.time.com/time/politics/article/0,8599,1779544,00.html.

129. Matt Corley, "Rove Ironically Attacks Obama for Not Wearing Flag Pins," *Think Progress*, April 2, 2008, https://archive.thinkprogress.org/rove-ironically-attacks-obama-for-not-wearing-flag-pins-58fddae4ae04/.

130. Heather Hendershot uses this phrase quoted from Kim Phillips-Fein to describe scholars of the American right who approach their research subjects with kid gloves and in the process smooth over the often intense surreality of what is being described. See *What's Fair on the Air: Cold War Right-Wing Broadcasting and the Public Interest* (Chicago: University of Chicago Press, 2011), 20.

131. Nickerson, *Mothers of Conservatism*, 105.

132. Nickerson, *Mothers of Conservatism*, 105; see generally 103–135.

133. Peck, *Fox Populism*, 55.

134. Peck, *Fox Populism*, 89–92.

135. Peck, *Fox Populism*, 147.

136. Don Gonyea, "'Joe the Plumber' and the Rise of MAGA," *All Things Considered*, NPR, August 29, 2023, https://www.npr.org/2023/08/29/1196641965/joe-the-plumber-and-the-rise-of-maga.

137. Larry Rohter, "Real Deal on 'Joe the Plumber' Reveals New Slant," *New York Times*, October 16, 2008, https://www.nytimes.com/2008/10/17/us/politics/17joe.html.

138. "Why Are Democrats Attacking Joe the Plumber?," *Hannity & Colmes*, Fox News, October 20, 2008, https://www.foxnews.com/story/why-are-democrats -attacking-joe-the-plumber.

139. Matzko, *Radio Right*, 233.

140. Linda Kintz, "Clarity, Mothers, and the Mass-Mediated National Soul: A Defense of Ambiguity," in *Media, Culture, and the Religious Right*, ed. Linda Kintz and Julia Lesage (Minneapolis: University of Minnesota Press, 1998), 133.

141. Critchlow, *Schlafly and Grassroots Conservatism*, 218, 227–229.

142. Razelle Frankl, "Transformation of Televangelism: Repackaging Christian Family Values," in *Media, Culture, and the Religious Right*, ed. Kintz and Lesage, 175.

143. Peck, *Fox Populism*, 192.

144. Chip Berlet, "Who Is Mediating the Storm? Right-Wing Alternative Information Networks," in *Media, Culture, and the Religious Right*, ed. Kintz and Lesage, 252.

145. Jen Schradie, *The Revolution That Wasn't: How Digital Activism Favors Conservatives* (Cambridge, MA: Harvard University Press, 2019).

146. Theda Skocpol and Vanessa Williamson, *The Tea Party and the Remaking of Republican Conservatism* (New York: Oxford University Press, 2016), 7.

147. Schradie, *Revolution That Wasn't*, 77–78.

148. Schradie, *Revolution That Wasn't*, 19.

149. Schradie, *Revolution That Wasn't*, 21.

150. Schradie, *Revolution That Wasn't*, 20.

151. Gabriel Sherman, *The Loudest Voice in the Room: How the Brilliant, Bombastic Roger Ailes Built Fox News—and Divided a Country* (New York: Random House, 2014), xiii.

152. Peck, *Fox Populism*, 6.

153. For a folkloric analysis of the kinds of anti-Obama rumors, conspiracy theories, and internet memes that engulfed the Obama presidency, see Patricia A. Turner, *Trash Talk: Anti-Obama Lore and Race in the Twenty-First Century* (Oakland: University of California Press, 2022).

154. Andy Barr, "Palin Trashes 'Lame-Stream Media,'" *Politico*, November 18, 2009, https://www.politico.com/story/2009/11/palin-trashes-lamestream-media -029693.

155. "Palin Defends Obama Terrorist Comment," *NBC News*, October 4, 2008, https://www.nbcnews.com/id/wbna27022487.

156. Whitney Phillips, *This Is Why We Can't Have Nice Things: Mapping the Relationship between Online Trolling and Mainstream Culture* (Cambridge, MA: MIT Press, 2015), 107–111.

157. Angie Drobnic Holan, "PolitiFact's Lie of the Year: 'Death Panels,'" *Politi-Fact*, December 18, 2009, https://www.politifact.com/article/2009/dec/18/politifact-lie-year-death-panels/.

158. Parker Molloy, "A Decade after Screaming about Nonexistent 'Death Panels,' Fox News Is Downplaying the Deaths of 200,000 Americans," Media Matters for America, September 23, 2020, https://www.mediamatters.org/coronavirus-covid-19/decade-after-screaming-about-nonexistent-death-panels-fox-news-downplaying.

159. Jeremy W. Peters, "Where Fox News and Donald Trump Took Us," *New York Times*, February 5, 2022, https://www.nytimes.com/2022/02/05/business/media/trump-fox-news.html.

160. Nina Mast, "Flashback: How Fox News Promoted Trump's Birtherism," *Media Matters for America*, September 16, 2016, https://www.mediamatters.org/sean-hannity/flashback-how-fox-news-promoted-trumps-birtherism.

CONCLUSION

1. Francisco Goya, *Saturn Devouring His Son*, 1820–1823, Museo del Prado, Madrid, Spain, https://www.museodelprado.es/en/the-collection/art-work/saturn/18110a75-b0e7-430c-bc73-2a4d55893bd6.

2. John Boehner, *On the House: A Washington Memoir* (New York: St. Martin's Press, 2021), 174.

3. Boehner, *On the House*, 174.

4. Boehner, *On the House*, 174.

5. Boehner, *On the House*, 174.

6. Boehner, *On the House*, 164.

7. Boehner, *On the House*, 164, 186.

8. Boehner, *On the House*, 179.

9. Boehner, *On the House*, 160.

10. Mark Z. Barabak, "How a Top Conservative Radio Host Took on Trump, Lost His Audience and Faith, but Gained a New Perspective," *Los Angeles Times*, January 30, 2017, https://www.latimes.com/politics/la-na-pol-sykes-talk-radio-2017-story.html.

11. Davis Richardson, "Why 'Never Trump' Godfather Rick Wilson Started Carrying a Gun in Public," *Observer*, August 13, 2018, https://observer.com/2018/08/rick-wilson-never-trump-strategist-death-threats/.

12. Carlos Lozada, "Bomb Squad: Anti-Trump Conservatives Want to Reverse the GOP's Destruction. But They Helped Light the Fuse," *Washington Post*, December

14, 2018, https://www.washingtonpost.com/news/book-party/wp/2018/12/14/feature/anti-trump-conservatives-want-to-reverse-the-gops-destruction-but-they-helped-light-the-fuse/.

13. Tim Miller, *Why We Did It: A Travelogue from the Republican Road to Hell* (New York: Harper, 2022).

14. Miller, *Why We Did It*, xviii.

15. Paige Winfield Cunningham, "For Never-Trump Conservatives, It's Never-Ending Misery," *Washington Post*, August 15, 2022, https://www.washingtonpost.com/politics/2022/08/15/never-trump-conservatives-it-never-ending-misery/.

16. Lozada, "Bomb Squad," 2018.

17. Mark Leibovich, "Romney, Defying the Party He Once Personified, Votes to Convict Trump," *New York Times*, February 5, 2020, https://www.nytimes.com/2020/02/05/us/politics/romney-trump-impeachment.html; Wendy Leonard, "Why Romney Voted to Convict and Lee Voted to Acquit Trump in 2nd Impeachment Trial," *Deseret News*, February 13, 2021, https://www.deseret.com/utah/2021/2/13/22281675/why-mitt-romney-voted-to-convict-trump-in-the-former-presidents-2nd-impeachment-trial.

18. Joseph Konig, "In Book, Romney Charges, 'a Very Large Portion' of the GOP 'Doesn't Believe in the Constitution,'" Spectrum 1 News, September 13, 2023, https://ny1.com/nyc/all-boroughs/news/2023/09/14/romney---a-very-large-portion-of--the-gop--doesn-t-believe-in-the-constitution-.

19. Charlie Sykes, "Mitt Romney and the Verdict of History," *Bulwark*, September 14, 2023, https://plus.thebulwark.com/p/mitt-romney-and-the-verdict-of-history; McKay Coppins, *Romney: A Reckoning* (New York: Scribner, 2023).

20. Paul Kane, "Liz Cheney Launches a New Brand in Wyoming," *Washington Post*, August 16, 2016, https://www.washingtonpost.com/politics/another-cheney-rises-in-a-republican-party-led-by-trump/2016/08/15/a2f817a0-6267-11e6-8b27-bb8ba39497a2_story.html.

21. Nick Mordowanec, "Liz Cheney Voted with Trump 93% of Her Congressional Career," *Newsweek*, August 16, 2022, https://www.newsweek.com/liz-cheney-voted-donald-trump-93-percent-congress-1734186.

22. John L. Dorman, "Rep. Liz Cheney, Who Was Just Ousted from House GOP Leadership, Says She Now Regrets Voting for Trump in 2020," *Insider*, May 15, 2021, https://www.businessinsider.com/liz-cheney-regrets-2020-trump-vote-election-false-claims-2021-5.

23. Brittany Shepherd and Tal Axelrod, "How Liz Cheney Went from Rising Republican Star to Primary Underdog after Jan. 6," ABC News, August 15, 2022, https://abcnews.go.com/Politics/liz-cheney-rising-republican-star-enters-primary-underdog/story?id=88415555.

24. Tim Murphey, "Liz Cheney Was Defeated by the Extremist Movement She Helped to Empower," *Mother Jones*, August 16, 2022, https://www.motherjones .com/politics/2022/08/liz-cheney-defeated-by-harriet-hageman-wyoming-primary -donald-trump/.

25. Shepherd and Axelrod, "How Liz Cheney Went."

26. Steve Benen, "Freedom Caucus Chair Pushes GOP Leaders to Oust Cheney, Kinzinger," MSNBC, September 2, 2021, https://www.msnbc.com/rachel-maddow -show/maddowblog/freedom-caucus-chair-pushes-gop-leaders-oust-cheney -kinzinger-n1278354.

27. Katherine Tully-McManus and Chris Marquette, "House Republicans Oust Liz Cheney from No. 3 leadership Post," *Roll Call*, May 12, 2021, https://rollcall .com/2021/05/12/house-republicans-oust-liz-cheney-from-no-3-leadership-post/.

28. Jonathan Allen and Henry J. Gomez, "Rep. Liz Cheney Loses Her Primary in Wyoming to Trump-Backed Challenger," *NBC News*, August 16, 2022, https:// www.nbcnews.com/politics/2022-election/rep-liz-cheney-loses-primary-wyoming -trump-backed-challenger-rcna43379.

29. David Bauder, "'Weak Ratings Make Good Journalists Do Bad Things': Fox News Panic over Trump's Loss Doing Bad Numbers Laid Bare in Court," *Fortune*, February 18, 2023, https://fortune.com/2023/02/18/fox-news-dominion-lawsuit -donald-trump-2020-loss-bad-ratings-rupert-murdoch/.

30. Jeremy W. Peters and Katie Robertson, "Fox Stars Privately Expressed Disbelief about Election Fraud Claims. 'Crazy Stuff,'" *New York Times*, February 16, 2023, https://www.nytimes.com/2023/02/16/business/media/fox-dominion -lawsuit.html.

31. Carlson quoted in Anthony Nadler and Doron Taussig, "The Deep Story beneath the Big Lie," *Los Angeles Times Review of Books*, August 16, 2023, https:// lareviewofbooks.org/article/the-deep-story-beneath-the-big-lie/.

32. Katie Robertson, "Here Are the Other Legal Cases Fox Is Entangled In," *New York Times*, April 18, 2023, https://www.nytimes.com/2023/04/18/business/media /fox-lawsuits-legal-cases.html.

33. Justin Baragona, "Trump Urges MAGA to Dump His Longtime Fox News Pal Laura Ingraham," *Daily Beast*, October 6, 2023, https://www.thedailybeast .com/trump-urges-maga-to-dump-longtime-fox-news-pal-laura-ingraham-over -hit-piece.

34. Tim Dickinson, "'The End of Fox News': MAGA World Reacts to Tucker Carlson's Departure," *Rolling Stone*, April 24, 2023, https://www.rollingstone.com /politics/politics-news/tucker-carlson-fox-news-reactions-far-right-1234722644/.

35. Tucker Carlson was fired the same week the settlement with Dominion was reached, though Fox claims it wasn't related to the settlement. Carlson insists that

it was. See Martin Pengelly, "Tucker Carlson Claims in Book Fox News Firing Was Part of $787.5m Settlement," *Guardian*, July 26, 2023, https://www.the guardian.com/books/2023/jul/26/tucker-carlson-fox-news-firing-condition -dominion-settlement; Dickinson, "'The End of Fox News'"; Isabella Simonetti, "Tucker Carlson's Fox Exit Helps Boost Newsmax Ratings," *Wall Street Journal*, July 24, 2023, https://www.wsj.com/articles/tucker-carlsons-fox-exit-helps-boost -newsmax-ratings-8aed0b57.

36. Tim Alberta, "How Politics Poisoned the Evangelical Church," *Atlantic*, May 10, 2022, https://www.theatlantic.com/magazine/archive/2022/06/evangelical -church-pastors-political-radicalization/629631/; Patrick Smith, "Why One Evangelical Pastor Left a Radicalized, Post–Jan. 6 America Behind," *NBC News*, April 18, 2022, https://www.nbcnews.com/news/religion/one-evangelical-pastor -left-radicalized-post-jan-6-america-rcna14869.

37. Jaweed Kaleem, "QAnon and Other Conspiracy Theories Are Taking Hold in Churches. Pastors Are Fighting Back," *Los Angeles Times*, March 3, 2021, https:// www.latimes.com/world-nation/story/2021-03-03/la-na-church-qanon-conspiracy -theories.

38. Sophia Ankel, "Pastors Are Leaving Their Congregations after Losing Their Churchgoers to QAnon," *Insider*, March 14, 2021, https://www.businessinsider .com/pastors-quit-after-qanon-radicalize-congregation-2021-3; A. W. Ohlheiser, "Evangelicals Are Looking for Answers Online. They're Finding QAnon Instead," *MIT Technology Review*, August 26, 2020, https://www.technologyreview.com /2020/08/26/1007611/how-qanon-is-targeting-evangelicals/; Smith, "Why One Evangelical Pastor Left"; VICE News, "QAnon Conspiracies Are Tearing through Evangelical America," YouTube, October 19, 2021, https://www.youtube.com /watch?app=desktop&v=rYMIozCKxGE&t=16s.

39. "Pastors Share Top Reasons They've Considered Quitting Ministry in the Past Year," *Barna*, April 27, 2022, https://www.barna.com/research/pastors-quitting -ministry/. The burnout and stress experienced by Evangelical pastors attempting to navigate the Trump era is also a recurring theme of Tim Alberta's *The Kingdom, the Power, and the Glory: American Evangelicals in an Age of Extremism* (New York: Harper Collins, 2023).

40. "The Pastors Being Driven Out by Trumpism," *The Daily*, podcast, September 23, 2022, https://www.nytimes.com/2022/09/23/podcasts/the-daily/evangelicals -trumpism.html.

41. David Bumgardner, "They Spoke Out against the Capitol Insurrection; One Year Later, They're No Longer Pastors," *Baptist News Global*, January 19, 2022, https://baptistnews.com/article/they-spoke-out-against-the-capitol-insurrection -one-year-later-theyre-no-longer-pastors/.

42. Bumgardner, "They Spoke Out."

43. Smith, "Why One Evangelical Pastor Left."

44. David R. Swartz, *Moral Minority: The Evangelical Left in an Age of Conservatism* (Philadelphia: University of Pennsylvania Press, 2012), 5–7, 28, 33.

45. Aaron Blake, "Tucker Carlson Puts Mike Pence in His Place in Today's GOP," *Washington Post*, July 14, 2023, https://www.washingtonpost.com/politics /2023/07/14/tucker-carlson-puts-mike-pence-his-place-todays-gop/.

46. Alia Slisco, "Evangelicals Are Now Rejecting 'Liberal' Teachings of Jesus," *Newsweek*, August 9, 2023, https://www.newsweek.com/evangelicals-rejecting -jesus-teachings-liberal-talking-points-pastor-1818706.

47. David E. Campbell, Geoffrey C. Layman, and John C. Green, *Secular Surge: A New Fault Line in American Politics* (Cambridge: Cambridge University Press, 2020); Michele F. Margolis, *From Politics to the Pews: How Partisanship and the Political Environment Shape Religious Identity* (Chicago: University of Chicago Press, 2018); Stephen Bullivant, "Flatline Protestants," in *Nonverts: The Making of Ex-Christian America*, ed. Stephen Bullivant (New York: Oxford University Press, 2022), 74–93.

48. Patricia Tevington, "Americans Feel More Positive than Negative about Jews, Mainline Protestants, Catholics," Pew Research Center, March 15, 2023, https:// www.pewresearch.org/religion/2023/03/15/americans-feel-more-positive-than -negative-about-jews-mainline-protestants-catholics/.

49. Alberta, *The Kingdom*.

50. For examples of journalists framing—and simultaneously decrying—Trump as an Evangelical messiah figure, see Ed Kilgore, "Do Evangelicals Think Trump Is Jesus?," *New York Magazine Intelligencer*, May 8, 2023, https://nymag.com/intelli gencer/2023/05/do-white-evangelicals-think-trump-is-jesus.html; Thomas B. Edsall, "The Deification of Donald Trump Poses Some Interesting Questions," *New York Times*, January 17, 2024, https://www.nytimes.com/2024/01/17/opinion/trump -god-evangelicals-anointed.html; Sarah Posner, "Listen Closely: Trump Wants to Be a 'Messiah' Figure for Evangelicals," *Daily Beast*'s New Abnormal, January 19, 2024, https://www.thedailybeast.com/listen-closely-trump-wants-to-be-a-messiah -figure-for-evangelicals.

51. Joe Sommerlad, "Trump Shares Bizarre Biblical Video Saying God Made Him to Be America's 'Caretaker,'" *Independent*, January 15, 2024, https://www.the -independent.com/news/world/americas/us-politics/trump-iowa-caucuses-video -god-b2478729.html.

52. Aaron Blake, "How Jan. 6—and Republicans—Enabled Trump's Domination of the GOP," *Washington Post*, January 6, 2022, https://www.washingtonpost.com /politics/2022/01/06/how-jan-6-republicans-enabled-trumps-domination-gop/.

53. Martin Pengelly, "Republican Party Calls January 6 Attack 'Legitimate Polit-ical Discourse,'" *Guardian*, February 4, 2022, https://www.theguardian.com/us

-news/2022/feb/04/republicans-capitol-attack-legitimate-political-discourse-cheney-kinzinger-pence.

54. Mychael Schnell, "Cheney Rips Claims Jan. 6 was 'False Flag Operation,'" *Hill*, November 7, 2021, https://thehill.com/homenews/sunday-talk-shows/580439-cheney-likens-claims-that-jan-6-was-a-false-flag-operation-to-9-11/.

55. Madison Czopek, "Taylor Swift: Singer, Songwriter, Psyop? How Conservative Pundits Spread a Wild Theory," *PolitiFact*, February 2, 2024, https://www.politifact.com/article/2024/feb/02/taylor-swift-singer-songwriter-psyop-how-conservat/.

56. Nadler and Taussig, "The Deep Story beneath the Big Lie."

57. Fatma Khaled, "Pizza Hut Slammed for Suggesting Drag Performer Book in Kids' Reading Club," *Newsweek*, June 3, 2022, https://www.newsweek.com/pizza-hut-slammed-suggesting-drag-performer-book-kids-reading-club-1712655.

58. Jordyn Holman and Julie Creswell, "Brands Embracing Pride Month Confront a Volatile Political Climate," *New York Times*, May 25, 2023, https://www.nytimes.com/2023/05/25/business/target-pride-lgbtq-companies-backlash.html.

59. Dee-Ann Durbin, "Bud Light Parent Says US Market Share Stabilizing after Transgender Promotion Cost Sales," Associated Press, August 3, 2023, https://apnews.com/article/bud-light-anheuser-busch-inbev-earnings-46b6412f84b5e8884caea941fc069d2f.

60. Eric Cortellessa, "Conservatives Aren't Just Boycotting Bud Light. They're Trying to Build a Parallel Economy," *Time*, September 26, 2023, https://time.com/6317479/bud-light-boycott-maga-economy-donald-trump-jr/.

61. For background on the parents' rights movement, see Jamelle Bouie, "What the Republican Push for 'Parents' Rights' Is Really About," *New York Times*, March 28, 2023, https://www.nytimes.com/2023/03/28/opinion/parents-rights-republicans-florida.html; Stephen Groves, "House Republicans Pass 'Parents' Rights' Bill in Fight over Schools," *PBS NewsHour*, March 24, 2023, https://www.pbs.org/newshour/education/house-republicans-pass-parents-rights-bill-in-fight-over-schools.

62. "Uncovering Who Is Driving the Fight against Critical Race Theory in Schools," *Fresh Air*, NPR, June 24, 2021, https://www.npr.org/2021/06/24/1009839021/uncovering-who-is-driving-the-fight-against-critical-race-theory-in-schools.

63. The state of Florida, helmed by Governor Ron DeSantis, is a hotbed for "anti-woke" legislative efforts. See Brooke Migdon, "What Is DeSantis's 'Stop WOKE Act'?," *Hill*, August 19, 2022, https://thehill.com/changing-america/respect/diversity-inclusion/3608241-what-is-desantiss-stop-woke-act/; "Governor DeSantis Announces Legislative Proposal to Stop W.O.K.E. Activism and Critical Race Theory in Schools and Corporations," DeSantis Press Release, December 15, 2021,

https://www.flgov.com/2021/12/15/governor-desantis-announces-legislative
-proposal-to-stop-w-o-k-e-activism-and-critical-race-theory-in-schools-and
-corporations/.

64. For more on the controversy around critical race theory, or at least the various things that get called "critical race theory," see "Uncovering Who Is Driving the Fight against Critical Race Theory."

65. For broader context on the homophobic and transphobic "groomer" slur, see Matt Lavietes, "'Groomer,' 'Pro-Pedophile': Old Tropes Find New Life in Anti-LGBTQ Movement," *NBC News*, April 12, 2022, https://www.nbcnews.com/nbc-out/out-politics-and-policy/groomer-pedophile-old-tropes-find-new-life-anti-lgbtq-movement-rcna23931.

66. Alex Woodward, "Republican Senator Reads Explicit Passages from LGBT+ Memoirs in Misleading Stunt at Book Ban Hearing," *Independent*, September 13, 2023, https://www.the-independent.com/news/world/americas/us-politics/john-kennedy-book-ban-hearing-b2410824.html.

67. Gabriel Hays, "Viewer Discretion: Kennedy Makes Dem Squirm with Mentions of Dildo, C—— While Reading LGBTQ Kids' Books," Fox News, September 12, 2023, https://www.foxnews.com/media/sen-kennedy-makes-dem-lawmaker-squirm-reading-excerpts-lgbtq-kids-books-hearing-disturbing.

68. Andrew Stanton, "Senator Reads Aloud from Pornographic Book in Hearing: 'Disturbing,'" *Newsweek*, September 12, 2023, https://www.newsweek.com/senator-reads-aloud-pornographic-book-hearing-1826531.

69. Taussig and Nadler, "The Deep Story beneath the Big Lie."

70. Turning Point USA home page, accessed February 29, 2024, https://www.tpusa.com/.

71. Turning Point USA, "Free the First," accessed February 29, 2024, https://www.tpusa.com/highschoolresources/freethefirst. Turning Point USA increasingly pushes a pro-Christian message that dovetails with its emphasis on freedoms and translates to various anti-liberal attacks, including against secular humanism, which founder Charlie Kirk says invented the "fabrication" of the separation of Church and State, as well as what Kirk calls the "LGBTQ agenda." Kirk summarized the *anti-* embedded in his organization's *pro-* during a 2024 Turning Point event held at a megachurch. "I worship a God that defeats evil," he stated. See Mike Hixenbaugh and Allan Smith, "Charlie Kirk Once Pushed a 'Secular Worldview.' Now He's Fighting to Make America Christian Again," *NBC News*, June 12, 2024.

72. Turning Point USA, "Professor Watchlist," accessed June 2023, https://www.professorwatchlist.org/search.

73. Campus Reform, "Mission," accessed March 2023, https://www.campusreform.org/about.

74. Ben Mincey, "UMaryland College of Education Welcomes Overwhelmingly Woke Cohort of New Professors," *Campus Reform*, September 14, 2023, https://www.campusreform.org/article?id=23999. As of March 2024, Campus Reform's section on free speech is labeled on the website as a "Free Speech Zone."

75. Daniel Golden, "Muzzled by DeSantis, Critical Race Theory Professors Cancel Courses or Modify Their Teaching," *ProPublica*, January 3, 2023, https://www.propublica.org/article/desantis-critical-race-theory-florida-college-professors.

76. Golden, "Muzzled by DeSantis."

77. "Trump's Full Speech at D.C. Rally on Jan. 6," *Wall Street Journal*, February 7, 2021, https://www.wsj.com/video/trump-full-speech-at-dc-rally-on-jan-6/E4E7 BBBF-23B1-4401-ADCE-7D4432D07030. For a full transcript of the speech, see Brian Naylor, "Read Trump's Jan. 6 Speech, a Key Part of Impeachment Trial," NPR, February 10, 2021, https://www.npr.org/2021/02/10/966396848/read -trumps-jan-6-speech-a-key-part-of-impeachment-trial.

78. Trump, January 6 speech.

79. Michael Gold, "'Maybe I've Gotten Worse': Trump Makes Clear That Unity Is Over," *New York Times*, July 28, 2024, https://www.nytimes.com/2024/07/28 /us/politics/trump-vance-unity-minnesota.html.

80. "Former President Trump Speaks at CPAC," C-SPAN, February 24, 2024, https://www.c-span.org/video/?533737-1/president-trump-speaks-cpac.

81. Lulu Garcia-Navarro, "Inside the Heritage Foundation's Plans for 'Institutionalizing Trumpism,'" *New York Times*, January 21, 2024, https://www.nytimes .com/2024/01/21/magazine/heritage-foundation-kevin-roberts.html. In 2023, Project 2025 published a policy guide titled "Mandate for Leadership: The Conservative Promise" that resembles the Contract with America and Contract with the American Family but with much more shadow gospel accelerant. Like the contracts, the mandate lends itself to rhetorical analysis at the conspiratorial, *anti-*, and *pro-* levels, and its paratext—all the media, information, and cultural happenings that surround a text—subsumes similar personalities as in the 1990s, with the role of anti-liberal crusader Newt Gingrich filled by current House Speaker Mike Johnson and the role of bombastic conspiracist Pat Buchanan filled by Georgia representative Marjorie Taylor Greene. See "Policy Agenda," Project 2025, accessed June 24, 2024, https://www.project2025.org/policy/.

82. Jacob L. Nelson and Seth C. Lewis, "Only 'Sheep' Trust Journalists? How Citizens' Self-Perceptions Shape Their Approach to News," *New Media & Society* 25, no. 7 (2021): 1522–1541, https://doi.org/10.1177/14614448211018160.

83. See Benjamin Toff and Rasmus Kleis Nielsen, "I Just Google It": Folk Theories of Distributed Discovery," *Journal of Communication* 68, no. 3 (2018): 636–657, https://doi.org/10.1093/joc/jqy009; Rasmus Kleis Nielsen, "Folk Theories of Journalism," *Journalism Studies* 17, no. 7 (2016): 840–848; Ruth Palmer,

Becoming the News: How Ordinary People Respond to the Media Spotlight (New York: Columbia University Press, 2017), 15, 195–196, https://doi.org/10.1080/14616 70X.2016.1165140.

84. Ariella Azoulay, *The Civil Contract of Photography* (Princeton, NJ: Princeton University Press, 2008).

85. Azoulay, *The Civil Contract*, 197–199.

86. Phillips defines the institutional-consensus "we" in a chapter titled "Both and Neither: Foregrounding Media History." The chapter explores the dueling emergency claims between demonologists and non-demonologists and will be included in *Truth after Post Truth*, ed. Anthony Nadler and Doron Taussig, forthcoming.

87. Ayana Archie, "A Lot Is Happening in Florida Education. These Are Some of the Changes Kids Will See," NPR, August 14, 2023, https://www.npr.org /2023/08/14/1193557432/florida-education-private-schools-prageru-desantis; Lexi Lonas, "Oklahoma Follows Florida in Allowing PragerU in Schools," *Hill*, September 5, 2023, https://thehill.com/homenews/education/4188167-oklahoma -follows-florida-in-allowing-prageru-in-schools/#:~:text=Oklahoma%20is %20the%20second%20state,be%20penalized%20for%20showing%20them; Sarah Schwartz, "PragerU, Creator of Controversial Social Studies Videos, Now Has a Toehold in Schools," *Education Week*, August 31, 2023, https://www.edweek.org /teaching-learning/prageru-creator-of-controversial-social-studies-videos-now -has-a-toehold-in-schools/2023/08; PragerU, "What Is PragerU," accessed October 25, 2023, https://www.prageru.com/about; PragerU, "Kids Shows You Can Trust," accessed October 25, 2023, https://www.prageru.com/kids.

88. Schwartz, "PragerU, Creator of Controversial Social Studies Videos"; Matt Gertz, "Public Schools Are the Latest Target of the Right's Con Culture," Media Matters for America, September 7, 2023, https://www.mediamatters.org /dennis-prager/public-schools-are-latest-target-rights-con-culture.

89. Caleb Ecarma, "From Florida to Oklahoma, PragerU's Propaganda Project Isn't Slowing Down," *Vanity Fair*, September 6, 2023, https://www.vanityfair .com/news/2023/09/florida-oklahoma-prageru-propaganda-isnt-slowing-down.

90. John Knefel, "The Lessons Florida Public School Students Will Learn from PragerU Kids," Media Matters for America, July 27, 2023, https://www.media matters.org/prageru/lessons-florida-public-school-students-will-learn-prageru-kids.

91. Tyler Kingkade, "How Oklahoma's Schools Superintendent Became the State's Top Culture Warrior," NBC News, August 23, 2023, https://www .nbcnews.com/news/us-news/ryan-walters-oklahoma-schools-superintendent -tulsa-rcna101235.

92. For representative framings, see Sudiksha Kochi, "'Fight This Battle Piece by Piece': Concerned Moms Are Shaping Culture Wars and 2024 Race," *USA Today*, September 19, 2023, https://www.usatoday.com/story/news/politics/2023/09

/19/moms-for-liberty-defense-of-democracy-2024-race/70834857007/, and Kiara Alfonseca and Mary Kekatos, "Debate over 'Parental Rights' Is the Latest Fight in the Education Culture Wars," ABC News, September 14, 2023, https://abcnews .go.com/US/debate-parental-rights-latest-fight-education-culture-wars/story?id =103024033. For examples of how news stories highlighting parents' rights election losses, or which otherwise minimize the extent of parents' rights successes, still reinforce the "culture war" frame, see Anya Kamenetz, "The Education Culture War Is Raging. But for Most Parents, It's Background Noise," *Morning Edition*, NPR, April 29, 2022, https://www.npr.org/2022/04/29/1094782769/parent-poll -school-culture-wars, and Katrina vanden Heuvel "The Moms for Liberty Platform Is Extreme—And Most Voters Are Loudly Rejecting It," *Guardian*, November 21, 2023, https://www.theguardian.com/commentisfree/2023/nov/21/moms -for-liberty-school-board-elections.

93. The title of George Lakoff and Mark Johnson's book, *Metaphors We Live By* (Chicago: University of Chicago Press, 1980), underscores the world-shaping power of frames. So does Erving Goffman's discussion of frames as "principles of organization" that help discern subjective reality and how to answer the question, "What is going on here?" Goffman, *Frame Analysis: An Essay on the Organization of Experience* (Boston: Northeastern University Press, 1986), 8, 10.

94. "Photos of the Trump Store in Boones Mill, VA," *Roanoke Times*, August 1, 2021, https://roanoke.com/gallery/photos-the-trump-store-in-boones-mill/collection _7cb60ca0-efca-11eb-b3ed-83fb62afd632.html#2.

SELECTED BIBLIOGRAPHY: ACADEMIC WORK AND OTHER SOURCES

Aiello, Thomas. "Constructing 'Godless Communism': Religion, Politics, and Popular Culture, 1954–1960." *Americana* 4, no. 1 (Spring 2005). https://american popularculture.com/journal/articles/spring_2005/aiello.htm.

Akenson, Donald Harman. *The Americanization of the Apocalypse: Creating America's Own Bible*. Oxford: Oxford University Press, 2023.

Alberta, Tim. *The Kingdom, the Power, and the Glory: American Evangelicals in an Age of Extremism*. New York: HarperCollins, 2023.

Ammerman, Nancy T. "North American Protestant Fundamentalism." In *Media, Culture, and the Religious Right*, edited by Linda Kintz and Julia Lesage, 55–115. Minneapolis: University of Minnesota Press, 1998.

Anderson, W. H. Locke. "Red Hunting in the Promised Land." *Monthly Review* 46, no. 1 (May 1994): 54–61.

Apel, William D. "The Lost World of Billy Graham." *Review of Religious Research* 20, no. 2 (Spring 1979): 138–149.

Asma, Stephen. "Possessing Demons and Witches." In *On Monsters: An Unnatural History of Our Worst Fears*, 103–123. Oxford: Oxford University Press, 2009.

Azoulay, Ariella. *The Civil Contract of Photography*. Princeton, NJ: Princeton University Press, 2008.

Baddeley, Gavin. *Lucifer Rising: Sin, Devil Worship, and Rock & Roll*. London: Plexus, 2016.

Baker, Kelly J. *Gospel According to the Klan: The KKK's Appeal to Protestant America, 1915–1930*. Lawrence: University Press of Kansas, 2017.

Baker, Tod A. *Political Parties in the Southern States: Party Activists in Partisan Coalitions*. Westport, CT: Praeger, 1990.

Balmer, Randall. *Evangelicalism in America*. Waco, TX: Baylor University Press, 2016.

Balmer, Randall. *The Making of Evangelicalism: From Revivalism to Politics and Beyond*. Waco, TX: Baylor University Press, 2010.

Barrett, Marsha E. "Defining Rockefeller Republicanism: Promise and Peril at the Edge of Liberal Consensus, 1958–1975." *Journal of Political History* 36, no. 2 (2022): 336–370. https://doi.org/10.1017/S0898030622000100.

Barthes, Roland. *Mythologies*. New York: Farrar, Straus and Giroux, 1972.

Başpehlivan, Uygar. "Cucktales: Race, Sex, and Enjoyment in the Reactionary Memescape." *International Political Sociology* 18, no. 3 (2024): olae026. https://doi.org/10.1093/ips/olae026.

Bates, Stephen. "'Godless Communism' and Its Legacies." *Society* 41, no. 3 (2004): 29–33.

Bednar, Nancy N., and Allen D. Hertzke. "The Christian Right and Republican Realignment in Oklahoma." *PS: Political Science & Politics* 28, no. 1 (2013): 11–15. https://doi.org/10.2307/420572.

Belew, Kathleen. *Bring the War Home: The White Power Movement and Paramilitary America*. Cambridge, MA: Harvard University Press, 2018.

Belew, Kathleen. "Veterans and White Supremacy." *New York Times*. April 16, 2014. https://www.nytimes.com/2014/04/16/opinion/veterans-and-white-supremacy.html.

Belfrage, Cedric. *The American Inquisition: 1945–1960*. Indianapolis: Bobbs-Merrill, 1973.

Berg, Thomas C. "'Proclaiming Together'? Convergence and Divergence in Mainline and Evangelical Evangelism, 1945–1967." *Religion and American Culture: A Journal of Interpretation* 5, no. 1 (1995): 49–76.

Berlet, Chip. "Who Is Mediating the Storm? Right-Wing Alternative Information Networks." In *Media, Culture, and the Religious Right*, edited by Linda Kintz and Julia Lesage, 249–274. Minneapolis: University of Minnesota Press, 1998.

Bernstein, Shana. "From Civic Defense to Civil Rights: The Growth of Jewish American Interracial Civil Rights Activism in Los Angeles." In *A Cultural History of Jews in California: The Jewish Role in American Life*, edited by Bruce Zuckerman, William Deverell, and Lisa Ansell, 55–80. West Lafayette, IN: Purdue University Press, 2009.

Binder, Amy. "Constructing Racial Rhetoric: Media Depictions of Harm in Heavy Metal and Rap Music." *American Sociological Review* 58, no. 6 (1993): 753–767. https://doi.org/10.2307/2095949.

Bivins, Jason C. *The Fracture of Good Order: Christian Antiliberalism and the Challenge to American Politics*. Chapel Hill: University of North Carolina Press, 2004.

Bivins, Jason C. *Religion of Fear: The Politics of Horror in Conservative Evangelicalism*. Oxford: Oxford University Press, 2008.

Bivins, Jason. "Tracing the Rise of Christian Media in American Political Discourse." *Pacific Standard*, May 30, 2018. https://psmag.com/news/the-rise-of-the-christian-media.

Blee, Kathleen. *Inside Organized Racism: Women in the Hate Movement*. Berkeley: University of California Press, 2003.

Boehner, John. *On the House: A Washington Memoir*. New York: St. Martin's Press, 2021.

Bokina, John, and Timothy J. Lukes, eds. *Marcuse: From the New Left to the Next Left*. Lawrence: University Press of Kansas, 1994.

Brackett, John. "Satan, Subliminals, and Suicide: The Formation and Development of an Anti-Rock in the United States during the 1980s." *American Music* 36, no. 3 (2018): 271–302.

Brands, H. W. *The Strange Death of American Liberalism*. New Haven, CT: Yale University Press, 2001.

Brennan, Mary C. *Turning Right in the 60s: The Conservative Capture of the GOP*. Chapel Hill: University of North Carolina Press, 1995.

Brennan, Mary C. *Wives, Mothers, and the Red Menace: Conservative Women and the Crusade against Communism*. Boulder: University Press of Colorado, 2008.

Bromley, David G. "Satanism: The New Cult Scare." In *The Satanism Scare*, edited by James T. Richardson, Joel Best, and David G. Bromley, 49–74. New York: Routledge, 1991.

Bryant, Anita. *The Anita Bryant Story: The Survival of Our Nation's Families and the Threat of Militant Homosexuality*. Old Tappan, NJ: Fleming H. Revell, 1977.

Buckley, William F. *God and Man at Yale*. Chicago: Henry Regnery, 1951.

Bullivant, Stephen. *Nonverts: The Making of Ex-Christian America*. New York: Oxford University Press, 2022.

Burge, Ryan. "American Religion in 2030." *Religion in Public*, October 24, 2019. https://religioninpublic.blog/2019/10/24/american-religion-in-2030/.

Burge, Ryan P. "Evangelicals Show No Decline, Despite Trump and Nones." *Christianity Today*, March 21, 2019. https://www.christianitytoday.com/news/2019/march/evangelical-nones-mainline-us-general-social-survey-gss.html.

Burge, Ryan. "44 Years of Religion and Politics in One Graph." *Religion in Public*, May 11, 2017. https://religioninpublic.blog/2017/05/11/44-years-of-religion-and-politics-in-one-graph/.

Burge, Ryan. "How Has Partisanship and Theology Shifted in America's Religious Traditions?" *Religion in Public*, May 22, 2017. https://religioninpublic.blog/2017/05/22/how-has-partisanship-and-theology-shifted-in-americas-religious-traditions/.

Busch, Andrew. *Reagan's Victory: The Presidential Election of 1980 and the Rise of the Right*. Lawrence: University Press of Kansas, 2005.

Butler, Anthea. *White Evangelical Racism: The Politics of Morality in America*. Chapel Hill: University of North Carolina Press, 2021.

Campbell, David E., Geoffrey C. Layman, and John C. Green. *Secular Surge: A New Fault Line in American Politics*. Cambridge: Cambridge University Press, 2020.

Campbell, Robert. *New Morality or No Morality*. New York: Bruce, 1969.

Canipe, Lee. "Under God and Anti-Communist: How the Pledge of Allegiance Got Religion in Cold War America." *Journal of Church and State* 45, no. 2 (Spring 2003): 305–323.

Cargill, Jack, Jr. *The American Far Right: A Case Study of Billy James Hargis and Christian Crusade*. Grand Rapids, MI: William B. Eerdmans, 1969.

Carlson, Shawn, and Gerald Larue. *Satanism in America: Final Report for the Committee for Scientific Examination of Religion*. El Cerrito, CA: Gaia Press, 1989.

Carmines, Edward G., and James A. Stimson. *Issue Evolution: Race and the Transformation of American Politics*. Princeton, NJ: Princeton University Press, 1989.

Carpenter, Joel A. "Fundamentalist Institutions and the Rise of Evangelical Protestantism, 1929–1942." *Church History* 49, no. 1 (March 1980): 62–75. https://doi.org/10.2307/3164640.

Carpenter, Joel A. *A New Evangelical Coalition: Early Documents of the National Association of Evangelicals*. New York: Garland, 1988.

Carter, Dan. *The Politics of Rage: George Wallace, the Origins of the New Conservatism, and the Transformation of American Politics*, 2nd ed. Baton Rouge: Louisiana State University Press, 2000.

Caute, David. *The Great Fear: The Anti-Communist Purge under Truman and Eisenhower*. New York: Simon and Schuster, 1978.

Celestini, Carmen. "God, Country, and Christian Conservatives: The National Association of Manufacturers, the John Birch Society, and the Rise of the Christian Right." PhD dissertation, University of Waterloo, 2018.

Cook, Anthony E. "Encountering the Other: Evangelicalism and Terrorism in a Post 911 World." *Journal of Law and Religion* 20, no. 1 (2004): 1–30.

Clifton, Brett M. "Romancing the GOP: Assessing the Strategies Used by the Christian Coalition to Influence the Republican Party." *Party Politics* 10, no. 5 (2004): 475–498. https://doi.org/10.1177/1354068804045384.

Coalter, Milton J., et al. *Vital Signs: The Promise of Mainstream Protestantism*. Grand Haven, MI: FaithWalk, 2002.

Cockrell, Amanda. "Harry Potter and the Witch Hunters: A Social Context for the Attacks on Harry Potter." *Journal of American Culture* 29, no. 1 (2006): 24–30. https://doi.org/10.1111/j.1542-734X.2006.00272.x.

Conley, Wm. "The Tracking of Evil: Home Video and the Proliferation of the Satanic Panic." In *Satanic Panic: Pop-Cultural Paranoia in the 1980s*, edited by Kier-La Janisse and Paul Corupe, 231–247. Surrey: FAB Press, 2015.

Connor, Claire. *Wrapped in the Flag: A Personal History of America's Radical Right.* Boston: Beacon Press, 2013.

Contract with the American Family: A Bold Plan by the Christian Coalition to Strengthen the Family and Restore Common-Sense Values. Nashville, TN: Moorings, 1995.

Coontz, Stephanie. *The Way We Never Were: American Families and the Nostalgia Trap.* New York: Basic Books, 2016.

Cooper-White, Pamela. *The Psychology of Christian Nationalism: Why People Are Drawn in and How to Talk across the Divide.* Minneapolis: Augsburg Fortress, 2022.

Corupe, Paul. "20-Sided Sins: How Jack Chick Was Drawn into the RPG War." In *Satanic Panic: Pop-Cultural Paranoia in the 1980s*, edited by Kier-La Janisse and Paul Corupe, 69–82. Surrey: FAB Press, 2015.

Coulter, Ann. *Godless: The Church of Liberalism.* New York: Crown Forum, 2006.

Cramer, Katherine J. *The Politics of Resentment: Rural Consciousness in Wisconsin and the Rise of Scott Walker.* Chicago: University of Chicago Press, 2016.

Critchlow, Donald T. *Phyllis Schlafly and Grassroots Conservatism.* Princeton, NJ: Princeton University Press, 2005.

Critchlow, Donald T. *When Hollywood Was Right: How Movie Stars, Studio Moguls, and Big Business Remade American Politics.* Cambridge: Cambridge University Press, 2013.

Crouch, Ben, and Kelly Damphousse. "Law Enforcement and the Satanism-Crime Connection: A Survey of 'Cult Cops.'" In *The Satanism Scare*, edited by James T. Richardson, Joel Best, and David G. Bromley, 191–204. New York: Routledge, 1991.

Daniels, Jessie. *White Lies.* New York: Routledge, 1997.

Davis, Nicholas T. "The Psychometric Properties of the Christian Nationalism Scale." *Politics and Religion* 16, no. 1 (2023):1–26.

Deckman, Melissa M. *School Board Battles: The Christian Right in Local Politics.* Washington, DC: Georgetown University Press, 2004.

Delton, Jennifer A. *Rethinking the 1950s: How Anticommunism and the Cold War Made America Liberal.* Cambridge: Cambridge University Press, 2013.

Denker, Angela. *Red State Christians: A Journey into White Christian Nationalism and the Wreckage It Leaves Behind.* Minneapolis: Augsburg Fortress, 2022.

Diamond, Sara. *Roads to Dominion: Right-Wing Movements and Political Power in the United States.* New York: Guilford Press, 1995.

Dionne, E. J., Jr. "Inevitably, the Politics of Terror: Fear Has Become Part of Washington's Power Struggle." *Brookings*, May 25, 2003. https://www.brookings.edu/articles/inevitably-the-politics-of-terror-fear-has-become-part-of-washingtons-power-struggle/.

Dochuk, Darren. *Anointed in Oil: How Christianity and Crude Made Modern America*. New York: Basic Books, 2019.

Dochuk, Darren. *From Bible Belt to Sunbelt: Plain-Folk Religion, Grassroots Politics, and the Rise of Evangelical Conservatism*. New York: W. W. Norton, 2010.

Dochuk, Darren. "The Other Brother Duo That Brought Us the Modern GOP." *Politico Magazine*, September 2, 2019. https://www.politico.com/magazine/story/2019/09/02/pew-brothers-politics-influence-wealth-227993/.

Doherty, Carroll, and Jocelyn Kiley. "A Look Back at How Fear and False Beliefs Bolstered U.S. Public Support for War in Iraq." Pew Research Center, March 14, 2023. https://www.pewresearch.org/politics/2023/03/14/a-look-back-at-how-fear-and-false-beliefs-bolstered-u-s-public-support-for-war-in-iraq/.

Donovan, Joan, Emily Dreyfuss, and Brian Friedberg. *Meme Wars: The Untold Story of the Online Battles Upending Democracy in America*. New York: Bloomsbury Publishing, 2022.

Dubler, Joshua, and Vincent W. Lloyd. "The Political Theology of Mass Incarceration." In *Break Every Yoke: Religion, Justice, and the Abolition of Prisons*, edited by Joshua Dubler and Vincent W. Lloyd, 65–104. New York: Oxford University Press, 2020.

Ellis, Bill. *Raising the Devil: Satanism, New Religions, and the Media*. Lexington: University of Kentucky Press, 2000.

Engels, Jeremy. *The Politics of Resentment: A Genealogy*. University Park: Penn State University Press, 2015.

Ersoz, Meryem. "Gimmie That Old-Time Religion in a Postmodern Age: Semiotics of Christian Radio." In *Media, Culture, and the Religious Right*, edited by Linda Kintz and Julia Lesage, 211–226. Minneapolis: University of Minnesota Press, 1998.

Estey, Ken. "WCP: Billy Graham and the Evangelical Origins of Organized Labor." Georgetown University, Kalmanovitz Initiative for Labor and the Working Poor. Accessed June 2023. https://lwp.georgetown.edu/visitingscholars/wcp-billy-graham-and-the-evangelical-origins-of-organized-labor/.

Evans, Curtis. "A Politics of Conversion: Billy Graham's Political and Social Vision." In *Billy Graham: American Pilgrim*, edited by Andrew Finstuen, Grant Wacker, and Anne Blue Wills, 143–160. New York: Oxford University Press, 2017.

Evans, Curtis J. "White Evangelical Protestant Responses to the Civil Rights Movement." *Harvard Theological Review* 102, no. 2 (2009): 245–273.

Evans, Stanton. *Revolt on the Campus*. Chicago: Henry Regnery, 1961.

Fanestil, John. *American Heresy: The Roots and Reach of White Christian Nationalism*. Minneapolis: Augsburg Fortress, 2023.

Ferguson, Kevin L. "Devil on the Line: Technology and the Satanic Film." In *Satanic Panic: Pop-Cultural Paranoia in the 1980s*, edited by Kier-La Janisse and Paul Corupe, 87–126. Surrey: FAB Press, 2015.

FitzGerald, Frances. *The Evangelicals: The Struggle to Shape America*. New York: Simon and Schuster, 2017.

Flippen, J. Brooks. *Jimmy Carter, the Politics of Family, and the Rise of the Religious Right*. Athens: University of Georgia Press, 2011.

Forsyth, Neil. *The Old Enemy: Satan and the Combat Myth*. Princeton, NJ: Princeton University Press, 1987.

Fowler, Robert Booth. *A New Engagement: Evangelical Political Thought, 1966–1976*. Grand Rapids, MI: William B. Eerdmans, 1982.

Frankl, Razelle. "Transformation of Televangelism: Repackaging Christian Family Values." In *Media, Culture, and the Religious Right*, edited by Linda Kintz and Julia Lesage, 163–190. Minneapolis: University of Minnesota Press, 1998.

Frisken, Amanda, and Gretchen Soderlund. "Editors' Introduction: Sensationalism's Enduring Power." *Feminist Media Histories* 8, no. 4 (2022): 1–32. https://doi .org/10.1525/fmh.2022.8.4.1.

Gage, Beverly. *G-Man: J. Edgar Hoover and the Making of the American Century*. New York: Penguin Books, 2022.

Garrett, James Leo, E. Glenn Hinson, and James E. Tull. *Are Southern Baptists "Evangelicals"?* Macon, GA: Mercer University Press, 1983.

Gibbs, Nancy, and Michael Duffy. *The Preacher and the Presidents: Billy Graham in the White House*. New York: Center Street, 2007.

Gibson, John. *The War on Christmas: How the Liberal Plot to Ban the Sacred Christian Holiday Is Worse than You Thought*. New York: Sentinel, 2005.

Gilbert, Jeremy. "This Conjuncture: For Stuart Hall." *New Formations* 96, no. 1 (2019): 5–37. http://dx.doi.org.uoregon.idm.oclc.org/10.3898/NEWF:96/97 .EDITORIAL.2019.

Giordano, Ralph G. *Satan in the Dance Hall: Reverend John Roach Straton, Social Dancing, and Morality in 1920s New York City*. Lanham, MD: Scarecrow Press, 2008.

Glynn, Kevin. *Tabloid Culture: Trash Taste, Popular Power, and the Transformation of American Television*. Durham, NC: Duke University Press, 2000.

Goffman, Erving. *Frame Analysis: An Essay on the Organization of Experience*. Boston: Northeastern University Press, 1986.

Gore, Tipper. *Raising PG Kids in an X-Rated Society*. Nashville, TN: Parthenon Press, 1987.

Gorski, Philip, and Samuel Perry. *The Flag and the Cross: White Christian Nationalism and Its Threat to American Democracy*. New York: Oxford University Press, 2022.

Graham, Billy. *Angels: God's Secret Agents*. Waco, TX: Word Books, 1975.

Graham, Joshua Benjamin. "Masters of the Imagination: Fundamentalist Readings of the Occult in Cartoons of the 1980s." In *Satanic Panic: Pop-Cultural Paranoia in the 1980s*, edited by Kier-La Janisse and Paul Corupe, 83–96. Surrey: FAB Press, 2015.

Greene, Robert, II. "National Review and Civil Rights Memory." In *News on the Right: Studying Conservative News Cultures*, edited by Anthony Nadler and A. J. Bauer, 174–190. New York: Oxford University Press, 2020.

Grem, Darren E. *The Blessings of Business: How Corporations Shaped Conservative Christianity*. New York: Oxford University Press, 2016.

Grem, Darren E. "'Christianity Today,' J. Howard Pew, and the Business of Conservative Evangelicalism." *Enterprise & Society* 15, no. 2 (June 2014): 353–354.

Griffith, Aaron. *God's Law and Order*. Cambridge, MA: Harvard University Press, 2020.

Grindstaff, Laura. *The Money Shot: Trash, Class, and the Making of TV Talk Shows*. Chicago: University of Chicago Press, 2008.

Groce, Eric C., Tina Heafner, and Elizabeth Bellows. "'Under God' and the Pledge of Allegiance: Examining a 1954 Sermon and Its Meaning." *Social Education* 77, no. 4 (2013): 185–191.

Grossberg, Lawrence. *Cultural Studies in the Future Tense*. Durham, NC: Duke University Press, 2010.

Grossman, Anita. "Shadows of War and Holocaust: Jews, German Jews, and the Sixties in the United States, Reflections and Memories." *Journal of Modern Jewish Studies* 13, no. 1 (2014): 99–114.

Gundlach, Bradley J. "The Fundamentalist-Modernist Controversy." In *The Oxford Handbook of Presbyterianism*, 97–115. New York: Oxford University Press, 2019. https://doi.org/10.1093/oxfordhb/9780190608392.013.11.

Guth, James L. "South Carolina: The Christian Right Wins One." *PS: Political Science & Politics* 28, no. 1 (1995): 8–11. https://doi.org/10.2307/420571.

Hall, Stuart. "Encoding/Decoding." In *Culture, Media, Language: Working Papers in Cultural Studies 1972–1979*, edited by Stuart Hall, Dorothy Hobson, Andrew Love, and Paul Willis, 128–138. London: Hutchinson, 1980.

Hamilton, Michael S. "From Desire to Decision: The Evangelistic Preaching of Billy Graham." In *Billy Graham: American Pilgrim*, edited by Andrew Finstuen, Grant Wacker, and Anne Blue Wills, 43–63. New York: Oxford University Press, 2017. https://doi.org/10.1093/acprof:oso/9780190683528.003.0003.

Hangen, Tona J. *Redeeming the Dial: Radio, Religion, and Popular Culture in America*. Chapel Hill: University of North Carolina Press, 2003.

Hankins, Barry. *American Evangelicals: A Contemporary History of a Mainstream Religious Movement*. Lanham, MD: Rowman & Littlefield, 2008.

Hankins, Barry. *Evangelicalism and Fundamentalism: A Documentary Reader*. New York: New York University Press, 2008.

Hankins, Barry. *Uneasy in Babylon: Southern Baptist Conservatives and American Culture*. Tuscaloosa: University of Alabama Press, 2002.

Harris, Harriet A. *Fundamentalism and Evangelicals*. Oxford: Clarendon Press, 1998.

Hartman, Andrew. *A War for the Soul of America: A History of the Culture Wars*. Chicago: University of Chicago Press, 2019.

Harvey, Charles E. "John D. Rockefeller, Jr., and the Interchurch Movement of 1919–1920: A Different Angle on the Ecumenical Movement." *Church History* 51, no. 2 (June 1982): 198–209.

Hemmer, Nicole. "The Man Who Won the Republican Party before Trump Did." *New York Times*, September 8, 2022. https://www.nytimes.com/2022/09/08/opinion/pat-buchanan-donald-trump.html.

Hemmer, Nicole. *Messengers of the Right: Conservative Media and the Transformation of American Politics*. Philadelphia: University of Pennsylvania Press, 2016.

Hemmer, Nicole. *Partisans: The Conservative Revolutionaries Who Remade American Politics in the 1990s*. New York: Basic Books, 2022.

Hendershot, Heather. *What's Fair on the Air: Cold War Right-Wing Broadcasting and the Public Interest*. Chicago: University of Chicago Press, 2011.

Henry, Carl F. H. *The Uneasy Conscience of Modern Fundamentalism*, 2nd ed. Grand Rapids, MI: William B. Eerdmans, 2003.

Hertenstein, Mike, and Jon Trott. *Selling Satan: The Evangelical Media and the Mike Warnke Scandal*. Chicago: Cornerstone Press, 1993.

Heyward, Carter. *The Seven Deadly Sins of White Christian Nationalism: A Call to Action*. Lanham, MD: Rowman & Littlefield, 2022.

High, Stanley. *Billy Graham: The Personal Story of the Man, His Message, and His Mission*. New York: McGraw-Hill, 1956.

Hochschild, Arlie Russel. *Strangers in Their Own Land: Anger and Mourning on the American Right*. New York: New Press, 2018.

Hofstadter, Richard. *The Paranoid Style in American Politics, and Other Essays*. Chicago: University of Chicago Press, 1979.

Holland, Jennifer. *Tiny You: A Western History of the Anti-Abortion Movement*. Berkeley: University of California Press, 2020.

House Republican Conference. *Contract with America: The Bold Plan by Rep. Newt Gingrich, Reps. Dick Armey, and the House Republicans to Change the Nation*. New York: Times Books, 1994.

Hummel, Daniel G. *The Rise and Fall of Dispensationalism: How the Evangelical Battle over the End Times Shaped a Nation*. Grand Rapids, MI: William B. Eerdmans, 2023.

Hunsicker, David Buckelew. "The Rise of the Parachurch Movement in American Protestant Christianity during the 1930s and 1940s: A Detailed Study of the Beginnings of the Navigators, Young Life and Youth for Christ International." PhD dissertation, Trinity Evangelical Divinity School, 1998. https://philpapers.org/rec/HUNTRO-10.

Hunter, James Davison. *Culture Wars: The Struggle to Control the Family, Art, Education, Law, and Politics in America*. New York: Basic Books, 1991.

Ivie, Robert. "Into the 21st Century." In *The Routledge History of the Devil in the Western Tradition*, edited by Richard Raiswell, Michelle D. Brock, and David R. Winter. New York: Routledge, 2025.

Ivie, Robert L., and Oscar Giner. *Hunt the Devil: Demonology in US War Culture*. Tuscaloosa: University of Alabama Press, 2015.

Johnson, David K. *The Lavender Scare: The Cold War Persecution of Gays and Lesbians in the Federal Government*. Chicago: University of Chicago Press, 2004.

Johnson, Eithne. "The Emergence of Christian Video and the Cultivation of Videoangelism." In *Media, Culture, and the Religious Right*, edited by Linda Kintz and Julia Lesage, 191–210. Minneapolis: University of Minnesota Press, 1998.

Johnson, Jessica. "White Terror and the Great Replacement." Paper presented at SPAWN 2022: White Supremacy, Misogyny, and the "New" Terrorism, June 25, 2022. Syracuse University.

Joo, Jeongsuk. "The Hollywood Red Scare: An Attack on the Labor and Progressive Politics of Hollywood." *International Area Review* 13, no. 3 (2010): 125–143.

Kenaston, Connor S. "Broadcasting the Gospel of Tolerance: Media, Capitalism, and Religion in Twentieth-Century America." Issue Lab, September 5, 2019. https://mediaimpact.issuelab.org/resource/broadcasting-the-gospel-of-tolerance-media-capitalism-and-religion-in-twentieth-century-america.html.

King, Martin Luther, Jr. *Letter from Birmingham Jail*. London: Penguin Classics, 2018. First published 1963.

Kintz, Linda. *Between Jesus and the Market: The Emotions That Matter in Right-Wing America*. Durham, NC: Duke University Press, 1997.

Kintz, Linda. "Clarity, Mothers, and the Mass-Mediated National Soul: A Defense of Ambiguity." In *Media, Culture, and the Religious Right*, edited by Linda Kintz and Julia Lesage, 115–140. Minneapolis: University of Minnesota Press, 1998.

Kintz, Linda, and Julia Lesage. "Religious Culture in the United States." In *Media, Culture, and the Religious Right*, edited by Linda Kintz and Julia Lesage, 51–55. Minneapolis: University of Minnesota Press, 1998.

Kirby, Dianne. "Religion and the Cold War—An Introduction." In *Religion and the Cold War*, edited by Dianne Kirby, 1–22. New York: Palgrave Macmillan, 2003.

Klinkner, Philip A. *Midterm: The Elections of 1994 in Context*. Boulder, CO: Westview Press, 1996.

Knight, Peter. "Introduction: A Nation of Conspiracy Theorists." In *Conspiracy Nation: The Politics of Paranoia in Postwar America*, edited by Peter Knight, 1–20. New York: New York University Press, 2002.

Kovel, Joel. *Red Hunting in the Promised Land: Anticommunism and the Making of America*. New York: Basic Books, 1994.

Kuersteiner, Kurt. *The Unofficial Guide to the Art of Jack T. Chick: Chick Tracts, Crusader Comics, and Battle Cry Newspapers*. Atglen: Schiffer Publications, 2004.

Kyle, Richard. *Evangelicalism: An Americanized Christianity*. New York: Routledge, 2017.

Ladouceur, Lisa. "The Filthy 15: When Venom and King Diamond Met the Washington Wives." In *Satanic Panic: Pop-Cultural Paranoia in the 1980s*, edited by Kier-La Janisse and Paul Corupe, 158–172. Surry: FAB Press, 2015.

LaHaye, Beverly. *Who But a Woman? Concerned Women Can Make a Difference*. Nashville, TN: Thomas Nelson, 1984.

LaHaye, Tim. *The Battle for the Mind*. Old Tappan, NJ: Fleming H. Revell, 1980.

Lahr, Angela M. *Millennial Dreams and Apocalyptic Nightmares: The Cold War Origins of Political Evangelicalism*. New York: Oxford University Press, 2007.

Lakoff, George. *Don't Think of an Elephant! Know Your Values and Frame the Debate*. White River Junction, VT: Chelsea Green, 2004.

Lakoff, George, and Mark Johnson. *Metaphors We Live By*. Chicago: University of Chicago Press, 1980.

Lane, Julie B. "Cultivating Mistrust of the Mainstream Media." In *News on the Right: Studying Conservative News Cultures*, edited by Anthony Nadler and A. J. Bauer, 157–173. New York: Oxford University Press, 2020.

Layman, Geoffrey. *The Great Divide: Religious and Cultural Conflict in American Party Politics*. New York: Columbia University Press, 2001.

Layman, Geoffrey C., and John C. Green. "Wars and Rumours of Wars: The Contexts of Cultural Conflict in American Political Behaviour." *British Journal of Political Science* 36, no. 1 (2006): 61–89.

Lesage, Julia. "Christian Coalition Leadership Training." In *Media, Culture, and the Religious Right*, edited by Linda Kintz and Julia Lesage, 295–327. Minneapolis: University of Minnesota Press, 1998.

Levendusky, Matthew. *The Partisan Sort: How Liberals Became Democrats and Conservatives Became Republicans*. Chicago: University of Chicago Press, 2009.

Levitt, Cyril. "The New Left, the New Class and Socialism." *Higher Education* 8, no. 6 (1979): 641–655.

Lewis, Hyrum, and Verlan Lewis. *The Myth of Left and Right: How the Political Spectrum Misleads and Harms America*. New York: Oxford University Press, 2023.

Lieberman, Robbie. *The Strangest Dream: Communism, Anticommunism, and the U.S. Peace Movement, 1945–1963*. Syracuse, NY: Syracuse University Press, 2000.

Lienesch, Michael. *In the Beginning: Fundamentalism, the Scopes Trial, and the Making of the Antievolution Movement*. Chapel Hill: University of North Carolina Press, 2007.

Limbaugh, Rush. *The Way Things Ought to Be*. New York: Simon & Schuster 1992.

Lindsell, Harold. *The World, the Flesh, and the Devil*. Moscow, ID: Canon Press, 1973.

Lindsey, Hal. *The 1980s: Countdown to Armageddon*. King of Prussia, PA: Westgate Press, 1981.

Lindsey, Hal. *The Road to Holocaust*. New York: Bantam Books, 1989.

Lindsey, Hal, with C. C. Carlson. *The Late Great Planet Earth*. Grand Rapids, MI: Zondervan Publishing House, 1970.

Lindsey, Hal, with C. C. Carlson. *Satan Is Alive and Well on Planet Earth*. Grand Rapids, MI: Zondervan Publishing House, 1972.

Luca, Tom De, and John Buell. *Liars! Cheaters! Evildoers! Demonization and the End of Civil Debate in American Politics*. New York: New York University Press, 2005.

Mahler, Jonathan. *Ladies and Gentlemen, the Bronx Is Burning: 1977, Baseball, Politics, and the Battle for the Soul of a City*. New York: Picador, 2006.

Margolis, Michele F. *From Politics to the Pews: How Partisanship and the Political Environment Shape Religious Identity*. Chicago: University of Chicago Press, 2018.

Margry, Peter Jan. "Envisioning and Exploring Mary's Theatre of War." In *Cold War Mary: Ideologies, Politics, and Marian Devotional Culture*, edited by Peter Jan Margry, 7–58. Leuven: Leuven University Press, 2020.

Marsden, George M. *Reforming Fundamentalism: Fuller Seminary and the New Evangelicalism*. Grand Rapids, MI: William B. Eerdmans, 1995.

Marshall, Susan E. "Who Speaks for American Women? The Future of Antifeminism." *Annals of the American Academy of Political and Social Science* 515 (1991): 50–62.

Martin, Daniel, and Gary Allen Fine. "Satanic Cultures, Satanic Play: Is Dungeons & Dragons a Breeding Ground for the Devil?" In *The Satanism Scare*, edited by James T. Richardson, Joel Best, and David G. Bromley, 107–126. New York: Routledge 1991.

Martin, Lerone A. *The Gospel of J. Edgar Hoover: How the FBI Aided and Abetted the Rise of White Christian Nationalism*. Princeton, NJ: Princeton University Press, 2023.

Mathews, Mary Beth. "The History of Black Evangelicals and American Politics." African American Historical Perspectives, March 30, 2017. https://www.aaihs .org/the-history-of-black-evangelicals-and-american-politics/.

Mathews, Mary Beth Swetnam. *Doctrine and Race: African American Evangelicals and Fundamentalism between the Wars*. Tuscaloosa: University of Alabama Press, 2017.

Matzko, Paul. "Radio Politics, Origin Myths, and the Creation of New Evangelicalism." *Fides et Historia* 48, no. 1 (Winter/Spring 2016): 61–90.

Matzko, Paul. *The Radio Right: How a Band of Broadcasters Took on the Federal Government and Built the Modern Conservative Movement*. New York: Oxford University Press, 2020.

May, Elaine Tyler. *Homeward Bound: American Families in the Cold War Era*, 2nd ed. New York: Basic Books, 2008.

McDaniel, Eric L., Irfan Nooruddin, and Allyson F. Shortle. *The Everyday Crusade: Christian Nationalism in American Politics*. Cambridge: Cambridge University Press, 2022.

McManus, Matthew. *The Rise of Post-Modern Conservatism: Neoliberalism, Post-Modern Culture, and Reactionary Politics*. New York: Palgrave Macmillan, 2019.

McRae, Elizabeth Gillespie. *Mothers of Massive Resistance: White Women and the Politics of White Supremacy*. New York: Oxford University Press, 2018.

Mehlman, Natalia. "Sex Ed . . . and the Reds? Reconsidering the Anaheim Battle over Sex Education, 1962–1969." *History of Education Quarterly* 47, no. 2 (2007): 203–232.

Miller, Douglas T. "Popular Religion of the 1950's: Norman Vincent Peale and Billy Graham." *Journal of Popular Culture* 9, no. 1 (Summer 1975): 66.

Miller, Jennifer M., and Udi Greenberg. "From Mental Slavery to Brainwashing: Anti-Catholic Legacies in Anti-Communist Polemics." In *Defending the Faith: Global Histories of Apologetics and Politics in the Twentieth Century*, edited by Todd Weir and Hugh McLeod, 119–140. Oxford: Oxford University Press, 2021.

Miller, Neil. *Out of the Past: Gay and Lesbian History from 1869 to the Present*. New York: Vintage Books, 1995.

Miller, Robert Moats. *Harry Emerson Fosdick: Preacher, Pastor, Prophet*. New York: Oxford University Press, 1985.

Miller, Tim. *Why We Did It: A Travelogue from the Republican Road to Hell*. New York: Harper, 2022.

Misztal, Bronislaw, and Anson Shupe. *Religion and Politics in Comparative Perspective: Revival of Religious Fundamentalism in East and West*. New York: Bloomsbury, 1992.

Mitchell, Travis. "In U.S., Decline of Christianity Continues at Rapid Pace." Pew Research Center, October 17, 2019. https://www.pewresearch.org/religion/2019/10/17/in-u-s-decline-of-christianity-continues-at-rapid-pace/.

Mohl, Raymond A. *South of the South: Jewish Activists and the Civil Rights Movement in Miami, 1945–1960*. Gainesville: University Press of Florida, 2004.

Mookas, Ioannis. "Faultlines: Homophobic Innovation in Gay Rights/Special Rights." In *Media, Culture, and the Religious Right*, edited by Linda Kintz and Julia Lesage, 345–362. Minneapolis: University of Minnesota Press, 1998.

Moses, Paul. "Old Anti-Semitism, New Audience." *LaCroix International*, November 12, 2022. https://international.la-croix.com/news/politics/old-antisemitism-new-audience/16885.

Mulder, John M. "The Moral World of John Foster Dulles." *Journal of Presbyterian History* 49, no. 2 (Summer 1971): 157–182.

Mulhern, Sherrill. "Satanism and Psychotherapy: A Rumor in Search of an Inquisition." In *The Satanism Scare*, edited by James T. Richardson, Joel Best, and David G. Bromley, 145–175. New York: Routledge, 1991.

Mulloy, D. J. *The World of the John Birch Society: Conspiracy, Conservatism, and the Cold War*. Nashville, TN: Vanderbilt University Press, 2014.

Murch, James DeForest. *Cooperation without Compromise: A History of the National Association of Evangelicals*. Grand Rapids, MI: William B. Eerdmans, 1956.

Nadler, Anthony. "The Great Anti-Left Show." *Los Angeles Review of Books*, October 2, 2020. https://lareviewofbooks.org/article/the-great-anti-left-show/.

Nadler, Anthony, and A. J. Bauer. "Taking Conservative News Seriously." In *News on the Right: Studying Conservative News Cultures*, edited by Anthony Nadler and A. J. Bauer, 1–16. New York: Oxford University Press, 2020.

Nadler, Anthony, and Doron Taussig. "The Deep Story beneath the Big Lie." *Los Angeles Times Review of Books*, August 16, 2023. https://lareviewofbooks.org/article/the-deep-story-beneath-the-big-lie/.

Nekola, Anna. "'More than Just a Music': Conservative Christian Anti-Rock Discourse and the U.S. Culture Wars." *Popular Music* 32, no. 3 (2013): 407–426.

Nelson, Anne. *The Shadow Network: Media, Money, and the Secret Hub of the Radical Right*. New York: Bloomsbury, 2019.

Nelson, Jacob L., and Seth C. Lewis. "Only 'Sheep' Trust Journalists? How Citizens' Self-Perceptions Shape Their Approach to News." *New Media & Society* 25, no. 7 (2021): 1522–1541. https://doi.org/10.1177/14614448211018160.

Nickerson, Michelle. *Mothers of Conservatism: Women and the Postwar Right*. Princeton, NJ: Princeton University Press, 2012.

Nielsen, Rasmus Kleis. "Folk Theories of Journalism." *Journalism Studies* 17, no. 7 (2016): 840–848. https://doi.org/10.1080/1461670X.2016.1165140.

Nuzum, Eric. *Parental Advisory: Music Censorship in America*. New York: Harper, 2001.

O'Donnell, S. Jonathon. *Passing Orders: Demonology and Sovereignty in American Spiritual Warfare*. New York: Fordham University Press, 2020.

Oldfield, Duane Murray. *The Right and the Righteous: The Christian Right Confronts the Republican Party*. Lanham, MD: Rowman & Littlefield, 1996.

Olmstead, Kathryn. *Real Enemies: Conspiracy Theories and American Democracy, World War I to 9/11*. Oxford: Oxford University Press, 2009.

Olson, Laura R., and Adam L. Warber. "Belonging, Behaving, and Believing: Assessing the Role of Religion on Presidential Approval." *Political Research Quarterly* 61, no. 2 (2008): 192–204.

Omer, Atalia, and Joshua Lupo. *Religion, Populism, and Modernity: Confronting White Christian Nationalism and Racism*. Notre Dame, IN: University of Notre Dame Press, 2023.

Onishi, Bradley. *Preparing for War: The Extremist History of White Christian Nationalism—And What Comes Next*. Minneapolis: Broadleaf Books, 2023.

O'Reilly, Bill. *The No Spin Zone: Confrontations with the Powerful and Famous in America*. New York: Broadway Books, 2001.

Orum, Anthony M. "Religion and the Rise of the Radical White: The Case of Southern Wallace Support in 1968." *Social Science Quarterly* 51, no. 3 (1970): 674–688.

Packer, James Innell, and Thomas C. Oden. *One Faith: The Evangelical Consensus*. Downer's Grove, IL: InterVarsity Press, 2004.

Pagels, Elaine. *The Origin of Satan: How Christians Demonized Jews, Pagans, and Heretics*. New York: Vintage, 1996.

Palmer, Ruth. *Becoming the News: How Ordinary People Respond to the Media Spotlight*. New York: Columbia University Press, 2017.

Parsons, Talcott. "Postscript to 'The Sociology of Modern Anti-Semitism.'" *Contemporary Jewry* 5 (1980): 31–38.

Pastor, Gregory S., Walter J. Stone, and Ronald B. Rapoport. "Candidate-Centered Sources of Party Change: The Case of Pat Robertson, 1988." *Journal of Politics* 61, no. 2 (May 1999): 423–444.

Paterson, Thomas G. *Meeting the Communist Threat: Truman to Reagan*. New York: Oxford University Press, 1988.

Peck, Reece. *Fox Populism: Branding Conservatism as Working Class*. Cambridge: Cambridge University Press, 2019.

Peffley, Mark, and Lee Sigelman. "Intolerance of Communists during the McCarthy Era: A General Model." *Political Research Quarterly* 43, no. 1 (1990): 93–111.

Peters, John Durham. *Speaking into the Air: A History of the Idea of Communication*. Chicago: University of Chicago Press, 2001.

Phillips, Phil. *Saturday Morning Mind Control*. Nashville, TN: Oliver-Nelson Books, 1991.

Phillips, Phil. *Turmoil in the Toy Box*. Lancaster, PA: Starburst, 1990.

Phillips, Phil, and Joan Hake Robie. *Halloween and Satanism*. Lancaster, PA: Starburst, 1987.

Phillips, Whitney. *This Is Why We Can't Have Nice Things: Mapping the Relationship between Online Trolling and Mainstream Culture*. Cambridge, MA: MIT Press, 2015.

Phillips, Whitney, and Ryan Milner. *You Are Here: A Field Guide for Navigating Polarized Speech, Conspiracy Theories, and Our Polluted Media Landscape*. Cambridge, MA: MIT Press, 2021.

Phillips-Fein, Kim. *Invisible Hands: The Businessmen's Crusade against the New Deal*. New York: W. W. Norton, 2010.

Pierce, Michael. "The Racist Origins of Right to Work." *Labor Notes*, August 3, 2017. https://labornotes.org/blogs/2017/08/racist-who-pioneered-right-work-laws.

Pohlman, Michael E. *Broadcasting the Faith: Protestant Religious Radio and Theology in America, 1920–50*. Eugene, OR: Wipf and Stock, 2021.

Poole, W. Scott. *Satan in America: The Devil We Know*. Lanham, MD: Rowman & Littlefield, 2009.

Putnam, Robert D., and David E. Campbell. *American Grace: How Religion Divides and Unites Us*. New York: Simon and Schuster, 2012.

Raiswell, Richard, Michelle D. Brock, and David R. Winter. "Introduction: Giving the Devil His Due." In *The Routledge History of the Devil in the Western Tradition*, edited by Richard Raiswell, Michelle D. Brock, and David R. Winter. New York: Routledge, 2025.

Ridgely, Susan B. "Conservative Christianity and the Creation of Alternative News: An Analysis of Focus on the Family's Multimedia Empire." *Religion and American Culture* 30, no. 1 (January 2020): 1–25.

Robin, Corey. *The Reactionary Mind: Conservatism from Edmund Burke to Sarah Palin*. New York: Oxford University Press, 2011.

Rogin, Michael. *Ronald Reagan: The Movie*. Berkeley: University of California Press, 1988.

Rolland-Diamond, Caroline. "Another Side of the Sixties: Festive Practices on College Campuses and the Making of a Conservative Youth Movement." *Revue Française d'études Américaines* 146, no. 1 (2016): 39–53.

Rosenthal, Michele. "Introduction: The Triumph of Televangelism and the Decline of Mainline Religious Broadcasting." In *American Protestants and TV in the 1950s: Responses to a New Medium*, edited by Michele Rosenthal, 1–5. New York: Palgrave Macmillan US, 2007.

Salzer, James. "Gingrich's Language Set a New Course." *Atlanta Journal-Constitution*, July 5, 2016. https://www.ajc.com/news/local-govt--politics/gingrich-language -set-new-course/O5bgK6lY2wQ3KwEZsY.

Saunders, Lowell Sperry. "The National Religious Broadcasters and the Availability of Commercial Radio Time." PhD dissertation, University of Illinois at Urbana-Champaign, 1968.

Sbardellati, John. *J. Edgar Hoover Goes to the Movies: The FBI and the Origins of Hollywood's Cold War*. Ithaca, NY: Cornell University Press, 2012.

Schäfer, Axel R. *American Evangelicals and the 1960s*. Madison: University of Wisconsin Press, 2013.

Schlafly, Phyllis. *Child Abuse in the Classroom*. Alton, IL: Pere Marquette Press, 1984.

Schneider, Gregory L. *Cadres for Conservatism: Young Americans for Freedom and the Rise of the Contemporary Right*. New York: New York University Press, 1999.

Schradie, Jen. *The Revolution That Wasn't: How Digital Activism Favors Conservatives*. Cambridge, MA: Harvard University Press, 2019.

Schultze, Quentin J. "Evangelical Radio and the Rise of the Electronic Church, 1921–1948." *Journal of Broadcasting & Electronic Media* 32, no. 3 (Summer 1988): 289–306. https://doi.org/10.1080/08838158809386703.

Schulze, Laurie, and Frances Guilfoyle. "Facts Don't Hate, They Just Are." In *Media, Culture, and the Religious Right*, edited by Linda Kintz and Julia Lesage, 327–344. Minneapolis: University of Minnesota Press, 1998.

Senter, Mark. "The Youth for Christ Movement as an Educational Agency and Its Impact upon Protestant Churches, 1931–1979." PhD dissertation, Loyola University Chicago, 1989. https://ecommons.luc.edu/luc_diss/2698/.

Shapiro, Edward S. "The Approach of War: Congressional Isolationism and Anti-Semitism, 1939–1941." *American Jewish History* 74, no. 1 (1984): 45–65.

Shelley, Bruce L. "The Rise of Evangelical Youth Movements." *Fides et Historia* 18, no. 1 (1986): 47–63.

Sherman, Gabriel. *The Loudest Voice in the Room: How the Brilliant, Bombastic Roger Ailes Built Fox News—and Divided a Country*. New York: Random House, 2014.

Shinn, George Wolfe. "What Has Become of Hell?" *North American Review* 170, no. 523 (1900): 837–849.

Silliman, Daniel. "An Evangelical Is Anyone Who Likes Billy Graham: Defining Evangelicalism with Carl Henry and Networks of Trust." *Church History* 90, no. 3 (September 2021): 621–643. https://doi.org/10.1017/S000964072100216X.

Simonelli, Frederick. *American Fuehrer: George Lincoln Rockwell and the American Nazi Party*. Urbana: University of Illinois Press, 1999.

Skocpol, Theda, and Vanessa Williamson. *The Tea Party and the Remaking of Republican Conservatism*. New York: Oxford University Press, 2016.

Smith, Gregory A. "More White Americans Adopted than Shed Evangelical Label during Trump Presidency, Especially His Supporters." Pew Research Center, September 15, 2021. https://www.pewresearch.org/fact-tank/2021/09/15/more-white-americans-adopted-than-shed-evangelical-label-during-trump-presidency-especially-his-supporters/.

Smyth, J. E. "Organisation Women and Belle Rebels: Hollywood's Working Women in the 1930s." In *Hollywood and the Great Depression: American Film, Politics, and Society in the 1930s*, edited by Iwan Morgan and Philip John Davies, 66–85. Edinburgh: Edinburgh University Press, 2016.

Soderlund, Gretchen. *Sex Trafficking, Scandal, and the Transformation of Journalism, 1885–1917*. Chicago: University of Chicago Press, 2013.

Stabile, Carol A. *The Broadcast 41: Women and the Anti-Communist Blacklist*. Cambridge, MA: MIT Press, 2018.

Starbird, Kate. "Information Wars: A Window into the Alternative Media Ecosystem." *Medium*, March 14, 2017. https://medium.com/hci-design-at-uw/information-wars-a-window-into-the-alternative-media-ecosystem-a1347f32fd8f.

Starbird, Kate, et al. "Eco-System or Echo-System? Exploring Content Sharing across Alternative Media Domains." *Proceedings of the Twelfth International AAAI Conference on Web and Social Media* 12, no. 1 (2018). https://doi.org/10.1609/icwsm.v12i1.15009.

Steensland, Brian, and Eric L. Wright. "American Evangelicals and Conservative Politics: Past, Present, and Future." *Sociology Compass* 8, no. 6 (2014): 705–717.

Stephens, Phillip, Jr. "The Demonology of Satanism." In *The Satanism Scare*, edited by James T. Richardson, Joel Best, and David G. Bromley, 21–41. New York: Routledge, 1991.

Stephens, Randall J. *The Devil's Music: How Christians Inspired, Condemned, and Embraced Rock 'n' Roll*. Cambridge, MA: Harvard University Press, 2018.

Stephens, Randall J., and Karl W. Giberson. *The Anointed: Evangelical Truth in a Secular Age*. Cambridge, MA: Harvard University Press, 2011.

Stouffer, Samuel. *Communism, Conformity, and Civil Liberties: A Cross Section of the Nation Speaks Its Mind*. New Brunswick, NJ: Transaction, 1992. First published 1955.

Strozier, Charles B. *Apocalypse: On the Psychology of Fundamentalism in America*. Eugene, OR: Wipf and Stock, 2002. First published 1994.

Suber, Howard. "Politics and Popular Culture: Hollywood at Bay, 1933–1953." *American Jewish History* 68, no. 4 (1979): 517–533.

Sundquist, James L. *Dynamics of the Party System: Alignment and Realignment of Political Parties in the United States*. Washington, DC: Brookings Institution Press, 2011.

Sutton, Matthew Avery. *American Apocalypse: A History of Modern Evangelicalism*. Cambridge, MA: Harvard University Press, 2014.

Swain, Carol M. *The New White Nationalism in America: Its Challenge to Integration*. Cambridge: Cambridge University Press, 2002.

Swartz, David R. "Chicago 1945: Youth for Christ and World War II." In *Facing West: American Evangelicals in an Age of World Christianity*, edited by David R. Swartz, 13–34. New York: Oxford University Press, 2020. https://doi.org/10.1093/oso/9780190250805.003.0002.

Swartz, David R. *Moral Minority: The Evangelical Left in an Age of Conservatism*. Philadelphia: University of Pennsylvania Press, 2012.

Swint, Kerwin. *Dark Genius: The Influential Career of Legendary Political Operative and Fox News Founder Roger Ailes*. New York: Union Square Press, 2008.

Tevington, Patricia. "Americans Feel More Positive than Negative about Jews, Mainline Protestants, Catholics." Pew Research Center, March 15, 2023. https://www.pewresearch.org/religion/2023/03/15/americans-feel-more-positive-than-negative-about-jews-mainline-protestants-catholics/.

Toff, Benjamin, and Rasmus Kleis Nielsen. "'I Just Google It': Folk Theories of Distributed Discovery." *Journal of Communication* 68, no. 3 (2018): 636–657. https://doi.org/10.1093/joc/jqy009.

Toole, John Kennedy. *Confederacy of Dunces*. Baton Rouge: Louisiana State University Press, 1980.

Turner, John G. *Bill Bright's Campus Crusade for Christ: The Renewal of Evangelicalism in Postwar America*. Chapel Hill: University of North Carolina Press, 2008.

Turner, Patricia A. *Trash Talk: Anti-Obama Lore and Race in the Twenty-First Century*. Oakland: University of California Press, 2022.

Victor, Jeffrey. *Satanic Panic: The Creation of a Contemporary Legend*. Chicago: Open Court Press, 1993.

Wacker, Grant. *America's Pastor: Billy Graham and the Shaping of a Nation*. Cambridge, MA: Harvard University Press, 2014.

Ward, Mark. *Air of Salvation: The Story of Christian Broadcasting*. Grand Rapids, MI: Baker Books, 1994.

Warnke, Mike. *The Satan Seller*. Plainfield, NJ: Logos International, 1972.

Watt, David Harrington. "The Private Hopes of American Fundamentalists and Evangelicals, 1925–1975." *Religion and American Culture* 1, no. 2 (1991): 155–175. https://doi.org/10.1525/rac.1991.1.2.03a00020.

Webster, Gerald R. "American Nationalism, the Flag, and the Invasion of Iraq." *Geographical Review* 101, no. 1 (2011): 1–18. http://www.jstor.org/stable/41303604.

Whitehead, Andrew L. *American Idolatry: How Christian Nationalism Betrays the Gospel and Threatens the Church*. Grand Rapids, MI: Brazos Press, 2023.

Wilcox, Clyde. "America's Radical Right Revisited: A Comparison of the Activists in Christian Right Organizations from the 1960s and the 1980s." *Sociological Analysis* (1987): 46–57.

Wilcox, Clyde. "Evangelicals and the Moral Majority." *Journal for the Scientific Study of Religion* 28, no. 4 (1989): 400–414.

Wilcox, Clyde. "Sources of Support for the Old Right: A Comparison of the John Birch Society and the Christian Anti-Communism Crusade." *Social Science History* 12, no. 4 (1988): 429–449.

Wilcox, Clyde, and Ted Jelen. "Evangelicals and Political Tolerance." *American Politics Quarterly* 18, no. 1 (1990): 25–46.

Williams, Anna. "Conservative Media Activism: The Free Congress Foundation and National Empowerment Television." In *Media, Culture, and the Religious Right*, edited by Linda Kintz and Julia Lesage, 275–295. Minneapolis: University of Minnesota Press, 1998.

Williams, Daniel K. *God's Own Party: The Making of the Christian Right*. New York: Oxford University Press, 2012.

Williams, Daniel K. "The Partisan Trajectory of the American Pro-Life Movement: How a Liberal Catholic Campaign Became a Conservative Evangelical Cause." *Religions* 6 (2015): 451–475.

Wilson, John K. *The Myth of Political Correctness: Conservative Attack on Political Correctness*. Durham, NC: Duke University Press, 1995.

Winston, Diane. *Righting the American Dream: How the Media Mainstreamed Reagan's Evangelical Vision*. Chicago: University of Chicago Press, 2023.

Wirt, Sherwood Eliot. *The Social Conscience of the Evangelical*. New York: Harper & Row, 1968.

Wojcik, Daniel. "Apocalypticism and Millenarianism." In *Encyclopedia of New Religions: New Religious Movements, Sects, and Alternative Spiritualities*, edited by Christopher Partridge, 388–395. Oxford: Lion, 2004.

Wojcik, Daniel. "Avertive Apocalypticism." In the *Oxford Handbook of Millennialism*, edited by Catherine Wessinger, 66–88. Oxford: Oxford University Press, 2011.

Wojcik, Daniel. *The End of the World as We Know It: Faith, Fatalism, and Apocalypse in America*. New York: New York University Press, 1997.

Wojcik, Daniel. "Fatalism." In *Encyclopedia of Millennialism and Millennial Movements*, edited by Richard Landes, 149–155. New York: Routledge, 2000.

Wojcik, Daniel. "Modern Mythology, Visionary Art, and Techno-Reenchantment." Keynote presentation for the conference, "New Approaches to 'Re-enchanted' Central and Eastern Europe." Institute for Theoretical Studies of the Moholy-Nagy University of Art and Design of Budapest, April 7, 2022.

Wolfinger, Raymond E., Barbara Kaye Wolfinger, Kenneth Prewitt, and Sheilah Rosenhack. "America's Radical Right: Politics and Ideology." In *Ideology and Discontent*, edited by David Apter, 267–269. New York: Free Press, 1964.

Wright, Joshua David. "'The Devil Hates That Doctrine': Hell in American Fundamentalism and Evangelicalism, 1900–2015." MA thesis, University of Colorado at Boulder, 2016. https://scholar.colorado.edu/concern/graduate_thesis_or _dissertations/th83kz71s.

Wuthnow, Robert. *The Struggle for America's Soul: Evangelicals, Liberals, and Secularism*. Grand Rapids, MI: William B. Eerdmans, 1989.

Zelizer, Julian E. *Burning Down the House: Newt Gingrich, the Fall of a Speaker, and the Rise of the New Republican Party*. New York: Penguin, 2020.

Zeskind, Leonard. *Blood and Politics: The History of the White Nationalist Movement from the Margins to the Mainstream*. New York: Farrar, Straus and Giroux, 2009.

INDEX

100 percent Americanism, 33, 34, 35, 36, 47, 48

2020 election conspiracy theories, 183, 184, 199. *See also* Big Lie

Abortion, political history of, 116–118, 119

Affordable Care Act (Obamacare), 175, 177, 179

Ailes, Roger, 138, 139–140, 143–145, 147, 148, 176

Alberta, Tim, 187, 212n70, 268n39

Amalgamation (shadow gospel media dynamic)
and definitions of liberalism, 17, 91, 153, 159
and the fusing of real and false things, 31, 43
and the liberal devil, 52, 99, 109, 161
and *pro-, anti-,* and conspiratorial frames, 74, 94 (*see also* Pandemonic rhetoric)
and rightwing media networks, 83, 84–87, 88, 123, 134

America First Committee, 75

American flag lapel pins, 152, 170–171

American Civil Liberties Union (ACLU), 1, 109, 151

American Legion, 31, 32, 33

Anti-Catholicism, and anticommunism, 36

Antichrist, 67, 101, 104, 127, 135, 138

Anticommunism
amalgamated targets of, 36, 43
and anti-Semitism, 35–36
and apocalypticism, 37
and attacks against Catholics, 36
bipartisan expressions of, 39, 219–220n81
and the Catholic embrace of, 36
consequences of, 24, 45–46, 48, 223n142
and corporate support for, 32, 33, 45, 222n119, 234n77
and Evangelicalism, 37, 49, 67, 73, 117
and fusionism, 91
and historical revisionism, 48, 74
history of, 31
as a mental health disorder, 41, 171
organizational forms of, 31–33
and overlap with anti-Communism, 31, 33, 42–43, 77
and the Pledge of Allegiance, 39
and religiosity of, 12, 36–37, 38, 39, 74
and Satan, 39, 41, 67–68
and segregation, 164
and sexual containment, 163
and the shadowy bizarre, 13, 45
two tracks of, 33
and white supremacy, 172
and women's activism, 164

Anti-liberal demonology, 7, 10, 14, 15, 18, 186, 196
and 1950s and 1960s rightwing media networks, 84